D0944992

DISCARD

# Understanding Magazines

# Roland E. Wolseley

# *Understanding Magazines*

SECOND EDITION

The Iowa State University Press
*Ames, Iowa, U.S.A.*

# About the author

ROLAND E. WOLSELEY is professor of journalism and former chairman of the Magazine Department, School of Public Communications, Syracuse University. His professional background includes years as a newspaper and magazine journalist, teacher, and writer. Author of nine books and co-author of ten, his writings have also appeared in over 100 magazines in the United States and abroad. Professor Wolseley earned the B.S. and M.S. degrees in journalism at Northwestern University and holds an honorary Litt. D. degree from Albright College. He was a Fulbright lecturer in India, and has long been active in professional organizations.

© 1965, 1969 The Iowa State University Press
All rights reserved. Printed in the U.S.A.

First edition, 1965
*Revised printing*, 1966

Second edition, 1969
*Revised printing*, 1972

International Standard Book Number: 0–8138–1708–0
Library of Congress Catalog Card Number: 69–18484

# Preface

T HE PURPOSE of *Understanding Magazines* is to provide at least four kinds of readers with an overview of magazines in the United States—their history, functions, organization, types, responsibilities, problems, vocational opportunities, and future. These readers are magazine publishing company employes wishing a broad knowledge of the field; persons who do business in the industry, such as writers, advertisers, authors' and artists' representatives, and promoters; magazine consumers who seek to know more about the periodicals to which they are exposed; and students thinking of entering or definitely preparing to enter the industry as an occupation.

Magazines first are placed in relationship to the other members of the journalistic family and to mass communications. The nature of the industry as a whole in the United States is then explained against the historical background of more than two hundred years.

This section is followed by an examination, department by department, of the operations of the modern magazine publishing company, after which various kinds of consumer and specialized periodicals are described and analyzed in detail. Social responsibilities and influence are described and discussed in a final section, as well as magazine education, training, and vocations. The book concludes with a look at the future for the magazine business in this country.

The reader familiar with *The Magazine World,* an earlier book by the same author, may wonder how the two differ. *Understanding Magazines* is more than a revision of the other. It has a different theme (the ascendancy of the specialized magazine in recent years) and an entirely new plan of organization; pays far more attention to various types of magazines and to individual magazinists; and contains much new material resulting from the author's closer connection with and continuing research in the magazine field in the decade and a half between the books.

The author of books on any aspect of communications is faced with the problem that confronts someone writing about weather—it always is changing. The magazine world is no different. Although this book first was published in 1965, so active is the industry that certain details were outdated by publication day.

The few years since the first edition have seen many more changes which an adequate report and analysis of the industry must recognize and note.

The intention of this new edition of *Understanding Magazines* is to reflect these developments and events—the deaths, retirements, and appointments of leading editors and publishers or other executives; the growth of such parts of the industry as business publications; the changes among the women's magazines; new evidence of the influence of periodicals in public life; the burgeoning of the magazine supplement to newspapers; and much more.

Also considered and in some instances accepted were suggestions of reviewers and of users of the book in industry or the classroom.

But nothing that has occurred in the period between editions has changed the basic theme, i.e., that the strength of the industry lies in the specialized or selective magazine. On the contrary; the same few giant consumer magazines go on adding millions to their circulations and advertising revenue, while the rest of the publications increase rapidly in number and their ability successfully to collect groups of readers intensely interested in segments of human activity. The genuine growth of the magazine world in the United States continues to be among the specialized periodicals.

# Acknowledgments

---

THE AUTHOR wishes to say thanks to numerous persons who assisted.
The published works of certain scholars provided facts and ideas it took them years to obtain; these were drawn upon and credited. Foremost, of course, is the work of the late Dean Frank Luther Mott, who until 1951 headed the School of Journalism at the University of Missouri. His four-volume *A History of American Magazines* proved to be a precious source, as it has been for so many other writers on magazines. The author wishes he could create a super "Oscar" to symbolize the debt of all professional journalists, teachers, and students to this fine work. Dean Mott's rare judgment and enormous amount of labor at least earned him Pulitzer and Bancroft prizes.

Another dean, Dr. Theodore Peterson of the College of Journalism and Communications at the University of Illinois, with his *Magazines in the Twentieth Century,* has dealt with a period which death prevented Dean Mott from reaching. And James Playsted Wood, through the two editions of his *Magazines in the United States,* suggested ideas for analysis and evaluation of the magazine that are highly original and fair-minded.

Another invaluable source of aid is that host of editors, publishers, department heads, fellow teachers, librarians, former students, and patient friends who supplied facts and illustrations cheerfully and promptly. The author is especially grateful to:

His wife, Bernice Browne Wolseley.

His colleagues at Syracuse University, Professor Edmund C. Arnold, Dr. George L. Bird, Professor Philip Ward Burton, and Professor Andre Fontaine; the late Professor Robert Root, of Eisenhower College; as well as Miss Evelyn E. Smith and Mrs. Elizabeth Gardiner, the former and present journalism librarians of the University.

These persons from the journalistic world:

Richard Bullock, Vance Publications; Robert D. Cole, business manager of the audio-visual division, Popular Science Publishing Company; Kenneth H. Constant, vice-president, advertising, Home State Farm Publications, Inc.; the late J. R. Cominsky, publisher, and Norman Cousins, editor, *Saturday Review;* James F. Coyne, photographer; Malcolm Cowley; the late Arch Crawford, formerly president, and Robert E. Kenyon, executive vice-president, Magazine Publishers Association; George J. Fine, director of promotion, Visual Panographics, Inc.; Dr. David P. Forsyth, vice-president and director, Hagen Communications, Inc.; the Rev. Carlton Frazier, former public relations director, Syracuse Area, The United Methodist Church; Samuel Grafton, editor, *Lithopinion;* Robert E. Harper, former president, National Business Publications; Miss Audrey Heaney, formerly of *Sponsor Magazine;* Clifford Hicks, former editor-in-chief and now special projects editor, *Popular Mechanics;* Mrs. Ronna Jacobi Telsey, former production editor, *Mademoiselle;* Ben Kartman, former executive editor, *Family Weekly;* Miss Barbara J. Love, formerly associate editor, *Sponsor;* Hazen H. Morse, retired vice-president, American Business Press; W. H. Mullen, formerly director, Magazine Advertising Bureau; the late Miss Mary E. Owen, editor, *The Instructor;* Norman F. Reber, secretary-treasurer, American Agricultural Editors Association; Albert G. Ryden, former editor, *The Boys' Outfitter;* Richard J. Sasso, assistant production manager, *Scientific American;* James J. Shapiro, editor, *Professional Builder;* Thomas W. Stephenson, manager, public relations division, E. I. du Pont de Nemours & Company; Mrs. Mary J. Tweedy, former director of education, Time Inc.; Mrs. Ellen Van Dusen, former editor, Crouse-Hinds *Family Circle;* H. David Whieldon, associate editor, *Medical Economics;* Mrs. Patricia Walker, editor, employe publications, Parke, Davis & Company; Dr. Donald Washburn, American Dental Association; Howard Watson, former director of public relations, Magazine Publishers Association; and Robert H. Williams, former editor, *Indiana Farmer,* and later managing editor, *Pennsylvania Farmer.*

Also, Carl Hamilton, vice-president for information and development, Iowa State University; Mrs. Ruth Kent, associate editor, The World Publishing Company; Professor George H. Phillips, head, Department of Printing and Journalism, South Dakota State University; and Vernon W. Smith, public relations staff, Syracuse University.

These magazine, newspaper, and book publishing companies and syndicates are thanked for permission to reproduce excerpts from their publications or for illustrations: Atlantic Monthly Company; Cahners Publishing Company; Chicago Tribune-New York News Syndicate; Chilton Company; Condé Nast Publications, Inc.; Cowles Communications, Inc.; Davis Publications, Inc.; The Reuben H. Donnelley Corporation; Harper & Row; Institute for Religious and Social Studies; King Features Syndicate; Local 1, Amalgamated Lithographers of America; Charles Scribner's Sons; Triangle Publications, Inc.; University of Illinois Press; *The Western Review;* and *Writer's Digest.*

*Syracuse, New York*                                                      **R.E.W.**

# Table of contents

# Part One

*The magazine in the communications scene*

*Chapter 1*

---

# The magazine
# in our time

The MAGAZINE is one outlet for an activity called journalism. The other main outlets are the newspaper, radio, and television. All four units are involved with related activities: administration, advertising, circulation, the graphic arts, the fine arts, promotion, publicity, public relations, and syndicating. And journalism itself is part of communications, which adds the motion picture, speech, the recording, and the book. Mass communication is a subdivision of communications.

Because the magazine is a part of both journalism and communications, we need to distinguish between them. *Journalism* is the systematic and reliable gathering, writing, interpreting, processing, and disseminating of public information, public opinion, and public entertainment for publication in newspapers, magazines, and broadcasts.[1] *Communications* is the study of the technique of transmitting symbols and signals as well as that technique itself; when the term *mass communications* is used we mean the study of the art or science of such communications when they involve newspapers, magazines, radio, television, movies, and books. For many years the newspaper—or some such early form of it as the news book or the newsletter—was the sole member of the journalistic family. But after the development of movable types in the fifteenth century, the family was enlarged

---

[1] Adapted from Roland E. Wolseley and Laurence R. Campbell, *Exploring Journalism* (New York: Prentice-Hall, Inc., 1949), p. 4.

3

by the addition of the magazine. Later, as journalists, aided by the improvement of transportation and means of communication, established the news-carrying and news-exchanging organizations and companies, the family expanded again.

Within our own century came the motion picture and radio-television communication. For a short time there was facsimile. The newspaper continues to dominate as the wise old man of the family, jealous of its age and long-held superiority, and still the most important news disseminator because it is a permanent record, it is swift, and it is timely.

## The family's purposes

Whatever we call a member of the journalistic family, each has certain purposes and functions in common with all the others. All function within society, and in the United States all are guaranteed freedom by society. All therefore have a responsibility to discharge in return for this protection. The idea of responsibility is conveyed in the definition of journalism.

*Systematic* means orderly, well organized, and thorough. *Reliable* means dependable, trustworthy, truthful, and accurate. Journalists are held responsible for these virtues as they carry out their duties as reporters, editors, administrators, and analysts.

Commonly the purposes of journalism are four: to inform, to guide, to entertain, and to assist commerce through advertising. Magazines inform chiefly by printing news, explanations of the meanings of events, and descriptions of conditions. They all strive to guide through editorials, special articles, and departments of opinion, even via entire periodicals. Many try to entertain and much of the material disseminated is for entertainment's sake: the greater the quantity of entertaining material, the less the amount of information and opinion. The commercial function, because the majority of magazines carry little or no advertising, is fulfilled mainly by the large consumer publications and the specialized ones issued for commercial purposes.

## The family is large

The family of journalism has only four main members: magazines, newspapers, radio, and television. But each of these has many units. In the United States general newspapers, which is the great majority, number about 10,000. Of these, approximately 1,750 are dailies and 7,600 are weeklies or of a frequency less than daily. Magazines number about 20,000, general and specialized together and of all frequencies. About 7,400 radio stations (of which about 4,300 are

AM type) and 850 television stations are on the air. Approximately 1,000 syndicates sell material to any of these media.

This big family turns out many copies of its periodicals, many programs for its stations. The daily newspapers have a circulation of around 62,000,000 copies a day and the weeklies and other non-daily papers have roughly 30,000,000 more. More than 322,000,000 copies in the aggregate is the circulation of magazines by issue. Three hundred and ten million sets receive radio programs and about 80,000,000 pick up the television programs.

In the United States the journalistic family is a business. If not always in aim, it must in practice be a business if it is to survive in a system where materials, labor, and services must be obtained by exchange of other materials, labor, and services or by payment in accepted currency. Elsewhere in the world, journalism is not nationally so large, independent, or influential as it is in the United States. But the journalistic family throughout the world has the same types of members.

## A big industry

Magazines develop as transportation and business expand. In the century beginning around 1850, most magazines in the United States ceased being upper-middle- and upper-class publications. As transportation lines fanned out from cities, connecting widely separated communities, magazines and newspapers shared a benefit intended for manufacturers of commodities. Their advertising managers could approach producers of hosiery, soaps, household appliances, and clothing, for example, because goods now could be shipped into the hinterlands. They could urge advertising in a magazine which now had entry to the same community as the goods.

Huge circulations, many new magazines, and rapid development of printing resulted. By comparison with today's brilliant picture-laden periodicals, magazines before the turn of the nineteenth century were drab. Yet many were sufficiently appealing to become powerful influences, either as molders of opinion or as media of entertainment. Scores were so successful as merchandisers through advertising that they helped to finance magazine publishing empires. Thus in the twentieth century we find the magazine at its peak in number of publications and persons employed, circulation, distribution, and advertising revenue.

## Number of magazines

Accurate statistics on the number of magazines published in the United States are not to be found. Part of the difficulty lies in disagreement as to what a magazine is. The term *magazine* connotes more than the consumer or general publication usually found on newsstands, in library periodical rooms, or in living rooms. It also is the business magazine, the company magazine, the technical journal, the religious, labor, education, or other such specialized periodical, the comic books, and any other issue of the press taking the physical form of the magazine. Almost none of these special interest periodicals appears for sale beside a subway kiosk or on a drugstore counter; the comics and a few others are the exception.

To the late Frank Luther Mott, foremost historian of American journalism, goes credit for the most useful definition of *magazine*. In the first volume of his authoritative study, *A History of American Magazines,* he clarified the meaning of *magazine, journal, review,* and *periodical,* four terms commonly confused.

All magazines are publications, for any issue of a press is a publication. Other common issues are newspapers, pamphlets, books, leaflets, cards, catalogs, and posters. Few of these familiar printed pieces are issued regularly. Only newspapers and magazines are published periodically, that is, with more or less regularity and under the same name. They, therefore, are the only ones to qualify as periodicals. But the newspaper, Dean Mott pointed out, never has been fully accepted in that status and for more than a century has been recorded under its own name, as distinguished from the periodical. [2]

The term *magazine* was used as part of the name of a publication for the first time in 1731, when it went into the title of the *Gentleman's Magazine* of London. That particular application was entirely suitable, for the word comes from the French *magasin,* and it originally meant *storehouse.* The early magazines in England and on the Continent literally were storage places for sketches, verse, essays, and miscellaneous writings on a variety of subjects. At least two military and two other journalistic uses of the word also exist. A storage place for gunpowder in a fort or on shipboard is called by that name, as is the cartridge chamber of a gun. Above certain types of cameras are two humps that shelter the reels of film: these also are magazines. At the top of a typesetting machine is a flat container in an inclined position which stores matrices. This, too, is known as a magazine.

In earlier years the term, as applied to the journalistic product, had to do with contents and not with format. Hence a publication with newspaper format but a wide variety of content was considered a magazine. As the newspaper more and more was devoted to news— in time, to spot news—and the magazine on the contrary made no effort to print up-to-the-minute news but tried to present fiction,

---

[2] Frank Luther Mott, *A History of American Magazines* (Cambridge, Mass.: Belknap Press of Harvard University Press, 1957), Vol. I, pp. 5–6.

travel articles, and other materials for entertainment, the word *magazine* was used to mean a bound and covered publication issued with regularity. The newspaper page size became large—in the 1840's and 1850's some pages measured three by five feet and were dubbed blanket sheets. They could be held together only by repeated folding. The magazine, however, usually consisted of sheets folded only once, vertically through the center. Since they tended to fall apart, it became the practice to bind them.

, Appropriately, therefore, Dean Mott defined a magazine as "a bound pamphlet issued more or less regularly and containing a variety of reading matter." [3]

The words *journal* and *review* have come to be virtual synonyms of *magazine*. Originally a journal (from *diurnal* or daily) was a diary or a daily record, covering official transactions. Certain journals were developed into magazines in format and content but retained the word *journal* in their names for the sake of tradition or sentiment. For many years a review was a periodical that contained literary materials, critical articles, and comment on current events; it reviewed what had taken place. Little remains of such distinctions. Fundamentally, today, all periodicals called journals or reviews are magazines.

The clause in Dean Mott's definition, "a variety of reading matter," seems to say that a magazine must have prose and poetry alike and be of general appeal. But the variety can be within the specialty it serves: a business magazine, for example, contains editorials, articles, advertising, photographs, diagrams, news stories, and other "varieties of reading matter." Thus Dean Mott's definition should not be confined to the general appeal magazines and admits all specialized types of periodicals.

To further complicate defining is the development of the consumer or general appeal magazines, that is, periodicals appealing to the whole population. These became powerful in the latter half of the nineteenth century, and are at their peak in circulation size and advertising revenue today, with *The Reader's Digest* and its multiple-million, world-wide circulation in the forefront, followed by more than sixty other magazines of a million to fifteen million circulation. At least several hundred magazines make mainly consumer appeal. The others—the industrial publications, the comics, business periodicals, juveniles, and those of various special interests—are specialized periodicals. But they all are magazines.

In the magazine world, the techniques are so interchangeable that persons who have worked on one easily adapt to another so far as skills are concerned.

The breadth of the magazine field is not always realized. Ayer's

---

[3] *Ibid.*, p. 7.

*Directory of Newspapers and Periodicals* omits several thousands of magazines from its listings, perhaps because they are company magazines or regional church publications. Most books on magazines and magazine techniques give the specialized periodicals short shrift. But the size of the field is recognized by Prof. Helen M. Patterson, now retired from the School of Journalism at the University of Wisconsin and author of a widely used article-writing text. In the third edition of her book, *Writing and Selling Feature Articles,* she includes tables which show that at the time of publication there were 8,220 magazines not including company magazines (often known as house organs). We find the division by types to be as follows:

| Type of Publication | No. of Magazines |
|---|---|
| Farm and agriculture | 1,068 |
| Education and social | 73 |
| Entertainment | 129 |
| Fraternal | 146 |
| Home and garden | 32 |
| General | 633 |
| Magazine sections of newspapers | 487 |
| Religious | 683 |
| Sports | 142 |
| Trade, technical, and class | 4,749 |
| Women's | 41 |
| Young people's and children's | 37 |
| *Total* | 8,220 |

Based on Ayer's *Directory,* Professor Patterson's figure is conservative, as we shall see in examining the periodicals of various specialties later. To her total, in any case, can be added the enormous number of magazines issued in this country by private business for its employes, customers, stockholders, and others. *Reporting,* the monthly of the International Council of Industrial Editors, reports the existence of 10,000 such publications, four-fifths being of magazine format. A few of these, perhaps, are included in her trade, technical, and class category.[4]

Magazines in the United States, therefore, total at least 20,000, conservatively, and comprise the largest single group of publications as defined by format. As indicated even by Ayer's *Directory,* although the value of its total figures is dubious in view of the many omissions, magazines are increasing numerically whereas newspapers are either declining or marking time. A comparison of the number of magazines and newspapers in recent years is shown in this list:

[4] Helen M. Patterson, *Writing and Selling Feature Articles* (Englewood Cliffs, N.J.: Prentice-Hall, Inc., 1956), p. 510.

| Year | No. of Different Magazines | No. of Different Newspapers |
|------|---------------------------|-----------------------------|
| 1964 | 8,900 | 11,346* |
| 1965 | 8,990 | 11,383* |
| 1966 | 9,102 | 11,355* |
| 1967 | 9,238 | 11,307* |

* Including papers of all frequencies and about 400 Sunday newspapers with magazine supplements.

Only magazines included by Ayer are covered in this list. Thus more than ten thousand are excluded. Whatever trends are noted may be deflected by the omitted magazines. But inasmuch as publications tabulated by Ayer are the chief business institutions in magazinedom, they are important to watch from vocational and commercial standpoints. A business depression which produced a sharp decline in the number of magazines of general circulation would even more seriously affect the industrial magazine or the periodical of music, sports, or some other specialty.

## Magazines by types

Broadly, the magazine in our time divides into two groups:
1.  The consumer or general interest *(The Reader's Digest)*.
2.  The specialized *(Dance)*.
The first can be subdivided further, if the group of consumers to which the general appeal is made is specialized, yet numerically extremely large. Thus:
1.  Women's *(McCall's)*.
2.  Men's *(True)*.
3.  Sophisticated *(The New Yorker)*.
4.  Quality *(Harper's)*.
5.  Confession *(True Story)*.
6.  News *(Newsweek)*.
7.  Sports *(Sports Illustrated)*.
8.  Travel *(Travel)*.
9.  Exploration *(National Geographic)*.
10. Humor *(Mad)*.
11. Shelter *(Better Homes and Gardens)*.
These are not mutually exclusive groups. Confession and shelter magazines, for instance, also qualify as women's magazines, but they appeal to special types of women or women with particular interests.

The second main group, the specialized magazines, has as many subdivisions as there are specialties of interest to human beings. Most

of these interests are acquired ones, not necessarily permanent, and
are gratified, for the most part, by small circulation periodicals. The
principal areas, either by type of content or by subject, include:

1. Juvenile *(Child Life).*
2. Comic *(Superman).*
3. Little literary *(Prairie Schooner).*
4. Literary *(Hudson Review).*
5. Scholarly *(Journalism Quarterly).*
6. Educational *(The Instructor).*
7. Business *(Business Week).*
8. Religious *(Christian Century).*
9. Industrial or company *(The Quaker).*
10. Farm *(The Missouri Farmer).*
11. Transportation *(Railway Age).*
12. Science *(Scientific American).*
13. Discussion or opinion *(The Nation).*

In addition there are the magazines of the labor movement, political and racial minorities, hobbyists, and countless more.

## *Circulations are astronomical*

If significance derives from bigness, magazines of the United
States are significant in circulation as well as in their total number.
This country is the homeland of the most widely circulated magazine,
*The Reader's Digest,* which in 1970 distributed 28,000,000 copies
throughout the world each month. Sixty-three others have circulations
of 1,000,000 or more. As gleaned from Audit Bureau of Circulations,
publishers', and Ayer's *Directory* reports, they are:

| | | |
|---|---|---|
| *American Home* | *Family Weekly** | *New York Times* |
| *American Legion* | *Farm Journal* | *Magazine** |
| *Argosy* | *Field & Stream* | *Newstime* |
| *Awake* | *Glamour* | *Newsweek* |
| *Better Homes and* | *Good Housekeeping* | *Outdoor Life* |
| *Gardens* | *Holiday* | *Parade** |
| *Boys' Life* | *House and Garden* | *Parents' Magazine* |
| *Changing Times* | *Junior Scholastic* | *Photoplay* |
| *Columbia* | *Ladies' Home Journal* | *Playboy* |
| *Consumer Reports* | *Life* | *Popular Mechanics* |
| *Cosmopolitan* | *McCall's* | *Popular Science* |
| *Decision* | *Mad* | *Monthly* |
| *Ebony* | *Mechanix Illustrated* | *Progressive Farmer* |
| *Elks* | *Motion Picture* | *Reader's Digest* |
| *Esquire* | *National Geographic* | *Redbook* |
| *Family Circle* | *New York Times* | |
| | *Book Review** | |

| | | |
|---|---|---|
| *Scouting* | *Today's Education* | *Upper Room* |
| *Seventeen* | *True* | *U.S. News and World* |
| *Sport* | *True Story* | *Report* |
| *Sports Afield* | *Tuesday** | *V.F.W. Magazine* |
| *Sports Illustrated* | *Tuesday at Home** | *Watchtower* |
| *Successful Farming* | *TV Guide* | *Woman's Day* |
| *Time* | *TV Radio Mirror* | *Workbasket* |

* Magazine supplements of newspapers.

More than four billion copies of consumer magazines alone are sold annually in the United States. Partial estimates are made each year by the Magazine Advertising Bureau, which finds that 270 magazines alone have 195,000,000 circulation combined and enter 44,000,000 of the nation's 52,000,000 homes. But the MAB reports only on Audit Bureau of Circulations publications and such non-ABC general and farm periodicals as are listed in *Standard Rate and Data*. It does not include the more than 2,000 business periodicals or the

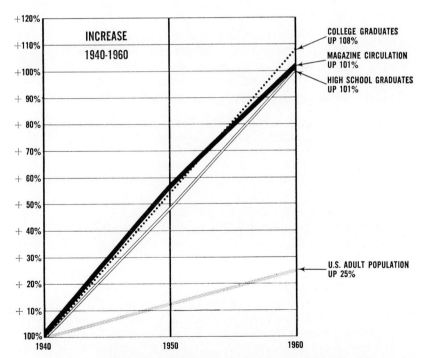

*Fig. 1.1.* There is a close relationship between higher education, reading, and the quality of the magazine audience. *(Bureau of the Census, Audit Bureau of Circulations Records, Magazine Advertising Bureau)*

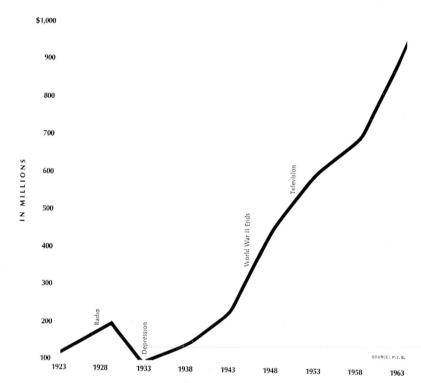

***Fig. 1.2.*** **Investments in magazine advertising increased nine times between 1923 and 1963. The sharpest growth was in the third decade. From 1963 to 1971 the figure rose to $1,321 million.** *(McCann-Erikson Research Dept.; Magazine Advertising Bureau and Publishers Information Bureau)*

8,000 company magazines. These, with various religious, labor, political, social minority, educational, and other magazines would increase the total by many millions more.

### *Advertising keeps pace*

An axiom of the business of journalism has been that large circulations bring high advertising revenue. Magazines are no exception to the general rule, although with the rise in cost of materials and production an extremely high circulation can be a liability if the advertising rate cannot, for reasons perhaps of competition, be raised to the point where it offsets the mounting costs.

Advertising in magazines is largely national. The agencies that record it do not attempt to calculate income from advertising of small periodicals or of regional magazines existing on minimum, local copy.

Consumer advertising revenue now amounts to more than
$1.3 billion a year, placing magazines third in annual total value of
advertising, with newspapers first and television second. This figure
by no means covers all magazines, for omitted are magazine supplements of newspapers and various specialized publications similarly excluded in reckoning circulation totals. The comparable figure for
1939 was $152,000,000, showing an increase since then of nine times.
Between 1957 and 1962, magazines (consumer type only) earned more
national advertising revenue than any other medium. But it must be
realized that increases in income can be the result of rate increases
and not sales volume, that is, space, increases. In this respect magazines are not in as strong a condition on volume sold as on revenue
received, although increases occurred between 1963 and 1971.

### Extent of employment

More than 40,000 persons are employed by consumer magazine
publishing companies alone. Untabulated thousands are on the staffs
of specialized publishers, such as the McGraw-Hill Company, which
issues thirty business magazines, the Chilton Company, and the Dun-
Donnelly Company, in the same type of magazine journalism.

The United States Department of Commerce has on record more
than two thousand magazine publishing firms. This figure probably
is far too small, for the government agency discovered only 68,000
persons employed on 4,610 periodicals at the time of its last study
(1947), whereas other counters show thousands more. Eight thousand
could be added as the employes of the house magazines alone, as these
are rarely listed by any of the usual calculators, since the firms that
issue them are not in any other way in the publishing business. Even
the figures between government agencies do not agree. The Census
of Manufactures has reported 182 labor publications, whereas the Department of Labor reports 800 such magazines and newspapers.

The actual extent of employment is also difficult to arrive at,
since magazine publishing companies generally contract for the printing of their publications. Thus any figure which reports the number
of printing employes would represent only those of firms that chose
to operate their own plants, which the vast majority do not. Unknown
numbers of engravers, printers, binderymen, and others are related to
the magazine publishing business, therefore. Similarly commercial
artists, promotion experts, and independent sales forces are dependent upon the magazine industry.

### Magazines as journalism

Although the magazine has long held an honorable place in the
world of journalism, until recently it has been subordinated to the
newspaper as a subject of study.

Usually it is the newspaper journalist, rather than the magazinist, to use Edgar Allan Poe's word to describe one who does magazine work, who has published his drama-filled memoirs. Until the second decade of this century only newspapers and news services commonly sent their staff writers on exciting and dangerous war, police, and disaster assignments. Not until World War I did any substantial number of magazines report the big stories at first hand.

Instruction in journalism was begun by newsmen and during its first quarter-century it remained in their hands. Curricula of schools of journalism were designed, as to a considerable extent they continue to be, mainly to prepare young people for newspaper work. Textbooks, courses, and classroom work were all centered in the newspaper as the matrix of journalism.

With one notable exception, historical research into journalism of the United States has been concerned largely with the newspaper. The newspaper appeared in the colonies earlier than the magazine, just as it appeared first in the mother country; for many years newspapers were more numerous and more influential than magazines.

Criticism of American journalism has been almost exclusively criticism of the general newspaper. Most of the milestone books, such as Upton Sinclair's *The Brass Check,* George Seldes' *Freedom of the Press,* Merle Thorpe's *The Coming Newspaper,* Oswald Garrison Villard's *The Disappearing Daily,* Hamilton Holt's *Commercialism and Journalism* and other volumes by Herbert Brucker, A. J. Liebling, Harold Ickes, James E. Rogers, T. S. Matthews, Silas Bent, Carl Lindstrom, and the Nieman Fellows say little or nothing about other members of the journalistic family; the magazine, in fact, although the other half of print journalism, is given less attention than the motion picture or television.

For many years even the dictionaries overlooked the magazine. The *press* was defined as "Newspapers or periodical literature collectively, or the body of persons collectively, as editors, reporters, etc., engaged upon such publications." The magazine used to be defined as "A periodical, containing stories, sketches, etc. and often illustrated." Now the magazine has won its fight for recognition in the word books. A recent definition reads: "A publication, usually paperbacked and sometimes illustrated, that appears at regular intervals and contains stories, articles, etc. by various writers and, usually, advertisements." This definition, however, actually is defining only the consumer magazine.

Even as the dictionaries have changed, so have biographers and autobiographers, teachers, historians, and critics. The life stories or memoirs of the notable magazinists Park Benjamin, John Bigelow, James T. Fields, Edward Everett Hale, George Creel, Theodore Dreiser, H. L. Mencken, George Horace Lorimer, Ellery Sedgwick, Kenneth Roberts, Briton Hadden, Harold Ross, Edward Weeks, Carmel Snow,

T. S. Matthews, Edna Woolman Chase, and Walter Lippmann all were published after 1947. Several of them have been treated in several books each; a half-dozen have been devoted to Mencken. Since 1947 books have been brought out on S. S. McClure, Sarah Josepha Hale, William Dean Howells, Isaiah Thomas, Oswald Garrison Villard, Henry R. Luce, Albert Jay Nock, the Harpers, W. E. B. DuBois, Henry B. Sell, and many others.

In 1948 five universities were found to have such well-developed programs for the study of magazine journalism that their sequences were accredited; others were later accepted. For the first time in its twenty-five years of existence to that time, *Journalism Quarterly* in September, 1948, devoted an entire issue to magazine journalism. The finest historical writing about American journalism has been a magazine study: Dean Mott's multi-volume work *A History of Magazines* won him a Pulitzer Prize for history and a Bancroft Prize in the same area after the first four volumes were published; no other books on journalism have been thus honored. To that set have been added three editions of James Playsted Wood's *Magazines in the United States,* two of Theodore Peterson's *Magazines in the Twentieth Century,* David P. Forsyth's *The Business Press in America,* and studies of individual or small groups of publications, notably *The Little Magazine, Endless Frontiers, Little Wonder, Decline and Fall,* and *Time Inc.*

The position of the magazines no longer is minor. They are significant enough to be examined as social influences, distinctive enough in techniques to be the subject of increasing numbers of textbooks, and attractive enough vocationally to deserve examination by career seekers.

### All techniques are used

Although the early dictionaries sought to imply that magazines were mainly storehouses of what is considered ephemeral copy, magazines long ago exceeded the function of being media of entertainment or escape. To do so they have employed all the tools and techniques of journalism. As evidence:

1. Commercial magazines in our time are financed through income from subscription and single copy sales and from advertising.
2. They use all the known varieties of written manuscript and a wider variety of illustration than any other publication.
3. They are issued by every known process of reproduction that has commercial feasibility; by the use of color they have exceeded in beauty all other journalistic forms.
4. Because of their relative infrequency of issue and their independence of immediate timeliness they have been able to use devices to gain circulation to such an extent that they have

achieved wide national coverage and international distribution equaled only by the sacred books.

5. They have joined consumer with advertiser and have thus become essential factors in modern business.

6. By using conventional public-opinion-forming techniques they have obstructed or advanced social causes, as the case may be, and as desired by their owners.

All these are characteristics, likewise, to some degree, of newspapers, radio and television stations, and other means of mass communication.

## Individual functions and qualities

Magazines now are capable not only of performing virtually all the functions of all other printed media, although not always in the same way, but they also have their own particular virtues and faults.

They long have performed all the press's usual functions of informing, influencing, entertaining, and supporting commerce. As daily newspapers and radio-television stations increasingly developed the spot-news functions, it was natural that magazines should prefer to present largely long-range information. So long as newspapers seek editorial influence and are in a position to comment promptly on news events, giving the short-range view, the magazine is content—except for a few, newspaperlike in their production methods, the newsmagazines—to exercise long-range influence. The entertainment function has been changing: it no longer clings to short stories, novels, jokes, humorous cartoons, plays, and verse as its major stock in trade. These, to some extent, have been supplanted by articles of many types.

In fulfilling its functions it has created certain distinctive journalistic products, characteristics, or procedures. Almost never are they typical of all magazines but all magazines possess some of them. They are:

## Individual strengths and weaknesses

**Magazine advertising.** Dominantly national, it is distinguished by a closer approach to technical perfection than any other advertising medium. High grade paper, color printing, original styling and design, and distinctive copywriting set magazine advertising apart from all other appearing in journalistic media.

**Circulation.** Home delivery and newsstand release on a national, uniform basis can be matched by other media only in smaller and therefore more easily traversed countries.

**Editing.** Because it is expected, the magazine must do more careful editing than is possible for a rapidly produced daily newspaper or a busy non-metropolitan weekly. Consequently, staff attention to completeness, accuracy, and originality of copy is at least as great as for any other product of the press except the book.

**Production.** Advertising and editorial page layouts, reproduction of paintings and photographs in black and white as well as in color, and durable and original covers are among the more obvious production distinctions.

**Research.** Study of readers and reading desires, for advertising, circulation, editorial, and sales departments, has gone as deeply and broadly into readership and reader interest problems as for any other medium, although not necessarily with satisfactory scientific methods and results.

**Specialization.** The magazine format has lent itself better than that of any other medium to use by special interest groups—scientists, propagandists, industrialists, and scores of other persons united by a special interest.

For the reasons that permit achievement of leadership in the areas noted above, the magazine also is characterized by certain weaknesses. They are:

**Untimeliness.** Superior printing cannot be produced at high speed without extraordinary expense. Timely and newsy copy, therefore, has place in few magazines. Often news is stale if reported straight; to compensate, editors must prepare interpretations and analyses that supplement newspaper and radio reports. At times this causes embarrassment. *Look* was on the newsstands and in the mail in early June, 1968, when Senator Robert F. Kennedy was assassinated. On its cover was a photograph of Mrs. Kennedy, happy and surrounded by her ten children; inside was an article making no mention of the tragedy. It had been written and printed long before the event.

**Internal competition.** Advertising and reading matter compete vigorously in magazines. Even radio and television do not in general allow commercials to dominate their programs, for in amount of time they are a small proportion of the total. Newspaper advertisements have reader interest, but they are not as compelling to the reader as the comics, news stories, feature articles, and picture pages. Magazines, however, print advertisements that use original art work, photographs, paintings, and individual typographic styling, often in full color. The reading matter must meet the competition of these attractive advertisements, and it is not well prepared to do so. It often is from free-lance sources and therefore not so well tailored and shaped as the copy provided to newspapers by reporters trained by the papers themselves, by experts writing for wire services and for syndicates. And it does not have the inherent compelling interest possessed by spot news.

**External competition.** A periodical is easily and frequently imitated, sometimes with success. The first two American magazines, each racing to win first place, were issued only three days apart. Such battles have been repeated. *Life* and *Look* did so sensationally. Each new idea gives rise to imitators, and imitators may spring up undeterred, for the magazine is not patented. When *Esquire* was founded it soon was faced with competition from *Sir, Mr., Ringmaster,* and much later from *Playboy.* It changed its formula to one of appeal to the sophisticated man interested in modern social problems and ideas as well as clothes, entertainment, and the arts. *Playboy,* in turn, soon was faced with a string of imitators. *Life* and *Look* were followed by *Click,* the early version of *Pic, See, Roto, Focus, Flash, Photo-History, Ebony, Sepia,* and numerous others, most of which did not survive. *Time* was followed successfully by *Newsweek* and *United States News,* and unsuccessfully by *U.S. Week, World Report,* (later joined to *United States News),* and a revamped *Pathfinder,* among others.

**Circulation limitations.** Magazines have the further handicap of requiring either intense circulation or wide national distribution before they can command lucrative national advertising accounts. Regional magazines (as distinguished from regional editions of national periodicals), therefore, are rarely more than moderately successful. *Cue,* sometimes considered a slight competitor of *The New Yorker,* is barely known outside metropolitan New York except to persons in the magazine business or frequent visitors to that city. The area is so large and densely populated that *Cue* obtains some consequential advertising. It also has succeeded in gaining a sufficient reader following. Chicago, however, never has had a magazine like *The New Yorker* or *Cue* for any substantial length of time, despite its four million population. The attempts (which included *The Chicagoan,* a close imitation of *The New Yorker,* and *The Tatler,* not unlike *Cue*) have failed not only because they did not obtain enough advertising but also because they were not indigenous to their city.

Magazines, of course, share with other media of communication all the common weaknesses attributed to the press: too great dependence upon advertising revenue; the tendency to give the public what it wants to assure the publication's survival; glorification of human self-interest, appearance, and monetary success; overemphasis on material goods; unwillingness to examine unpopular ideas objectively and thoroughly; and creation of social waste by misdirecting effort and resources. Some of these failings are examined in more detail in Chapter 22.

### The quality of dynamism

If there were a magazine to record the life of the magazine world itself, each issue would be crowded with the reports of changes occurring in that world. The stories would be about new magazines being born and old ones dying, as they do every week; about the condition of the magazine economy as it alters year by year; about

American publishers expanding into other countries; and about mergers of publishing firms. We would see accounts of new types of diversification, of specialization becoming more intense, of the effects of the computer age, of the rise in various costs, and of the social changes in the nation and their impact on periodicals.

The magazine industry is a changing one. The changes come from two sources: the tradition of variety and movement that has been attached to the industry since the early 1800's and the necessity to meet the problems facing the print media in the communications world. The typical diversity of the magazine field results in dynamism. Let a publisher try printing his magazine with three covers instead of two or a fold-out center spread and other publishers see an application to their periodicals and experiment also. Or let a new specialty be born, such as space exploration, and shortly a magazine appears, concerned with the production and use of the equipment needed for such astral experiments.

But in recent years the impetus to change has come as well from the battle with the broadcasting media. When, in the 1950's, television seized more and more of the time of the American people, it deflected their attention from radio as well as from newspapers and magazines for a time. But after the novelty wore off the print media recovered and circulations now are higher than ever.

The real inroads on newspapers and magazines were made in the big pocketbook known as advertising. Companies that had devoted major portions of their advertising appropriations to newspapers and magazines found the mass audiences offered by television tempting. Magazines, being national rather than local publications, suffered more. To meet this competition, their publishers have launched regional editions with special advertising rates, speeded production, splashed more color on the pages, opened additional outlets for magazine sales (such as supermarkets), and stressed as significant the quality of readers rather than their number.

Thus a magazine publisher today is ready for new changes, considers constantly what changes are possible, and fears more the costs of change than the idea of change itself. We see diversification taking place steadily, with magazine publishing companies now operating radio and television stations, book publishing firms, and even such unrelated industries as the manufacture of lighting equipment, cartons, globes, and fabrics.[5]

Modern publishers of periodicals must look back with longing to the days when magazines were simple black and white booklets, the sole enterprise of those who owned them, and beset by no such prob-

---

[5] Sherilyn Cox Bennion, *A Study of Diversification of Operations Among United States Magazine Publishing Companies* (Syracuse, N.Y.: School of Journalism, Syracuse University, 1963), p. 9.

modern periodicals elsewhere. *Constanze* in Germany, *Alle Kvinner* in Norway, and *Elle* in France are only a few that resulted. In the nineteenth century, however, it was Germany's magazines for women that influenced the appearance and content of those in the United States.

American publishing methods and procedures are studied and adapted where possible, although those of the consumer magazines are not necessarily suitable to nations which are considerably smaller than the United States. Overseas magazines often have simpler problems of distribution and geographical diversity and usually can get along with much smaller press runs.

The European and American influences, while traceable in the Far East, are not as dominant there as in Latin America, since most nations of South and Central America were under Spanish or Portuguese rule at one time. The magazines of Japan, China, India, Indonesia, Burma, and other Asian countries are a mixture. That is, sold along with periodicals not unlike those of Europe in format and content, if not in language, are others that are markedly different. In Japan, for example, among the most popular periodicals are monthlies that more nearly resemble thick paperback books than magazines, for they measure 4½ by 5½ inches, run to about 300 pages, contain much text on low quality stock, with line drawings and occasional inserts of engravings, and advertising sprinkled throughout, even on the covers.

Probably of the most influence, beyond basic format and formula, are American advertising solicitation and presentation methods. Much less conscious of advertising than is the United States, other nations have only in recent years set up more elaborate and systematic means to solicit it and used space, where not restricted by government, to carry more of it. They also are publishing types of advertising not much printed heretofore, such as institutional and goodwill copy. In some countries the shortage or high cost of newsprint and other printing papers as well as restrictions of legislation have imposed obstacles in the way of development of magazine advertising.

Although many of the nations of the world have a high enough literacy rate to sustain numerous magazines, certain large ones, such as India and Brazil, have high illiteracy rates. And in scores of others the educational level is extremely low, college education being possible only for the well-to-do. Therefore inexpensive mass magazines are supported but periodicals of ideas and opinion, the arts, and various important specialties have small readership and usually require subsidy.

Publication of magazines by different levels of government is common in low literacy countries. Made necessary by the difficulties of sustaining magazines on a profit basis, this provides periodicals but also leads to their use as propaganda tools.

Multilingual nations have special publishing problems. India, for example, has fourteen major languages and hundreds of sublanguages and dialects. English and Hindi, the former and present national languages, are not spoken by a majority of the people and are read only by a minority. The problem of a publisher who issues magazines for those who can read only some major language other than Hindi or English, such as Marathi, is complex. To reach readers outside his own language area he must issue editions in translation. Even in Canada a publisher who wishes to be read by people anywhere in the nation must issue English and French editions, as does *Maclean's,* the largest consumer magazine in that country.

# Chapter 2

# Magazines have a history

Frome can be considered the mother of magazines. The earliest ones have been traced to the first catalogs issued by the booksellers of Europe in the seventeenth century. French dealers included in their lists descriptions, somewhat like little book reviews, of volumes offered for sale. These periodicals continued more or less in this style while the newspaper was developing into the London *Gazette* of the latter half of the same century. After a time essays and other types of content were added.

A cross between a newspaper and a magazine was issued in 1704 in London by a writer described in the advertisements for his arrest as a "middle-sized spare man about forty years old of a brown complexion and dark brown-coloured hair, but wears a wig; a hooked nose, a sharp chin, grey eyes, and a large mole near his mouth."

This man was Daniel Defoe, who later was to become famous as the author of *Robinson Crusoe*. Because he attacked the Church of England in a pamphlet called "Shortest Way with Dissenters," Defoe was placed in the pillory for three days and then sent to prison. Soon after his release from Newgate, this journalist began publishing the first British periodical: *The Review*. The Facsimile Society of New York has issued a 22-volume set of the entire publication in recognition of its importance. This antecedent of the modern magazine usually had four small pages. It was issued for nine years, sometimes as often as three times a week. Defoe wrote and edited all of it, producing articles on domestic affairs and national policies and commenting on the news. He added a department on literature, manners, and morals. It was this section that inspired other editors to found what rightly can be considered regular magazines, although they were not so called then.

Richard Steele and Joseph Addison, with their *Tatler* and *Spectator,* started five years after the *Review,* are known to all who have studied English literature. Their publications were literary and the work of contributors whose aim was to influence public taste and morality as well as politics. Many imitations followed, including magazines titled the *Guardian, Englishman, Town Talk, Tea-Table, Chit-Chat,* and *Grub Street Journal.*

Despite its name, it would be an error to consider the *Gentleman's Magazine* the first in the English language. It was simply the first to call itself a magazine. Edward Cave, an English printer who used the name Sylvanus Urban, brought out the first issue in 1731. Selection of the name *magazine* for the periodical is worth at least brief examination so as to gain greater understanding of the differences, in the early years of journalism, between newspapers and magazines. The variety of material in the *Gentleman's* justified its label. It truly was a storehouse or repository. Space was given to current affairs, poetry, biography, obituaries, bibliography, songs, and features of various sorts, illustrated with engravings. Because it reprinted materials from other publications it was in that function a predecessor of the modern digest.

Among the most prolific contributors to this periodical was Dr. Samuel Johnson, whose main work was reporting Parliamentary activities. He is credited with writing some of the speeches he put into the mouths of statesmen who spoke in Parliament. The *Gentleman's* had a circulation of 10,000 during most of its life, and 15,000 when Johnson was its reporter, article writer, and assistant editor. He went on to form his own famous *Rambler* and to do his later writing for *The Idler.*

### Early colonial magazines

Just as homeland newspapers inspired colonials to set up weeklies and dailies in what was to become the United States of America, so these early British magazines, numbering about 150 in England in the middle of the eighteenth century, gave rise to colonial imitators.

Dean Mott, in one of his other books, *American Journalism,* described the publication of the earliest magazine in colonial British America. Benjamin Franklin conceived the plan, but Andrew Bradford was the first to execute it. A Philadelphia editor, John Webbe, was expected by Franklin to be his editorial assistant. Instead Webbe took the story of Franklin's intentions to Bradford and that printer, with Webbe's help, managed to get his *American Magazine* on sale three days before Franklin, who did all his own work, was ready with his *General Magazine*.

Both, however, dated their monthlies January, 1741. Both ventures failed, Bradford's in three months, Franklin's in six. Mott declares that Franklin's was "much more varied and interesting." They contained mainly government documents, printed in type now difficult to read. Yet they are worth examining for what they tell us of the events of 1740–41. Modeled after British magazines, they are preserved in facsimile form. Franklin's contained seventy pages, twice as many as Bradford's. Both were colonies-wide in their viewpoints.

This breadth of view was characteristic of the magazines born around the turn of the eighteenth century. They were intended, also, to influence homeland opinion. A few lived one or two years during the period from 1741 to 1775, including *Christian History,* the *American Magazine and Historical Chronicle,* the *American Magazine and General Repository, Censor, Royal American* and the *Pennsylvania Magazine.*

Philadelphia soon was to become the hub of the magazine publishing industry. Until recently it remained one of the important centers as the home of the huge Curtis Publishing Company and still is the source of numerous trade and special interest magazines. By 1800, sixty years after the attempts by Bradford and Franklin, almost one hundred publications had been founded, although in format they were more nearly newspapers than magazines. They were edited by men now widely regarded as literary figures, including Mathew Carey, Charles Brockden Brown, Thomas Paine, and Hugh Brackenridge. In New York the leading editor was Noah Webster, the dictionary-maker; in Boston, Isaiah Thomas, the printer. Among their periodicals was the *Pennsylvania,* in which Paine printed the work of David Rittenhouse and Benjamin Rush.

Carey, an anti-British Irish journalist, worked for Franklin as printer in France and came to America after twice being imprisoned in Ireland for publications offensive to the Crown. He started *The Columbian Magazine, or Monthly Miscellany* and also *The American Museum,* hiring and paying an editor as well as a contributor, a new idea in the last quarter of the eighteenth century. Carey was responsible for other professional innovations. He did not depend so much as did others on free-lance contributions that he could have had for nothing, but paid professional writers for assigned work.

Fourteen months was the average life span of magazines at this time, for they were largely dependent upon subscriptions, at a shilling a copy. Little advertising space was sold. Circulations were low, rarely running beyond five hundred copies, although readership was far greater than might be gathered from such a low figure. A few hit a high of 1,600 circulation.

## The early eighteen-hundreds

As the nineteenth century begins, the first important names we encounter are those of Joseph Dennie and *The Port Folio*. Dennie, Harvard graduate and good friend of John Quincy Adams, was in the words of James Playsted Wood, "bohemian, bibulous, a wit, a dandy, an Anglophile, a reactionary, a writer of sharp and polished prose."[1] He was called the American Addison. Dennie was no newcomer to journalism when he started his magazine in 1801. He had edited a Boston publication called *The Tablet* and in Walpole, New Hampshire, the *Farmer's Weekly Museum*. His prospectus for *The Port Folio* resembles the formula of *Esquire*. It was to be "Submitted to Men of Affluence, Men of Liberality, and Men of Letters." He and Adams wrote most of the first issue; the contributions of the future sixth president of the United States included installments of his book, *Tour Through Silesia*. The magazine printed satire, reviews, criticism, quotations, "Lay Preacher" essays, and political articles.

Dennie was against the Revolution as well as the separation of the colonies from England. He attacked Jefferson and declared that the Declaration of Independence was full of grammatical errors and faults of diction—"a false and flatulent and foolish paper." Democratic government, he wrote, would lead only to "civil war, desolation, and anarchy."[2]

He was indicted for seditious libel. Acquitted on July 4, 1803, he continued his attacks, using the name Oliver Oldschool, Esq. Nevertheless Dennie was more than an unsuccessful political force, for *The Port Folio* became a distinguished and literate weekly magazine with a high cultural standard. It ran from 1801 to 1827, but passed into other hands in 1812, when Dennie died at 44. Wood points out that Dennie illustrates well the comment of Emerson that an institution is but the lengthened shadow of a man.

"A strong editor," Wood writes, "even a strongly wrongheaded editor, has usually meant a strong and influential magazine; whereas intelligent editors of moderate means and no firm opinions have often produced colorless and comparatively ineffective magazines."[3] Wood illustrates his point successfully by references to modern editors: Harold Ross of *The New Yorker* and Henry Luce of Time Inc. To them might be added George Horace Lorimer of the *Saturday Evening*

---

[1] James Playsted Wood, *Magazines in the United States* (New York: Ronald Press Co., 1956), p. 28.

[2] *Ibid.*, p. 30.

[3] *Ibid.*, p. 36.

*Post,* Oswald Garrison Villard of *The Nation,* William Lloyd Garrison of *The Liberator,* Frederick Lewis Allen of *Harper's,* Norman Cousins of *Saturday Review,* and Herbert Mayes of McCall Corporation.

The other outstanding magazine editor of the early nineteenth century was the novelist Charles Brockden Brown, sometimes called the first professional man of letters in American literary history. He wrote for the *Columbian;* in 1803 he founded the *Literary Magazine and American Register* in Philadelphia.

## *The* Saturday Evening Post

For many years the original *Saturday Evening Post* insisted it was founded in 1728 and for a long time printed that statement on its cover. The *Post* said it was descended from the *Pennsylvania Gazette* and therefore that it was founded by Benjamin Franklin, who owned the latter. However, the *Gazette* was not founded by Franklin but by Samuel Keimer in 1728. Franklin and a partner bought it in 1729. In format the *Gazette* was a newspaper, not a magazine. It died in 1815. Actually the *Post* was founded in 1821 by Samuel C. Atkinson and Charles Alexander, two printers. It had no physical resemblance to the *Gazette.*[4] It merely for a time used the same office and presses as the *Gazette* had six years before.

Whenever it may have been founded, the magazine's history has been dramatic. By 1831 it was developing into a genuine periodical, borrowing less and less in appearance and content from newspapers of its time, although it still was a self-styled "Family Newspaper, Devoted to Literature, Morality, Science, News, Agriculture, and Amusement." During its first fifty years it was an important weekly. Among contributors in those days were William Cullen Bryant, who filled a front page on one occasion with a poem; Edgar Allan Poe, who wrote for it "The Black Cat"; Harriet Beecher Stowe; James Fenimore Cooper; Bayard Taylor; N. P. Willis; Ralph Waldo Emerson; James Russell Lowell; and Nathaniel Hawthorne. By Civil War time it had achieved a circulation of ninety thousand and had absorbed some of its rivals, including *The Saturday News* and the *Saturday Bulletin.* Only one of its early editors, Rufus W. Griswold, is now recalled. He also in his time edited *Graham's* (of which Poe likewise was editor) and the *International.* The *Post* at this time was politically neutral. Even up to 1848 it was printed on but four pages and was dominantly a literary magazine of the unintellectual sort. Although Bayard Taylor, Charles Dickens, and Hawthorne were contributing, so were T. S. Arthur and Ned Buntline, writers of pot-boilers of their time.

After the Civil War it went into a decline and nearly disappeared. It became more literary, to be sure, but in a serious and dull way. More and more trivia appeared. Little attention was given to the war.

---

[4] John E. Drewry, *Contemporary American Magazines* (Athens, Ga.: University of Georgia Press, 1938). See Mott letter, p. 65.

In its pages then was found the prose of the type one might expect under such titles as "Davy Crockett on the Track or The Cave of the Counterfeiters." The now famous "East Lynne" was offered. By 1895 its publisher, A. H. Smyth, was going bankrupt. When he died suddenly in 1897 the magazine was put up for sale.

Cyrus H. K. Curtis, now also well remembered as a newspaper publisher, was asked to buy it, which he did for $1,000 which now is approximately the cost of one-tenth of the present *Post's* advertising. The subscription list had sunk to two thousand. Editing it was a Philadelphia newspaper reporter who for $10 a week clipped other publications in his spare time. There was virtually no advertising. Although Curtis had bought a magazine seemingly about to die, he took his time reviving it. He left it much as it was until he could find the right editor, finally selecting an experienced magazinist. During the new editor's absence in Europe, Curtis decided to hire a stop-gap editor, George Horace Lorimer. That young Boston *Post* reporter issued four numbers and so impressed Curtis that he cancelled his original deal and Lorimer remained to make the magazine famous as a conservative and commercially successful weekly. He succeeded in the face of competition from large and flourishing general periodicals like *Collier's, Leslie's,* and *Harper's Weekly.* It remained on the path of economic success from the turn of the century until the 1950's.

Before the *Post* came into being in 1821 only one significant general magazine had lasted more than five years: the *North American Review*. Among the important short-lived ones were *Portico*, the *American Review, New England Galaxy, American Farmer, Plough Boy*, and two with jaw-breaker names reminiscent of the 1700's, *The Literary and Scientific Repository* and the *Genius of Universal Emancipation*.

The *North American* was founded in 1815 and published until 1941, when it lapsed until revived as a little magazine in 1964. It was the only twentieth-century survivor from the first decade and a half of the nineteenth among magazines of this type, which was general with emphasis on literature. Its list of contributors surpasses that properly claimed by any other magazine with the possible exception of the *Atlantic*. On its contents page were the names Richard Henry Dana, John Adams, Daniel Webster, George Bancroft, Edward T. Channing, James Russell Lowell, Charles Eliot Norton (Lowell and Norton also served as editors), and almost every other important literary figure in the first 125 years of its existence. To appear in its pages was the desire of every writer of serious work. At the time the United States entered World War II it fell into the hands of enemy agents, who sought to use it for propaganda purposes, although it long since had lost most of its popularity. It was revived in 1964 at Cornell College, in Iowa, to carry on the original traditions.

The *Saturday Evening Post* seemed to usher in a period of magazine stability that continued more or less steadily to the beginning of the second half of the century. Mortality naturally was great during Civil War and Reconstruction days. Some loss occurred during the depression and war periods from 1900 to 1950. The fortunes of magazines after 1950 are related later.

The roll call of memorable magazines started after the *Post* came into being also includes the fondly remembered friend of children, *Youth's Companion*. In its pages appeared the stories and poems of scores of important writers, from Alfred Lord Tennyson to H. L. Mencken, for this publication spanned the years, with only one short lapse, from 1827 to 1929. In that time it had as staff members Nathaniel Willis (father of the poet), Edward Stanwood, Charles Miner Thompson, Harford Powel, Jr., Joseph Edgar Chamberlin, Roswell M. Field (brother of Eugene), M. A. DeWolfe Howe, John Macy, Ellery Sedgwick, and Dallas Lore Sharp.

Unforgettable, too, is Sarah Josepha Hale's *Godey's Lady's Book*. In many a modern home hang framed pages of the engravings from this early magazine for what its editors called "females." It is remembered equally, however, for Mrs. Hale, a forthright editor who thought women deserved more from magazines than they had been receiving in the early nineteenth century. She was supported in her ambition by Louis A. Godey, who had bought her *Ladies' Magazine* so as to obtain with it her services as editor, combining the monthly with his *Lady's Book*, begun in 1830.

Mrs. Hale, also recalled because she wrote a poem beginning "Mary had a little lamb," proceeded to make the new magazine one of the most successful, both financially and in influence, of the seventy-year period it covered. She printed over-size pages that folded, accordion-like, and followed other practices which anticipated those of the smart magazines of our own time. She championed women persistently, striving to improve what she labelled "female education," and advocating that women be allowed to practice medicine. She also must be remembered as responsible for the national celebration of Thanksgiving Day. By obtaining manuscripts of the most popular writers, men and women alike; by printing stories, articles, poems, editorials, fashion, cooking, and sewing guidance (but ignoring political and social problems, an attitude not yet fully abandoned by many a magazine for women), the circulation was run to an astounding figure for this type of magazine in its time, one hundred and fifty thousand.

Paralleling *Godey's* during the first half of that magazine's existence was another thought of in connection with it, *Graham's Magazine*. It, too, emphasized the literary, which it could well do with such contributors as Lowell, Poe (who was its literary editor), Mrs. Sigourney, Park Benjamin, Bryant, Cooper, and Longfellow. A leading feature, likewise, was its illustrations, many the work of the noted

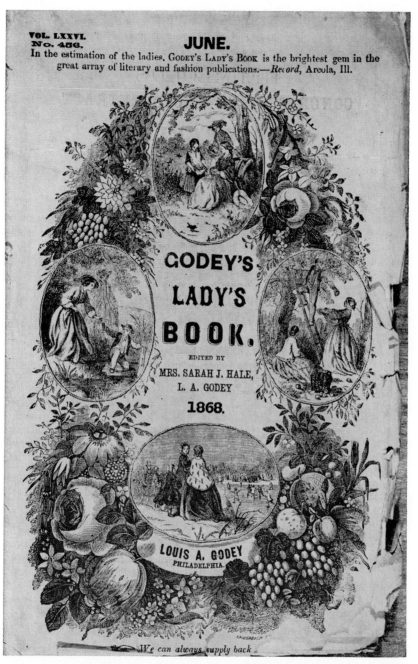

*Fig. 2.1.* The cover of an 1868 *Godey's Lady's Book.*

John Sartain, who later established a magazine bearing his name. Editor George R. Graham not only published these writers but also paid them well, an innovation.

Edgar Allan Poe's magazine career began on one of the several other outstanding periodicals of the same period. This was *The Southern Literary Messenger* of Richmond, Virginia, which ran from 1834 to 1864. To it he contributed his famous story, "Berenice— A Tale," which began a relationship that led to the editorship in 1835. Book reviewing occupied much of the poet's time on the *Messenger*. Another had a similar life span, the *Knickerbocker*, a New York monthly, named in honor of a famous contributor, Washington Irving. The humor and variety of its content may remind present-day readers of *The New Yorker*.

Another pre-Civil War magazine, the *Democratic Review,* during some of its years from 1837 to 1859 was known as the *United States Magazine,* a popular title in those days. Magazines of public affairs had an important place, for this area of interest engaged the attention of religious magazines as well as those devoted solely to current events. Here should be mentioned also numerous antislavery periodicals, edited sometimes by the nation's most eminent literati as well as by its most vigorous advocates of reform, led by Garrison and his *Liberator.* Farmers were beginning to support their own magazines, also.

*Harper's Monthly, Harper's Weekly,* the *Atlantic Monthly, The Nation,* and *Leslie's Illustrated* are the famous magazine names of the Reconstruction Period. The story of *The Nation* is told in Chapter 17, but since the other four have either disappeared or changed considerably, they will be examined briefly here as important markers in magazine history.

### *The careers of the* Atlantic *and* Leslie's

Founded in Boston in 1857, the *Atlantic* was announced as a magazine devoted to literature, art, and politics but later science was added to its subtitle. It still is deeply interested in these and virtually all other subjects. It has had only ten editors-in-chief, but few other periodicals could list as many distinguished names: Lowell, Howells, Aldrich, Page, James T. Fields, Horace E. Scudder, Bliss Perry, Ellery Sedgwick, and Edward A. Weeks. The *Atlantic* had the literati of the Hub among its early advisers, for it was intended for the Brahmins. Heavily literary and for a time distinctly regional, it has had an uneven career.

Sold three times, it never has been a magazine of large circulation, as figures for even the general literary magazines go. Up to 1874, the year of one of its sales, it had thirty to fifty thousand. It continued a distinguished but economically uncertain history until it nearly disappeared in 1909, when Sedgwick, experienced from work on several other magazines, rescued it. Since he rejuvenated it, the *Atlantic* has been a magazine of public affairs as well as letters. Sharing with most others the general rise in circulations of the past four decades, by the middle of the twentieth century it had four to five times its highest nineteenth-century circulation, had retained its place as one of the few quality magazines capable of survival, and was exerting its share of influence on American life and culture.

Sharply different in character was *Leslie's*. Henry Carter, its founder, was an English wood engraver who took the name Frank Leslie. He succeeded in making it famous with several periodicals but largely through a picture weekly successively called *Frank Leslie's Illustrated Newspaper, Frank Leslie's Illustrated Weekly, Leslie's Weekly,* and other variations. It had a colorful life from 1855 to 1922. *Leslie's Weekly* was at times considered a newspaper and even so called. Nevertheless it was progressively a true miscellany. It also was thoroughly journalistic, for it stressed news in pictures and in text.

From the circulation standpoint it was one of the sensationally successful magazines of its century. Just before the Civil War it had 164,000. Later an issue reporting the Heenan-Sayers prize fight in London sold 347,000. Wars, which often increase circulation, at least temporarily, did not benefit *Leslie's;* despite magnificent picture coverage of the Civil War, after it was over the magazine dropped to below fifty thousand. Mrs. Leslie carried on after her husband's death in 1880 and revived the magazine, but not to its former vigor. A picturesque editor, she pushed the circulation closer to one hundred thousand than it had been for some years. When she sold the magazine successive editors and owners kept it an alert, superficial, general publication through World War I; during the early war years circulation shot up to four hundred thousand. But the economic state of the nation after that war killed off *Leslie's* as well as other magazines that could not stand high production costs.

## The Harper magazines

The Harper family of book and magazine publishers was responsible for successful rivals to both the *Atlantic* and *Leslie's*, although the first might more properly be thought of as a rival to *Harper's*, which was founded earlier. Four magazines have been associated with the famed firm, now known as Harper & Row. They are:

*Harper's New Monthly* (in 1900 the word *New* was dropped and in 1925 likewise *Monthly*). It celebrated its centennial in 1950.

*Harper's Weekly,* established in 1857 and running until 1916.

*Harper's Bazaar,* a monthly founded in 1867, a magazine for women, and now the high fashion monthly published by the Hearst Magazine Company.

*Harper's Young People* (later renamed *Harper's Round Table),*

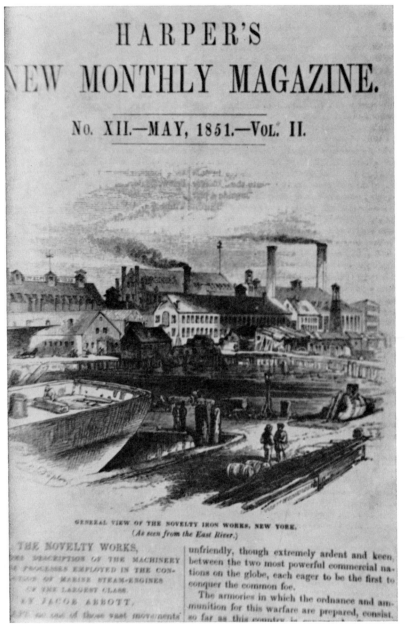

HARPER'S

NEW MONTHLY MAGAZINE.

No. XII.—MAY, 1851.—Vol. II.

GENERAL VIEW OF THE NOVELTY IRON WORKS, NEW YORK.
(As seen from the East River.)

THE NOVELTY WORKS,

WITH A DESCRIPTION OF THE MACHINERY
AND PROCESSES EMPLOYED IN THE CON-
STRUCTION OF MARINE STEAM-ENGINES
OF THE LARGEST CLASS.

BY JACOB ABBOTT.

... so one of these vast movements

unfriendly, though extremely ardent and keen,
between the two most powerful commercial nations on the globe, each eager to be the first to
conquer the common foe.

The armories in which the ordnance and am-
munition for this warfare are prepared, consist,
so far as this country is ...

Fig. 2.2. The present *Harper's* as it looked as a two-year-old in 1851.

a weekly established in 1879, and lasting, after conversion to a monthly, until 1899.

The two most significant were the *Monthly* and the *Weekly*. The former, edited as was the *Atlantic* by eminent literary men, had had only seven editors by the mid-1960's. Best known were Henry J. Raymond, remembered more for his establishment of the New York *Times,* of which he also was the first editor; Henry Mills Alden, Thomas B. Wells, Frederick Lewis Allen, and John Fischer. It grew out of a company magazine, *Harper's Family Library,* as have numerous other magazines issued by book publishing firms *(Scribner's, Century, Appleton's,* and *Putnam's).* The new monthly began immediately (1850) to print the work of prominent authors, sometimes pirating them from English publications and thereby creating a controversy.

A New York publication, it gained a fifty thousand circulation promptly. By the early years of the Civil War it achieved two hundred thousand. Much as did the *Atlantic,* the *Monthly* dealt with literature, politics, science, and the arts but became especially known for its illustrated travel articles. It spent large sums on pictures. As the big consumer periodicals of a more general appeal succeeded in selling large quantities of advertising space, the general literary magazine formula was abandoned and *Harper's* owners converted it, in 1925, to a magazine of comment on current affairs, with place for literature. Today it and the *Atlantic* have a common business department, a device used to cut down operating expenses and to offer likely advertisers the larger circulation of two somewhat similar magazines. By the early 1970's both had circulations higher than ever in their history *(Atlantic,* 330,000; *Harper's,* 360,000). Both also had appointed new, young editors, each with practical news experience and magazine writing as background.

The *Weekly* had a far more colorful but also a fateful career. Started by the Harper brothers, principally Fletcher, as a competitor to *Leslie's,* it was inspired by the *London Illustrated News.* Much as with *Leslie's,* pictures dominated, some filling two pages. It covered the Civil War about as did its rival, and had the advantage of the services of the famous cartoonist, Thomas Nast. Its circulation exceeded one hundred thousand during the war years and ten years after stood at 160,000. Probably the *Weekly* is best remembered for the successful fight with Tammany which made Nast famous and raised the circulation. But in a new political campaign, that of 1884, the magazine lost support, never to regain its full strength despite attempts by noted editors and subeditors to provide it with new power. These included George William Curtis (not to be confused with Cyrus H. K. Curtis), connected with it since its early days; Richard Harding Davis, the novelist and war correspondent; John Kendrick Bangs, the humorist; and Norman Hapgood, an experienced magazinist fresh from success at *Collier's.* It finally was merged with the *Independent.*

MARCH 1967 / 75 CENTS

# Harper's
*magazine*

# Ralph Ellison on American Writing

**The author of "Invisible Man" discusses Negro and Jewish writing, Hemingway, Faulkner, Wright, and the "Movement"...**

**The Real Masters of Television**
**Robert Eck**

**A Way Out for Homosexuals**
**Samuel B. Hadden, M.D.**

**God, Man, and William F. Buckley**
**Larry L. King**

*Fig. 2.3. Harper's* as its cover looked one hundred and sixteen years later, in 1967, in red, white, blue, and gold.

### *Wars, Depressions, and Magazines*

These were only the more vital magazines in America up to the end of the century. Less important but not to be overlooked were the popular *Lippincott's,* which ran from post-Civil to World War I days; *Appleton's Journal;* the *Delineator,* a woman's magazine once edited by Theodore Dreiser, the novelist; and *Munsey's.* Begun in the 1870's or 1880's were several periodicals for women still published today: *McCall's, Ladies' Home Journal,* and *Good Housekeeping.* This, too, was the period of *The Literary Digest,* which was declining in 1936 when an inaccurate election poll brought it bad publicity and it soon was put on the block to *Time.* At one time, however, the *Digest* had several million circulation and offered an influential summary of press opinion on current events. This was the day also of *Collier's,* the *American,* and *Woman's Home Companion,* all destined to be discontinued in the late 1950's when in their prime.

The historical events in the magazine world during the first half of the twentieth century were the result of a succession of depressions and wars. During World War I several important small magazines of opinion, such as *The Masses,* were censored out of existence. Casualties for another reason were specialized magazines that lost circulation because normal reading habits were disturbed and because advertisers could see no reason for buying space when the usual consumers were elsewhere and not exposed to the magazine. In World War II periodicals of unpopular opinion were not removed or closed by government edict. Major advertisers, some of whom learned that not to advertise for a protracted period results in the public forgetting about a product (the classic example being Pear's Soap), continued their schedules and consumer magazines held firm.

During the depression years in the late 1920's and early 1930's, the victims of events were hundreds of industrial magazines of the type ordinarily known then as house organs and now as company magazines: small periodicals intended mainly for the employes of a single concern. Often financed out of an advertising, personnel, or public relations budget, hundreds of these were lopped off as an unnecessary expenditure. But during later periods of economic stress, now dubbed recessions rather than depressions, this policy of destruction was less often followed and the magazines for the employes as well as customers, stockholders, and dealers of oil firms, pharmaceutical companies, machinery manufacturers, and others in the business world generally were continued.

The effects of the social and economic changes were not uniform on the magazine world. These changes included not only more social legislation originating chiefly with the federal government but also shifts within the world of business that decreed changes for certain industries, as for example the growth of the manufacture and use of rocketry as distinguished from aviation and the development of new processes and devices, such as pressurized containers, air conditioners, and air control equipment. Also, there was the rise in popularity of sports, outdoor living, and other leisure time activities. Add to this the increase in the number of women working in both industry and the professions, the interest in foreign as well as domestic travel, the changes in transportation resulting from the greater use of automobiles and the spread out from the cities, and the shrinking of the farm population. The arrival of new nationalities—the Hungarians, the Puerto Ricans, the Mexicans, and the Cubans—for the American melting pot, which for several decades had received merely trickles into it from foreign lands, was another social movement with which magazine publishers had to reckon.

Changes on the communications scene are equally important in backgrounding the magazine events of the period. Facsimile reproduction of newspapers, thought to be a possibly important rival to printed newspapers as we know them, never materialized beyond a few experiments. Television was the fair-haired boy instead. It grew to be a colossus, offering advertisers as many as forty million viewers for a single program, a greater exposure than could be promised by even *The Reader's Digest,* with its monthly domestic circulation in the early 1950's of ten million. Motion pictures went into a slump, video providing the public with a home screen, and the number of movie houses as well as studios decreased sharply. Radio, robbed by television of drama and virtually all other types of visually desirable programs, also went into a decline for a time and then settled down to news and music as standard fare. Both newspapers and magazines lost advertising revenue to radio, in the early years, and then to television when the latter was able to provide the impact of the picture that radio lacks.

Underlying all of this were the steadily rising cost of materials and labor, higher taxes and increased postal rates. These pressures, plus the usual incidence of mismanagement, publication of unneeded or duplicating periodicals, and inept editing, all serve to explain the inability of some magazines to continue publishing. Because certain popular magazines were among those affected, the impression exists that the entire industry has been in jeopardy since 1955. The troubles have been selective, for at the same time that certain magazines were dying, others were born and lived to be healthy members.

The losses during the past fifty years are impressive, but so are the additions. The list of the dead includes, among those with large circulations, the following: *American, Collier's, Coronet, Today's Woman, Charm, Woman's Home Companion, Country Gentleman, Ballyhoo, Everywoman's, Better Living, Quick, Life* (the humor magazine), *Judge, Blue Book, Household, Literary Digest, Liberty, Pictorial Review, Delineator, Farm and Fireside, Look, Living for Young Homemakers,* and *Holland's.* Among the widely known but more specialized that did not survive were *The Etude, Musical Courier,* and *Southern Agriculturist.*

But in that time we saw the rise of such large magazines as *Time, Life, Newsweek, United States News and World Report, Woman's Day, Playboy, Holiday, Family Circle, Jet, Look, Fortune, Sports*

*Illustrated, Hot Rod, Cavalier, True, Ebony, The Reader's Digest,* and *TV Guide.*

Specialized new periodicals other than company magazines appear at the rate of about one a week; not all survive, but a considerable number do. Among those in recent years serving highly particularized fields are *Better Camping, Skin Diver, Antique Airplanes, United Church Herald, Interpreter, Antique Automobile, Church Administration, Road and Track,* and *Change.*

Also among the newcomers are the magazine-book combination periodicals, such as *American Heritage, Horizon, US–The Paperback Magazine, New American Review,* and *Smithsonian.* These "magabooks" or "bookazines" have influenced publishers of certain older magazines, such as *Art in America,* to try—not always successfully—the same format.

In addition are the extraordinary magazines for the blind, sometimes called the products of the Inkless Press. These, such as the *Zeigler Magazine,* are printed in Braille, i.e., a system of writing with raised dots so that the readers may read through their fingers.

As will be seen in later chapters, where the histories of some of these and other magazines of the present century are introduced, the American magazine industry is one of fluidity and movement. Fundamentally it gains and loses units as do all industries in a country as large as the United States, with its dynamic economic system, moving from the uninhibited individualism of the last half of the nineteenth century to the social controls taken for granted in the last half of the twentieth.

## The notable magazinists

We have seen that such leading American writers as Poe, Lowell, and Howells were closely identified with the magazine world of the nineteenth century. Eminent as they were in the literary field, it is often forgotten that not a few of the literati of that day had journalistic careers as well. Dreamy poets and absent-minded novelists at times, perhaps; during other hours they were persons with journalistic jobs that they performed well enough to leave their impression. Even if they are thought of as journalists, which is rarely, the fact that they were magazine journalists sometimes is overlooked.

We have seen the famous names on the roster of contributors to the *North American Review.* Others have been mentioned only in passing. But when grouped as a journalistic rather than a literary list their significance takes on new meaning.

We remember Thomas Paine mainly as an Englishman who became an American revolutionary writer, a producer of propaganda essays called *Common Sense,* and a man at first misunderstood and hated by some critics but later accepted as a genuine patriot. He also was a magazine writer; the *Pennsylvania Magazine* carried his own and, while he edited it, much other revolutionary writing. Isaiah Thomas is known today chiefly as a printer and historian whose history of printing in this country was used as a basic work for more than a century. But Thomas also was a newspaper and magazine journalist and edited two periodicals: the *Massachusetts* and the *Royal American.* These editorships were less exciting than his operation of the newspapers, the *Halifax Gazette* and the Worcester *Spy.* He introduced innovations, including the use of copy beyond that of interest only to the so-called intelligentsia. In other words, he popularized content more than had his predecessors. His magazines and the *New-York Magazine* were the few of the latter part of the eighteenth century that lasted as long as eight years.

We think of Noah Webster only as the man who prepared a dictionary. But he also edited the first magazine in New York State, the *American,* which he established in 1787. He printed in it more material for women than had anyone previously; he also was more hospitable to fiction than were earlier editors. Later he edited the *American Minerva,* commonly considered a newspaper but possessing many magazine features.

Three famous American writers were joint editors, and therefore magazinists, of *The Dial,* a literary periodical, the original of four bearing that name. Although it lived only from 1840 to 1844, it had a disproportionately large influence on American writers and writing, for it was hospitable to new authors, most of whom later became noted; the editors were Ralph Waldo Emerson, Margaret Fuller, and Henry David Thoreau. More than a century later this comparatively obscure magazine became the subject of new studies of its importance and an anthology of its content was issued.

Another significant editor was James Russell Lowell, the poet, who at first edited a literary magazine, *Pioneer,* later translated his social principles into the *National Anti-Slavery Standard,* then became the first editor of the *Atlantic,* and finally editor of the *North American Review.*

Still another famous poet, John Greenleaf Whittier, author of "Snow-Bound," "Maud Muller," and "The Barefoot Boy," was a magazinist. A strong enemy of human slavery, he edited the *Pennsylvania Freeman.* For his pains his office in Philadelphia was burned by proslavery rioters and he later was mobbed. He also was an editor of *National Era,* which in 1852 printed "Uncle Tom's Cabin."

Like Whittier, Thoreau was a social pioneer. He remains close to modern interests because his ideas were concerned with many issues which still press us today. For example, he believed in nonviolence, a philosophy now widely discussed and used in consequence of its acceptance by such modern leaders as Gandhi, Kagawa, and Schweitzer, and playing a vital part in the civil rights protests of minority groups in the United States.

# Part Two

## *The business side*

# Chapter 3

# Ownership and company organizations

**B**ECAUSE *journalism* signifies only an editorial activity to many persons, it sometimes comes as a shock to them to find out that in the United States this occupation is an intimate part of the entire business system of the nation. Nor is it merely a part; it also is heavily dependent upon that complex engine.

One of the reasons for the fluidity of the magazine business in this country is that there are no requirements of registering or obtaining licenses to publish. This freedom is a product of the democracy which characterizes the American philosophy of government.

Thus it is possible for anyone to go to a printer and contract for the production of a magazine. Such a new publisher requires no permission from any official body. All he needs is editorial material, advertising copy if he is selling his space, money to pay his bills, and a place to put the finished magazines when they come off the presses. The only restrictions are those democratically agreed upon years ago: the laws relating to libel, sedition, and obscenity in the magazine's content. This freedom explains the rapidity of birth and death of new magazines, for the liberty is no assurance of continuance, which depends upon survival in the market place.

Anyone, therefore, can become a magazine publisher. Such publishers, as they sometimes are, can be groups of students who are dissatisfied with the academically approved periodicals and go off campus to start a different publication. Similarly, one or more literary or social experimentalists have during the past century started dozens of obscure but important "little magazines" (see Chapter 17), some of which became aged: *Story, Poetry, Prairie Schooner, Kenyon Review,* and *Partisan Review,* for instance.

In contrast with such simple forms of ownership of a publication is the complex structure behind such firms as Time Inc., the McCall Corp., or the Condé Nast Publications Inc., complicated further by their international divisions, subsidiary operations, and intricate internal organizations.

Forms of magazine company ownership, however, conform to the usual patterns of all American business. These are three:

1. *Individual proprietorship.* This form is suitable particularly to a small magazine which is supported by one person who desires to keep control in his own hands. If it is intended to be a profit-making venture the earnings come to him alone, but if there are debts instead of profits it is his sole responsibility to pay them.

2. *Partnership.* If two or more persons join to conduct a magazine publishing company they may form a legal organization called a partnership. This joining may increase the amount of capital available with which to float the enterprise. But it does not divide financial responsibility, for each partner is wholly responsible for the firm's liabilities. Profits are shared by agreement.

3. *Corporation.* A common form of ownership of large firms especially, a corporation is formed under state law and operates as if it were a legal person, separate from the persons who serve as its officers. The owners of the business, under this form, are known as stockholders. They elect a board of directors which controls and manages the firm. In the magazine world most corporations do not make their stock available to the public on the open market, restricting it for sale instead to family members and other associates of those in control. Stockholders are not liable for debts except in amounts equal to their investment. A controlling stock percentage usually is 51 or more, but it may be less if no single other owner or group holds as much.

These three forms of ownership are subject to tax laws in different ways; there always are various advantages and disadvantages to each form which must be taken into consideration before a new publisher decides on the final type of ownership under which the publication is to function.

Whatever the form of ownership, its form affects the magazine. If privately owned for profit, it has a different motivation than if privately owned as a public service, or if issued by a government, or if coming from a group of persons who wish to use it, not for money-making, but for propaganda purposes.

Not all magazine publishing corporations are formed to make a profit. Nation Associates and the Christian Century Foundation, which issue *The Nation* and *Christian Century* and *The Pulpit,* are examples of non-profit corporations. Another variation is government ownership. The U.S. federal government alone issues several hundred periodicals, ranging from *Amerika,* a handsome magazine the size of *Life* containing articles about this country, for sale in Soviet Russia and Poland as propaganda, to *Higher Education,* a small and unpretentious periodical containing news, book reviews, and articles.

Nor is the federal branch the only government in the magazine business: states and cities have found magazines useful. *New York State Conservationist* and *Vermont Life* both could compete with many newsstand magazines in attractive appearance.

However it may be owned, the company must have plans and these must be carried out through an organization, unless the enterprise is so tiny that one person can perform all the duties. Even then he must organize his efforts in some fashion.

## Magazine formulas

The plans for a magazine issued by a publishing firm generally are based on a formula, which may be defined as the organized concept of the magazine held by those in charge of it and translated into type, advertising ideas and facts (if it is to carry advertising), and reading matter ideas and facts, including illustrations.

Every magazine's owners, consciously or unconsciously, operate on a formula. The better organized the magazine the more likely it

*Fig. 3.1.* Five of the persons shown here owned at that time magazines which aggregated 44,000,000 circulation. From left to right, Mrs. DeWitt Wallace, *(The Reader's Digest),* Samuel I. Newhouse *(Vogue, Mademoiselle,* and others), the late Henry R. Luce *(Time, Life,* and others), former Chancellor William P. Tolley of Syracuse University, Dean Wesley C. Clark of the university's School of Journalism, Dewitt Wallace (co-owner of the *Digest),* and Mrs. Newhouse. *(Jon Bird Photo)*

is to be functioning on an articulated formula, for such a concept is part of scientific business operation. It may be successful or unsuccessful, social in purpose or predatory in aim, depending upon the objective selected or upon its effectiveness in achieving this objective.

Before the magazine administration and staff can do the most intelligent work of buying manuscripts, planning the periodical's typographical dress, and obtaining buyers of its advertising space and its issues, the owners must decide upon the formula they will follow.

The more original and yet popular the formula the more certain is the magazine to succeed financially. An original formula may not be popular and therefore may not succeed because the public is not ready for it or because of some other handicap. Or the printer may not be able to translate the formula into type, for physical reasons or because of costs.

Among the successful formulas of commercial magazines of the day are these:

**The Reader's Digest.** The husband-and-wife team of DeWitt and Lila Acheson Wallace realized in the early 1920's that people like to clip articles, jokes, anecdotes, and other material that pleases them that they want to reread and refer to again. They realized, also, that in a nation in which the ideal of keeping up with the Joneses economically and culturally is strong, a short cut to information would be popular. They saw the desire, also, for a readily portable magazine (meaning pocket size) of not too many pages, and an impression of much material in small compass. Their formula took account of these facts and has been successful financially as well as from the standpoint of influence. The original formula excluded paid advertising; to maintain its ratio of profit, the publishers have had to include it, and the present formula also is gradually including more and more color printing and illustrations.

**Time.** Briton Hadden and Henry R. Luce knew that Americans want not only quips and articles but also condensed news, that they wanted to be spared reading numerous publications, and that they appreciate an overview of what is happening. They were right, as the circulation and advertising revenue figures of the magazine now reveal. As part of their formula, Hadden and Luce devised at first a writing style which enabled them to make stale news sound fresh; later they added considerable original reporting. A basically similar formula is followed by *Newsweek* and by such specialized newsmagazines as *Business Week*. *U.S. News and World Report,* often grouped with these, has altered the newsmagazine formula, to make a place for itself, by covering only certain types of events, de-emphasizing departmentalization, and running materials in greater length and at greater depth. Both *Newsweek* and *U.S. News and World Report* avoid *Time's* anonymous authorship.

**TV Guide.** Profiting from *The Reader's Digest* experience with small size and from the rapid acceptance of television in the American home, this weekly by 1970 had achieved a fifteen million circulation in less than fifteen years. Although its core is program listings, its editors were aware that they must give readers certain typical magazine content: humor, articles, photo features, letters, editorials; further, they had to localize the basic content and publish as many editions as possible, already in excess of eighty. This formula has been extremely successful even though local newspapers in all areas print similar guides, some outrightly imitative of *TV Guide's* format.

**Life.** Luce was aware, in addition, that Americans like picture pages in newspapers as well as news stories; the surveys rated them first or second in popularity. Why not have, in addition to a summary of the news *(Time)*, a picture digest of the news? Various titles and sizes, all part of the formula, were considered; to signify its general character the name *Life,* then belonging to a dying humor magazine, was purchased. The large size was chosen as being the most effective for picture presentation. This concept was immediately successful. It later was modified to admit more text and emphasize feature pictures and picture narratives, and illustrated long-range material, such as pieces on art and science. A variation on *Life's* formula was that of *Look,* which used more controversial public affairs material, humor, and a biweekly frequency, but it failed to maintain a personality. *Ebony* is another application, merely with a different group of readers.

Unsuccessful formulas might be engraved on the headstones of hundreds of magazines in the graveyard of dead publications. Some formulas were outlived, as in the instance of *The Etude.* For almost 75 years it was a successful magazine for music teachers and students. As private lesson-giving gave way to more study of music at conservatories, university schools of music, and other institutions, the content of the magazine was not sufficiently adjusted to fit into the new environment.

Other formulas are too imitative; a small market cannot sustain several magazines with the same aims, appearance, and content. An example was *Common Sense,* published between World War I and World War II, which was much like *The Nation* or *The New Republic* and others in the opinion group. Later examples of unsuccessful imitation are *U.S.A.-1,* a monthly news interpretation magazine; *Show Business Illustrated,* which was too much like its parent publication, *Playboy;* and *Better Living,* which sought to compete with *Family Circle* and *Woman's Day,* as did *Everywoman's,* but could not survive; *Everywoman's* was merged with *Family Circle* but *Better Living* died.

Late in the 1950's and the early 1960's it appeared that failure to adjust their formulas to the times had doomed three of the Curtis Publishing Company's famous magazines: the newly acquired *Ameri-*

*can Home,* the *Saturday Evening Post,* and the *Ladies' Home Journal.*
They were in trouble. Not only had television made heavy inroads
on their advertising but also competition from magazines with more
successful adjustment to the television age was injuring them.

A sharp change of formula was made by Curtis for the *Journal*
and the *Post* especially; even other magazines in the concern were
affected, as when *Jack and Jill* opened its pages to advertising. The
alterations in the *Post* were too sudden and too extreme both typographically and in content, so far as readers were concerned, and the
editors received numerous complaints. Matters became worse instead
of better. With the sale of the firm to new owners, physical and content changes again were made, more conservative ones this time.
These, coupled with new financing, extraordinary salesmanship in
obtaining advertising contracts, and drastic economies, pulled the
magazines out of their doldrums. But the surcease was only temporary,
and the *Post* was discontinued in 1969 and then revived by new
owners as a quarterly.

Thus far, we have judged formula success or failure entirely on
an economic standard. Making profits, however, is not the sole or even
the most desirable yardstick to use, economically necessary as it happens to be if there is no other source of income or if the owner wishes
to remain independent of those who might provide subsidy.

Subsidized magazines, however, are no novelty in any country,
and certainly not in the United States, despite its business achievements. Hundreds of religious, educational, literary, scholarly, and
other special interest magazines are published by institutions that
underwrite their budgets. All company magazines, furthermore, are
so supported. Thus, well over half the magazines published in the
United States are issued not for profit, do not make a profit, and
are not expected ever to make a profit. This situation does not mean
they are independent of the profit system, for their subsidy comes, in
many instances, out of profits earned by the subsidizers from other
sources.

Influence is as legitimate a measurement of magazine success as
is commercial effectiveness. And the non-profit magazine has influence beyond its own small circle of specialization. From the
strictly profit-and-loss in dollars and cents point of view the formulas
of *The Progressive, The Nation, Commonweal, Black World, The New
Leader, Liberation, Commentary,* and several others like them economically are a failure, for much of the time most must be underwritten.
But from the standpoint of being an influence on society they have
successful formulas. (See Chapter 17.)

An ideal magazine formula is one that is successful in all ways,
because in the choice of dependencies (on advertising or on under-
writers) it is possible for a big profit-earning magazine to be more

independent of advertisers than for a small one lacking advertising to go counter to the wishes of its "angel." *The Reader's Digest* has a more generally successful formula, for it is both economically and philosophically effective, regardless of the quality of its influence.

Whatever the formula, it must be understood and democratically worked out and supported by all responsible officials. Magazine staff sessions are necessary and are likely to be lengthy. On a well-managed publication, formulas are changed only after much discussion. And, in addition to such meeting of minds, there must be knowledge of the field to be served by the magazine.

How is the formula determined? It may be arrived at by studying certain basic factors. If the standard is one of monetary success, the purpose of the formula is to achieve the ideal situation of a large enough group of readers and/or advertisers to support the magazine by direct subscription and sale or through sale of advertising space or both. The factors include:

1. *Purpose of the publication.* Why is a magazine to be issued at all? Motives usually are mixed. Catering to public taste for the sake of financial return will produce a formula different from one based on catering for the sake of political support.

2. *Market for the publication.* How many persons are interested in the area and how many are active in it? The more interest and activity, the greater the possibility of serving that market. This question also must be raised: Are these readers organized into associations, clubs, or other groups that have accessible mailing lists?

3. *Standard of living.* What is the financial condition of potential readers as possible buyers of the magazine, of products advertised in it, or of space sold for advertising use? What is standard at any given time?

4. *Educational level.* What are the levels of education of the circle of readers? What are the cultural positions of the group?

5. *Competitors.* What are the competing magazines? What are *their* formulas?

6. *Tested formulas.* How have existing formulas worked? Circulation and advertising volume and revenue reports and readership surveys are helpful sources.

7. *Climate of opinion.* What is the temper of the public, generally? To what new idea would it logically respond at the particular time in the nation's or the world's history? Is there a craving or a need exhibited by the public's conduct or habits in other types of communication (movies, personal habits, newspaper reading, book use, recreation, radio, television, and church going)?

8. *Financial horizon.* What limits are set by the financial condition of the magazine's owners? A particular formula may be beyond the reach of the magazine founder. If, for example, the formula

can be carried out only with quantities of color printing, it had better be abandoned if the company can hope to use only black and white.

All formulas are not thought out in advance, of course. Sometimes they are hit upon accidentally or by repeated experiment and change. *Holiday* is an example of the result of experimentation. In its first form, in 1946, it expressed a formula which resulted in a conventional magazine of travel except that it was glamourized. Newsstand sales declined soon after a brilliant circulation start, so another formula was used. An aura of sophistication was cast around it, liquor advertising was accepted (the first Curtis periodical permitted to do so), and *Holiday* developed into a magazine of special interest with a million circulation and a strong advertising medium.

Formulas are not necessarily put on paper. They are not achieved by staff discussion or study alone, although this is the soundest method. Sometimes they come from the exercise of inherent editorial skill. *The New Yorker,* for example, is an expression of its founder's unwritten and unorganized formula. The editorial genius of Harold Ross, although he has been dead since 1951, continues to express itself through a concept which is consistent, original, and perceptive even though not bandied at a staff roundtable, put down in memoranda, or tried out on public taste testers.

### Advertising and magazines

From time to time, attempts are made to produce magazines that will be independent of advertising revenue. Most of these have not succeeded. From 1922 to 1955 this operating policy was followed by *The Reader's Digest* in its domestic and by far largest edition. But mounting costs to produce the enormous number of copies each month finally opened the pages to paid space. Otherwise this magazine functioned with a conventional financial organization.

A variation occurred in 1946 when Jerome Ellison, experienced as managing editor of *Collier's,* editor of *Liberty,* and associate editor of *The Reader's Digest,* launched an adless pocket-size magazine he called *'47—The Magazine of the Year,* and the next year issued *'48.* The formula here was not so different in content as it was in a variation on the form of ownership. The owners were the more than three hundred writers, artists, photographers and other contributors, plus John Steinbeck, Pearl Buck, Gjon Mili, John Hersey, Maxwell S. Stewart, and other leaders in each occupation. This plan was a form of mutual ownership. In content *'47* and *'48* resembled the early *Coronet,* with articles on the arts, travel, and significant individuals, and some color printing. But the public did not respond in sufficient numbers to bring enough circulation revenue nor did the contributor-owners often enough provide their best copy. The firm went into bankruptcy in its second year, after spending $2,000,000.

Nine years later Mr. Ellison attempted another experiment, the publication of *Best Articles and Stories,* in which he reprinted complete fiction and non-fiction. These were "Editors' Nominations from Selected Magazines," concentrating on the less popular publications, such as the *Antioch Review, Michigan Alumnus, Yale Review,* and *Arizona Quarterly.* Before it ceased in the fall of 1961 it had added photography, an occasional color reproduction of a painting on its cover, and issues of as many as seventy pages, flat size. Of this experience he has written, on announcing that his magazine had to cease publication but that its subscriptions would be fulfilled by a similar one, *Current*:

> The editors of both magazines have been inspired by the same awareness that the important new thoughts of our day often appear first in publications seldom seen by the general reader—the learned journals and quality reviews of the world.
>
> The editorial choices were two: (1) to publish a few important selections in each issue, in full; or (2) to print a larger number of selections, under the more urgent and topical subject headings, in briefer form. BA&S followed the former course, Current the latter, allowing a much wider survey of current thought, events and opinion. We are glad our readers will continue to have regular access to these vital thought currents.[1]

*Current* continued, unaffected physically by the change. Its formula included several innovations: on its rear cover appeared a list of leaflets, booklets, and other free or low cost materials available to subscribers which they could obtain merely by filling out a prepaid card which was part of the over-size cover; the excerpts of reprinted materials, speeches, broadcasts, and other statements were carefully classified and printed with side heads for easy reference.

Other adless magazines of recent years include *Atlas,* subtitled "The Magazine of the World Press," which reproduces translations of material from publications overseas; *Changing Times,* a general periodical for young families, in the 1,250,000 circulation group; *Horizon,* a quarterly bookazine or magabook of the arts; and *American Heritage,* an older sister-publication of *Horizon,* devoted to making history readable. The latter two are handsome products of the press, saved by their readers like books in a continuing series, and compensate for the lack of advertising by high subscription rates (*Horizon,* at $20 for four copies a year, had reached 160,000 circulation by the early 1970's; *American Heritage* had a $20 a year rate for six copies and a 300,000 circulation).

## New factors

Being businesses, magazine publishing companies are subject to factors of success or failure much as are other commercial enter-

---

[1] Undated letter to subscribers to *Best Articles and Stories* from Miriam and Jerome Ellison.

prises. They respond to the fluctuations of world business as well as to economic conditions in the country of publication. It stands to reason that if manufacturers, for example, lose access to raw materials because of economic stress or crop destruction at their source of supply and cannot produce and distribute goods as usual, advertising budgets will be cut and the magazine volume and revenue will decrease.

Sound management is essential to any business and no less so to magazine publishing houses. Overexpansion, waste of materials, excessive inventory, failure to maintain reserves, inadequate expenditures for promotion, faulty internal or external public relations—these and other practices are not peculiar to magazines but can explain one failure or another just as the opposite practices can help explain success.

Insufficient, inaccurate, or inadequate market analyses before publishing are often the reasons for the quick death of a magazine. Although unlimited capital resources may coax an unpromising infant magazine into a profitable life, the growing pains will be costly.

Misgauging of competition or inexperience with meeting a new type of competition is no less a serious threat to the continued life of a publication than downright incompetence on the part of staff members or profligacy with his earnings by a sole owner.

Troubles set in for magazines, as for other business, that are beyond their control, such as inflation. The inflationary cycle in the United States which has been affecting all industry has shot up every basic cost of magazine publishing, but especially charges for postal services, salaries, paper, and printing, in that order. This trend has directed the attention of the owners of the firms to savings that are possible through automation and profits that might be earned by diversification of their operations.

Several new factors have entered the scene since the early 1950's; if not exactly new, they are accentuated old ones. These are:
1. Rise of the television industry.
2. Success of paperback book publishing.
3. Decline of magazine newsstand sales.
4. Multiplication and duplication of periodicals.

Mainly the consumer magazines have been affected by these trends, but since this is an interdependent industry some of the specialized periodicals have been under stress as well. As already indicated, not all magazines in any category, nor even a majority, have been affected; those that anticipated social and economic changes were able to meet the new problems.

These four factors are interlocked. The rise of television diverted some advertising expenditures from magazines and other print media, at first sharply, and then less so as advertisers realized that the media have different uses and that all media must be employed to some extent to obtain full impact. The existence of television as a competitor also had a psychological effect upon the sales staffs of publishing companies. They believed they had to outdo video numerically. For a time they worked so hard to build circulations that production costs went awry, in proportion to income from advertising. For a period, also, magazines lost readers to the screen. On the other hand, documentary television as well as some regular programing can move viewers to read specialized magazines as they search for more information on a subject of deep interest.

Paperback books similarly have had double effects. They, too, occupy reading time with matter that is not magazines (except for the bookazines) but which is distributed much like them and is available in many of the same outlets. As paperbacks have tended to become more expensive, costing as much as $1.95 to $3.75, this competition has lessened. They continue to appeal, however, because the reader often buys a pig in a poke when he purchases a consumer magazine whereas with a paperback he knows—or at least he thinks he knows—what he is getting: a single novel, a collection of short stories, a cookbook, a science manual, or a biography. And books traditionally are more free to print what magazines cannot in vocabulary and imagery. Disposable as they are, paperbacks, being books, nevertheless are more nearly permanent than magazines.

Drops in newsstand sales are the result mainly of the other two trends, although improper display on stands and the need to find room for too many magazines also are important factors. The reader now may choose between a paperbound novel and a mass magazine, for they are side by side in racks or on stands at sales outlets. Instead of stopping by at a newsstand to pick up his favorite or some new magazine he now may rush home to see the favorite tv program of the early evening. If the habit of nighttime television viewing is heavy in a household, magazines pile up unread and there is little incentive to buy new copies.

In a fully developed nation like the United States, with its high literacy rate and standard of living, printing presses work constantly to produce more and more billions of copies of newspapers, magazines, leaflets, booklets, brochures, books, and other printed materials. These now flood into the homes of most citizens. The paper deluge makes it impossible for a businessman, for example, to keep up with all the printed matter that comes to his desk.

The magazine publishers who see a success and set out to imitate it contribute to the swamp of publications. The copies of some successful magazines that one sees on newsstands are of little importance as expressions of new opinion or as divulgers of new facts. Often they are inferior imitations, issued by firms seeking only to assure themselves of some of the profits they see going to the successful publications that have survived the costly period of experimentation and launching of a new idea in magazines.

The public, consequently, has not enough time to read many of these and also receives the impression, when they fail, that the magazine industry is irresponsible, unsettled, peopled with unoriginal moneygrubbers, and economically unstable.

To meet these problems, that portion of the industry most affected by the trends has adopted new policies. These include printing covers that will be more effective in attracting newsstand buyers, improving display methods, making magazines available at new types of outlets, such as supermarkets, offering cut prices for subscriptions, experimenting with new cover prices for newsstand copies, and periodically re-examining formulas. Publishers also try offering advertisers regional editions, selling through charge accounts in department stores, emphasizing to advertisers the nature rather than the number of readers, reapportioning expenditures so as to increase circulation promotion, and attempting to offer higher quality editorial content.

## The Curtis story continues

In recent years four books have been devoted to the troubles in the 1960's of the Curtis Publishing Company, a major magazine publishing firm in American journalistic history.

Because of various situations: slowness to modernize its point of view on social developments in the country; in-fighting of staff; alert competition from rivals; and the impact of television, the company began having financial troubles in the 1950's, and has continued to do so in the 1960's despite changes in management and experiments with new formulas. Most of these were used on the magazine for which Curtis was best known: the *Saturday Evening Post.* (See Chapter 2.) That weekly, under the direction of its two famous editors, George Horace Lorimer and Ben Hibbs, was the flagship of the fleet and a remarkably influential and successful book until the destructive factors began their work.

By 1968 different policies were followed by the firm when its new owner, Martin S. Ackerman, president of a film and chemical company, banker, and a professional at doctoring sick businesses and industries, decided on a dramatic course.

He sold two of the company's major magazines, the famous *Ladies' Home Journal,* a household name since the late 1800's, and *American Home,* a more recent acquisition, but both multimillion in circulation. They were bought by Downe Communications, a relative newcomer in the field as publisher of a newspaper magazine supplement. And Ackerman caused further stir in the industry by lopping 3,000,000 subscribers from the *Post's* list and by buying a small, jet-set-appeal monthly called *Status.*

His formula was intended to take Curtis out of the monster circulation class and turn its efforts to the moderate-sized, specialized area of magazine publishing, hoping to attract advertising that appealed to the better-heeled citizens. In the letter written by the director of circulation to subscribers to be decapitated this aim was put delicately thus: "Unfortunately, the economics of publishing often dictate major changes in policy, and occasionally this means a program of austerity."

The real reason was that the subscriber supposedly lived in a rural or other relatively low income area. Time Inc. had arranged to take over these discarded subscribers by supplying them with *Life*. Oddly, among the supposedly small earners thus notified of their severance were Ackerman himself and Governor Winthrop Rockefeller of Arkansas, two slips attributed to a defenseless computer.

None of these and other stratagems saved the magazine from what proved to be a temporary departure from the newsstands, although it seemed permanent. In January 1969, Ackerman announced that he had been unable "to reduce expenses and increase sales fast enough to halt mounting losses." Soon other Curtis magazines were sold: *Holiday, Jack and Jill,* and *Status.* The Saturday Evening Post Company, the remainder of the Curtis empire, now had only its paper mill and a printing plant. The magazines went, with the Curtis name, to Beurt Ser Vaas, a wealthy auto parts manufacturer. About a year after the *SEP* had died Ser Vaas acquired control of it and Curtis. By summer of 1971 he had revived the *Post* as a quarterly at $1 a copy and made it strongly reminiscent of the original magazine in both advertising and editorial content. A few issues later it was carrying original as well as reprinted *Post* material, and rising to beyond a half million circulation. In format it was exactly like the *Post* of the 1940's; in content it was calculated to arouse nostalgia for the good old days. The firm aimed at monthly frequency in a few years, with emphasis on American life.

## Businessman or magazinist

Many of the decisions about such policies as those described are made by the owners, publishers, and other administrators, including editors. Editors of large magazines sometimes reach the point where they wonder if their work is editing or operating a business.

Careers of numerous magazinists are related in various sections of this book. The business character of their careers is clearer in some accounts than in others. Writers still are dominant in the writing field so far as publicity for the individual is concerned. Editors, too, still are important figures in the magazine world, but the major rewards, the power, and the influence, as in all areas of modern journalism, go usually to the men and women active in the business operations, particularly management.

Sometimes the path to administrative and business leadership in the magazine industry is through the editorial department, as in the case of Herbert R. Mayes. In his heyday during the 1960's, he became known as a challenger of magazine publishing's accepted conventions.

Mayes entered the door of magazine journalism by getting a job as editor of *The Inland Merchant,* a New York business publication. It turned out to be a one-man operation and he was the one man. Four years later he became editor of the trade paper division of the Western Newspaper Union; from there, in 1927, he joined the Hearst management as editor of *The American Druggist.*

In another seven years, having studied the consumer magazines of the nation, especially those for women, he proposed so many new ideas about them to the Hearst management that it made him editor of *Pictorial Review,* a rival for *Woman's Home Companion* and *Ladies' Home Journal.* Within four years he was editor of Hearst's still larger *Good Housekeeping.* As a result of a disagreement in 1958 with the Hearst management, he resigned. Within a day he was named editor of *McCall's* which he was destined to lead into circulation and advertising dominance of its field. When he became editor the magazine had 5,300,000 circulation and advertising revenues of $18,400,000 annually.

Within five years the circulation rose to more than 8,000,000, leading not only the women's field but most other magazines; and revenue from advertising equalled nearly $42,000,000. Mayes was promoted to president of the McCall Corp., thereby becoming executive head of its operations, which included not only publication of *McCall's, Redbook,* and several business publications, but also two printing divisions, and an interest in an investor's service. He was retired in 1965 but became a consultant in 1968 when *McCall's* began slipping. After the crisis he moved to England to live in retirement.

### Magazines and the law

Whatever their background, these executives must supervise departments that perform various business operations. Most of these are standard in any business. But there is one aspect that touches the magazine industry in special ways—the law of the press, including postal regulations.

The press laws of this country apply fully to magazines. The greater national distribution of magazines, as compared with newspapers, for example, does not exempt them from state laws. In fact, their wide distribution makes them subject to more different laws than locally distributed publications. And those with international circulation encounter enormous problems.

Magazine publishing companies, therefore, are guided by the usual manuals relating to printing of libel and obscene matter. They leave to a lawyer settlement of fine points. Copy may be submitted to a company attorney, in a big firm, or to one on a retainer fee or hired for one opinion only, in the instance of a small company.

The laws a magazinist might inadvertently violate are in these areas:

1. Libel, which may be criminal or civil. Criminal libel tends to incite violence against government. It includes publication of obscenity or blasphemy. Civil libel is malicious publication tending to blacken the reputation of a living person or to expose him to ridicule, hatred, or contempt.
2. Right of privacy.
3. Copyright.
4. Postal regulations.
5. Censorship.
6. Use of photographs for business purposes.
7. Labor and other laws with sections restricting printing.

These apply to both reading matter and advertising.

## Libel law violations

Magazines are in danger of violating libel laws in exactly the same manner as other publications—by printing prohibited materials. A news story appearing in a magazine may defame a reputation as much as one in a newspaper; it may do even more damage because many magazine circulations are larger. Examination of typical cases indicates the kind of suit that may result from careless or well-intentioned but mistaken writing and editing.

**Dall *vs.* Time Inc.** *Time* magazine printed an article under the foreign news heading that began:

> "Yesterday Curtis B. Dall, son-in-law of President Roosevelt, shot himself in the White House in the presence of his estranged wife and Mrs. Roosevelt. He died later in the day."
>
> If such an event were so briefly reported in the U.S. Press, neither readers nor publishers would be satisfied. Yet almost an exact parallel of that tragedy occurred in the Hotel Continental apartment of Premier Gaston Doumergue last week. Mention was limited to a few slender paragraphs in New York newspapers and a close-mouthed silence on the part of French officialdom.

Under a "France" heading, this and details of the suicide of Enzo de Bonze, son-in-law of France's prime minister at the time, followed.

Curtis B. Dall sued Time Inc., for libel. Although the opening paragraph referring to him was in quotation marks, what followed was not, he pointed out, and also declared that his business affairs were greatly disturbed by the publication. *Time* sought to defend itself by explaining that its intention was merely to get the attention of the readers with a startling statement, that the beginning of the article was purely fictitious. Justice Dore decided that the article was libelous *per se*.[2] That is, the words in the article are actionable in themselves; when they are not actionable the material is said to be libelous *per quod*.

---

[2] William R. Arthur and Ralph L. Crosman, *The Law of Newspapers* (New York: McGraw-Hill, 1940), pp. 138–39.

**Rosenfeld** *vs.* **Curtis Publishing Company.** The *Saturday Evening Post* of July 1, 1944, carried an article with a one-column picture called "How To Beat the Races." The photograph showed a man partly facing the camera, with one hand on the shoulder of another man, whose back was to the camera, and into whose ear the first man apparently was whispering. A crowded grandstand formed the background. The cutline read: " 'How can we lose?' This race-track question is often the prelude to a very bad investment." In the text of the article beside the picture were these statements: ". . . what chance has the average bettor, influenced by hunches, seedy touts and vagrant tips, of picking one horse out of a large field completely unknown to him and making a buck for himself?" and also "All systems are extremely fallible, but any one is infinitely better than picking horses haphazardly or listening to hangers-on." The men's names were not given in either article or cutline.

But an Ezra Rosenfeld sued, contending that because of the proximity of offending language and picture, he had been held up to contempt and ridicule as a "seedy tout" or "hanger-on" at race tracks and that he could be identified as the first man in the picture. The *Post* had obtained the photograph from Wide World, an agency, after it had accepted the article. The photographer testified that he had taken it in 1938 at the Empire City Race Track as part of a horse-racing picture assignment. The case became exceedingly complicated. Originally entered in the Supreme Court of New York, it was removed on petition of Curtis, as a citizen of another state, to the Circuit Court of Appeals, Second Circuit, where it was heard July 9, 1947. Rosenfeld lost his suit, appealed, but lost again.[3]

Any magazine that muckrakes or crusades is likely to bring upon itself numerous libel suits. One of the most often involved in recent years has been the *Post,* especially after it changed its formula from that of a conservative magazine carrying more or less bland articles, romantic fiction, and humor to one publishing numerous exposes of supposed maldoings in the sports and gang worlds and personality or biographical pieces sometimes thought to reflect upon their subjects. At one time during 1963 the company was facing $38,000,000 in libel suits. These included:

One for $7,500,000 by a manufacturer of a machine to treat arthritis who claimed the company was defamed by an article in the *Post* called "The Hucksters of Pain."

One for $10,000,000 brought by Paul Bryant, University of Alabama football coach, who claimed libel in an article that charged him with conspiring with Wally Butts, a former athletic director at the University of Georgia, to rig a game.

An earlier one was filed by Bryant for $500,000 for an alleged libel

---

[3] *Federal Reporter*, Second Series, Nov. 10, 1947, pp. 660–64.

in an article which declared that Bryant condoned brutality among his players.

Both suits by Bryant were settled for $300,000 in 1964.

Butts also sued, asking $10,000,000. At first he won a jury award of $3,060,000, but later it was ruled as excessive, and Butts agreed to take $460,000 damages instead.

Marlon Brando, the actor, sued for $5,000,000—alleged libel to have been committed in a 1962 article entitled "Mutiny on the Bounty."

The $2,000,000 libel suit, begun in 1966, of Barry Goldwater, 1964 Republican candidate for President, against Ralph Ginzburg, publisher of *Fact,* was significant in setting guidelines about the Constitutional rights of a publication to criticize a public figure. Ginzburg lost the suit, which did not come to trial until 1968.

The action was based on the October, 1964, issue, dated a month before election, and labeled a "special issue on the mind of Barry Goldwater." A lead article by Ginzburg described Goldwater as "paranoid" and compared him to Hitler. Also in the issue was a summary of the results of a questionnaire mailed to psychiatrists across the nation. *Fact's* cover reported: "1,189 Psychiatrists Say Goldwater Is Unfit To Be President!"

Goldwater's contention was that Ginzburg and his co-defendant, a staff member, published false, scandalous, and defamatory statements knowing them to be false or "recklessly not caring if they were true or not."

Goldwater was awarded a verdict of $75,000 in punitive damages.

An aspect of press law that applies particularly to magazines is libel in fiction. Charles Angoff, former managing editor of the *American Mercury* and author of an extensive study of libel, has called it "one of the most troublesome sections in the whole realm of libel." The issue is: Are publishers or authors liable if a reprehensible fiction character invented by an author bears the name of a real person?

One of the best known cases is Corrigan *vs.* Bobbs-Merrill Company, which came up in 1920. In it a New York judge sued for $25,000 damages because a novel portrayed a fictional judge who could be himself. The plaintiff sustained the verdict. In commenting on this case Philip Wittenberg, specialist in laws affecting literature and journalism, pointed out that the question is not particularly who was aimed at as it is who was hit.

"When one considers the population of the United States alone," he later wrote, "and the impossibility of finding a name not somewhere borne by a living person, the lurking danger appals."[4]

---

[4] Philip Wittenberg, *Dangerous Words* (New York: Columbia University Press, 1947), p. 87.

A magazine, therefore, always is in danger; all an editor can do is remove names known to be possessed by real people and hope for the best. The safest names are not odd ones but common ones. Somerset Maugham once changed the name of a character in an uncompleted story when he learned that a person of that exact name existed.

## Right of privacy

A typical definition of *right of privacy* is "the natural right of every person to demand that his private affairs shall not be exhibited without his consent."[5] It applies to both type and illustrations; legal action often involves photographs. Among magazines that have lost cases is *True Detective Mysteries,* which printed a courtroom picture showing the plaintiff as "the broken-hearted mother." This use was held to be a commercial and not a legitimate one. The judge declared that the woman in the picture had no connection with the crime's history or the detection or trial of the criminal.[6]

## Copyright

The laws of copyright provide a magazine protection for its content if the proper steps—depositing two copies and a fee in Washington—have been taken to obtain it. Once this action has been taken the material may be used only by permission, which may or may not entail payment of a fee.

Only the way something is written, not the statements of fact, is covered. Other basic facts about copyright are that a notice of it must be printed with the material, the order of facts and ideas in another magazine's material cannot be paraphrased or rearranged so as to avoid infringement of copyright law, and extracts and quotations can be quoted directly only in small amounts. Material exceeding approximately fifty words in length offers possibility of violation; use of even smaller passages without permission is risky, especially if it is poetry. It is the value, however, rather than the length of material that is central in any case. Highly valuable extracts, such as quotations that make a magazine more salable, could be basis for a suit. Also, the copyright must be obtained as quickly as possible and it must be maintained.

A classic case is the Atlantic Monthly Company *vs.* the Post Publishing Company in the District Court of the United States, in 1928, in Massachusetts. The *Atlantic* printed an article, actually an open letter, by Gov. Alfred E. Smith of New York. It arranged with him to allow newspapers to reprint it, with or without copyright acknowledgment, after a certain date. The article was copyrighted

---

[5] William G. Hale, *The Law of the Press* (St. Paul, Minn.: West, 1948), p. 299.
[6] Frank M. Thayer, *Legal Control of the Press* (Brooklyn, N.Y.: Foundation Press, 1962), pp. 535–36.

promptly and in an unusual way—by selling a proof to the magazine's treasurer for a dime, so that it became property of the company. But the Boston *Post* procured a copy of the letter from the printing plant and published it two days before the general release. The suit against the newspaper was not filed until after the second day; the judge denied the plea and dismissed the suit. He said that the magazine, by its own agreement, held no copyright after the day the press in general was allowed to reprint the article without credit; it was like a suit on a patent that had expired before the bill was brought.[7]

Another aspect of copyright is plagiarism, a subject closer to writers than committing libel, close as that is. Such cases are difficult to decide because lawyers are able to cite numerous historical instances of noted authors using the works of others as the basis for their own. Sometimes copying is unintentional, as in using exact notes from some source and forgetting that they are not the writer's own language.

Writers who are unable to sell their own material to magazines are sometimes tempted to type, with minor changes, stories or articles from back numbers of similar periodicals. Editors, of course, cannot remember every piece that has appeared in even their own magazines, much less what has been published in every other like it. Nor is there a complete check list which they can consult. That many plagiarisms of this sort are discovered is testimony to the excellent memories of certain editors and the alertness of the true authors, if they are still alive to defend themselves against the thievery.

An instance of this occurred some years ago when the *Saturday Evening Post* carried a certain short story. A free-lance writer who had never managed to sell to that weekly, although he was successful with other big magazines and had submitted as many as twenty-five pieces to the *Post* without success, discovered that it was a tale he had sold to *Good Housekeeping* a half dozen years earlier. But the story had another title, another by-line, and different names for the characters; otherwise it was exactly the same. He sued the *Post,* and the plagiarist was brought to light and indicted (he had earlier stolen a story similarly from *Blue Book* and sold it to *Argosy*). *Good Housekeeping* then sold the *Post* second publication rights and overlooked the matter, but the original author was not remunerated for the use of his work.[8]

Sometimes a magazine is involved in a reverse situation, as in 1954 when Time Inc. sued the New York Central Railroad for infringement of copyright by unauthorized use of an article and an editorial in *Fortune*. The railroad company had quoted the *Fortune*

---

[7] Arthur and Crosman, *op. cit.,* p. 431.
[8] "This Looks Familiar," *Newsweek,* Feb. 18, 1957, p. 94.

materials in a newspaper advertisement and mailed reprints to stock-holders. Time Inc. won a $7,000 judgment.[9]

Although magazine names cannot be copyrighted, they are pro-tected by laws relating to trademarks and unfair competition. Among the cases in this area of supposed violation of the law are the suits filed by the Simplicity Pattern Company, publisher of *Modern Miss,* against the Miss Publishing Company, publisher of *Miss* and the Macfadden Publications' unsuccessful suit against Time Inc., because of the fear that the latter would drop the second word from *Sports Illustrated,* thus leaving it too closely like *Sport;* and a complicated case in which one publisher sued two others, both of which planned to use *Quick* as a magazine name.

### Postal regulations

Either the business office or the circulation department must be informed about postal regulations pertaining to magazines and must keep up with changes issued by the United States Postal Service from time to time.

The texts of basic regulations usually are on file in the company offices (or with the printer or firm entrusted with mailing) in printed form. The chief records of regulations are in the *Postal Service Man-ual.* The text of the regulations is available at all central post offices.

A professional user of this information must consult and study the full statements which cover hundreds of pages. These high-lights, however, may enable the newcomer to the magazine world to obtain some understanding of the complex problems involved in dis-tributing periodicals by mail.

Mailable matter is classified in four ways:
1. *First class*—Written matter, such as sealed letters and postal cards, both surface and air mail.
2. *Second class*—Periodical publications (newspapers, magazines), both single copy and bulk mailings.
3. *Third class*—Printed and other matter not over 15 ounces and not in other classes.
4. *Fourth class*—Merchandise and printed matter 16 or more ounces and not in other classes, known as parcel post.

Magazines go second class. To have that privilege they must meet certain requirements:
1. Be regularly issued at stated intervals.
2. Be from a known office of publication.
3. Bear date of issue and other data.
4. Be issued as frequently as four times a year.

[9] "Time Sues N.Y. Central . . . ," *Editor & Publisher,* May 8, 1954, p. 75.

5. Be formed of printed sheets, without boards, cloth, leather, or other substantial binding.
6. Not be made by stencil, mimeograph, hectograph, or imitation of typewriting.
7. ". . . be originated and published for the purpose of dissemination of information of a public character, or they must be devoted to literature, the sciences, art, or some special industry."
8. Not be designated primarily for advertising purposes, have free circulation, or be sold at excessively low rates.
9. Be regularly issued to maintain privileges.
10. Be mailed only at the office where entered.
11. Have a legitimate list of subscribers.

Also in the second class are publications known as fraternal, benevolent, lodge institutions, trade unions, professional, literary, historical, scientific, charitable institutions or societies. These must be published, not to benefit the income of an individual, but to further the objects and purposes of the institutions issuing them. Foreign publications coming from outside the country may also be admitted if they obey this country's copyright laws.

Illegitimate subscribers are defined as those who receive subscriptions at 50 per cent less than the advertised rate through clubbing and those who pay less than 30 per cent through a subscription company.

Certain characteristics can prevent second class privileges from being allowed. Four are:
1. If a magazine is conducted as an auxiliary to and as advancement for a particular business.
2. If advertisers pay for having certain copies sent to certain persons.
3. If the magazine contains editorial puffs of businesses.
4. If the expired list of subscribers is not kept up to date.

One of the most important points is that there must appear on one or more of the first five pages the following information:
1. Name of the publication (also on first page).
2. Date of issue.
3. Statement of frequency.
4. Issue number.
5. Name of known office or place of publication and zip code.
6. Subscription price.
7. Imprint.

Other regulations affect the postage rates, according to the county of publication. Outside that county the requirements are: filing of a sworn statement relating to ownership, designating what is unmailable matter, and folding and wrapping so as to coincide with requirements.

Controlled circulation magazines come under different regulations. These are periodicals issued mainly in the specialized fields and heavily by business magazine publishers. They do not have newsstand circulation and mainly do not charge a subscription or per copy fee but mail issues to selected readers.

The post office provides a special pound rate for mailing such magazines. This charge is lower than that for second class. Controlled (also called free or qualified) circulation magazines must:

1. Contain at least 24 pages.
2. Contain not less than 25 per cent non-advertising.
3. Appear regularly and at intervals of four or more times annually.
4. Be circulated free or mainly free.
5. Not be owned and controlled chiefly to advance the business or individuals owning them.
6. Carry a publication name on the front, date of issue, frequency, publisher's address, subscription price, if any, a specific controlled circulation imprint, a specific notice of pending application, and a specific printed or stamped notice on envelopes or wrappers. (The texts of such notices are in the *Postal Service Manual.*)

## *Censorship*

Laws relating to censorship function only in wartime. During most recent conflicts censorship has been on a voluntary basis, its rules being drawn up by representatives of the industry itself.

In the interest of national defense, however, publishers are expected to exert caution about what they publish. For example, in 1950 the Atomic Energy Commission ordered 3,000 copies of *Scientific American* burned because it contained an article on the hydrogen bomb with supposedly classified information from a noted atomic scientist. This official action was protested by the editors and scientists, who declared that the material had been disseminated previously and that it actually was of a non-military nature. Yet the destruction cost the magazine firm thousands of dollars.[10]

Enforcement of postal regulations leads the public to think that the federal government censors magazines. In a literal sense that is true, for if the post office refuses to transport a periodical it must seek some other way to be delivered, a costly and difficult procedure in a country so large as the United States. Generally this refusal leads to at least temporary cessation of publication. In practice, few publications have been restricted thus.

Defined as mailable publications by the U.S. Postal Service, so as to qualify for second class privileges, are those whose copies do "not contain obscene, treasonable, lottery, or other kinds of material

---

[10] "Publisher Bows to A.E.C., Burns His Magazines," New York *Herald Tribune,* April 1, 1950.

that would cause them to be unmailable under the provisions . . . ," according to the *Postal Service Manual.*

An instance was the suit by *Eros,* a magazine which described itself as a publication "devoted to love and sex," in Federal Court to force the New York Post Office to accept it as second class matter. A quarterly magabook, it sold for $10 and first was issued in 1962; it was sold at bookstores as well as mailed. Its publisher issued as well a newsletter of sex called *Liaison* and a book on promiscuity by housewives which he also mailed and which were included in the 28 charges of mailing obscenity. He was sentenced to five years in jail and fined $42,000 in 1963.[11] In 1970 it was reduced to three years but by 1972 he had not yet been jailed.

*Confidential* and *Whisper* each paid $5,000 in fines in 1957 when found guilty of conspiracy to publish obscenity in expose-type stories. They agreed to discontinue the practice.

Not all restrictions stem from postal regulations, however, nor do they relate only to allegedly obscene content. School trustees in Los Angeles, in 1962, limited two magazines in the El Segundo High School library. They ordered that *The Reporter* and *The New Republic,* a biweekly and a weekly of national affairs, literature, and the arts, were to be available only in the library to students who had a teacher's permission to use them. They were prohibited from use in classrooms. Only *Time* and *Newsweek* were allowed there. Teachers labelled the action as book banning.

## Photographs

Use of photographs for business purposes is closely related to violations of the right of privacy. An additional point, however, goes beyond invasion: the matter of obtaining releases. This requirement is made in connection with pictures used in advertisements appearing in periodicals, inasmuch as such use is more clearly commercial. A civil suit for damages may be entered if a release is not obtained.

Cautious editors therefore ask persons posing for commercially used pictures or even for others that may have some commercial use to sign a statement agreeing to the use for business purposes.

As we have seen in the case of Rosenfeld *vs.* Curtis, a photograph can bring legal difficulties upon a magazine when used in proximity to a possibly libelous article or can enhance that alleged libel. It also can cause legal difficulties by being positioned in a layout in such a way as to have libelous implications; also, it can be thought to be held in contempt of court.

## An organized business

In the magazine world, overhead organization begins with for-

---

[11] United Press International dispatch from Philadelphia, Dec. 19, 1963.

*Fig. 3.2.* **Three present or former officers of the Johnson Publishing Company, Inc.** *(Ebony, Jet, Black World,* and *Black Stars)* **at a meeting of the Magazine Publishers Association. Left to right: Jay C. Wade; William P. Grayson, vice-president,** *Ebony;* **and John H. Johnson, founder of the firm and board member of the MPA.** *(MPA Photo)*

mation of groups of companies or of individuals on a national scale; in a nation the size of the United States regional organization may precede national in some instances. Such activity does not mean that any one group dictates what magazines shall print or how they shall conduct their affairs. Advertising policies, general business standards, and suggestions for uniformity emanate from these groups but without compulsion.

A worldwide organization in which publishers of the United States play a prominent part is the International Federation of the Periodical Press, whose members represent magazine publishing companies in about twenty nations. Founded in Paris in 1925, its objectives are to further good relations among publishers, protect the interests of the press, and to "develop education, science, and culture by free exchange of ideas and information." Other international groups in which magazine representatives take part include several for special areas, such as the International Association of Business Communicators (house magazines), International Federation of Catholic Journalists, and the American Newspaper Guild, which, despite its name, signs contracts with magazine companies.

Among the principal groups dealing solely with the magazine on the national level is the Magazine Publishers Association (MPA). Comprised mainly of the representatives of large consumer magazines, it has its headquarters and permanent staff in New York. Founded in 1919, it acts as spokesman for these periodicals in their relationships with government. Through its committees and meetings it seeks to solve mutual problems relating to policy and operation. Its meetings consider, among other matters, price of paper, postal rate changes, projected surveys, advertising and editorial trends, and demographic changes.

The Magazine Advertising Bureau, Inc. (MAB), associated with MPA and also with its headquarters at Magazine House in New York City, is supported by about two dozen firms that publish consumer magazines. These publishers of large quantities of advertising authorize research studies in the advertising field; the MAB also develops plans for increased use of magazine advertising and revenue for comparative study with other media. In recent years both MPA and MAB have used institutional advertising as a means to stimulate reading and purchase of magazines and use of magazine advertising. One such appeared as an inside back cover of more than 12,000,000 copies of *TV Guide,* and said:

### How are you spending tonight?

There's not much choice—or fun—if everything's the same.

It's because you *do* have free choice that you have so many good things to choose from. Tonight's movie. Tomorrow's groceries. Next year's car. And it's all the competition that makes these things get better all the time.

Of course, some people think you have *too much* choice in the marketplace.

For instance, wouldn't it be simpler if there were only four brands of toothpaste instead of 68? And who needs all those flavors?

Most people like peppermint so why shouldn't they all be peppermint? Don't laugh. There really are people—well-meaning people—who think the government ought to regulate the number of brands on the market and standardize their contents. In other words, they want to do your shopping for you. That's nice of them. But, <u>maybe you don't like peppermint.</u>

**Magazine Publishers Association**
An association of 365 leading U.S. magazines

Above this text appeared a typical movie house listing, but at each of the thirty theaters the same film, "Goldthumb," was being shown.

The Publishers Information Bureau, Inc. (PIB), formed early in the century, compiles records on national magazine advertising. It checks and classifies advertising and measures coverage. For many years a private agency, in 1948 it was taken over jointly by a number of publishers.

Three major organizations, the Audit Bureau of Circulations (ABC), Business Publication Audit of Circulation, Inc. (BPA), and Verified Audit Circulation Corporation (VAC), serve magazines (see Chapter 5).

One of the most active groups of magazine publishers in the United States is the American Business Press, Inc. (ABP) with headquarters in New York.

ABP, founded in 1906, has as its purposes to provide opportunities for publishers and their staffs to exchange experiences, conduct workshop sessions led by experts in advertising, circulation, editorial, and other operations, promote the business press, and to "foster greater awareness of quality business papers . . . ."

The Association of Publication Production Managers is concerned with standards and problems in magazine manufacture and production. It cooperates with MPA and other groups in efforts to improve quality of production. Its members are active in periodical production or represent publishers on advertising production problems.

Numerous special groups of magazines or their publishers and editors exist in the United States. Editors of industrial, association, and some other specialized publications have an organization, the International Association of Business Communicators. Within it are about forty state or regional groups, such as the House Magazine Institute in New York, the Industrial Editors of Chicago, and the Upstate New York Council of Industrial Editors.

Farm publications, many of which are magazines, have their Agricultural Publishers Association. The Association of Screen Magazine Publishers has as members group magazine firms that issue one or more cinema periodicals. Protestant religious magazines and papers have the Associated Church Press and the Evangelical Press Association. The Catholic Press Association unites the editors of that church's many publications. Other regional or denominational groups also exist. The Associated Construction Publications and the Associated Purchasing Publications are two other highly specialized groups.

The rank and file employes of magazines have little unity and consequently practically no organization. The Newspaper Guild, which is an AFL-CIO affiliate intended mainly for newspapers and wire services, has contracts with approximately twenty magazines (see Chapter 24). Most magazines are printed on contract with outside firms, some of which have union shops. Many big publishing companies have no agreements with unions. Magazines that own their own plants generally are not unionized. If there is a union in a plant, however, it is usually not exclusively in the magazine field.

### Group publishing

A further type of organization in the magazine world results from the publishing of more than one magazine by the same firm. In the newspaper world, chain or group publishing is common. Several of the most important newspaper group owners also are in the magazine field, as for example the Hearst Publications (*Cosmopolitan, Harper's Bazaar, Good Housekeeping, House Beautiful, Town and Country, American Druggist, Motor, Motor Boating, Popular Mechanics,* and *Sports Afield*). Among the about forty firms of this type in the magazine field are Time Inc. *(Life, Time, Sports Illustrated, Fortune, Panorama* [in Argentina], and *President* [in Japan]); Curtis *(Saturday Evening Post, Holiday,* and *Jack and Jill);* Condè Nast *(Vogue, Mademoiselle, Glamour, House and Garden,* and *Analog);* and Ziff-Davis, with a diversified group, including *Flying, Plastics, Popular Pets,* and *Popular Photography.* In the business field McGraw-Hill, Chilton, Haire, and Cahners are among the largest, the first with more than thirty periodicals.

Group publishing leads to great economies in operation. Paper may be bought in quantities, printing contracts are advantageous, and office operations can be consolidated. It also leads to mass production, with the questionable effect upon the creative work of writers and artists of standardizing ideas, facts, and workmanship.

### Internal organization

Internally, magazines in the United States are organized, in general, like other businesses: by operating departments. Whether one or ten magazines are issued and whether they are large or small, there may be from one to a dozen major departments, divisions, offices, or other operating units, with any number of subdivisions to handle minor activities. The usual departments are administrative or business, advertising, circulation, editorial, production, promotion, public relations or publicity, sales, art, photography, research, and international operations.

In some companies accounting, personnel, and other standard business divisions are ranked along with the others; in others those mentioned earlier may be subordinated. Both major and minor divisions may serve several magazines in common or exist separately for each magazine unit. Editorial departments often but by no means always serve only one periodical; perhaps two or three magazines will have separate editors-in-chief and two or three associate editors each, but a number of assistant editors and editorial assistants assigned to all three publications. Administrative, advertising, circulation, production, and promotion departments usually serve all units in a firm with a group of magazines.

The most important and distinctive of these departments and divisions are examined in succeeding chapters.

### Diversification

A development of the 1960's which was heightened in the early 1970's by generally bad business conditions in the nation, diversification increased when magazine publishing companies realized that ownership and operation of varied types of industry, so common in other businesses by then, had its applications to communications.

As a result we find a New York consumer magazine publishing firm owning several companies that produce lighting fixtures or are active in pollution control, and a middlewestern home and farm periodical publisher with an interest in globe manufacture producing other educational materials as well as operating television stations and several book companies.

A magazine firm today not only publishes a wide variety of periodicals but also is likely to be engaged in book publishing, newspaper publishing, broadcasting, and some other enterprises. So broad are these ventures that "publishing" no longer describes some activities; "communications" is sometimes used instead and even it may be dropped altogether as being too limited.

The values of such distribution of effort are several, as are the dangers. Such a firm is protected against temporary losses in its publishing activity, i.e., a weak member can for a time be kept alive until or if there is recovery. If there is an unexpected growth in some segment, as occurred for a time in educational book publishing, a magazine firm that serves the field already is prepared to benefit from and serve it more. On the other hand, diversification can lead to a too-great spread of effort and attention, to a loss of interest in the original *raison d'être* of the firm.

# Chapter 4

# Advertising and sales

THE ADVERTISING DEPARTMENT of a magazine publishing firm plays
little part in the interests of persons considering a career in magazine
journalism. Usually, if they are young people pondering their professional futures, they have their minds on the more widely publicized
editorial departments or free-lance writing, the supposed way stations
on the road to literary fame.

To be sure, the advertising department is not the place where
journalism as we commonly understand it is practiced. Yet it uses
words, employs writers and artists, and requires the services of editorial practice experts. Because it finances most self-supporting magazines and because on small periodicals editorial-side people may also
do advertising work, the need for aspiring journalists to know something about its functions should be obvious.

One day a young man just out of journalism school called on the
editor of a regional and community magazine about a job. He had
written sports for his home town daily, helped edit his college paper,
and had studied magazine editorial techniques. He was surprised to
find that this editor was a woman with several years' experience in a
New York City advertising agency and that she spent at least 75 per
cent of her time soliciting advertising for her magazine. Her editorial duties were relatively unimportant; they had to be. She planned
deadlines and publication dates, not on the importance or timeliness
of editorial content, which was reasonably newsy, but in relation to

times when she could expect advertising managers in shops and stores to purchase space. The young applicant was repelled by what he considered commercialism and indifference to the literary amenities, as he characteristically put it, but when he undertook to solicit advertising for the magazine on a commission basis he understood the editor's situation.

### Departmental organization

The general lack of absolute standardization in journalism organization is characteristic of magazine advertising departments. Big consumer magazines organize according to the number of periodicals issued by one firm, types of advertising handled, and amount of advertising or related work, such as promotion and research. Small magazines turn the job almost entirely over to an agency or company, trust a small staff, engage sales representatives, or combine these methods.

Advertising for *The Instructor,* one of the most widely circulated and read magazines in the education field, with a 297,358 circulation, is handled inside as well as outside the publishing headquarters in Dansville, N.Y. Its manner of organizing its advertising operations is typical of that of many moderately sized magazines.

The F. A. Owen Publishing Company, which issues the magazine and also is in the book printing business, distributes advertising responsibilities between Chicago and New York branch offices and two firms of advertising representatives. Each branch has a manager, a space salesman, and a secretary; both managers also are directors of the company; one also is vice-president in charge of advertising. The firms of representatives serve the Midwest and West. The vice-president visits those firms about four times a year. Managers and space salesmen work on a salary and commission; the representatives on a straight percentage basis.

At the Dansville office the person in charge receives the advertising orders and copy, sees to the placement of copy in the magazine according to specifications, sends out proofs, handles plates, and supervises billing.

*The Instructor's* advertising activity does not cease there, for another part of the publishing firm's work is offering what it calls The Instructor Educational Service: the preparation of educational teaching kits for industry as well as for associations, services, and counsels. These consist of teachers' manuals, wall charts, posters, student work sheets, and similar materials. This service also prepares advertising pieces coordinated with school curriculums. These are intended "to give teachers and their classes practical knowledge of advertised products and services." The office also tests products and conducts surveys within schools.

General magazines expect their advertising departments to cover

much the same ground but may organize them differently. The Meredith Publishing Company in Des Moines, Iowa, publisher of *Better
Homes and Gardens* and of *Successful Farming,* has offices for research, sales, merchandising, and order-filling for both publications.
Curtis Publishing Company has one division to service its magazines.

Whatever the size or scope of a magazine advertising department, it is itself departmentalized. All functions may be carried out
in one office, as on a small periodical, or in large publications they
may be distributed over the country to branch offices, which in turn
are departmentalized. Names of subdepartments indicate their functions: research, promotion, merchandising, sales, order, accounting,
statistics, and classified. Not in all instances are these subordinate;
some occupy separate departmental status. Only the largest publishers
have these subdivisions; sometimes two or more are combined.

Advertising printed in magazines generally is placed through
agencies; in the United States these operate on a commission of 15
per cent, a standard rate paid by magazines. Clients of these agencies
are national advertisers, who spend $25,000 or more annually for na-
tional advertising in magazines.

## The function of advertising

To understand the work of an advertising department it is necessary to understand advertising itself. Thorough analysis of advertising as a business and social tool and influence is found in the
numerous extensive studies on the subject. It will suffice here to summarize the nature of advertising, the principal views about it, and its
relationship to the magazine.

Advertising is a tool intended to create immediate sales and a
climate favorable to future sales. Before the advent of radio and television it was sufficient to speak of *printed selling,* a definition still
satisfactory for magazine advertising, which differs from other forms
in that it appears in a regularly issued bound pamphlet, generally in
more than one issue, and is representational rather than functional.
Readers are expected only to examine the advertisement and possibly
clip a part of it or remove a coupon, with a view to a future purchase.
Direct mail advertising may put in the reader's hands a sample pack-
age as well as a printed leaflet, a reply envelope or card, and even
coins, stamps, and other functional materials.

Kleppner has found seven advertising forms: national, retail
(that is, local), mail-order, trade, industrial, professional, and that
intended to get leads for salesmen.[1] National is used to establish a
trademark in the minds of consumers. Magazines clearly present
this form; in recent years they have been the leading medium for it,

[1] Otto Kleppner, *Advertising Procedure* (Englewood Cliffs, N.J.: Prentice-Hall,
1966), p. 26.

although television also is powerful, yet fleeting. Local or retail advertising also appears in periodicals, but relatively little is in nationally circulated publications; regional editions are being used slightly for this purpose. This type aids movements of goods in stores near the publication's point of issue or area of distribution. Retail advertisers increasingly tie into advertising of nationally distributed goods in national magazines.

Mail-order advertising is used by magazines themselves to stimulate circulation and is not carried in their pages. The consumer is expected to buy by mail and receives the advertising by that means, not from the pages of the magazine. But the request forms for direct mail information are commonly printed in business magazines and increasingly in those for general consumers.

Advertising to get leads for specialty salesmen, Kleppner explains, is often used by firms that specialize in selling their product in the potential buyer's home rather than in a salesroom. Such items as encyclopedias, insurance, and house insulation are sometimes sold in this manner. The ad usually invites the reader to "write for further information." These inquiries are passed on to area salesmen who then call. Magazines of all kinds are popular for this form.

Trade advertising differs from other forms in being addressed to those who sell to consumers rather than to consumers themselves. Specialized magazines commonly sell space for this type. Industrial advertising is similar; it is aimed at producers of raw materials and parts needed by producers in creating consumer commodities. Technical magazines obviously are most suitable carriers.

Professional advertising is aimed at persons who may not necessarily buy a product directly but are in a position to recommend its purchase: dentists, opticians, and other professionals. Medical journals and other technical publications are desirable outlets for this form.

Six of the seven forms noted by Kleppner appear in magazines, although more often in the specialized than in the consumer. Since the specialized serve as clearing houses for information about industry, trade, the professions, and various special interests, they are logical carriers of most of these forms of advertising.

In whatever form, what is advertising intended to accomplish in the magazine, with the magazine, and for the magazine? It is expected to:

1. Bring in revenue (payment for space) to pay all or part of the cost of manufacturing, distributing, and maintaining the publication.
2. Earn a profit for the owner of the company issuing it.
3. Serve readers by informing them about commodities or services.
4. Serve producers of commodities or handlers of services by cultivating sales.

The purpose of the advertising department of a magazine is to carry out all these basic functions in the way most beneficial to all concerned.

## Advantages of magazine advertising

Magazine advertising executives for many years have pointed to specific advantages of their publications as an advertising medium, as follows:

1. Distribution of magazine advertising is national in extent, in contrast to media whose circulation or reach is local.
2. Magazines generate "confidence and believability . . . in the minds of their readers," as the Magazine Advertising Bureau phrases it. Magazines were the first medium to guarantee certain products advertised in their pages.
3. Magazines can provide a selective audience. An advertiser using newspaper, radio, or television reaches a general audience. Through magazines he can reach the special group most likely to purchase his product or service.
4. Magazine advertising is comparatively economical. A consumer magazine charges much less per impression for a black and white page than the advertiser would have to pay to send each reader a postal card, which is technically inferior.
5. Magazine advertising has greater permanence than any other form. Because the periodical is read at leisure, the reader accords longer attention to its message than that of newspaper advertising, which has a tone of urgency, change, and perishability. Radio and television rarely repeat programs under the same sponsorship. Surveys made by magazine groups, show that magazines are still being read weeks after publication and often retained for years.
6. Advertising can be presented with greater craftsmanship by magazines than by other media, for they use better paper, color printing, and elaborate art work; and, having more time, they can achieve a greater degree of accuracy of presentation.
7. Having been selected deliberately by readers, magazines go into their homes and remain accessible.
8. Magazines have prestige value. A widely known national magazine that has won public respect transmits its prestige to its advertisers.
9. Magazines provide more pass-along readership than other media.
10. Magazines offer circulation guarantees and refunds if guarantees are not reached.

## Disadvantages of magazine advertising

The principal disadvantages of magazine advertising are:

1. The most effective of such advertising is too costly for advertisers who do not need elaborate presentation, as in multicolor. This particular drawback is intensified as production costs mount.

2. Some duplication of readership exists among consumer as well as specialized magazines; advertisers in some instances consider this wasteful.
3. Magazine advertising is static, as any printed matter must be. It does not have the ear appeal of radio or the eye-ear appeal of television. As noted, radio and television are impermanent, but their advertising presentation is alive and dramatic.
4. Advertising copy and plates for magazines must be submitted so long in advance of publication that they sometimes lose accuracy or timeliness. Magazine advertising cannot always be adjusted quickly to changing conditions.
5. Magazines cannot easily serve local advertisers, who gain little advantage from multimillion circulations, as compared with the local newspaper's ability to announce their goods and services in detail and their addresses.
6. Because of page size and wide use, the volume of advertising has become so great that it is difficult to make any particular advertisement stand out. Attention value in thick magazines is lessened. This handicap does not exist so much for specialized as for general periodicals, because readers of the former are more intensely interested in the advertising that is displayed; to them it is more properly thought of as *newsvertising*.

### *Who does what?*

The various duties in a magazine advertising department are performed by full-time members of the publishing company staff, aided by outside experts. If a group of magazines is served by one department, there may be an art division which services both advertising and editorial sides by making original drawings to be used as illustrations, retouching photographs, painting covers, and similar work. On some magazines the advertising staff plans some advertisements but advertising agency employes lay out others that are to appear.

Staffs of large magazines include clerks, stenographers, researchers, space salesmen, copy writers, media analysts, merchandisers, accountants, writers, artists, statisticians, and administrators, to name the principal personnel. On a small magazine the positions are telescoped or farmed out to companies that make a specialty of doing them on a concession or contract basis. Work on a small periodical calls for versatility. As a result, employes in the small office receive excellent training and experience and sometimes exceptional rewards.

A magazine advertising office is concerned primarily with sales. Its director, practically speaking, is a sales manager, responsible to the publisher or owner for the sale of space. He must, directly or through subordinates, obtain and develop new sources of business; plan sales strategy, materials, and procedures; manage the staff, including hiring, training, and supervising; take responsibility for preparation of advertising pages in the publication; and, unless separate divisions handle such work, direct the promotion, publicity, and public relations of the company.

So much advertising department work is done by salesmen under direction of the department head that their jobs may profitably be examined in some detail. They are among the best paid of magazine-dom's employes. Men rather than women handle such work for large magazines, for it is highly competitive and arduous and requires considerable travel. Working on commission or salary or both, they sell advertising to firms in allocated territory or according to types of accounts. Modern selling long since passed the stage at which it was merely a matter of talking prospects into buying. Space salesmen use elaborate presentations, ranging from table displays to slide shows and motion pictures. They must educate potential advertisers to the magazine's characteristics and to the market it reaches. They must convince the advertiser that the magazine can help him by meeting specific problems or needs.

Associated with the advertising department is another group of salesmen: publishers' representatives. These men are independent of any one publication and may represent several in a given territory. Their commission is higher than that of salesmen working out of a magazine's home office or branch. But they make it unnecessary for a magazine firm to have many branch offices.

Even though sales personnel succeed in obtaining contracts for hundreds of pages of space, their work may be ineffective if the copy supplied is badly translated into type and engravings. Production managers therefore are necessary on large magazines. Their respon-sibility is to carry the advertisements through to successful presenta-tion. These persons are responsible for obtaining text and illustration copy, plates, and other materials. These come directly from the ad-vertiser or his agency. The production office sees to it that the page make-up as planned by other executives is followed by printers, and supervises the keeping of records of contracts, schedules agreed upon, and materials obtained from printers. On small publications this office is responsible for proper billing for the space sold to advertisers.

Much business is done by small magazine firms with advertising service and supply houses, such as printers, engravers, photographers, mailing companies, artists, and typographers.

The newcomer to magazine advertising does not begin in such positions as copy chief or production department head. Depending upon his background, he may start as a clerk or stenographer. If he has art talent and sufficient training, however, he may begin by pre-paring layouts or sketches for illustrations, or editing photographs. If he shows promise with words, he works with an experienced copy writer on the production of suggested advertising displays. Or he may, for example, write the text of a simple booklet about a product being advertised. If he is facile with mathematics and statistically minded, he shares in research work.

All these jobs in advertising are common to it, wherever practiced. Consequently, magazine advertising departments employ persons with agency, newspaper, outdoor, or other non-magazine advertising experience.

### Department scope

The breadth of the work in a magazine advertising department stretches from the making of basic decisions to the doing of detailed chores. What is done differs, depending upon whether the magazine is of general or specialized appeal. Few periodicals attempt to appeal to all persons but instead are aimed at categories. Each department, therefore, reflects the magazine's specialization in the kinds of advertising it handles.

Whether specialized or not, advertising falls into two main classifications: display and classified. Classified consists of small announcements, usually in small type, arranged in special columns under classifications. Sometimes these are called *want ads* or *help wanteds,* although the classifications cover far more than employment. Not entirely typical, this example at least is amusing:

> TOMBSTONE for sale with the name
> of John Murphy carved on it, stone
> contracted for in 1937 and uncalled
> for. Opportunity for right party.

The advertising director may decide that classified advertising is not lucrative for his periodical or does not offer an important service to readers. Certain magazines traditionally have sold it: *Popular Mechanics, Saturday Review, Dance,* and most business magazines.

But virtually all commercial magazines sell space for display advertising, which uses various sizes and faces of type and drawings or photographs as illustrations, and may occupy any amount of space up to one page or several dozen for a single advertiser.

After policy on types of advertising has been decided by the department or other executives, the matter of rates must be settled.

### Advertising rates

The rate structure of magazines is more nearly standardized, within the same magazine category, than is that of general newspapers. That is, consumer magazine rates have some comparability as do the rates among farm magazines that are regional. But rate structure and practices relating to such advertising vary as between general and specialized magazines. Business magazines, for instance, offer sliding scale rates with discounts, but general magazines have a flat rate with no discounts for more frequent use of space.

Costs of advertising space in magazines vary according to circulation, specialized appeal of the publications, size of the space, and whether black and white or color. The more exposure received by an advertisement the more it costs, if for no other reason than that printing of more copies involves greater expense to the publisher. Therefore one of the high advertising rates per page is that of *The Reader's Digest,* with its more than seventeen million circulation in the U.S. alone. Its black and white page costs about $45,000 for one insertion in one issue. The cost per thousand readers to that advertiser comes to about $3. *The New Yorker,* because it is a more selective medium, charges about $4,800 for a page of black and white advertising, although its circulation is under five hundred thousand copies a week. Color advertising always brings a higher rate than black and white, in some instances an increase of as much as from 20 to 40 per cent over black and white.

Some magazines charge, on a space basis, a directly proportional amount; others a higher rate in proportion. Two half-pages in some publications cost more than a single page, for example.

Such facts as rates, frequency discounts, guaranteed circulations, and the deadlines for advertising copy are presented by most magazines on rate cards, folders, or sheets. In coming to an agreement, advertiser and magazine sign a contract. Typical contractual clauses cover the publisher's right to cancel under given conditions, the rule that a contract must be completed within a given period, and the publisher's liability for error.

## Expenditures

The amounts of money spent on printed and broadcast advertising in the United States in any one year are more than ordinary citizens can grasp. In recent years the media on which statistics have been kept were found to have collected, in one year, more than $15 billion. Consumer magazines received about 8% of this sum in the usual statistical records. But since many hundreds of specialized magazines were omitted in the figuring, the $600,000,000 of farm and business magazines justifiedly being added to the consumer amount, and all television was taken into consideration, a full picture of magazine advertising undoubtedly would show that magazines as a whole in the United States collected more than any other medium.

The expenditures by individual national advertisers also are in figures we associate more with astronomy than with journalism. One firm, Procter & Gamble Company, spends close to $187,000,000 a year (all but $7,555,000 of it on television and about $5,000,000 of the rest on magazines). Another big investor in advertising is General Motors Corporation, which divides its expenditures differently (out of about $74,000,000 spent, magazines often attract the most, sometimes $24,000,000 for it, $5,000,000 for outdoors, and $3,000,000 for radio).

## *Regional editions*

A new element in modern magazine advertising is the sale of space in regional editions, with special rates for them. An outgrowth of what sometimes is called split-run publishing, it is exemplified by the policies of certain national magazines which adopted the plan toward the end of the 1950's. Regional buying occurs when one advertiser uses one or more geographical portions of the circulation but not the entire distribution. Variations include adding Canadian distribution, appearance of one advertisement in newsstand copies and another piece of copy by the same advertiser in subscription copies, or the running of several different pieces of copy in various segments of the circulation and involving the total circulation.

Such split runs are commonly available in many major national magazines. *TV Guide,* which has about one hundred regional editions, offers as many split runs as that number might indicate, in various combinations. *Time* and many others have what are called *demographic editions,* such as sale of space in copies that go only to college and school people, or to doctors.

The advantages to the advertiser and publisher alike are clear, although the publisher must offset high costs of such splits by charging special rates. The advertiser whose product is distributed only in certain geographical areas, or who wishes to test a new product in a limited market, need not pay for the printing of his copy in issues which will bring him no revenue. Or if his service or commodity has a greater interest to readers in a certain geographical area (persons living in a resort country, for example, will respond to advertisements of new kinds of fishing lures or a new type of cruiser more than would residents of an urban, waterless area dominated by the oil industry), he can pinpoint that area.

Publishers have the advantage of being able to charge far higher rates for the segment of circulation thus purchased by an advertiser than if the national rate were prorated. For instance, advertisers using certain regional editions of *The Reader's Digest* in 1971 paid from 15 to 60 per cent more for black and white pages, per thousand circulation, than the same circulation would have cost on a national basis. But had they bought the entire circulation they then would have had to pay for all the other regions, and their total bill would be vastly greater.

Linage gains made by magazines in recent years are thought to have come about largely through this plan of selling regional edition space. They have been of particular benefit to the small advertiser, who earlier could not afford the entire run of an issue. During 1970 such regional advertising (about $202,500,000) was reported to have been 17 per cent of the total magazine advertising revenue for the year. A 9 per cent increase over 1960, it covered only the 94 publications measured by PIB.

## Advertising acceptability

Because magazines are published by private businesses, they may accept or reject advertising (or reading matter copy) as they wish. Nothing in the law forces a magazine company to *accept* an advertisement it does not wish to print.

The more prosperous a magazine the more it can afford to reject advertising. A certain amount of undesirable advertising is rejected by all magazines because it may violate the law. The legal restriction is imposed after publication, not before.

Certain magazines are known for their independence in the matter of accepting or rejecting advertising accounts. One of these is *The New Yorker,* which carries more advertising than most of the nation's magazines. It limits the total number of pages to be sold in a year so that, as its advertising department has been quoted as saying, the magazine does not get "to be a catalog." It urges advertisers to use less space at times and rejects hundreds of thousands of dollars in contracts each year. Why this unusual policy? Because it does not want to unbalance the ratio of editorial to advertising content, a possibility since, its editors say, the magazine does not receive manuscripts of high enough quality in sufficient quantity. This statement would seem to be an invitation to authors to be more productive, which indeed it is. Furthermore, *The New Yorker* has strict rules about the types of advertising it will accept. It objects if copy violates what it considers good taste or is inappropriate in its appeal.[2]

Other magazines also reject copy, for ethical reasons. During the discussion of reports on the effects of cigaret smoking in recent years a number of magazines adopted the policy of refusing tobacco advertising entirely, among them *Good Housekeeping, Saturday Review, National Geographic,* and *The Reader's Digest;* in the case of the latter this was a long-standing policy, for it refused $17,000,000 in such advertising between 1954 and 1963.

## Advertising research

The department helps advertisers by obtaining facts about readers as well as about the markets in which in they work and about the advertising effectiveness of the periodical itself. The chief aim of all this research is to show the potency of the magazine as a sales medium, especially in comparison with broadcasting advertising.

Advertising and editorial content both draw certain types of readers by education, income, sex, age, and other characteristics. The department, or an agency or research firm hired by the publishing

---

[2] " 'New Yorker' Treats 'Em Rough; Admen Love It," *Advertising Age,* Feb. 21, 1955, pp. 2, 70, 72; " 'New Yorker' Bars Ads for Girdles, Bras, Etc.," *Advertising Age,* pp. 3, 102; "Out, Damned MacBird," advertising column, New York *Times,* April 3, 1967.

company, conducts readership studies to determine pertinent facts, which also are placed at the disposal of the editors. In the parlance of magazine advertising, readers are known collectively as the *audience* (see Chapter 8).

Pioneer among advertising researchers was Daniel Starch, who made his early studies for the American Association of Advertising Agencies. For many years his firm has maintained an organization for research and twice each year since 1932 released findings known as the Starch Consumer Magazine Report. His firm's work generally is confined to the consumer magazines.

In reporting on readership, Starch ratings have been expressed in three levels. Advertisements that readers remember having seen are listed as having been *noted;* if readers associate the advertisement with the product or advertiser the rating is *seen associated,* and if they read more than 50 per cent of the copy it is rated *read most.*

Advertising departments depend heavily upon the findings of Standard Rate & Data Service, which regularly issues reports, in general appearance like magazines, on rates, circulation, and mechanical requirements of consumer, farm, and business magazines and comparable facts about broadcasting stations.

Also important as a source of research information is the Magazine Advertising Bureau. All the media have their organizations to promote the increased use of their medium as an advertising tool or outlet. The trade press—*Advertising Age, Advertising and Sales Promotion, Madison Avenue, Western Advertising* and the like—refers to such groups as MAB, the Radio Advertising Bureau, Television Bureau of Advertising, American Newspaper Publishers Association's Bureau of Advertising, and others more specialized in scope.

MAB explains that it functions in two main areas: (1) To do research about magazines and advertising; (2) To promote the idea of magazines "by telling people about magazine advertising and its advantages."

A variety of reports and studies, charts, film presentations, and other materials useful to magazine advertising departments and to advertisers has come from this organization. They report on the size of the magazine market, the success of specific advertising campaigns, periodic expenditures by advertisers, comparison with volume sales and revenue of previous years, changes in rates, trends in different phases, and many other facts. Its officers are executives of magazine publishing firms, as are its members, although it has a paid staff in Magazine House, the New York City headquarters.

Similar research and promotion activities, although on not so large a scale, are carried out by the trade associations of the specialized magazines, such as the Agricultural Publishers Association (for farm magazines), Western Society of Business Publications, and American Business Press, Inc.

*Chapter 5*

---

# Circulation

O NE SUMMER DAY the author of this book walked into the circulation department offices of a large weekly magazine in New York City. He found at work two graduates of a school of journalism where he once had taught. Both men had gone through the editorial sequence; one, in fact, had been in the author's own writing classes at the institution.

Both were holding important writing positions in the magazine's sprawling circulation department. That sentence does not contain an error. They were indeed writing and doing other editorial work.

If this situation, by no means rare in the magazine business, comes as a surprise it may be because the circulation department is one of the least known to the general public and scarcely ever is set before prospective magazinists as an outlet for their abilities. Yet increasingly it offers some of the most brain-cracking problems and important tasks anyone can face in journalism.

Would an alert mind not be aroused by seeking to tackle these questions, some of which beset all magazines and others only the larger ones:
1. How can a publisher educate or train retailers of magazines to display them more effectively, keep them clean, discourage free reading, and prevent piling up so some periodicals are not obscured by others?

2. How can one find what motivates people to buy certain magazines at newsstands and not others; to prefer some by subscription and others by newsstand purchase?
3. How effective are various types of covers in the sale of magazines? With people of what education? What economic level? What social level? And why?
4. What difference does one price or another make in circulation? In newsstand sales alone? In subscription sales?
5. With postal delivery of magazines becoming increasingly costly, what other methods are practical for delivery? Local delivery trucks, like those used for milk and parcel post? Newsboys? House-to-house delivery?

These problems are only a few of the scores that magazine circulation departments face all year around. The managers of such departments look to trained people for help, once they have learned the routines of the business, in solving them. One publishing executive put it this way: ". . . it is often more difficult to find a person who can write about a publication than it is to find one who can write for a publication."

And writing about the publication is only one of the kinds of work done in a magazine circulation office. Such offices are hospitable to people with preparation in mass communications research methods, who understand the business side of the magazine world, who can prepare copy for letters, posters, leaflets, advertisements, and many other kinds of printed matter, and who have new ideas for improving sales and distribution of magazines.

### The nature of circulation

At one time in the history of magazines publishers were content merely to send their issues to subscribers and sell copies in bookstores. But in our time circulation is much more complicated. With more than half a hundred publishers counting their subscribers and newsstand buyers in the millions, and many more with circulations ranging from a quarter of a million to a million, distribution requires a huge staff and complex mechanism. Magazine circulation itself has become a separate occupation. Numerous firms, including some affiliated with large publishing companies, are in the business.

Even the small business magazine or scientific journal must keep records of business transactions, subscriptions, and sales, compile lists of prospects, sell copies to commercial distributors, change addresses, cancel and renew, meet post office regulations, return inaccurate orders for clarification and correction, wrap, tie, and address, deliver to dispatch points, and promote sales. It does little good to cram a magazine with pungent articles, alluring fiction, and potent advertising layouts if the finished copies pile up in warehouses.

## The circulation department

Small magazine companies combine their advertising, circulation, promotion, and other business-side operations into one general business department. Large ones need a separate unit. A typical department in a firm publishing one or more consumer magazines is larger than the entire staff of any small magazine. Advertising, in any case, is linked logically with circulation, for these departments and their operations are closely related. Advertising, for example, studies circulation trends, watches geographical distribution, and is responsible for readership surveys; it must call upon the circulation department for records and other assistance.

The three most important departments of a magazine publishing company—advertising, circulation, and editorial, in alphabetical order —often are likened to the three-legged stool that will fall if any one leg is removed.

**TABLE 5.1.** *Circulation Department Organization\**

| Title of Personnel | Major Duties |
|---|---|
| Director | Directs and manages the department. Accepts responsibility for all areas of the department. |
| Copy Chief | Has charge of circulation promotion. Supervises other promotion copy writers. Produces such copy. |
| List Manager | Finds lists of possible new subscribers. Rents such lists; negotiates with dealers in lists. Keeps lists up to date. |
| Agency Manager | Supervises selling through subscription agencies. Writes advertisements dealing with circulation. |
| Newsstand Manager | Works with national distributor. Supervises special promotion of newsstand sales. |
| Fulfillment Manager | Supervises fulfilling of subscriptions. Checks auditing reports. |

\* This form of organization is typical of moderate-size or large firms. It is based on that of the Popular Science Publishing Company, which issues *Popular Science Monthly* and *Outdoor Life*. These officials serve both magazines and in some instances also devote time to other operations, such as the company's book clubs.

The circulation department is watched as a doctor watches a pulse. Much of its basic work is clerical; some of this routine is now being performed by machines. Its personnel prepares or orders addressing plates for new subscribers, fulfills subscription orders, keeps back copies, and does other work of an unglamorous nature. Depending on the size and content of the magazine, the department does outside work also; it may employ persons capable of training and leading solicitation crews in the field.

Young men and women contemplating magazine journalism as a career consider circulation department work as a possibility so rarely that about one student in eighty mentions it, surveys made by the author at several universities show. Magazines arrive so efficiently and quickly that students assume there is nothing to the work. Now and then, one finds a summer job with a circulation crew and returns to placid college life having learned lessons in social psychology. A taste of work in this department creates better writers and editors, for after six months or a year the novice is more sharply aware of the financial workings of a magazine firm and the nature of readers.

Although it works closely with the advertising department, the circulation department also provides much information for the editorial unit. Phillips Wyman, while a McCall Corporation official, illustrated this point in the first substantial study made of magazine circulation operations.[1] The analysis that follows includes some of his findings, most of which are as valid for these times as for Wyman's day.

### *External circulation factors*

The most powerful factors on which magazine circulations depend are outside the magazine. These change rapidly as national and world conditions alter.

First of the external ones is growth of education, especially at high school level. The world as a whole, and the United States particularly, is becoming more literate, although world literacy progresses slowly. The greater the number who can read, the larger the number of magazine buyers or readers or both. Only certain magazines, however, benefit from the creation of new literates, as in the developing countries of the world, for many of these at first can read only the simplest materials and may never increase their ability beyond a low minimum point. In the United States, as well as within other nations, more and more citizens are being formally educated; many of these will read magazines as well as newspapers and books.

The increase or decrease in amount of leisure at the disposal of the average citizen is a second factor pointed out by Wyman.

---

[1] Phillips Wyman, *Magazine Circulation: An Outline of Methods and Meanings* (New York: McCall Company, 1936).

When he segregated this factor, the United States was recovering from a severe economic depression. During such times a sort of leisure exists that makes for an increase in reading but also a decrease in the buying of magazines. Dependence upon libraries and exchange of magazines are greater.

During World War II, which broke out abroad three years after Wyman's analysis was published, magazines were in greater demand than ever but restricted by paper shortages. The prosperity of the postwar years was reflected in mounting circulations. As working hours were shortened through labor-management agreement, time for reading increased. Although leisure time is no guarantee of magazine reading, it offers a challenge and an opportunity to maga-zine publishers to win attention. The midcentury years saw the ar-rival of commercial television. It, as we have noted already, along with the reading of paperback books, offered new competition for the use of leisure time.

Closely coupled with the second factor is another already touched upon: the standard of living. If it is high, more money is available for purchase of magazines; if low, less. The standard in the United States is one of the highest in the world; magazine circulations reflect this dramatically.

## Internal factors

The internal factors are both more numerous and more subtle than the external. Two involve some understanding of psychology.

Historically and logically the most powerful internal factor is edi-torial content. Important, vital, and appealing as advertising content may be, no publisher offers a magazine containing advertisements only. A few commercial publications assemble publicity for new products and sell their magazines with advertising thus disguised; many firms print company publications of the external type which boost specific products, as do mail-order catalogs and advertising circulars. But readers recognize this advertising for what it is. When they pay cash for a magazine they want articles, editorials, columns, stories, poems, helpful hints, news, and other accepted content. Some readers are satisfied with less content than others; the medical journal reader does not expect to find fiction nor does the buyer of a short story magazine want technical dissertations on medical science.

Editorial content is a factor in circulation because it influences reader interest. If the staff is to arouse the response of potential readers it must know their reading interest and attempt to gratify them sufficiently, at least, to retain the reader's desire to continue seeing the periodical. The narrower the reader's interests, the less the appeal of the general magazine. The narrower the content of the publication, the less the appeal to the general reader. Through research departments hired for the purpose, magazine publishers constantly seek to understand the reader's psychology, so as not to offend it or fail to satisfy it.

Advertising matter also has reader interest, even if it appears not to be so powerful as that of editorial matter. Although consumers may not wish to pay for advertising as the only ingredient of a magazine, the reader who is considering buying the commodity or using the service offered nevertheless is deeply interested in the advertising pages of a magazine he bought primarily for reading matter. Proof of this reaction lies in the purchases and response to invitations to send for samples, literature, and other materials. Advertising departments recognize this second internal factor sufficiently to study carefully the reasons for reader response to types of advertising copy and appeal.

The third factor—the reader's desire that his magazine appear on the newsstand or in the mailbox dependably, with the usual recognizable appearance plus freshness and newness that are appealing—sets up a problem for both the editorial and the circulation departments. It can be likened to a family situation. A husband always wants to be able to recognize a particular woman as his wife, but he appreciates her all the more if she has a new hair-styling now and then or makes him look twice because of her smart appearance and the presence of some new effect, be it even so little as the addition of a small piece of costume jewelry. The circulation department can assure dependability and regularity of issue if the departments behind it—advertising, editorial, and production—do their work efficiently. But the task of giving a magazine a new look and an old look simultaneously is up to editorial, with help from production.

Whether a magazine continues or ceases publication depends upon the success of its editors in resolving this paradox. For, Wyman declares, "The relation of reader and magazine is essentially emotional," a fundamental statement the truth of which is not realized by all professionals in circulation work. Many periodicals are read by habit, which is upset by issues that look unfriendly, odd, too much like some other magazine, or in some way too startlingly unusual. The *Saturday Evening Post* learned this when it indulged in some unusual typographical innovations in the late 1950's.

Wyman also points out that in preparing sales letters or other copy for new-subscriber promotion material, a list of features generally is ineffective. A reader occasionally may buy a magazine because he sees an article listed in a leaflet or on the table of contents page, for the piece may be by his favorite author or on a subject of absorbing interest; but unless the magazine runs such material regularly he will not buy the book regularly. The effectiveness of this third factor is most clear when the magazine succeeds in building loyalty to itself.

Once the reader becomes habituated to a certain magazine, which he does when he is confident almost every issue will contain material suitable, valuable, or pleasing to him, he will procure it regularly.

Typical is the attitude of a subscriber who wrote enthusiastically: "Please print more Charles F. Kettering articles. I have read your magazine about 75 years and 'Get Off Route 25' is one of the best you ever published." To which the editors replied with appreciation for friendship: "We're glad that our old friend liked the article— even though our magazine is a mere youngster of 62." Magazine reading is passed along within families like clothing and political allegiance.

A factor of strictly economic character is the periodical's cost to the reader. As with any other commodity the reader must feel that he is getting value received. He was impressed with the size of the *Saturday Evening Post* when it cost only a nickel. He has been willing to pay two to four times as much for his magazines because he knows that other costs have increased proportionately. The practically universal desire to get much for little explains in part the public's indifference to small experimental magazines issued by literary or artistic groups, although lack of knowledge and interest are the main reasons. Nevertheless, these periodicals are high priced (often from one to two dollars a copy), small in physical size, and with few pages compared with large commercial magazines, glowing as they are with color and weighing pounds each issue. The bookazines, like *American Heritage,* can charge several dollars for a copy and obtain sufficient sales because the reader realizes that physically, as well as in other ways, he is getting what he considers his money's worth. Many a reader responds to an expensive color-printed magazine of conventional content and ignores a plain one of stimulating ideas and facts of which he is unaware and which may even be important to his life.

The business managers of a publishing company must consider the price factor with utmost concern. But now and then they are influenced by the examples of magazines who defied the view that price must be decided carefully. *Fortune* and *Esquire,* at their founding, defied the experts and set comparatively high per copy and subscription costs for their day, the second quarter of this century. *Fortune* was ten dollars a year and a dollar a copy at the newsstand, *Esquire* five dollars a year and fifty cents a copy. These were unheard of high prices for periodicals of their class and in a time when the economy was in trouble. Both magazines were successful, however. *Fortune* has held to its original price; *Esquire* has raised its several times. But scores of other magazines have increased their charges.

Appealing content and presentation, it was shown, can overcome the handicap of high price and that price is high under certain conditions only. A prosperous business executive or one who can subscribe to a magazine like *Fortune* as a legitimate company expense is not much concerned over price. Magazines that readers believe will save them money—*Consumer Reports* and *Consumer Bulletin,* for example—also can disregard this factor in circulation if readers can reasonably be expected to possess sufficient means. Magazine pricing is extremely variable; experiments with it are conducted constantly. *Cosmopolitan, Life,* and others have tried temporary newsstand price reductions in regions of the U.S.A. and found them useful in attracting new readers. Other magazines accept installment subscription payments. Still others give short-term subscriptions free. Discounts, cut-rates, and tie-ups with newspapers are common.

Some authorities hold the view that the public will have to pay still more for magazines because advertising rates have gone so high that advertisers will not tolerate further increases. Edward A. Grey, senior vice-president in charge of media for McCann-Erickson, Inc., an agency that places much advertising in magazines, puts it this way: "Magazines will have to start passing their increased costs along to readers instead of advertisers. The advertisers have had it on rate increases." [2]

A physical factor is perishability of magazines. Advertisers count this important. If a publication is cheaply printed on easily torn paper, with few illustrations, and deals only with passing subjects or carries unimportant fiction by hacks, it is not likely to be kept on library and home bookshelves. Nor will it remain long in family living rooms or professional reception offices. Only the most unsentimental, calloused, or unappreciative readers lightly throw into the trash can copies of handsomely produced magazines containing important or beautiful writing and unforgettable art work. Usually perishability is in balance with cost; the lower the cost the higher the perishability rate. The lower the cost, also, the less reluctant is the reader to part with the magazine; the more he pays the greater the reluctance to part with it. Scarcity also plays a part in his reactions. He is more likely to dispose of a magazine that is easy to replace than one he obtained only with considerable effort.

This physical factor does not affect over-all circulation so clearly as it may affect the fate of single issues. Magazines worth saving often are so expensive that comparatively few readers can afford to buy them and so to keep them. On the other hand, those not worth preserving may cost so little that many readers buy them, believing that they lose almost nothing from their investment. Publishers know that there are readers who avoid magazines they feel they must keep because these offer a storage problem, and others who decide on cheap magazines (as well as paperback books) because they are readily disposed of.

---

[2] Edward A. Grey, "Media Futures—," *Media/scope,* April, 1964, p. 48.

Magazines cannot have the widest distribution unless they reach all communities. To accomplish this their publishers must confront the final factor: distribution.

## Distribution as a factor

The fundamental problem in magazine circulation work is "the distribution of the periodical to a circle of readers large enough to maintain it," as Bakeless phrases it. [3] This vital factor has been given meticulous study by magazine owners. They have discovered, in the United States, that as the educational level rose and buying power became widespread, giving the country a large middle class and comparatively small poor and wealthy classes, magazines had an opportunity to reach many communities and various types of readers.

Two means of distribution developed: newsstand sales and paid-in-advance subscriptions. Later some publishers decided to give their magazines away. These methods did not arise overnight. The first newsstands, if shelves and counters of bookstores and railway stations a century ago could be so called, were not numerous. Publishers succeeded in interesting local stores in becoming agencies. But this was before the day of wide distribution of manufactured products. As railways spread a network over the United States, frontiers were pushed back by the building of roads and settlement of towns, and all types of vehicles were improved; national distribution became faster and easier, and it proved a stimulus to advertising. For now it was valid for a publisher to solicit advertising from producers shipping goods to the same towns the magazine was entering.

Paralleling this business development was improvement of editorial content, speeding of production, and lowering of magazine prices. Publishers found it lucrative to send crews into the countryside to obtain subscriptions. The premium fad, actually a form of price-cutting, grew popular. Books were popular rewards to new subscribers, as were hunting pictures and lamps, reminding one of the offers of banks in our own day. Club plans were made, also, enabling subscribers to have a group of magazines at lower cost than by contracting for each separately. Premium-giving has virtually disappeared, but clubbing is increasingly popular and now includes combinations with newspaper subscriptions.

More magazines were sold on trains. Retail outlets became so varied and numerous that the bookshop was smothered under competition. Once the principal middleman for magazines, the bookstore now sells fewer than the drugstore or pipe shop. Street stands displayed so many magazines that newspapers were subordinated. Canvassing was put on a more professional basis by careful training of personnel and by organization of crews over geographical districts.

[3] John Bakeless, *Magazine Making* (New York: Viking Press, 1935), p. 234.

Now the outlets include drugstores, supermarkets, airports, bus terminals, hotel and motel lobbies, and tobacconists as well as the usual outlets of city street corner newsstands. Book and stationery stores, once the main outlets, are minor. Vending machines that would make it possible to buy a magazine at any hour of the day, without dependence upon newsstands or shops being open for business, have been tried experimentally by Time Inc. for *Time, Life,* and *Sports Illustrated.* It has not proved to be the cure-all for lagging newsstand sales, however. Advertising in newspapers and in other magazines has aided both newsstand and subscription sales.

Direct mail sales became and still are another productive means of obtaining subscribers, newsstand purchasers, and readers. Sales, promotion, advertising, and circulation departments, one or more of which may be responsible for direct mail attempts, have developed carefully planned series of letters to bring in new or renewal orders.

As the advertising department sometimes farms out much of its work to advertising companies and agencies, and the production department allows typesetting, engraving, and binding to be done under contract (except where the publishing company owns its own plants), so the circulation department often employs a subscription agency or other means to help bring in subscriptions. These firms will go so far as to set up individuals in small community businesses to solicit magazine subscriptions.

### Types of subscription agencies

Five types of agencies serve as channels through which publishers sell magazines. These are:
1. Catalog agencies.
2. Salesmen employed by the publisher himself.
3. Salesmen employed by independent agencies.
4. Newspaper agencies.
5. Organization members, such as in schools and churches.

Catalog agencies actually are wholesalers of subscriptions. They employ individuals who sell subscriptions. The agency annually issues a catalog describing the magazines it has to offer, with prices and other information. These lists cover as many as four thousand titles. About a dozen large firms constitute this channel.

Publishers naturally set up agencies to sell their own magazines but also commonly sell subscriptions to other periodicals as well. This channel, known as the Publisher-Owned Subscription Agency, emphasizes the long-term subscription. The salesmen these groups employ do door-to-door solicitation and telephone selling. They work from the firm's branch offices.

The independent agencies hire itinerant salesmen who form crews and move constantly.

Magazine and newspaper publishing companies cooperate in this area of magazine subscription sales. Newspaper carrier boys are organized also to offer magazine subscriptions to their customers; the newspapers push these sales in display advertising and flyers or dodgers as well. Payment is made at the time the boys collect for the paper. Subscriptions of this sort are long term.

Subscription campaigns are conducted by local organizations—schools, clubs, churches, fraternal and military organizations, and many other groups of those types. Being local, they obtain extraordinary cooperation in a community. Professional canvassers and subscription solicitors carry out the campaign under auspices of the home town organization. If a school is involved, pupils do the canvassing rather than professionals. On college campuses students circularize and canvass fraternities, sororities, and other groups. In some instances special, low-cost editions are printed for school use. Organizations which solicit subscriptions are given a discount which enables them to earn money.

### Physical distribution

Whatever the means of obtaining subscriptions or stimulating newsstand purchases, the publications must be moved from printing plant to sales point. Physical distribution is neither magical nor romantic and, like the mails, must go through. And, thanks to the mails, it does "go through" to subscribers. Other means carry copies to newsstands.

Magazines are accepted for mailing under one of four standard classifications explained in Chapter 3. They are considered second class matter as distinguished from first class, which is sealed, written matter, like letters, or third or fourth class printed matter, which is classified according to weight, like catalogs.

The unliterary job of preparing copies of a magazine of extremely small circulation for mailing is open to many aspirants to a place in the world of writing. Except to the most modest would-be authors, wrapping, labeling, and sorting magazines must seem to have only the slightest connection with an editorial career. Such work must be done by someone, however, and the experience provides understanding of one side of the business.

The wrapping of a magazine, for instance, may be a problem. To begin with, not all publishers are agreed on the necessity of a separate wrapper. The larger the circulation the less the probability that a wrapper will be used, because of cost. On the other hand, if a magazine cover is an especially important element of its appeal and is likely to be marred in the mail, the publisher will protect it by a wrapper or an envelope despite the cost.

Wrappers are made of different qualities of paper, with at least the source of the magazine printed upon them and sometimes with special instructions to the U.S. Postal Service to expedite delivery (such as NEWS—RUSH on business magazines); they range in size from half the magazine's width, when wrapped, to the entire width plus enough to tuck into the ends.

Pasting wrappers around magazines, attaching prepared labels or addressing the wrappers directly, sorting the copies, and other clerical operations in a small office involve details that must be attended to carefully. Big firms now do much of this work with automated machinery. Once the rules for preparation have been followed, the Service sees to the rest, at considerable saving to publishers, whose magazines in some instances are so heavy that the owners would be bankrupt if they had to mail them first class. Yet handling magazines at a loss to the U.S. Postal Service, as it declares is the case, is part of the guarantee of freedom of expression provided by the United States government. In a democracy it should be possible for anyone, within the limits of democratically passed laws, to disseminate ideas, and for publications issued for the public good to continue their service. Many hours could be consumed, however, in debating whether all magazines are published in the public interest.

Uncle Sam's part in magazine circulation is not one way. The mails also are used to solicit and receive subscription orders and renewals and to carry promotion for advertising content.

### Magazines go to newsstands

The mailman takes small numbers of magazines to outlets too expensive to reach by standard means: distributing and wholesaling companies. Newsstand distribution is almost altogether in the hands of these firms, which are hired, controlled, or operated by magazine publishing companies.

That newsstand underground on a subway platform or beside the kiosk upstairs or outside Flack's cigar store on Main Street blossoms with magazines all year around but rarely does a customer see the copies arrive. They reach the retailer via distributors or wholesalers. The former are firms of two kinds of ownership but are the same in function. One group is owned by the publishing companies, such as the large Curtis Circulation Company, the Dell Distributing Company, Inc., and Macfadden Publications. The other is comprised of independent companies engaged by publishers to distribute their magazines. About twenty of both types do the major amount of business. Wholesalers, of which there are about one thousand, are local firms that receive the issues and distribute them in turn to city and nearby suburban outlets, usually by truck.

After being printed, the magazines are bundled and shipped to the national distributor and thence to the wholesaler. The independents receive a commission on the basis of quantity delivered to the wholesaler. Under another plan, payment is based on a system of returns or proof of non-sale. If copies are unsold at the end of the sale period the cover or perhaps only the logo or title line of the cover is returned to the publisher, who then pays only for the copies sold. Sometimes these coverless copies are destroyed by the wholesaler but other times are sold at small cost by secondhand, back number dealers.

This machinery of distribution and sale is important, not only so that magazines reach newsstands and other sales outlets but also because it is a factor in the difficulties encountered by new or small magazines in reaching the public.

"The difference between the new systems is important because the national distributor who receives his income from quantity delivery to the wholesaler has a tendency to flood the outlet," a study of magazine circulation reveals. "The wholesaler on the other hand must be concerned with the overhead accrued in processing tons of publications. The national distributor frequently can make a profit on a volume which would put the wholesaler out of business if he had to handle everything sent to him.

"In defense, the wholesaler starts setting aside a large percentage of those publications which he knows he cannot move and warns the distributor that smaller shipments must be made."[4]

Because of the steady rise of postal rates, magazine publishers experiment from time to time with other methods of delivering subscription copies. In Darien, Connecticut, and nearby communities, for example, Time Inc. and several other publishers undertook private delivery of their magazines in certain areas. A series of two-foot-long plastic tubes, on wooden poles, was set up to receive the magazines and protect them from weather. They were trucked to a delivery service in Darien. This would be a less expensive plan than the present one if postal rates become much higher, but is practical only in communities where many copies are subscribed for.

Some firms find it economical to ship quantities to cities that are distant from the printing plant and then deliver them to the local post office for mailing, rather than mailing them from the printing center itself.

Even such apparently routine operations as these involve excitement at times. One day a fast Santa Fe train bound for Los Angeles hit a rock slide in an Arizona canyon. In one of the eleven cars that buckled and crashed into the desolate canyon walls were advance pages being used by *Time* and *Sports Illustrated* from Chicago for joining to the current pages to be printed in Los Angeles for West

---

[4] Vernon W. Smith, "January 1963 Distribution of Magazines in Syracuse, New York" (Unpublished report, Syracuse University, 1963), p. 2.

Coast subscribers to the two weeklies. Also in that car were all the mailing labels for copies of *Time* and part of *Life's* circulation on the West Coast. By the next morning new labels had been sent to Los Angeles, and the reprinted pages were being trucked in 5,000-pound loads to a Chicago airport, where they filled unused cargo space on any plane going to Los Angeles. By the end of another twenty-four hours almost 60,000 pounds of printed magazine pages had been airlifted to the West.

## Central Registry

One of the headaches of magazine circulation for publishers is maintaining high standards of operation by subscription solicitors. Because of the abuses of a minority of people working in crews, Central Registry, sponsored by the Magazine Publishers Association, was formed. This organization is "a voluntary self-regulatory organization for industry improvement." Its purpose is to "serve the public interest by maintaining ethical selling standards among door-to-door . . . salesmen and to protect the public against fraud and loss in magazine transactions."[5]

The type of abuse this group seeks to correct is the practice of solicitors pretending to be medical, nursing, or other students or orphans, or the failure of agencies or crew managers to live up to agreements, such as proper registration. Central Registry issues credentials to acceptable agencies and cooperates with Better Business Bureaus and Chambers of Commerce.

## Circulation checking agencies

Another form of self-government within the publishing industry is a circulation checking organization. Originally this need arose because years ago some publishers falsified their circulation figures. The auditing groups set up standards conducive to confidence between those who buy and those who sell advertising space.

Three major organizations, as noted earlier, measure magazine circulations.

The Audit Bureau of Circulations was formed in 1914 by the union of two older groups with similar aims, the Bureau of Verified Circulation and the Advertising Audit Association. Representatives from two general magazine publishers, two farm, and two business magazine companies made up the first board of twenty-one members. Its objects are explained in Article I of its bylaws as "to issue standardized statements of the circulation of publisher members; to verify the figures shown in these statements by auditors' examination of any and all records considered by the Bureau to be necessary; and to dis-

---

[5] "Central Registry in Action Serves the Public" (New York: Central Registry of Magazine Subscription Solicitors, 1964), p. 2.

seminate circulation data only for the benefit of advertisers, advertising agencies and publishers."

Prof. William H. Boyenton has related in his history of the ABC the reaction of Cyrus H. K. Curtis to the verification of circulations. When Curtis was asked to allow his publications to join, he said: "No one doubts the circulation statements of my company." To which ABC officials agreed while reminding him that the same confidence is not justified in the circulation figures of all other publishers. "By staying out of the Bureau," they said, "you are withholding your endorsement of the uniform standards of circulation measurement that are so necessary to the welfare of advertisers and publishers."[6]

Newspapers, magazines (both consumer and specialized), advertisers, and advertising agencies are ABC members. Charges of dues are on the basis of circulation size. Advertising agencies and advertisers pay according to the number of reports issued. Bureau reports cover the total number of copies sold and describe the means used to obtain circulation. Only publications with dominantly paid circulation are admitted, for ABC holds that such a publication is "one of which 70 per cent or more of its distribution qualifies as paid under the standards of the Bureau."

Business publication Audit Bureau of Circulation, on the other hand, audits magazines with less than 70 per cent paid circulation. Founded in 1931 and known until 1954 as Controlled Circulation Audit, it has aims similar to those of ABC otherwise. It came into being because ABC did not accept as members publications with mainly free circulation. Proponents of paid circulation insist that free circulation is not as valuable, because people do not give attention to what they do not have to pay for, or at least to the same degree. Readers who have paid for a magazine are assumed to want to read it. The extent to which this is not true can be gauged by the response to offers of premiums, discounts, club prices, and other inducements to subscribe, and the reader interest surveys made by publishers.

Controlled, or qualified, circulation, as opposed to paid, can be aimed exclusively at persons known to be interested in the advertising and editorial content, thus eliminating waste, and of having great flexibility by rotation of copies sent free to readers according to the season or some other basis.

Some publishers issuing groups of magazines, such as Chilton and McGraw-Hill, employ both methods of auditing. Chilton's fifteen business magazines have been divided, with six ABC audited and nine BPA audited.

Both ABC and BPA are membership organizations. A third group,

---

[6] William H. Boyenton, *Audit Bureau of Circulations* (Chicago: Audit Bureau of Circulations, 1948), p. 12.

Verified Audit Circulation Corporation (VAC) differs from the other two in several respects. Not being a membership group, it is available to all magazines. It is organized for profit, audits publications regardless of the field they serve or the nature or amount of their circulation (such as being paid or unpaid), and may be distributed in any way between them. The publications audited do not elect members of the directing board.

VAC also declares that "the space buyer is entitled to know just how many copies of the publication are actually being received by the person the advertiser wants to reach" and points out, as "an exclusive feature," the provision of this information on its circulation reports. It also makes semiannual reports and audits; others are annual.

All groups use generally similar methods of checking. Auditors examine all records relating to circulation, including postal receipts, supplies and services bills, ledgers, address files, and lists of subscribers. Circulation department employes are interviewed. Tests and samplings are conducted, press-runs are verified at printing plants; binderies and other divisions pertaining to circulation are inspected and visited as necessary.

### The precious renewals

An enthusiastic magazine publisher with confidence in his periodical is certain that if readers will merely expose themselves to his publication they will want to continue renewing it. He realizes that there are all sorts of barriers to this hope, but after having lovingly produced a handsome, striking issue he cannot see why many millions of persons do not buy it eagerly and renew subscriptions without urging.

The barriers—apathy, lack of money, vanishing interest, pressure of too much to read, competition from other time-consumers—seem to be just as serious when it comes to persuading subscribers to renew as it is to coax them to put down their coins for a newsstand copy.

Yet subscription renewal is one of the most vital measurements of a magazine's financial success. A high percentage of prompt renewals not only shows that the magazine is desired by its readers but also cuts down costs of operation. For it reduces the need for extra reminder mailings (with their preparation of specially printed pieces, mailing costs, and record-keeping), and eliminates another source of error in the records.

So precious are renewals that publishers of consumer periodicals offer considerable savings on subscription costs by giving special two-, three-, and five-year rates; a subscriber usually can save himself from two to five dollars as compared with the regular mail rate and as much as eight to ten by comparison with the newsstand price. A few magazines have a lifetime price.

Renewal rates of business publications and other specialized periodicals are far higher than those of consumer magazines because the specialized one becomes something of a text, source, reference, or guidebook for its reader whereas the consumer magazine is not considered so essential.

To large national magazines the problem of obtaining renewals becomes a major enterprise and keeps a large promotion department busy (see Chapter 7). *The Reader's Digest,* for example, has records for more than 17,000,000 subscribers to its U.S. edition alone; in one year most of these subscriptions come up for renewal. It uses computers to check the records, putting the names of all whose subscriptions are up for renewal on tape and comparing these with a list, on another tape, of names of persons who renewed or resubscribed within six months after the expiration date covered by the year.

Experiments, not yet proved successful, have been tried with another approach: asking the subscriber to agree that he will be billed annually for his subscription unless he notifies the publisher that he wishes to discontinue it, much as book clubs operate. *Life, The Reader's Digest, Popular Science Monthly,* and other magazines have used this continuing subscriber service, but it has met some resistance. Readers, in some instances, have objected. Advertisers are not certain that readers who continue to receive the magazine in that way actually want it and read it, since they exert no effort to obtain it beyond paying their bill. Publishers find additional billing necessary under the plan.

## Fulfillment

However the subscription may be obtained, it must be serviced or, as the magazine business calls it officially, fulfilled, i.e., the contract with the subscriber carried out. Seeing to it that his records are kept up to date would seem to be a simple enough matter, but both large and small magazine firms that operate on a subscription basis find this area of magazine work complex. An office handling millions of subscriber records, even only hundreds of thousands, is bound to be the victim of much human failure, even with automated machinery. The various electronic devices now being used by the larger firms or companies in the business of handling subscription fulfillment have cut down the possibility of error, however.

Elaborate systems have been set up to carry out the aims of this division of a magazine company. One such involves the use of computers and printers of labels. For many years magazines kept their subscribers' names, addresses, and other information on cards. Punch cards became so bulky, however, that large modern offices began feeding the information from them into a computer which compressed the facts onto tape reels. Time Inc. used 47,000,000 cards, at one time, to record subscribers to its various magazines. A computer reduced this bulk to one hundred reels of tape, with 100,000 subscriber records on one reel. Each reel saved the publisher fifty square feet of floor space that once was occupied by card file cabinets. The new system also made a number of calculators, printer machines, and other pieces of equipment obsolete. Correlated with the computer is an address-label printer which produces thirty-six labels a second. That rate is a dozen times faster than even electronic printers spewed forth labels earlier.

*Chapter 6*

---

# Production

AFTER HEARING about the thundering, giant presses of the publishing and printing business, the remarkable results of color reproduction, and the almost human performances of machines that assemble and bind magazines, a visitor can be disillusioned on entering a magazine office to see only desks and files and no special quarters or building for production facilities.

Production miracles are performed every day, but they rarely take place in printing and engraving plants owned by publishing companies, most of whom sign contracts with printing firms to produce their magazines. When they make such agreements they need at most an office or two for production editors so they have a place from which to control traffic between printers and engravers on the one hand and editors and artists on the other.

Here, again, magazine publishing is nearer kin to book than to newspaper publishing. Practically all book firms engage printers to produce their volumes; virtually all newspaper publishers own their plants, and print not only their own papers but also specialized newspapers for industry or education and hundreds of jobs common to all small printing plants: letterheads, posters, menus, signs, booklets, fliers, and advertising mailing pieces.

Not even the big consumer magazines all operate their own plants. Time Inc. engages the services of printing establishments in different parts of the world to obtain uniform production and delivery of its magazines, two of which have such huge circulations that one plant could not produce them quickly enough to deliver them in all areas simultaneously. The McCall Corp. prints, in addition to its own, about one hundred other magazines in its Dayton plant.

Here occurs the distinction between publishing and printing, which are not interchangeable terms. A publisher sponsors, as a business venture usually, a magazine, book line, or newspaper. Publishers can do their work in hole-in-the-wall offices, with no more equipment than desks and lamps, typewriters, file cases, coat racks, chairs, and wastebaskets. A printer literally produces, by machine, the physical commodity: book, magazine, newspaper. He does not sponsor the publication, he manufactures it.

Independence of large investment in printing machinery is significant to the publishing business. It may or may not be economical, depending upon what use is made of the equipment. But what may be more important is that it is part of journalism's never ending fight to preserve freedom of expression. If all publications had to be produced by companies fully equipped with machines worth millions, not two hundred important magazines could exist in the United States. Literary societies, religious bodies, scientific groups, and minority organizations could not afford publications. Even the newspaper world is finding it increasingly difficult to maintain small papers under present production costs, as is shown by the enormous decrease, since the early part of the century, in number of papers, daily and weekly. Although the survivors are economically sounder than before, they tend to become monopolistic and conformist in viewpoint.

### Departmental organization

The relatively few magazines with their own printing plants maintain a large separate production staff and carefully integrate its work with that of the editorial and advertising departments. The production department of the typical specialized magazine, say a religious journal or an educational periodical, is hardly a department at all but only one (or not even the full time of one) person. This individual may be responsible for dummying and laying out pages and serving as liaison between editorial and advertising departments on the one hand, in production matters, and printers, engravers, and other graphic arts services on the other. Moderate-size magazines employ production directors for the advertising and editorial departments. Usually the advertising production manager also takes care of graphic arts details for the promotion department.

On most magazines, production details and relationships with printer and engraver are a duty of an editor who understands in general the graphic arts process being used. These duties are not necessarily associated with any one title; they fall to the person who knows something about typography, make-up, printing, and engraving.

## *Production is creative*

Whether directed by an individual or a department, production is the physical creation of the magazine. The process begins in the editorial and advertising departments but depends finally upon machines. The cooperating departments supply certain of the raw materials and the pattern or design for each page. The mechanical department provides the remaining raw substances—principally paper, ink, metal, and binding materials.

Compared with individualistic works of art, such as paintings by masters, magazines are stereotyped. Like all American journalism, they are somewhat standardized in both content and appearance, although by groups of publications rather than up and down the whole industry. They have been less regimented than books or newspapers: color is used in some but not in others; size varies from small pocket to big flat; paper stock is pulp to enameled; pages number from eight to many hundreds; they are issued with or without covers. These physical variations are more than matched by differences in content. Consider the content dissimilarity of *Newsweek, Nucleonics,* and *National Live Stock Producer.*

Opportunity to exhibit creative ability lies mainly in the part of production having to do with make-up and typography. Creative ability is not imperative in journalism but it makes for distinction. Beginners can survive by imitating; they can achieve attractive layouts by studying those in use and copying the ones that please them. Within limitations of the type holdings of their printers, they can duplicate the typography as well. But the persistent imitator is not likely to become an outstanding craftsman.

Innovations and new effects are achieved by applying certain principles. What the creative journalist may do in the way of distinguished production depends upon his mastery of the fundamental principles of good typography. These principles, explained by Edmund C. Arnold, Charles L. Allen, Albert A. Sutton, and other writers on the graphic arts, apply to any piece of printed matter. By way of illustration they are here applied to the present-day magazines of different typographical dress, drawing mainly on Dr. Allen's explanation.[1]

**The optical center.** The magazine page ordinarily is a rectangle. It has two centers: the mathematical or mechanical and the optical. The first is the actual physical center by measurement. It is exactly half-

---

[1] Charles Laurel Allen, *The Journalist's Manual of Printing* (New York: The Ronald Press Co., 1929), Chapter XIII.

way between top and bottom and halfway between the sides. The optical center is somewhat above the mathematical center. It is five-eighths of the way from the bottom and three-eighths of the way from the top but is exactly the same distance from each side. These two centers are not the same because the human eye does not function perfectly. It does not automatically find the exact mathematical center. The reader thinks the optical center is the same as the mechanical one. He prefers the optical, for it is more pleasing to him than the mechanical.

The magazine cover or page designer, therefore, does not place at the exact center the object for which the greatest attention is wanted. He raises it slightly to the optical center, to accommodate the normal adjustment of the reader's eye.

**Balance.** Since all nature and all objective art (as opposed to non-objective) must conform to the law of balance (achieved when a force pulling in one direction offsets a force pulling in the opposite direction), all orthodox magazine typography directed at the reader of popular periodicals also should conform. On the magazine page balance occurs around the optical center. Two kinds of balance exist in this type of journalism: (1) centered or perfect and (2) off-center or occult. In the first, each mass is so placed that half its weight is on each side of the optical center. In the second, mass is so arranged that the weight is off-center but compensated for by the position of the remaining elements.

Important to magazinists is the fact that color-strength as well as the area covered must be considered. An area in boldface is not balanced by an area of the same size in lightface. Tone, in other words, adds weight; the darker the heavier. The apparently casual but actually carefully planned balance in editorial and advertising pages using colors can be noted in any leading consumer periodical.

**Position.** The principle of position depends upon the number of units in the material being placed or spotted. A painting, photograph, drawing, or any other illustration with a border (excluding the vignette) has depth, which is provided by background as contrasted with objects in the foreground. The one portion providing most density belongs around or directly upon the optical center. If there are several dense areas rather than one, their position should be away from the optical center, nearer to or farther from it according to their respective weights.

**Contour.** As any dictionary tells us, *contour* means the shape of objects. But shapeliness does not always equal pefection in typography. Old English type, for example, offers difficulty because, though shapely, it is confusing to decipher. Simple, streamlined types, a preference dating back several decades, are liked today. Ornate types do not return for any but decorative printing use. In magazine typography it is not only a matter of choosing type faces that are graceful and readable but also of planning pages or pairs of pages that, possessing shapeliness, are pleasant to the eye.

**Proportion.** This principle is one of the most difficult to apply because of disagreement among designers about it. The objective is to attain correct proportions between typographical elements. The magazine typographer's aim is to attract the reader's eye. Concepts as to what is proper proportion are varied, as a glance at today's consumer magazines reveals.

Dr. Allen notes an important convention: "in determining proportions for the parts of a rectangle [i.e., the ordinary magazine page] . . . the smaller part should be to the larger part as the larger part is to the whole." Almost any standard magazine page carrying a headline or title over an article or short story illustrates this rule; the literary, business, and opinion magazines provide ready examples. Magazines may display pages that are out of proportion because of failure to follow this principle or because of deliberate intention to violate it, as do some slicks dominated by art work rather than type or some of the little literary magazines and art journals.

Known to all art students is the shape for a rectangle devised by the Greeks, the Golden Section or Golden Rectangle, with the width three-fifths of the length. This proportion must be known to a staff person making or supervising layouts.

**Unity.** One of the more widely known and obvious principles, unity applies to typography as well as to writing. It is best achieved not by using borders and other type gadgets to unite elements but by putting the elements in proper position and relationship to one another. They must appear as a whole rather than as separate parts. Invariably, simple arrangements provide greater unity than do ornate ones.

**Simplicity.** This final principle, like unity, generally is recognized and sought but not easily achieved. Even the most experienced magazine staffers violate it in their attempts to avoid the trite and commonplace. A test is a study of the physical features of magazines that encountered difficulty pleasing the public when first issued. One such is *Holiday,* which did not do well in its first year. Its early issues carried complex and confusing page layouts; with some a reader could not tell where to begin reading. After changes in staff and revamping of the typography this expensive magazine became successful. Recall also the *Saturday Evening Post's* troubles already noted.

Complex design is not the only cause of consumer magazine illness, but it is one. Simplicity of design is no guarantee of survival, but it helps. Confusingly intermixed pictures and type masses offer optical barriers that a reader should not have to contend with and will not undertake to penetrate except out of dogged loyalty, a reader-response magazines rarely engender, especially in their first months.

Simplicity of typography and typographic design is all the more necessary if the publication seeks general consumer appeal. Non-objectivists among artists can comprehend typographic complexities but the average magazine reader is unschooled in artistic principles and theories. He is impatient with anything that forces him to stop to figure out what path his eye should follow. An occasional experiment, yes, but not a long sequence of complex pages. The failure of *Flair,* a women's magazine containing fold-out inserts, Dutch door pages (horizontal half pages) and other variations for the time, 1950 and 1951, was in part attributed to its sometimes complicated typography and make-up.

The genius among magazine typographers is he who can avoid the stereotyped, achieve originality, preserve legibility, and provide beauty.

### *Machines make magazines*

Printing is the mechanical basis of the magazine. Three methods are in use. *Letterpress* or relief printing is the most common. By this process paper is pressed against an inked surface that is higher than the body of type or the plate from which the printing is done. *Intaglio* printing, the second most commonly used, is done from plates on which what is to be reproduced has been etched or engraved. The image to be transferred is below the surface level so that ink goes into the sunken portions and can be wiped from the surrounding, higher surface. Other forms of intaglio printing are *rotogravure, coloroto,* and *photogravure.* The third method of printing is the *lithographic,* called *planographic.* In the basic process the material to be reproduced is placed on a plate with the use of ink or pigment that later is wetted. The portions that are to print reject the water, the image remaining greasy or oily. Now commonly known as *offset lithography,* this method is used on small magazines with short press-runs and many pictures or for prepared-in-advance inserts in large magazines. Printing is achieved by transferring the image to a rubber blanket which then transmits it to paper.

The body type for magazines is set by machine. Various composing units are used. The machines principally relied upon to produce the strip material required for the body type are known by their trade names of *Linotype, Intertype,* and *Monotype.* All cast lines. The first two compose each line as a solid and separate unit, but the last casts individual characters which then are arranged into a line.

Type for headings also is set by line-casting machines. The most often used is the *Ludlow,* which can produce type ranging from 8-point through 144-point.

These types are metal; use of the equipment mentioned is known as the *hot metal* process, for the metal—an alloy of lead with small amounts of tin and antimony—is heated to a molten state before being cast into lines.

In contrast to this is the cold metal or *cold type* process, which produces type through photography. That is, a picture of a character is projected on film or paper. By varying the lenses, different sizes of type can be obtained. Printing plates are prepared from the photographs of the type matter.

A still more recent development is the use of computers in composing type. These can cut the time for such editorial operations as digesting and arranging copy and can speed up the composition of type. Equipped with high-speed tape devices, the computer can punch out as many as 85 fully justified and hyphenated single-column lines a minute or more than four times faster than by manual operation of the composing machine.

Cold type production and the use of computers make for increased speed and higher quality, according to proponents of these devices and systems, as well as economies in operation. As more commercial printers use them they will be employed more widely in magazine production. Resistance to them is being encountered, however, from the printers' unions because of a natural fear of reduction in employment.

In varieties of types available the magazine publisher is restricted by what his printer possesses or can obtain by farming out all or part of the job to another printer. Small magazines are printed directly from type; large ones use plates from type, the plates being rubber, plastic, or metal. Stereotyping, electrotyping, and photography produce these plates. Stereotyping, common as a newspaper printing process, is quicker and cheaper than electrotyping, but also is less effective, being cruder, heavier, and faster wearing. An impression of the type page is made on papier-mâché, hot metal is poured into this impression, and the metal is cooled by water. The procedure is useful for magazines to be produced quickly, especially if multiple plates must be made for simultaneous running. Electrotyping uses electrolysis to produce a plate that exactly duplicates the type. Copper or nickel in acid solution is deposited upon a wax or lead mold, taken from the original type. This method is used for the finest printing work.

Photoengraving is the basic process of production of all magazine halftones. Zinc etchings are widely used for reproducing cartoons or any other copy consisting of lines and of black and white masses.

Three types of presses are used: platen, cylinder, and rotary. The first two also are called flatbed because each uses a flat surface on which the printing source rests. The rotary press, used for high speed work, runs the paper between two cylinders, on one of which are the printing plates, curved to fit. In a given period it can produce four or five times as many impressions as either of the other two. Depending upon its size, a printing plant may have one or more of each; the production manager must know which can produce best results for a specific purpose.

The machines used in two of the three principal operations of magazine production have now been noted: those for setting type and those for printing. There remains a third operation: binding. It is a basic difference between newspapers and magazines, and far more important to the latter than to the former. The sheets of the newspaper are large and kept folded at least once even during reading. They do not, therefore, separate readily. Magazines have many more pages, smoother and more slippery paper, and only center folds. Binding makes for permanence, which magazine publishers desire for their product. Also, magazines are passed from reader to reader and must survive considerable wear.

Cutting the sheets, folding them, trimming to size, gathering or assembling, and fastening the assembly: all these are included in the binding operation. Magazines usually are held together by staples inserted through the backbone. This is called saddle-stitching, and the signatures, or folded sheets, are one inside the other so that the staples grip them all and permit flat opening. Or they are held together by threads sewn through the back similarly or by staples, wire, or thread inserted through the sides of the signatures, which rather than being placed one within the other are piled one upon the other. Sometimes the cover is not included in the sewing or wiring but as a last operation is pasted around the signatures at the spine. Light magazines can be bound by gluing alone. A few use spiral, plastic, and loose-leaf bindings.

## *Ink*

Magazinists need some knowledge of ink and paper to obtain better results with type and illustrations and to understand defects in basic production.

The neophyte thinks that ink is ink, and that's that. But the surfaces on which ink is used are so varied that many different kinds of it had to be developed. An unsuitable grade can block the printing operation altogether. A halftone can come out black as night if the wrong ink is applied. Letters may fill and print as mere blobs. Magazine publishers, therefore, must have a definite understanding with their printers as to the inks to be used. The speed at which printed pages are to be produced also governs the type of ink. A high circulation weekly in color needs special inks whereas a small circulation monthly that prints only in black does not. Innumerable shades can be obtained by special mixing, although enough stock colors are available for ordinary purposes.

Ink has three principal constituents: pigments, vehicles (or solvents), and driers (or binders). Those used by rapidly produced magazines are compounded so as to flow freely and dry quickly, and are comparatively inexpensive. Periodicals have developed several types of instantly drying inks. One type sets immediately when printed sheets are passed over gas flames; another, solid at ordinary temperature and looking like lumps of coal, is used at a 200° F. temperature and resolidifies at once when it hits the paper's cold surface. Still another dries as soon as exposed to water vapor.

Improvements in inks and equipment enable large printing firms to produce two or three times as many magazines (printed 80 per cent in color) as they did in the first quarter of this century. Heat-set inks enable them to handle color advertising on the same schedule as black and white.

Inkless printing, a recent development, is used by small periodicals which need only from a few hundred to several thousand copies. One method is known as Xerography. It uses static electricity to form a pattern on paper. Powder is distributed over the surface of the paper into the pattern. The paper then serves as a plate for offset printing. Portions of magazines, such as embossed inserts, also are produced without ink.

Magazine production workers expect printers to keep abreast of improvements. They consult with them about the effects of certain inks or inkless processes in particular jobs, obtaining proofs of material in different inks to decide upon the most satisfactory.

The printer usually buys the paper as well as the ink, but the publishing office should know what he buys and why. A novice may specify paper sizes that are not standard, which results in great waste and extra expense.

## Paper

Papers used in magazine production fall into three groups: newsprint, book, and cover stock.

*Newsprint,* sometimes called *news,* is the cheapest grade. In its crudest form it is used by the comics and the few remaining pulp magazines, which received their nicknames, *pulps* and *pulpies,* from the paper. Yellowish, thick, and so porous that it does not take engravings but only line cuts, it becomes brittle and disintegrates quickly. Newspapers and magazines other than pulps use a grade of newsprint suitable to take coarse-screen engravings.

*Antique* is one in a category of book papers. It is bulky, flexible, and rough in surface. *Machine-finished,* another book paper, has a harder surface than newsprint and is of such quality that it has become the basic paper for large circulation magazines. It is smoothed by being passed between rollers, a process known as calendering. It reproduces illustrations with satisfactory, if not perfect, detail.

*Super-calendered* paper, also in the book group, has been more highly processed than machine-finished. Called *super* in the shops, this paper is hard, with a glossy surface, and is used by many high-priced magazines to obtain first class results with printing.

*Coated* stock is still more expensive paper providing an especially fine surface for printing effects and supplying extraordinary durability. It results from brushing paper with coatings of clay, casein, and other elements that give it weight. The finish ranges from dull to enamel coats.

*Special* finishes are for the wealthiest publications only. They include satin and linen finishes, laid paper—a wire-screen-like surface—woven finish, pebbled finish, and many others. Usually heavy, these papers are for special effects not requiring the high polished surface of calendered papers.

Cover stock naturally is heavier and more durable than the paper used in printing the body of the magazine. Numerous small periodicals that do not illustrate their covers with halftone engravings use the same stock for the cover as for the remainder, wrapping it around the signatures.

Magazines print some signatures on one grade of paper and others on another, mixing them in the final assembly. Another variation is to print certain signatures or inserts by the offset method and other parts by letterpress, encouraging the use of several paper grades in one issue.

The paper selected depends upon the use to be made of it. A different grade is required for the best results from different printing methods. Whoever selects paper in consultation with the printer must check on kind, quality, weight, and size for the body of the magazine as well as for the cover.

### A magazine in production

Like all modern journalism, magazine production has much in common with the assembly-line technique of motor car or washing machine manufacture. A few publishers, engaged mostly in amateur journalism or issuing small-circulation literary and art magazines, pride themselves on setting type by hand and printing their pages on hand-operated presses. But all other publishers, whether or not they like standardization, use assembly-line techniques and profit by them.

Magazine production in one sense begins with the concept of content outlined by an editor or editorial board. Actual physical production starts with the assembly of raw material, i.e., copy. This word usually means typescript received from staff or free-lance writers. It logically includes also photographs, drawings, charts, and other material used by the editorial department and text and illustrations for advertising matter.

This raw material, whatever its source, must be processed. Editorial department staff members and advertising department employes do this. It was aptly defined once by Austin C. Lescarboura, former managing editor of *Scientific American,* as "fitting it to the readership." Since advertising copy originates not only in the office of the magazine but also in those of agencies equipped to do their own processing, the editorial copy gets the greater share of attention from the magazine staff.

When the copy of different kinds has been made ready (see Chapter 12) it is sent to the printer and engraver. The printer sets type for a letterpress or relief printing job, such as being described here, according to the specifications on the copy. He produces body type (the fundamental reading matter) and type for titles, blurbs, and other sorts of headings. He provides cutlines, decorations, and various materials known as standing matter (repeated from issue to issue), masthead, folio lines, nameplate, and department headings. He delivers to the editorial offices sets of proof of all this material. He also sends proofs of hold-over—material not used in previous issues—unless he already has done so in the interval between issues.

Printers do not receive—should not, in fact—all copy for a magazine issue at one time. They stipulate in their contracts that copy is to be delivered by certain dates, so production can be spread. A certain percentage is expected by the first date, other quantities thereafter. A smooth flow of copy is the ideal. But the proofs may or may not be returned in one sheaf. If editors keep to their schedules, the likelihood is that the printer can return proofs on schedule. But the work of editorial and advertising offices is impeded less by receiving proofs in one batch than is that of the printer if he receives copy that way.

While type is being set, engravings and line drawings are made in the same or another plant. These, too, may be sent for processing as ready; a magazine using a large number either must send them in small quantities or allow a generous period between deadline and delivery. Proofs of these are provided by the printer via the engraver. Proof sequences vary if offset printing is employed.

Editorial and advertising departments, when processing copy, provide for its appearance in a certain fashion. They specify size to conform to a concept of final appearance which, at first a thing only of the imagination, finally is expressed through layouts. All copy must be precisely fitted. When proofs and original materials are returned the staff fits the proofs together according to the pattern shown on the

layout sheets. Methods of following layouts vary according to magazine size. A small one produced by a staff occupied with many other
duties may not use layout forms but may assemble proofs into dummies, by no means exact but giving a general idea of placement, hoping that everything sent to the printer will fit into the available
space. Not precise, this method is wasteful, expensive, and results
in unplanned pages. A more careful method is to rough out layouts
before copy is processed by the mechanical department, hold them
until proofs are returned, and then assemble a dummy as precon-
ceived in the rough drawings. Many magazines send layout sheets
along with processed copy and leave to the printer the work of simultaneous arrangement of pages and pairs of pages until the dummy
arrives after proof checking.

The well-staffed magazine is equipped to take great pains with
its page and issue planning. The art division, in conference with
the editorial department, prepares layouts (called *shop layouts* in
some offices) that are striking in their originality and make full use
of color and fine typography. Galley proofs are read and corrected,
the printer assembles the corrected type into pages according to
professional layouts, sends page proofs to the magazine offices, and
then awaits a dummy showing exact sequence of pages. The dummy
is assembled either jointly by editorial and advertising departments
or in two parts, one by each, and later combined. Revised proofs of
all pages in the issue then are pulled by the printers and examined
carefully by all responsible persons in the mechanical department
before the foundry or stone proofs are taken. Finally, the press
proofs are pulled (these are the first copies of the finished magazine
or of certain signatures or forms) and an opportunity for final examination by the editorial and advertising departments is offered before
presses begin rolling.

The cover may be printed at the time the rest of the magazine
is being produced or may be made up separately but is ready before
the running of the press. Covers often are produced in another plant,
for they may require special color work not available from the printer under contract. Or they may be stock covers to be overprinted
locally, a situation in which non-competing magazines may use the
same covers.

On the presses may be type, as in the case of the flatbed, or plates,
as for rotary presses. One set of plates, reproducing each page with
one complete revolution, may be sufficient for a magazine of moderate circulation. But a large circulation magazine is produced by the
use of sets of the same plates running on several presses simultaneously. These are mounted on presses running in tandem or are shipped
to plants in widely separated areas so that the magazine is printed
simultaneously, at different points, from duplicate plates. It is

printed in parts, as it was set in type and engraved in parts. Forms or signatures of four, eight, sixteen, or thirty-two pages are produced in one operation. The signatures then are collected and bound by one of the methods already described. As the binding machine completes its work the new issue is born. A magazine has been produced.

## Format and formula

Put all the layouts together and add the cover and the whole becomes the format of the magazine—what it looks like in size and shape of page and over-all physical appearance.

*Format* and *formula* sometimes are confused, as are layout and make-up. The formula is the concept of the magazine's purposes and aims that is held by its owners (see Chapter 3). A new owner may have a formula for a magazine which he expresses through format. The layouts he uses, the make-up of each page or set of pages, are merely parts of the formula carried out physically.

*Current* magazine's formula is that of a magazine which will give serious readers generous excerpts of important pieces of writing on current political, economic, and social problems. This idea is expressed typographically by use of a moderate-sized page, neither as small as that of a pocket magazine nor as bulky as that of a picture magazine, with bold headings that make it easy to find material and also to identify the subject covered, a system of classifying the content for ready reference, and clear indication of sources and further information.

Selection of format for a new magazine or a change in an old one is a serious step in the creation or redesigning of a periodical—something like changing one's name or entering an entirely different occupation. Too frequent or sudden changes of format reduce confidence in a publication. Adoption of an unsuitable format can hasten death, or at least add to financial difficulties. The consumer magazine is especially vulnerable to the whims of readers and advertisers. Many a pocket-size magazine, for example, is unable to obtain certain advertising accounts because standard-size plates are too large for its tiny pages. Only an enormous circulation magazine like *The Reader's Digest* is able to overcome this problem. It can do so because advertisers want the multimillion reader exposure and are willing to make adjustments.

The magazine format, as distinguished from that of the newspaper and the book, has certain inherent advantages and disadvantages. It permits attractive printing effects, can develop recognition of its personality, connotes prestige, is durable, uses color, and offers variety in size. It suggests leisurely reading, lack of newsiness, and involves higher production costs than do newspapers.

Format includes, also, the sequence of the material. Does the magazine run all its advertising in the front and back and none in the center? Or does it deploy it all through? Are significant articles, stories, or departments concentrated at the beginning of the issues or distributed evenly? Shall an article or short story that starts at the front be jumped after a page or two or shall it be completed at once, on succeeding pages? These are some of the problems faced by editors and production staff members.

Magazines cannot be designed by a set of rules. A magazine with a 6,000-word short story encounters a problem of page readability that makes jumping to another page essential; otherwise too little will appear in the opening section of the publication, which is the portion traditionally earning most attention from readers. If, in consumer magazines, advertisers are to get fair exposure to readers their copy may be lost if concentrated in a limited number of pages devoid of reading matter. Some readers, on the other hand, complain because distributed advertising interrupts their reading of articles and stories.

Placements of the elements is called *pacing* the magazine. Editors and publishers debate various methods of arranging content; fashions change in magazines as well as in women's dress. About the only rule that can be devised at all is that format should be functional in so far as possible. Thus a magazine whose readers value the advertising almost as much as they do the editorial matter can run scores of ad pages effectively. Many a business and other specialized magazine follows such a policy.

### Layouts for magazine pages

In this quick review of magazine production, layouts have been shown to play a big part. What they are, physically, has been indicated: patterns or plans for pages containing editorial matter or advertising or both. Layout also is a mental operation. It may be defined as the distribution of page elements—body type, by-lines, illustrations, captions, blurbs, decorations, and white space—in such a way as to achieve a pleasing effect.

It also has been called harmonious arrangement of page elements. But this definition no longer is accurate because some layouts are deliberately disharmonious. The trends are toward using variety in layout and keeping it unobtrusive. Some layouts may be disharmonious for the sake of contrast but in any case can be thought to be best when not obviously harmonious or disharmonious. Yet they must attract attention to the whole.

Depending upon the basis of classification, there are two or three broad groups or kinds of magazine page layouts. If the basis is artistic design we may use Charnley and Converse's classification into *symmetrical* and *asymmetrical*. [2]

Arnold varies this by calling them *formal* and *informal* balance, noting also that the latter sometimes is called *occult* or *dynamic* balance.[3] If the basis is ease of production we may use the classification by Bentley of *simple* and *complicated*. [4] If the basis is the magazine's function there is the grouping suggested by Gale Spowers, who advances *literary, display,* and *technical*.[5] A magazine designer, his literary layout is for the opinion or the quality magazine, such as *Commonweal* or *Harper's*; display is for the popular, mass magazine, like *McCall's*; technical is for the business magazine, such as *Swimming Pool Age*.

Professor Arnold, a graphic arts teacher as well as former editor of *Linotype News,* subdivides his classifications still further.

Formal balance is the type in which "everything balances on a vertical axis down the middle of the page . . . In its simplest form it follows the old printshop dictum . . . center everything."

Under informal balance he puts six categories, noting that "most layouts combine one, or even several, characteristics of these groups. . . ." The first is *classic,* which includes the S or reverse S and the pyramidal forms. *Geometric,* the second, is related to classic, and uses pictures, blocks of type, or other groups of elements to define geometric shapes more specifically. Third is the *vertical axis* (also called by him the *totem pole* and *Christmas tree*), an asymmetrical layout, with projections from an axis not running in the center of the page. *Rectangular* layouts are those made by breaking up larger areas with small units of different shapes and sizes in some harmonious relationship. An *expanded* layout is one that transmits a feeling of motion and of being larger than it really is; this one is accomplished by using pictures and large headings. The final type, *connotative* or *jazz,* consists of a suggested but not entirely defined pattern, the various elements connoting each other but not carrying out the suggestion of resemblance completely. [6]

Matlack Price, one of the few writers on editorial page layout for magazines, believes that at the level of design, "as well as of editorial intention," there are two broad divisions in the field of magazine layout: *straight presentation* and *dramatization*. [7] The first, he

---

[2]Mitchell V. Charnley and Blair Converse, *Magazine Writing and Editing* (New York: Dryden Press, 1938), p. 127.

[3] Edmund C. Arnold, *Ink on Paper* (New York: Harper & Row, 1963), p. 107.

[4] Garth Bentley, *How To Edit an Employee Publication* (New York: Harper & Brothers, 1944), p. 159.

[5] Gale Spowers, "The Technique of Magazine Layout," *Magazine World*, December, 1946, p. 2.

[6] Arnold, *op. cit.,* p. 107–14.

[7] Matlack Price, *Advertising and Editorial Layout* (New York: McGraw-Hill, 1949), p. 222.

explains, confines itself mainly to plain, rectangular shapes, formally or semiformally arranged so as to look well on facing pages. The second permits use of all layout devices known, with unique combinations as well. Here, he declares, it is possible to use editorial sense. The aim is to "sell" the copy, as in advertising. In this type the goal may be achieved by making the most of size, by the display of unusual objects, by using many shapes, or by combining art work and photography.

A more detailed classification for layout types is not necessary here and is not even practical to provide, for layouts in the most carefully edited magazines have scores of different patterns. They are the individual expressions of editors or artists. Bentley's classification is too general, for what is simple for one editor may be complicated for another, depending upon the ability of each. Spowers' classification is weak because it is not desirable or always workable to learn layout by means of it. For example, while it is true that certain literary magazines follow a simple pattern of a page with article or story title at top, followed by the by-line, and then body type in two or three columns, with succeeding material running on pages that carry a folio line and two or three columns of body type, many periodicals are varying from it. Two leading literary and public affairs magazines, *Harper's* and the *Atlantic,* in the years near the publication date of Spowers' article, scrapped this design to some extent and are using systems based on methods of mass circulation magazines or Spowers' own display group. The *Atlantic* is an example; in the 1960's its circulation was at its peak. His classifications are disintegrating in practice.

A classification system should rest upon long-term principles that seem destined to survive. The distribution of page patterns into the groups selected by Charnley and Converse, Arnold, or Price is the only sound one. It is possible to define sub-classifications, much as zoologists and botanists make order out of their material, but it would not be a particularly useful set of definitions. Magazine production conditions differ sufficiently in major details to make difficult the imitation of thousands of possible combinations and sizes of elements.

A slight breakdown in layout patterns can be made, however. It must be remembered that newspapers and magazines differ on page designing. Newspapers are chiefly of two sizes, standard and tabloid. Generally the standard has an eight-column page and the tabloid five. Because of the need for speedy production, newspaper editors find it easier to follow a half dozen well-established designs, some for the front page and others for inside pages, including those departmentalized. All these have been classified and illustrated by such writers on newspaper editing and design as Leland D. Case, Floyd K. Baskette, Charles H. Brown, Bruce Westley, Edmund C.

Arnold, and others whose books are in common use in both class-room and newsroom. A working editor responsible for a magazine imitating newspaper design (*Variety, Advertising Age,* and scores of business magazines with news sections are examples) can use their analyses and follow the procedures with excellent results.

To achieve originality in the pages not supposed to look like those of newspapers, the magazines that are most concerned about layout problems reverse the magazine procedure of former years. Editors planned their pages from type; that is, they began with type as the core or center of page content. Drawings and photographs were thought of as extra, desirable if available but not required. As publishers realized the tremendous importance of illustrations, however, they changed the emphasis at least for the opening page or two of an article, story, or novel. The editor now seeks in the big circulation magazines, and increasingly in the small ones, smart appearance. He wants to sell his material to the reader through art work or photography as much as through writing or by subject matter as conveyed by the title or headline.

## Layout procedures

In the offices of large magazine companies the art department designs the layouts. Editors and artists confer. The editor participates in the work in a general way, since he knows what is to be emphasized. But on many magazines layouts are left entirely to the art department. Artists work from carbon copies of typescript and from the original illustrations or photostats of them. In small offices —the majority—the editor or a member of his staff plans the layouts or a commercial artist does them on a free-lance basis. The work uses especially printed layout sheets or old pages of the magazine. The special sheets have wider margins than the magazine page, to permit writing instructions to the printer. The type area is indicated by lightly inked printing of any body type; sometimes sheets have marginal numberings to indicate the units of size in inches. The faintly inked sheets are called *phantom pages*.

The place of each element is first sketched on a smaller sheet in the position it is to occupy on the final page or pair of pages. These thumbnail sketches highlight the basic appearance of a future page. From this small sketch a rough is made on the phantom, to normal size. Another layout method is to paste down all the elements from proofs, as in making a final dummy (i.e., actually skipping the layout stage and combining laying out and dummying of pages in one procedure). This plan is not feasible for any but the simplest magazine format, for it limits the layout by the dimensions of the elements. Paste-up layouts permit little original display and tend to be hasty and haphazard. Yet many company magazines, business publications, and other specialized periodicals are laid out in this fashion. It is a cheap

*Fig. 6.1.* Leonard F. Pinto, while production director of Davis Publications, Inc. *(Science & Mechanics, Ellery Queen's,* and others) looks over cover proofs of two of the magazines. *(Davis Publications, Inc., Photo)*

and quick method and satisfactory to the extent that the editor is indifferent to the results.

Dummying a magazine is largely a mechanical operation. Two methods are used: the paste-up and the diagram. Usually the work is done by one of the least experienced staff people, often as not an editorial assistant or clerk. Its aim is to show the printer precisely where each element in the issue is to run. The paste-up type is more nearly accurate than the diagram, since proofs of all elements are fixed in exact position, as a guide. The work is tedious unless combined with planning or laying out of pages. But often it is the operation in which the beginner learns much about editorial office routine.

## Covers

An editor who can provide original, effective, and not too expensive covers for his magazine is highly valued. Much time and money are spent on covers, especially for competing magazines. Newsstand periodicals are ever on the lookout for new ideas for cover content.

What readers see first, obviously, is the cover. It also is what they see longer than anything else related to the publication. If the magazine is left on living room table, doctor's waiting room magazine rack, or newsstand, either the front or back cover faces the world. If a magazine seeks to maintain or establish its personality, content and type of cover must be carefully determined. Readers sometimes have vigorous reactions to covers. There was the one who wrote to *This Week* that he was tired of covers featuring "glamour dames, clad or semi-nude." He added that intelligent people prefer Siamese cats, penguins. About the same time the editors received one from a woman reader who said: "Congratulations on your good taste in selecting covers. My only complaint is that you seem overly fond of animals." [8]

*McCall's,* wishing to dramatize an editorial formula of equal emphasis on food, fashion, home, and fiction, one month used two covers, one showing an angel food cake dripping with strawberries and the other a picture of a girl. The press run was split: the presses were stopped midway through the run and the second cover substituted. Subscribers voted for the girl cover and newsstand buyers preferred the cake to the girl.

Handling the cover problem is easier with a new periodical than an old one. An established magazine has a tradition to maintain. It does not want to change its appearance too much lest it become unrecognizable and lose its friends. Only an unsuccessful magazine or one changing its content drastically in hope of making an altogether new appeal can risk drastic changes.

When preparing covers for a new magazine, an editor is free to consider all possibilities, come to some conclusion on policies, and start fresh with the advantages of discoveries and the experiences of others.

What kinds of covers are available?

By paper quality, these:

**Self-cover type.** The cover and the inside pages are printed on the same quality of paper. The cover is part of the regular signature or form. Although economical, it is not impressive. The cover can do no more to appeal than the rest of the magazine. Halftones can be used neither in the body nor on the cover if the paper quality cannot reproduce them. The self-cover magazine is not likely to wear well; it is most suitable for perishable, small circulation magazines.

**Separate-cover type.** Here the cover is on different stock than that used for the insides. Depending upon paper quality, varied effects can be achieved. This cover is wrapped around the signatures and stapled, pasted, or sewed to them. The main disadvantages are high cost and slower production. Often it must be printed at a plant other than that of the main printer. Content cannot be changed as easily as on the self-cover. Some big magazines using separate covers have had the misfortune to find serious mistakes or untimely material on them just as they were being used. For example, when President John F. Kennedy was assassinated, several magazines had either to delay publication, suffer criticism because their covers contained title words considered in bad taste, or remain untimely. The covers could not in each instance be recalled; the substitutions made were expensive.

Magazines that can afford to do so have several covers prepared, as

[8] "Editor's Dilemma," *This Week,* Dec. 31, 1950, p. 2.

before an election, print them, and await the outcome. During the 1968 presidential election both *Time* and *Newsweek* prepared covers of Nixon, Humphrey, and Wallace. When the election results were certain the useless ones were withheld.

By content, these:

**Lettering and/or decorations.** This cover is one drawn by an artist; it remains more or less the same issue after issue. It still is used by scholarly magazines and others satisfied with this plan because their readers are unconcerned. They are not in direct competition; their content is wanted for its own sake and not for its appearance or power of diversion.

**All-type.** All effects are achieved by type only; borders, reading lines, and so forth are produced by machine. This one, also, is used widely by scholarly journals and other magazines that do not need or care to sell themselves by more than the messages on their covers.

**Photographs.** Pictures are used for all or part of a cover in black or in colors.

**Paintings.** Paintings in colors are employed as a basis for cover engravings.

**Drawings, sketches, other art work.** Used in both black and white and color, they are particularly appropriate for cartoons and caricatures.

**Combination.** Generally combinations are: (1) fixed-type designs with picture or drawing changing from issue to issue; and (2) fixed lettering or drawn design with changing picture, painting, or sketch.

By format, these:

**Four-page regular cover.** The cover size is the same or a slightly larger size than the inside pages.

**Folding cover.** This one employs three or five pages instead of four because two are half- or quarter-size and one is full-size.

### Cover content

What is put on a cover depends upon the use made of the magazine. A minimum for a company magazine or other more or less privately circulated one is name and date. To a newsstand periodical are added art work, the title of one or more of the materials inside for the sake of emphasis, and the identification of the cover photograph or painting, if needed. The volume and issue numbers sometimes are included, especially if there is no backbone or spine.

Four factors determine choice of cover content:

**Method of circulation.** Magazines circulated chiefly by mail need not compete with other magazines on a newsstand rack. To be sure all compete in homes and offices, where they may be side by side, but less intensely. The name may be placed along the side or at the bottom, a policy not advisable for newsstand magazines. If the periodical is mailed unwrapped it must have sturdy cover stock to withstand wear in transit.

If it is mainly a newsstand publication, it must use at least as attractive a cover as do others in its class. Color is important for eye appeal.

The magazine whose newsstand and subscription sales closely balance has a difficult problem which generally is solved by giving newsstand necessities right of way.

We have assumed that the editor is responsible only for the front cover, the advertising department providing copy for the inside-front, inside-back, and back covers. This brings up the second factor.

**Advertising policy.** The policy may be: (1) to sell three of the covers; (2) to sell all four or most of the front and all others; (3) to sell only the inside covers; (4) to sell only the rear cover; or (5) to sell none.

If the editor has full responsibility for all covers, he decides what to put on them, depending on what he makes available to the advertising department. Covers are choice spots that the editor actually covets, although it sometimes is so costly to print on them that he leaves them blank unless they can be sold for advertising. *The Reader's Digest* uses its covers to print institutional or promotional material about itself or runs its front cover illustration across on to the back cover. Organizational magazines sometimes put standing matter on these pages: staff names, officers of the sponsoring group, and similar data.

Few magazines put changing editorial copy on inside and back covers because doing so adds to production costs. If type is left unchanged from issue to issue cover manufacture is less expensive.

**Use by the reader.** *Where* the reader reads his magazine is important. If he sees it at home, generally the cover is of one kind. If he is most likely to see it in offices or waiting rooms, it is of another. If he reads it in transit, still another is more effective.

Magazines read in lobbies, foyers, and waiting rooms should have eye-catching covers that serve as distractions. The waiting person wants to read, and competition for his attention is not stiff. If the magazine is read on public transportation the cover—indeed the whole periodical—must provide optical ease, must not be embarrassing in any way, and must not be bulky. It also must be durable.

**Purpose of the magazine.** Magazines are published to inform, entertain, or guide. One which informs, other factors being taken into consideration simultaneously, emphasizes the factual content through its cover, using catchlines and possibly the entire contents page as cover matter; or it may use pictures of an informational nature, such as those of newsmagazines and business periodicals. Entertaining magazines put comic cartoons, pictures of scenes from the entertainment world, puzzles, or other types of amusement matter on covers. Those that seek chiefly to provide editorial leadership depend upon provocative words in type that may cause the reader to look inside.

As with so much else that goes into magazines, publishers and editors can learn from reader interest surveys and sales figures which are the most successful covers for their purposes. At least from the standpoint of effectiveness, practices of the day are reliable guides. The newspaper is much less able than the magazine to learn from sales figures what its readers want in the way of typography and format because so few papers compete directly. Only 10 per cent of the daily papers have competition from other newspapers. But newsstands piled high with colorful magazines are testing grounds of a severe kind. Only the publisher of a specialized magazine not subject to direct competition can afford to neglect the cover, and then only from the financial standpoint. If he wants his magazine read thoroughly, the cover must be used to its greatest typographical advantage.

# Chapter 7

# Public relations
# and promotion

UBLIC RELATIONS, publicity, promotion—whichever of these words is used in the title of the department—calls for editorial skills, knowledge of psychology and marketing, and selling ability.

Its purpose is to create a more favorable opinion of the magazine and to make it more effective in attracting newsstand and subscription purchases and as an advertising medium. It is intended to boost the magazine in every possible way; hence the people who work in such a department could be called the booster corps.

The more elaborate the organization of the magazine company, the more distinct the functions. Separate units will be maintained for public relations, publicity, and promotion. We therefore should distinguish between them before examining their operations.

*Public relations* has many definitions; it is a term often and erroneously used interchangeably with *publicity* and *promotion* in the magazine world and with *propaganda* and *press agentry* outside that area.

A popular definition of it is "doing good and getting credit for it." Another is "the science of attitude control." In the magazine field its ordinary function is to carry on activities that will develop and maintain good relations with the various publics that confront a publishing firm. The techniques rest heavily in knowledge of psychology and human relations and are carried out through publicity and promotion work.

A magazine publishing concern has several publics: (1) the general public without whose support it cannot survive and is its major reason for being, i.e., its readers and potential readers; (2) that segment of the public to which most commercial periodicals look for their chief financial support—the advertisers and potential advertisers; (3) the market, another segment of the public that must be convinced of the merit of cooperation with the advertisers, and which consists of retailers, dealers, and others expected to distribute and sell the products advertised; and (4) a small public comprised of the magazine industry itself: other publishing houses and organizations of the people in the industry.

A magazine company's public relations is handled in three ways: by a staff whose director is an executive on a par with the heads of other major departments, by a person in almost any regular department, such as advertising or editorial, who has public relations as one of his duties, or by a specialist firm engaged in public relations counselling. The first is the choice of a large company; the other two are the procedures in smaller firms.

Whoever has charge of the work, inside the company or on a retainer basis outside it, is a counsellor who functions for a publishing house no differently than for any other business. He diagnoses its internal and external problems and recommends policies and procedures to correct difficulties and to make its operations more effective with the various publics. Such a counsellor is an adviser who is—or should be—taken into the inner life of the company.

To carry out the public relations officer's proposals it usually is necessary to call upon the publicity and promotion office staffs, who have similar functions and often are joined. But there is a difference in their work. *Publicity* commonly involves letting the general public know the news—or what is called news but in reality may be free advertising—emanating from the publishing house. This information goes out as news releases, aimed at general newspapers, radio and television stations, wire services, and the trade press. These releases announce staff changes, alterations in advertising rates and circulation figures, extraordinary types of content and production techniques, and corporate news in general. The publicity department may be expected also to prepare an internal company publication as well as special leaflets and booklets about the magazine but logically these belong to the promotion department.

The line between promotion and publicity activities is vague, for on one magazine some duties are arbitrarily assigned to promotion that on another are performed by publicity. This decision may be determined by budget or personnel. *Promotion* has as its major activity finding ways to attract more readers, more newsstand buyers, and more paid-in-advance subscribers and devising schemes to make

the advertising more effective by making sure it is seen and to persuade advertisers to come into the pages.

The volume of work varies by the size of the publication and its
resources, by the energy, skill, and imagination of the departmental
staffers, by the activities of the competition, and by the climate of
opinion and economic condition of the public.

Promotion work can pull a new magazine over the one-, two-, or
three-year period of travail while the public and the advertisers are
deciding whether they like it and will support it. Unless it has the
capital to enable it to catch the attention of its various publics and
hold it, the most beautiful and readable magazine in the world will
die—and many noble efforts have died for lack of that financing and
boosting. This hard circumstance has to do with the fact that the
United States is such a huge country in population as well as in
geography and that the public already is pressed with many calls upon
reading time.

Public relations, publicity, and promotion activities, therefore,
are closely related to the business operations of the company and are
important tools. If sufficient and efficient they can dig a sound foundation and help erect a magazine of stability. If the opposite, they
can dig its grave quickly.

However fitted into the managerical scheme, the booster corps is
a busy one. Perhaps no American citizen ends his day without having
been touched by it in some way: a poster about the contents of a new
magazine's issues glimpsed from a subway train, bus, plane, or railway train terminal; a fancy mailing piece in the mailbox at home
or on the office desk; a spot radio or television advertisement noting
a special issue—these and dozens of other means to reach the various
publics are thrown out steadily by the magazine industry.

The boosting is not all one-sided. Many of the plans have a companion value of offering the public a benefit at the same time that
the magazine itself is aided. Take the contests conducted for college
students. Deans and counsellors of women each fall, for example,
find in their mail letters that start something like this:

> *This fall* Mademoiselle *again is recruiting outstanding
> students from your college for its College Board. We real-
> ize, of course, that you may not find time to recommend
> key students to try out for the Board, but we hope you will
> pass this letter on to the proper authorities, perhaps to the
> English department or to the heads of student publica-
> tions.*

This letter, on pink stationery appropriate to a periodical aimed
at young women, goes on to review the organization and purposes of
the College Board. An obvious but not announced purpose is to in-

terest more girls in reading *Mademoiselle*. One consequence of the promotional plan is training for a picked group interested in journalism, advertising sales, copy writing, fashion writing and design, and other types of publication work. Even coeds who fail to be appointed to the Board have practice in writing and magazine analysis.

To compete, aspirants are required during the year to prepare various types of assignments. Educators are asked to take into consideration high scholarship as well as natural talent when making recommendations. From the more competent girls who compete, a dozen are selected to go to New York in spring and spend a month as Guest Editors, as they are called, at the magazine's expense. They help on the August issue, which emphasizes college life.

The remarkable economic success of *Mademoiselle* cannot be credited entirely to the College Board plan, but this idea undoubtedly has been an important factor. Founded in 1935, the periodical was intended for girls from 18 to 30. After the first year its circulation was a discouraging 37,000. By 1940 it had reached 400,000. In another 30 years it had reached nearly 700,000. Until recently advertising has kept pace. The Guest Editor plan is basically a promotion, since promotion is any activity planned to attract readers and advertisers to the magazine.

Originally, modern methods of promoting a publication were confined to blatant self-advertising and direct means of calling attention to the magazine. Schemes made famous by commercial advertising were imitated, with large wall posters the most compelling. Such mild forms of promotion as the contest for contributions by the *American Museum* in 1789 did not satisfy publishers once they had big money to allocate to the booster corps.

Seven major purposes are behind promotion effort, except for magazines that are adless, not circulated via newsstands, or given away. They are to:
1. Stimulate sales of the magazine on newsstands and other public places.
2. Encourage buying paid-in-advance subscriptions.
3. Promote sale of advertising space.
4. Build goodwill.
5. Gain understanding of the magazine's content.
6. Make editorial content more effective.
7. Make advertising content more effective.

The first three are accomplished by direct sales effort; the others usually are by-products or the result of special campaigns aimed at achieving them. From this it may seem that the promotion department usurps the powers and duties of the advertising and circulation divisions. It is, however, a supplement—an extension of the basic efforts of these departments, not a substitute. It cooperates with them—studies their problems and attempts to solve them.

Departmental organization of the promotion work is parallel to that of other divisions of the publishing company. Under a director or manager are promotion specialists, whose work is divided according to the type of device to be used. Other departmental personnel are borrowed as feasible, or such employes, say artists or photographers, are engaged with the understanding that they work jointly for several groups in the publishing firm. Production work on promotion assignments may be left to such related departments as editorial, art, and production. This type of activity is akin to advertising; it naturally may be under the direction of, or coordinated with, the advertising department. Small firms find it uneconomical to maintain their own promotion departments and engage professional concerns to undertake the work.

## Kinds of materials

Only an organization with the resources, reputation, and range of one of the giant consumer magazine publishing companies could use all the promotional techniques and materials available. A firm that must be selective should base its decisions on knowledge of all techniques, so that it can be discriminating in its choice of tools. The most commonly used are:

Window posters, cards, and racks

Truck and wagon banners and posters

Newsstand posters, signs, and stands

General publication advertising

Motion pictures

Film slides

Sample copies

Reprints of advertisements

Reprints of editorial matter

Contests

Question and answer bureaus

Publicity releases

Recordings

Special issues

Gift booklets

At-cost gift books

School demonstrations

Letters

Institutional advertising

Specialized press advertising

Radio and television advertising

Radio and television programs

Cookbooks and other special books

Special events, such as cooking schools

Readership surveys

Market surveys

Tapes and cassettes

The nature of most of these materials is evident from their names; a few may need explanation. Magazine promoters have found that an attractive issue is among the best drawing cards, so they arrange for extra copies of certain issues and mail them to prospective subscribers. There are many varieties of promotion letters. One intended for a possible new subscriber differs from one sent to a subscriber who has failed to renew. Considerable thought is given to production of clever, compelling letters, which always include several mailing pieces, such as return envelopes and cards, leaflets listing features to come, or testimonials from present subscribers. *Time* is noted for its unusual letters. It has sent prospects postage stamps, with the statement that it is willing to "pay the freight" on a new subscription blank if returned with promise to pay; it also sends a tiny red pencil to be used in filling out blanks. Another letter began with a drawing of the human brain, with a play on the words "keep this in mind." *The Reader's Digest* has sent 3,000,000 shiny copper pennies to potential subscribers. Dozens of others have sent what seem to be certificates or bank checks made out for the amount that can be saved by accepting the offered special rate. So many letters relating to subscriptions are received by readers that *Saturday Review* mailed one with a different quirk:

Dear Subscriber:

(Text omitted at the suggestion of the
Society for the Suppression of
Cheery Renewal Letters.)

Sincerely yours,

George Emerson
For SATURDAY REVIEW

Realizing that this was not quite enough, however, the magazine added a P.S. which in eight lines explained it a bit and called attention to the values of the magazine and the renewal form with the letter.

Contests include not only the College Board program but also home-remodeling competitions, essay and other literary contests (such as those of the *Atlantic* and *Scholastic* primarily for the schools), and the Prix de Paris of *Vogue*.

Organization magazines, often beset with special problems because advertisers are not certain that a publication is read by persons who receive it by virtue of membership, use a device which promotes interest rather than subscriptions. They design programs for the local chapter or supply background materials that involve use of the magazine. Numerous church periodicals, especially those for young people, use this plan, and so do the magazines of service clubs, such as *The Rotarian*. Program chairmen of local clubs are notified of forthcoming articles that provide resource materials for weekly Rotary programs. Bibliographies as well as discussion questions are supplied.

Since building of loyalty is an invaluable aid to continued purchase and reading, numerous magazines print a department or column in which they talk over with readers their internal problems, invite comment and suggestions, and generally attempt to foster friendly relations. *Time's* publisher chats weekly with readers, telling of extraordinary journalistic feats of the staff or explaining problems of timing and selection involved in producing covers. *The Progressive* reports each month on the financial status of the magazine, which receives its support mainly from contributors' gifts. A youth magazine for a time printed a column headed "You're the Editor!" in which the young girl readers were asked to check on a small questionnaire whether they wanted some, more, less, or none of certain types of content. The various small departments of *The Reader's Digest,* such as "Life in these United States," are important as promotion. The magazine believes that the more readers participate in the magazine the more loyal they are to it. Consequently each issue carries a page listing the departments for which contributions are wanted and the prices paid, which range from $2,500 for a "First Person Article" to $10 for "Toward More Picturesque Speech" items.

## Advertising and sales promotion

Although promotion offices plan and carry out ways to call attention to reading matter and design ways to bring in more subscribers and move more magazines off newsstands into readers' hands, they give more time to advertising and sales promotion than to these other standard activities. Advertising and advertising sales promotion are in the foreground because, for the commercial magazine, from 50 per cent to 70 per cent of the revenue obtained comes from purchase of its space by advertisers. Whatever can be done to expedite this selling makes the company more stable.

Advertising sales promotion is intended to make it easier for the staff salesman and the advertising representatives to close their sales. Let us suppose a potential advertiser in his office at some point distant from the magazine's headquarters receives attractive mailing pieces about the magazine's sales power. When the salesman arrives an informed prospective client faces him—if the literature prepared by the promotion staff has been compelling enough. Perhaps a leaflet has brought an inquiry, which makes the sales call all the more promising. With him the salesman brings a film, a set of cards on a folding easel, or a portfolio of sketches or photographs—all the work of the advertising sales promotion office. He does not always clinch the sale, by any means, but when he does the materials thus provided usually have assisted in a major way.

Behind such films, film slide presentations, booklets, and portfolios are many hours spent in research in the market served by the magazine. Such research is concerned with the magazine's readership, its circulation reach, and its mechanical characteristics. The promotion staff is involved in planning and designing literature; in preparation of text, art, and photographic copy; or in the writing of scripts and taking of films or slides to be coordinated with the text of the presentation.

The larger advertising sales offices, serving major consumer magazines or groups of specialized periodicals, turn out other types of materials also: displays for exhibits, sometimes enough to fill one half the side of a hotel ballroom; entire programs for meetings of the sales staff, including all of the many details of a half-day session, with speakers, sound equipment, projectors, printed matter, luncheon and dinner arrangements, and even housing for those attending.

Advertising promotion work is that done to increase the power of advertising already, or about to be, printed.

Literally scores of types of merchandising aids are offered to advertisers to supplement their use of space, all intended to make the advertising more effective and productive to the business it is expected to stimulate. Examples are leaflets to be inserted in correspondence, tags to be attached to merchandise, postal cards, restaurant table cards, folders, booklets, reproductions (full size or in miniature) of advertisements, counter cards, stickers for use with correspondence when the advertiser writes to retailers, window displays of innumerable types ranging from a cardboard base with board risers on which to place samples of the product advertised to a battery-driven revolving display sold at cost if not free, sample copies of the magazine containing the particular ad with specially printed markers calling attention to it, direct mail letters to retailers and to their customers in local areas, and matrices which the retailer can use in his local newspaper advertising of the product advertised in the magazine simultaneously.

As that last type of merchandising assistance indicates, magazines seek through such means to overcome the fact that most of the commercial periodicals are national in scope. These devices enable a salesman of magazine advertising space to say to a potential customer that the magazine can move merchandise in the local area; this assertion is a talking point versus newspapers, radio, and television which can localize their effect more easily since they originate locally.

Certain types of magazines have special kinds of sales promotion that help advertisers, such as the erection of model homes or the furnishing of existing homes with advertisers' products, which then are featured in issues of the magazine. These are policies popular with the shelter magazines, such as *American Home* and *Better Homes and Gardens*.

Promotion of any of these sorts is not carried on solely by individual magazines. Through national or regional organizations plans are made to boost periodicals as a group. The publicity attending the annual conferences and other meetings of the Magazine Publishers Association benefit all periodicals to the extent that attention is called to the industry's concern for national problems. Prominent government leaders and other persons of note in public life are speakers. Their views on current affairs of national and international importance are reported widely.

On a smaller scale are the special weeks or months observed each year by a group of religious periodicals, sponsored by the Evangelical Press Association, the Associated Church Press, and the Catholic Press Association.

## Varied skills used

The advertising department is not the only one that needs advertising skills, and the editorial department is not alone in employing writers, editors, and artists or photographers. We have seen that the circulation department needs both types of employe. So do the related areas of public relations, publicity, and promotion. The countless brochures and leaflets, pamphlets and company publications, articles and columns, display advertisements and radio-television scripts produced in the public relations work are turned out by trained men and women who could be employed in the other departments if promotion did not need their services.

Promotion copy admittedly is not "literature." It is sales material, seeking only to persuade and to propagandize. But most journalism—magazine type or any other—is not literature with a capital L either, a fact that anyone who aspires to be in the magazine world should realize. Literary skill may be required now and then of the promotion department employe. Creative writing is appropriate at times in commerce. Extraordinary ability with camera or sketching pencil likewise is needed sometimes. But in this department these skills are being put to the service of journalism as a business, and a successful one at that, if journalism on the mass scale so typical of our time is to continue.

The promotion department's function is to help keep the magazine afloat financially. It naturally makes less use of literature than does the editorial department. It is on the business side and like all business, it is constantly in need of new ideas. To generate them employes in such departments formed their own organization, Magazine Promotion Group, with meetings planned to examine problems facing all members.

The challenge in this phase of magazine work can be grasped from observations made to MPG at one of its meetings by Ray Weber, general advertising manager of Swift & Company, which usually spends about four million dollars in magazine advertising annually. Mr. Weber said he was "deeply concerned about magazines in this marketing upheaval, because I believe in magazines. Magazines made a nation out of our collection of individual states. If the rest of the world had only one language, magazines would be the first to unify minds.

"But I am concerned about your sly, silly statistics that puff up Block 6 in Peoria. I am concerned about the stuffy trade journal ads and direct mail that I haven't been reading for two years because it is the same old stuffiness."

He also said that he was concerned because he did not see any new ideas erupting. "These are times that try magazine promoters' souls," he added. "We are in a communications explosion, and explosions take their toll." Among the communications explosions he listed were speed reading courses, instructional programs on television, changes in teaching, increases in FM and UHF channels on radio and television, self-service shopping, social and political awakening of underdeveloped nations, world's fairs, increased book reading, and developments such as Telstar.[1]

### Promotion paradox

Mr. Weber's comment about Block 6 in Peoria points up a paradox of the magazine business which centers in the promotion and publicity departments. Although most large firms invest heavily in various types of promotion, some of the leaders are proud of the fact that whereas they spend little on it they thrive.

Scientific American, for example, points out that its circulation has climbed steadily, moving from 50,000 in 1948 to 454,000 in 1970, while at the same time circulation promotion has been reduced; in 1959 it was abandoned altogether. "The direct-to-publisher truly voluntary circulation of Scientific American has been assembled— not by promotion—but by its editorial content," said an executive.

And The New Yorker advertises widely the fact that it does no merchandising promotion for its advertisers, as do most large magazines. "Imagine," says one advertisement, "152 companies advertising in a magazine for 25 or more years without receiving free merchandising tools." The magazine comments: "Perhaps they believe that a vital magazine and the response it evokes are the best merchandising tools, free or not." But in recent years it has brought space to advertise itself.

It will be noted that these two magazines represent areas of special interest or types of readers. The more a magazine is tailored to a particular group of readers and succeeds in satisfying their needs, the less it must spend on boosting circulation. And if advertisers' copy

---

[1] "Magazines Need New Ideas, Not 'Stuffy' Statistics: Weber," *Advertising Age,* Dec. 9, 1963, p. 50.

is so effective with the readers that promotion by merchandising is superfluous, there is no point in spending money on it.

But the magazine that appeals to the highly diversified audience has a different problem. To begin with, it probably has several competitors for both the same readers and the same advertisers. Therefore extraordinary measures—promotion—must be taken to meet the competition's plans and schemes for increasing readers and advertising accounts. The great volume of circulation means an enormous expense simply for printing the publication. Efforts must go on constantly, therefore, to keep this circulation up to par, to offset the natural loss of readers by death, moving, and other causes.

C. D. Jackson, a Time Inc. official who had been publisher of *Fortune* and held other top posts in that firm, once said: "One of the ways to run the magazine business badly is to saddle yourself with so much circulation expense that you have to get an awful lot of additional advertising revenue to support that expense." Promotion is part of that expense, but if wisely spent can be productive enough to justify itself. It gives a magazine company a way to offset the fact that its scope is national rather than local, a factor in competing with other media.

Nevertheless a trend toward more controlled promotion efforts is noted. Some advertising and magazine executives have realized that a magazine which must offer many free merchandising services evidently does not believe its advertising space is powerful enough by itself.

Similarly, readers can say that if a magazine must spend many dollars on a subscriber by pelting him with tricky subscription appeal letters or entreating him to renew, he must not want the magazine or he would subscribe or renew with little nudging. Once again, the more the magazine appeals to the reader's special interests and concerns the less expense is involved in putting him on or keeping him on the subscription lists. The broad-based consumer magazine, one of the giants of magazinedom, can make so little consistent and deep appeal to a large number of readers' concerns, however, that it must compensate with the pressure of promotion.

The booster corps heads right into this paradox, understands it, and proceeds to do its share of the work needed by that large section of the magazine world that depends upon promotion to operate effectively in a highly competitive industry.

# Chapter 8

# Research

THE PROBLEM was this: although *Popular Science Monthly* is a magazine of specialized interest its management wanted to convince the manufacturers of trucks and truck tires that the periodicals of its type can provide an audience and savings on costs that could not be equalled by the consumer magazines or the magazines devoted to truck operation.

Research enabled it to accomplish its aim. A three-state pilot study was made to learn the reading and buying habits of a certain type of truck owner and the results were placed before potential advertisers.

Magazines of moderate circulations have a higher advertising cost on a per-thousand basis than large consumer publications. An advertiser who wants to reach owners of fleets of trucks turns naturally to the business magazines intended for such fleet operators and to the weekly newsmagazines. But *Popular Science* pointed out that it and the other science and mechanics popular magazines are more effective in reaching the owners, not of large fleets of trucks alone but also the small businessmen who own only one or two. It was this segment that *PSM* wanted to isolate.

This idea actually came from one of the magazine's advertisers already in the fold, the Firestone Tire & Rubber Company, which had conducted its own research showing that the three leading science and mechanics magazines at that time were being read by one-truck and two-truck owners. But *PSM* wanted more evidence.

It engaged Richard Manville Research, Inc., which conducted a mail questionnaire survey. It gained almost 60 per cent response and uncovered the fact that *Popular Science, Popular Mechanics,* and *Mechanix Illustrated* together had many readers of the type suspected. And it indicated, also, that research along these lines has marketing as well as media importance and that research can be pin-pointed to the needs of a particular publication and small segment of an industry.[1]

## *What is research?*

Research is study and investigation to discover facts or establish principles. Research functions of a magazine publishing company or professional groups engaged in such work for magazines may be said to include survey, analysis, and distribution of information, gained through research, about magazine content, readers, markets, and internal operations.

Magazines have shown greatest interest in marketing research but also have conducted experiments or investigations into readability, reader interest, readership, legibility, content analysis, and more specialized areas.

Each department of a magazine company undertakes different types of research, according to its need for information. Research done by several score magazines of different sizes and by such groups as the Magazine Advertising Bureau, Advertising Federation of America, and Publishers Information Bureau can be classified into six major types: marketing, product, reader, internal magazine, retailer, and editorial.

**Marketing research.** As defined by the American Marketing Association, marketing research is "the gathering, recording, and analyzing of all facts about problems relating to the transfer and sale of goods and services from producer to consumer." Magazines are instruments that help achieve that transfer by providing information and by arousing desires and helping to gratify felt needs of readers.

In seeking to gather, record, and analyze marketing facts the magazine and advertising worlds have produced two main types of studies: *geographic* or *area* and *audience distribution.* In making the first type, research work has been done in city, county, state, or other defined area in which the magazine circulates. The purpose is to uncover information chiefly on population and income. Usually, geographic studies by magazines are national, since circulation is

---

[1] "Special Interest Magazine Stresses Cost Per Prospect," *Media/scope,* December, 1961, pp. 56–58.

national. An example is a report titled "Today's Customers for Dishwashers," issued by *U.S. News & World Report.*

Audience distribution research seeks to discover where the readers or consumers within a given market are to be found and what use they make of a given magazine. "Magazine Audiences in 594 Local Markets," issued by *Look,* is an example of the results.

**Product research.** Highly specialized, with only a remote connection with the magazine world, product research consists of analysis of a particular product and of its market.

A product is tested or analyzed as a special inducement to a manufacturer considering an advertising campaign for a new one, or it is done for the sake of the consumer. As a test of a new commodity it is sold in a limited geographic area only and the magazine—or a firm especially engaged—studies the sales results. Good Housekeeping Institute is maintained by that magazine in the interest of its readers as well as for its own protection and as a stimulus to high-grade advertising.

An assembly of market facts about a specific product results from this type of research. It describes the present market and forecasts its future. It deals with distribution, pricing, and other facts. Annually *Industrial Marketing* magazine, through its market data book number, issues a large body of information gathered about specific types of industrial products.

**Reader research.** Readers have become objects of study by all magazine departments. Editorial wants to know which ones read which magazines and how they react to the content. Advertising would like to discover which types of copy are most effective and what commodity brands the reader prefers. Circulation is eager to find out why readers select one magazine rather than another from a newsstand. At least four kinds of studies of this prized guinea pig, the reader, are being turned out: brand preference, audience purchase estimates, readership, and reader interest.

Brand preferences are discovered by studies of the audience's buying practices or stated preferences, usually made by selecting a typical family cross section in a substantial geographical area. One example is the "Use of Foods and Beverages by 1047 *Redbook* Families," issued by the McCall Corp.

Surveys to learn what items readers expect to purchase, rather than what they have purchased, constitute audience purchase research. A given list of products usually is included, estimates being made of sums represented by projected purchases. "The Cream of the Market," put out by *Eastern Breeder,* is an example.

Readership or audience research is a study of the persons who buy and read magazines or at whom they are aimed. This investigation is concerned with selection of magazines by readers and their reactions to content, time and place of purchase, age, income, education, sex, marital status, and other characteristics. All these are factors to be considered by every magazine research department and those depending upon its findings. Having wide applicability and usefulness, readership studies have become the most elaborate type of magazine research with the exception of marketing studies. Typical of published results for popular use are reports like "The Reading Habits of Registered Nurses," produced by the *American Journal of Nursing* and *"Woman's Day* Studies Women Who Buy It," issued to influence potential advertisers in this magazine distributed largely through a giant chain store system.

Time Inc. wanted to find out which magazines college students read regularly. It employed a research service to survey men and women in 168 accredited four-year colleges and universities. The sample was small. From the 1,844 men and women covered, 1,250 returns were received. This was a response of 69 per cent. But it was thought to be a dependable study since it covered a valid cross section of educational institutions.[2]

An example of audience research involving more than one publication is a study released by *Newsweek* called "The Audience of Five Magazines." Covered were *Newsweek, Time, U.S. News & World Report, Life,* and *Saturday Evening Post.* Its findings dealt with number of readers, cost of readers per dollar spent on advertising, percentages of position in the household, incomes, and appliances used.

*The Reader's Digest* released one embracing itself, *Life, Post, Look, Ladies' Home Journal, McCall's, Woman's Day,* and *Sunset.* For the study almost 60,000 field interviews were made; it attempted to define regional differences in household characteristics, such as what people own and buy.

When reader response is separately studied, such research is classified as reader interest. It discloses information on reaction to editorial as well as to advertising content of one or more periodicals. An example is "How To Increase Reader Interest in Your Printed Material," by Jack B. Haskins and Douglas E. Stuart, based on studies made for the Curtis Publishing Company and reported in *Graphic Arts Monthly.*

**Internal magazine research.** Also known as media research, internal magazine research is the type of investigation or experiment that analyzes editorial and advertising content and circulation. Content analysis research is measurement, with or without subsequent evaluation by researchers or experts acting as judges, who apply standards determined by general practices. One example is "Contents of 339

---

[2] *Magazine Industry Newsletter,* Nov. 30, 1963.

Employee Magazines," prepared by a division of the Metropolitan Life Insurance Company. Another is "Validation of the Abstraction Index as a Tool for Content-Effects Analysis and Content Analysis," by Jack B. Haskins, then of Curtis, which appeared in the *Journal of Applied Psychology*.

Such studies give an editor or advertising executive an overview of his magazine's content for a substantial period, indicating amount of copy dealing with different subjects, placement and typographic treatment, and editorial positions taken by the publication. If research is done on quantity and types of advertising space sold, it is known as an advertising linage study. This type may cover a single magazine or compare competing media, such as newspapers and magazines. The Magazine Advertising Bureau's "National Advertising Investments" is an example of published results.

By studying reports from circulation auditors or facts derived from audience surveys that provide circulation data, researchers produce circulation analyses. Typical of the results is "Look Behind the A.B.C. Statement of the *Engineering News-Record*," issued by Mc-Graw-Hill.

Is the magazine's choice of words for its editorial content setting up barriers between intended meanings and readers' minds? Is the type face selected for titles and other headings difficult to read because the letters are too small or too ornate? Such questions are attacked by researchers concerned with readability and legibility. Readability research studies the ease with which the reader grasps the meaning of facts and ideas that content is intended to convey, concentrating on word choice, sentence length, vocabulary, and other characteristics of writing. Legibility research, left in the hands of auxiliaries to the magazine world such as type manufacturing companies, psychologists, journalism school graduate students and faculties, and typographic experts, studies the ease with which the reader discerns correctly the physical properties of the magazine: the shapes of letters, relationship of types, and clarity of other symbols and signs used in magazine production.

**Retailer research.** Magazine firms have found it useful to study not only readers, industries, industrial products, and themselves, but also retailers or dealers who act as middlemen between magazines and advertisers. Important to discover are retailers' preferences among magazines as media to help sell goods, guide in stock selection, and facilitate business operations; for if a substantial group reveals dependence upon a given magazine, other dealers may be induced to use it.

Still more valuable is the report to advertisers not already in the magazine who might buy space if they realized that dealers find it effective in stimulating buying, either by readers as individuals or by dealers in quantity. The study made for *Popular Science Monthly*, described at the outset of this chapter, is an example of the results of such research.

**Editorial research.** In a sense, editorial research also is internal, inasmuch as it takes place within the magazine's own confines; but it does not deal with the magazine as an entity.

It consists mainly of study related to checking and verifying, i.e., using research methods to establish the accuracy of content, and to background, i.e., obtaining historical or statistical information that will provide documentation for editorial content. These studies are made by staff members especially assigned to them or by contributors who perforce do them in the course of preparing materials for publication (see Chapter 12).

## *Picture of a department*

At 56th and Chestnut Streets in Philadelphia are the offices of the Chilton Company, the second largest publisher of business magazines in the United States. It issues 24 periodicals and five directories. Among the better known are *Iron Age, Boot & Shoe Recorder, Hardware Age, Motor Age, Commercial Car Journal,* and *Marine Products.*

Chilton, as have many magazine publishing firms, has diversified its activities. It has a book division which issues about 75 titles a year and is greatly involved in language teaching aid programs. It also owns a paper mill in upper New York State with McGraw-Hill and controls half of Drug Topics Publishing Company in New York.

Chilton Research Services, Chilton's research arm, was founded in 1956 and is now one of the busiest of its various units. As a regional magazine put it: "Luring some of the top talent from National Analysts, Philadelphia-based marketing firm, Chilton set up its own numbers-counting department and started making marketing and readership surveys for its magazines and for advertisers and advertising agencies on a fee basis."[3]

By 1967 the division had a staff of 140 (see organization chart, pages 140–41) and more than 900 trained field interviewers available to it. The staff had access to a data center and a list of duties worked out in elaborate detail. Comparable to such departments in the big consumer publishing firms with numerous periodicals on their lists, its activities are described here not necessarily as typical but to show the extent of the work and the possibilities there for people bringing the needed skills.

Three main objectives are set down by Chilton for its research division: "(1) To serve the Chilton Company, its various magazines and departments; (2) To provide marketing assistance and research services to Chilton advertisers, potential advertisers, agencies and other

---

[3] "Chilton's Inky Empire," *Greater Philadelphia Magazine,* March, 1962, p. 59.

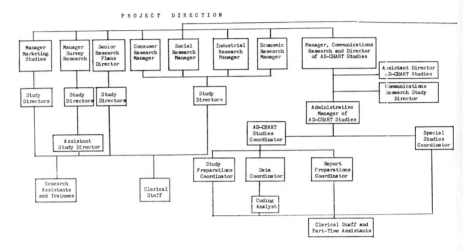

organizations, primarily non-competitive with Chilton products; (3) To make available, on a fee-paid basis, a wide range of total marketing and communications research capabilities to any organization requiring such service."[4]

The description of the details of these objectives, and of research policies, facilities, activities, and job specifications of the managerial staff of the department alone would fill twenty pages of this book. Some highlights of each, to indicate the scope, are reproduced. The objectives for internal research work at Chilton include these:

1. Provide management with information necessary to sound planning and operation.
2. Inform management regarding the uses of research data.
3. Serve as a clearing house of research information between segments of the company, and between the company and its clients.
4. Coordinate the research activities of the various magazines within the framework of Chilton policy.
5. Advance knowledge of marketing and the advertising process through sound research.
6. Provide research on Chilton magazines as an additional channel of communication between the company's magazines and their advertisers.

---

[4] This quotation and others relating to the department were provided by Dr. David P. Forsyth, while manager, Communications Research, Chilton Company, or appear in literature issued by the company.

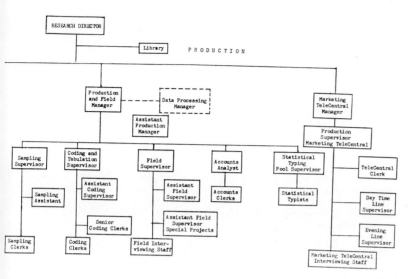

*Fig. 8.1.* Organization of the Chilton Company's research services, serving a firm with a score of business periodicals.

7. Afford an additional means of fortifying Chilton's image in the eyes of advertisers, potential advertisers, agencies, and readers.

The specific objectives of the external work, major objective No. 2, are:

1. Provide, indirectly, an additional means of communication between Chilton and its advertisers.
2. Enhance Chilton's image and the image of its various magazines in the eyes of advertisers, agencies, and other groups pertinent to Chilton success.
3. Provide an additional source of income for Chilton.

The document that provides a detailed statement of the principles and policies which guide the operation of the division comments that: "These are the usual ethical and operating policies of a professional research organization."

The facilities are different from those of an independent marketing research firm because Chilton is itself in the publishing business. They are described thus:

> *A National Area Probability Sample,* designed by our own statisticians, designed to allow regional or national sampling of engineers, retail establishments, manufacturing plants, consumers or other units of advertisers' or magazines' markets. . . .
> *A National Staff of Professional Interviewers,* located in each of our 100 sampling locations. These interviewers conduct surveys for Chilton publications, and are now used also for non-Chilton projects.

Interviewers are paid on an hourly rather than a piece-work basis as a motivation for quality work. . . .

*Professional Market Researchers.* While the professional staff is necessarily versed in publishing, they are primarily market researchers. Personnel have a variety of academic backgrounds, including mathematical statistics, engineering, marketing and the social sciences. Experience of our executive personnel sum to more than fifty years of problem solution. On-the-job experience includes industrial engineering sales, design engineering, marketing, social science and media research, and marketing research embracing a wide variety of marketing problems. Personnel have graduate training in these fields and are active in a number of marketing and academic societies.

*A Research Library and Reference Service.* Staffed by two full-time research librarians. Covers a multitude of subjects pertinent to various industrial and consumer markets. Available for information searches.

*A Trained Gunning Staff.* The library staff conducts Fog Index studies on Chilton magazines and competitors. This staff was personally trained by Robert Gunning.

*A Trained Space Analysis Staff.* The library staff also conducts on-going analysis of ad page sales in Chilton and competitive magazines. They have been especially trained for this activity by publishing personnel in various Chilton magazines.

*Chilton Market Data.* Masses of data on hundreds of markets provided by Chilton magazines are available to the department in its market research activities. There are few non-governmental research operations in the country that have as much data immediately available.

*Market Specialists.* Chilton's publishers, editors, marketing and circulation managers are available for consultation on research projects. These men are in close contact with the markets they serve, and are a source of great insight into marketing problems. They help to make the department a unique research operation.

*Special Censuses and Lists.* Chilton's censuses and direct mail lists add greatly to the department's outside research facilities, as well as provide an important element in research on Chilton magazines. From an advertiser's standpoint, they are a strong research sales point.

*Data Processing Center.* The Company's tabulation unit has worked closely with the department since the unit was established in 1960. It has facilitated research processing and decreased the department's tabulation costs.

In summary, there are few research operations in the country that provide this wide a variety of facilities and services.

The work of the department subdivides into internal and external activities in line with the objectives. The internal include: using research to determine reader interest in the editorial and advertising content of the publications, readability, and the nature of the readership. The external work relates to what Chilton calls its M-A-P (Marketing Assistance Program), i.e., providing marketing information for manufacturers. This includes "Marketing guidance, product and market studies, buying influence studies, distribution data, and many other services."

Also available to clients are services from what is called the Information Handling Services Division, which employs what is known as the VSMF system (Visual Search Microfilm File), an information retrieval system used to "cut time spent [by companies] in product search, eliminate filing, and speed comparison of competitive data." A final external service is that offered under the name Chilton Research Services, covering marketing consultation, statistical sampling, company image studies, new product acceptance, buying habits and motivations, and editorial readership.

## Research methods

So far we have examined kinds of research done for and by magazines, but not methods used by researchers. These range from the simple mechanical act of counting coupons to the more complex operation of analyzing assembled data. The work of the entire range of activities has been enormously expedited by the use of computers.

**Visual checking** consists of observation at newsstands or other distribution points (inside industrial plants, for example, to gain information about magazine purchase or use). Observers watch the public's reaction, record facts about the means of purchase or handling by the buyer, time when it is obtained from the outlet and other such information. Visual checking also is used with brand preference surveys and "pantry" surveys. The interview method sometimes is added.

**Questionnaire surveys** are among the oldest research methods in use. They may be as elaborate as a nine-page booklet sent regularly to a changing group of subscribers or as simple as one-page sheets inserted loosely between pages. While most commonly used by editorial, they are employed by all departments. Questions generally are about the reader and his content preferences.

**Personal interviews** are more thorough and dependable than either visual observation or questionnaire techniques because they are individualized and under better control by the researcher. Interviewers carry questionnaires and copies of the magazine, ask general and specific questions, and in the most careful studies mark portions of the publication read by the subscriber; these portions are determined by questions in depth revealing the reader's recollection and understanding of what was printed.

**Letters to the editor** have been an accessible source of information about reader interests and reactions since magazines first were issued, but only in recent years has any systematic research been done with them. They now are analyzed carefully, for they reveal not only what features are preferred or disliked but also how pressure groups stimulate them. They also provide correction of errors.

**Contests** among readers for letters or editorial contributions likewise are among the older methods, but they qualify more as promotion than as research. Their analysis, however, requires some research knowledge.

**Ballots** or forms printed in the magazine on which readers may comment on content or offer criticisms and suggestions provide a limited amount of superficial information for analysis.

**Premium offers,** such as free pamphlets, recipes, or other lures, are made to readers. Well hidden in the body of an article or department, these announcements sometimes bring amazing response. This marketing research device can make slight claim, even in its analysis, to being scientific.

**Telephone surveys** occasionally are made by and for magazines, but they have been used most successfully by radio and television researchers. Strictly to be limited to one of the business departments, these surveys are substitutes for the personal interview. Sometimes a questionnaire is used to learn if a person was satisfied or dissatisfied with his purchase, and the queries bring out the intentions of persons who have returned a coupon indicating interest in some advertised product. In some telephone surveys households are dialed without knowing the name of the person in whose name the telephone is listed.

**Panels** are made up of a group of families or individuals who are consulted regularly by mail or interview for answers to specific questions. Their reactions are gathered and noted over a definite period, giving a clue to response to be expected from the total audience.

### Who does the research?

The University of Michigan Survey Research Center at one time conducted a "Survey of Consumer Finances" for the Federal Reserve System of Governors. *Parents'* magazine researchers, using these data, prepared a report, "Families of Children Buy More Refrigerators," which indicated that such families spend 72 per cent more than families without children, and also compared expenditures for washing machines and television sets. Three sets of research workers were engaged in a study that resulted in a pamphlet eventually sent free to advertisers.

Some research agencies or individuals specialize in certain types of study. Others undertake to obtain almost any desired information. Consumer magazine publishers, especially those issuing several periodicals, do enough research to justify maintaining a staff for the purpose. Small magazines turn to companies that specialize in media research or they engage university and college specialists who are in a position themselves to do certain types of such work as content analysis or are able to form teams of graduate students to conduct more elaborate study.

Typical of the small firms commercially engaged in these investigations is Eastman Research, operated by George Kiernan Associates, Inc., in Long Island, N.Y. This company has done research since the early 1940's for a variety of specialized magazines, such as *American Journal of Nursing, Christian Herald, Iron Age,* and *Architectural Record.* Its method is to interview readers three or more times annually and from these interviews summarize the results and recommend "ways and means of making . . . publications more interesting and more useful."

Among the large companies engaged in such work are Daniel Starch of Mamaroneck, N.Y., one of the oldest; SRDS Data, Inc., New York; Gallup & Robinson, Princeton, N.J., of which the prominent pollster and former journalism teacher, George Gallup, is a partner; A. C. Nielsen Company (Nielsen Media Service), of New York; W. R. Simmons & Associates, New York, and Reade, Inc., of St. Paul, Minn. From the research results of firms such as these the multimillion circulation magazines of the nation are able to make fundamental changes in policy on formula, advertising rate schedules, and market appeal.

Several magazine publishing companies undertake research for their own periodicals as well as for others, at a fee. Among them are McGraw-Hill, Chilton, Hayden, and Penton. A few also do research work for advertisers, much as does a separate commercial testing or market research firm.

Research projects that require extensive personal interviewing or protracted observation are directed by experienced researchers who have under their management crews trained in techniques. Preliminary to field work are training sessions in which the study's purpose is explained carefully and methods are systematically rehearsed. Analysis of the findings is undertaken by statisticians familiar with the best ways to gauge and present them. Findings generally are confidential, being released only to the agencies that finance the studies.

To encourage university research in the magazine field, MPA, through its education committee, has sponsored fellowships. Awards from $500 to $1,000 were made annually during the 1960's to faculty or students at associate member institutions. Several of these studies have been published.

### Research in action

How is such research as has been described carried out? We shall look at the methods used with two different studies, one relating to consumer and the other to specialized periodicals.

"The Characteristics of the Reading Audiences of *Newsweek, Time* and *U.S. News and World Report*" is the title of a national study conducted by Sindlinger & Co., Inc., a Ridley Park, Pa., firm of business analysts, for *Newsweek*. Andrew J. Cullen, then director of research for the magazine, explained in the final report that *Newsweek* had "requested the Sindlinger organization to go back over its past interviewing records and develop audience characteristics data on the reading audiences of the newsweekly magazine field."

Mr. Cullen pointed out that *Newsweek* believed that "this project involves several major accomplishments: (1) It makes available for the first time total reading audience characteristics of the newsweekly magazine field. (2) It is the first time in the history of magazine research that a sample as large as this has ever been used. (3) It represents the application of a unique and powerful research instrument—the telephone—to the measurement of reading audiences of magazines of relatively small circulation size."

The study was intended to report the "quantities and qualities of the audience delivered by three magazines." It discusses two technical problems that handicap researchers seeking to evaluate magazine audiences accurately: (1) what is a reader? and (2) how can an accurate population sample be attained? Readership was scaled according to a system used by the research concern. These were preliminary questions, such as asking the respondent if he ever had heard of the magazine named.

The sample consisted of individuals twelve years old and older living in households having telephones and in metropolitan areas and counties of this country. The telephone interviews were conducted in the evening, with some exceptions, and 5,711 were attempted. Of these, 4,952 or 86.7 per cent were completed. Of the respondents, 2,283 were females and 2,714 males. Various projections were used in evaluation of the study, such as projecting it to the number of subscriptions for major magazines.

The findings were tabulated, for each newsmagazine, under the occupation of readers, their household income, and their age, each table subdivided as well into male and female readers.[5]

A readership study made by *U.S. Camera* itself is considerably simpler. Reported in a 9 x 4 pamphlet of a dozen pages, it is described as "a report of a survey conducted by mail among representative subscribers to *U.S. Camera* magazine in order to study their ownership and buying intentions with respect to photographic equipment and related products."

A questionnaire that covered both sides of a legal-size sheet was sent with a brief, duplicated request for cooperation. Part of the form itself, this memorandum was kept impersonal and "no inducement to reply was offered. . . ." A single mailing was made to 10,000 names selected at random from the continental United States subscription list. Every thirty-fifth name was used. A total of 1,405 replied, or a 14.0 per cent response. Since these were many more than needed, eight hundred were selected at random from this stockpile of replies.

"To make sure that the 800 were an adequate sample," the report explains, "the questionnaires were tabulated in batches of 200 each, and the percentages were compared at the 600 and 800 marks. In almost all cases there was little or no variation—only rarely more than half a percentage point."

Among the thirty-four questions asked were: "How do you rate yourself as a photographer? How many years have you been actively

---

[5] "The Characteristics of the Reading Audiences of *Newsweek, Time* and *U.S. News and World Report*," New York: *Newsweek*, 1959. 24 pp.

interested in photography? Do you own a projection screen? What brand? What surface?"

Typical of the form of reporting answers is this excerpt:

> 2a. How many years have you been reading *U.S. Camera?*
> Of the 765 who replied to this question:
>
> | | | |
> |---|---|---|
> | 3.0% | said | Less than one year |
> | 30.7 | " | One to two years |
> | 34.9 | " | Three to five years |
> | 23.8 | " | Six to ten years |
> | 7.6 | " | More than ten years |
> | 100.0% | | |
>
> One-half of the new subscribers (less than a year) are beginners. The median or typical subscriber has been reading *U.S. Camera* for four and one-half years.[6]

## Reader interest studies

Because magazines mean little without readers, owners are keenly concerned about the success of the content. Only subsidized periodicals can afford indifference to reader interest. Even these, however, at times use as many devices to discover readers' desires as do commercially supported magazines.

To increase understanding of what readers want, editors and publishers have found it useful to study readers themselves. Readership and reader interest studies are closely related. Readability also is related, for it can affect reader interest.

The virtue of the dependable reader interest survey is that it saves the editor from making decisions largely on editorial hunch. Certain editors, however, appear to understand reader desires even when they know personally but few of the millions who read their magazines.

One such was George Horace Lorimer of the *Saturday Evening Post.* How did he do it? No one seems to know; possibly he did not know himself. His biographer, John Tebbel, gives some clue when he declares that Lorimer's mind was on the *Post* constantly, in the office and out of it; that he read prodigiously, old and new books but especially the classics.

"Fortunately," writes Tebbel, "his likings covered such a tremendously wide range that they inevitably encompassed the likings of the majority of readers." [7]

Another part of his secret may have been his versatility. He not only was an editorial genius in the popular magazine field but also a strong man on the business side, playing a decisive part in the management of Curtis publications.

---

[6] *"U.S. Camera* Readership Survey 1960–1961," (New York: U.S. Camera Publishing Corp. Undated [c. 1962]), 12 pp.

[7] John Tebbel, *George Horace Lorimer and the Saturday Evening Post* (New York: Doubleday & Co., 1948), p. 214.

Tebbel concludes that the explanation finally was that Lorimer edited the magazine to suit himself and that he was a typical American editing it for other typical Americans. He knew what his readers wanted because he was one of them; despite his personal success he remained one of them.

This formula for successful editorship, while apparently true in general, has its exceptions. Editors of several highly successful women's magazines have been men or women with little resemblance to their readers. Carmel White Snow of *Harper's Bazaar* and Diana Vreeland of *Vogue* were perhaps what their readers would want to be like but were hardly typical. Probably no one of the readers of *The New Yorker,* or even its staff members, was like its eccentric editor and founder, Harold Ross. Successful editing is giving readers not only something they want but also something they do not know they want but gladly accept. The latter element cannot be measured by reader interest surveys, for it is positive and creative. The surveys cannot discover public reaction to what it has not yet been given. Editors and publishers who base upon them all or most of their decisions are bound to produce magazines that meet only half the requirements set by psychologists: that a magazine must seem to be the same and to be different.

The advertising department finds surveys more useful than does editorial because measurement of results is more nearly accurate. Concrete information has been obtained by the department if it learns that copy containing a halftone sells more dresses than does one carrying only reading matter. If repeated tests substantiate the original findings, the department has a generalization to go on at least until all other advertisers, by using photographs, minimize reader attention to this practice.

Although research techniques and findings do not solve all problems, editors are increasingly using these means of ascertaining readers' interests. Those who do not employ research may be deterred by costs, which are prohibitive for the small publications comprising the bulk of magazinedom.

### Clues to reader interest

The main clues to reader interest already have been mentioned under types of research. The chief methods of discovering it include the following:

**Study of letters received from readers.** This method is at once the commonest and the least dependable of clues. Few readers write letters to editors, although the more brash or controversial the magazine and the higher the educational level of its reader, the more likely it is to receive mail of this sort; witness the letter departments of *Time, Harper's, Newsweek, Life,* and *Esquire.* Numerous periodicals of much wider circulation than these have no letters-to-the-editor departments. Even though the Voice of the People be the Voice of God, many an editor has no dependable flow of advice, comment, and reaction on which to rely. Lobbyists, special pleaders, propagandists, and professional writers of letters interfere with the democratic function of this department. Yet an editor who receives several hundred independently written letters reflecting more or less the same reaction to some article or story is bound to be influenced. Little is scientific about the creation or use of these missives, although they may play some part in further statistical analysis by being combined with results of interviews.

**Mailed questionnaires to subscribers.** Like observation of letters, this technique is one of the oldest. If the questions are incisive and the reader responds honestly, returned questionnaires provide more guidance than random letters but hardly as much as personal interviews with random subscribers, qualified readers, or panelists. This generalization holds only when questions seek to learn reader reactions to content: the mailed questionnaire is far more reliable in obtaining readership information. The more conscious a reader is that his opinions or habits are being measured or recorded, the less reliable are the results. Hence the use of one-way-vision mirrors by some researchers to note readers' practices without revealing their presence. But a reader is likely to be sufficiently reliable when asked on a questionnaire to indicate sex, age group, amount of education, and similar questions.

**Making reader traffic surveys.** In this method, readers meeting certain qualifications, of age-grouping, say, and degree of familiarity with a magazine, are interviewed personally and asked prepared questions about a set of articles, stories, editorials, cartoons, or other units of reading matter. The researcher, for example, asks if the reader recalls having seen a given item, whether he read it, if so, how much, and if he thought it "excellent, good, fair, poor, or very poor." He is asked, also, to rate covers, give reactions to the entire issue, and provide background data on himself.

**Conducting surveys of a controlled group of readers.** Readers studied through questionnaires are a changing group. Under this fourth technique, a jury or panel reports regularly to the magazine or company conducting the survey. Readers are shown experimental materials or published content. A typical consumer magazine experiment was to ask a panel of women to read duplicated, untitled, and unillustrated copies of certain stories and to rate them.

What becomes of the findings of these studies, surveys, and analyses? Are they filed and forgotten? In many instances they are set aside because applying them would require too costly a retooling of the magazine. But in scores of cases they have become decisive factors in editorial policy. Ernest C. Ludeke, while director of the Development Division of Curtis, described the use of the results of reader traf-

fic type interviews and the "controlled experiment survey" made by
the *Saturday Evening Post*. Among the resultant changes in the magazine were adoption of subtitles on stories and articles, use of a more
legible type face for headings, addition of a regular feature explaining the cover, inclusion of a letters-to-the-editor column, and publication of long stories and novelettes.[8] Among the most responsive to
results of these studies are numerous small specialized magazines
which may be edited by experts in some subject matter area but
novices in editorial operations.

## Readability experiments

Although they have not called it readability research, teachers
of journalism long have recommended to magazine writers and editors
the adoption of practices now commonly accepted. Examination of
journalism textbooks and classroom lectures in news writing, editing,
article writing, and other journalistic writing techniques proves that
novices and professionals alike have been advised to use shorter
sentences and paragraphs and simpler words, or at least to adjust
to the vocabulary level of readers.

But it was not until 1946, when a Columbia University scholar
named Rudolf Flesch issued in popular form a book based on his
doctoral dissertation, that readability became a by-word in magazine
and newspaper editorial offices, advertising agencies, and press association bureaus. Dr. Flesch asserted that all writing would be made
more readable by shorter sentences, simpler words, and more personal
references. Although Dr. Flesch brought public attention to readability, he was not the pioneer.

In 1935 the Gray-Leary formula, published in an English textbook, predicted reading difficulty on five points; the formulators
were William S. Gray and Bernice Leary:

1. Proportion of different "hard" words used by the writer.
2. Proportion of prepositional phrases.
3. Average sentence length.
4. Proportion of pronouns used.
5. Relative number of different words used.[9]

Four years later a Columbia professor, Dr. Irving Lorge, announced another formula, one containing the first three elements of
the Gray-Leary, but weighted or emphasized differently. Then, in
1943, Dr. Flesch completed his dissertation, *Marks of Readable Style*,
setting forth his formula of three elements:

1. Proportion of prefixes and suffixes.
2. Relative number of references to people.
3. Average sentence length.

---

[8] Ernest C. Ludeke, "The Role of Research in the Editorial Reconversion Problems of a Magazine." *Journalism Quarterly*, September, 1948, pp. 213–17.

[9] George R. Klare and Byron Buck, *Know Your Reader* (New York: Hermitage
House, 1954), p. 102.

Realizing that the book in which this formula appeared was itself not sufficiently readable for general use, Dr. Flesch revised it, while retaining the formula, and published it under a new title. [10]

When it appeared it gained attention immediately from the Associated Press, which engaged its author to test AP materials, and from innumerable book publishing firms, magazine editors, advertising copy writers, public speakers, and many others.

Another formula appeared in 1948, the Dale-Chall, devised by Dr. Edgar Dale and Jeanne S. Chall of Ohio State University. It also is pertinent to the magazine. It relies on two elements only:

1. Average sentence length.
2. Percentage of unfamiliar words; that is, words not on a list of approximately three thousand familiar words known in reading by at least 8 per cent of children in fourth grade.

The authors, who first published it in an educational magazine and later in a pamphlet, [11] with complete explanations of its use, believe it to be an improvement over preceding formulas because it is simpler and overcomes some shortcomings in Flesch's. It provides, in their view, a more discriminating instrument for testing the upper levels of reading ability, because the accompanying word list is about four times as long as that of Flesch. Also, affixes are ignored, as are personal references. The latter are not used because a high personal reference score may be found in otherwise abstract writing and because personal references, if unfamiliar to the reader, become abstract.

Dr. Flesch altered his formula in 1949, reissuing its new form in another book.[12] It is presented clearly as a way to help writers measure their work for interest value and ease of reading. Its four parts are:

1. Relative number of references to persons.
2. Proportions of personal sentences.
3. Average number of syllables per one hundred words.
4. Average sentence length.

Other formulas for measuring adult materials followed rapidly. Dr. Flesch in 1950 made one more change, in an attempt to meet the objection about abstractness. He constructed categories of definite words and counted the average word length in syllables. [13]

One other formula of value to the magazinist is that of Robert Gunning; it has been applied by periodical editors. Its purpose is to find what he calls "The Fog Index," which is determined by:

1. Determining the average number of words per sentence in a 100-

[10] Rudolf Flesch, *The Art of Plain Talk* (New York: Harper & Brothers, 1946).

[11] Edgar Dale and Jeanne S. Chall, "A Formula for Predicting Readability," Bureau of Educational Research, Ohio State University. Undated.

[12] Rudolf Flesch, *The Art of Readable Writing* (New York: Harper & Brothers, 1949).

[13] Rudolf Flesch, *How To Test Readability* (New York: Harper & Brothers, 1951).

word sample, treating independent clauses as separate sentences.
2. Counting the number of polysyllables in each 100-word segment.
3. Adding the average number of words per sentence to the poly-
syllable count and multiplying the sum by 0.4.[14]

In 1953 there appeared a procedure or test (but not a formula)
which has received considerable attention from researchers but comparatively little application in the practice of journalism. This is
known as the Cloze Procedure, its name being derived from *closure,*
which is "the term some psychologists use to refer to the notion that
humans tend to perceive a familiar pattern as a whole even when the
parts of it are missing, obscured, or distorted."[15] Dr. Taylor, who
developed this method, recommends deleting words from the passage
of writing, replacing them with blanks. Each reader is then asked
to guess the missing words; he scores a point each time he fills a
blank correctly. "His 'cloze procedure' for any passage is the total
number or percentage of its missing words he fills in correctly."

Applications of all these formulas are described in detail in the
books and pamphlets that set them forth. All may be studied to advantage by anyone who desires to write more clearly, simply, and
directly. They can alleviate vagueness, obscurity, and wordiness.

Formulas of this sort, however, must be used with discretion. Not
all are intended for adult readers, some are for children only. Figures
can mislead, furthermore. A certain survey revealed that the families
of Princeton graduates, a men's university, average 1.8 children,
whereas those of Smith graduates, a girl's college, average 1.4. It
would be erroneous to conclude from these figures that men have
more children than women.

The readability testers do not expect their formulas to be used
as absolute yardsticks. Yet some persons have gone to extremes, as in
the case of a somewhat flowery and ornate magazine writer who now
writes like a child, using only short sentences more or less uniform
in length. He did not note that the researchers do not recommend
that every sentence be short, but only that average sentence length
be short.

### Researchers are backstoppers

Occasionally a contributor deceives an editor, but a magazine
with a reliable research department need worry less about this possibility than one which leaves copy unverified. No magazine editor,
however, can rest entirely easy. Despite the greatest care, incorrect
information can creep in.

Justification for meticulous checking was brought home by an
incident in the *Coronet* office. Mrs. Lucille Beckhart contributed an

---

[14] Robert Gunning, *How To Take the Fog Out of Writing* (Chicago, Ill.: Dart-
nell Corp., 1959), pp. 9–10. A pamphlet.
[15] Wilson L. Taylor, "Cloze Procedure," *NPAC Agrisearch*, February, 1956, p. 1.

article about Cat Island, which, she said, was near Tahiti and had first been invaded by rats from a sinking ship. To get rid of the rats, she related, hundreds of cats were imported. When the cats multiplied and grew vicious, the people on the island were forced to desert it, leaving it to be ruled by the tabbies.

After publication of the article, William Kennedy, a Los Angeles *Herald & Express* reporter, tried unsuccessfully to find Cat Island on a map. *Coronet* referred him to the governor of Tahiti, who cabled that there was no island so named. The reporter had begun his investigation because a Pasadena millionaire announced his intention to undertake a trip to Cat Island in his 136-foot schooner. *Time* published a story that cast doubt on Mrs. Beckhart's accuracy. But both Dr. Fritz Bamberger, then *Coronet's* head researcher, and the author insisted on the story's accuracy. They shortly were vindicated by two letters to *Time* that added the documentary evidence. The full story of Cat Island had been told in one of Frederick O'Brien's books, originally published in 1922. One letter to *Time* identified the man who imported the cats as Dr. Walter Johnstone Williams, dentist and British consul at Papeete, Tahiti. It also reported on the number of cats imported, and traced present ownership of Tetiaroa, the island's real name, to Dr. Williams' widow.

## Skeptics about research

Although published reports of readership, reader interest, and marketing are impressive, usually being handsome presentations, sometimes in four colors, considerable skepticism about them is expressed inside as well as outside the advertising and magazine worlds. Adverse critics doubt the objectivity of these studies, in some instances, declare that the basic assumptions are not always valid, and insist that waste attends them.

The general criticism is that media research tends to be vulnerable because it sets out to prove a point rather than to arrive at facts. The almost total absence of published studies that reveal findings unfavorable to a given magazine supports this criticism. Such words as "one-sided," "slanted," "axes being ground," and "half-truths" are used by adverse critics, but dubious research continues.

Blair Vedder, while on the staff of Needham, Louis & Brorby, Inc., pointed out that "what most advertisers really want to know . . . is *not* simply how many people are exposed to the medium, but how many are apt to be exposed to his advertisement on whatever page it may appear in a periodical. . . ."[16] He doubted that the consumer magazine audience studies conducted up to the time of his writing contributed real answers, because the definition of *reader* is so vague. Failure to agree on who or what a reader is long has been a point of

[16] Blair Vedder, "What Is Exposure Opportunity for Magazine Advertisements?", *Media/scope*, March, 1958, pp. 48–49.

argument among researchers. Is reading the first page of an article reading the article? How much of a 260-page magazine must be read before one is a reader?

A survey of opinions of 236 members of the National Panel of Media Buyers brought out the fact that four out of five buyers feel that "research studies by specific media are not completely honest." [17] This panel, maintained by Standard Rate & Data Service, complained of the lack of facts in media research. The members were particularly critical of what they considered slanted questions and techniques and "omission of study results when they were unfavorable to the media conducting the story. They also criticized "distorted claims and questionable interpretations," the report of their views noted.

One of the most flagrant abuses of magazine research, although not confined to that area of publishing, is door-to-door selling of subscriptions disguised as market research.

### Researcher at work

No such being as a typical researcher exists in the magazine world. He or she may be young, fresh from college, assigned to the simpler jobs in a research department or employed as researcher for any regular department. He or she may just as likely be a holder of a doctor of philosophy degree, have considerable standing as a statistician or social psychologist, and be attached to a research organization serving magazines, advertising agencies, research companies, or university research institutes.

Out of the grand total of more than 20,000, few magazines, and only the more affluent, maintain their own research departments. A research office generally is connected with the advertising or promotion department. The bulk of the work behind innumerable reports is done far from the magazine offices, which only in rare instances are staffed or equipped to do more than routine factual background and verification or statistical analysis.

The type of research position open to the beginner in this area of magazine work and the sort of preparation needed are described in Chapters 23 and 24. From them it can be seen that habits of accuracy and thoroughness learned in study and practice of news writing and reporting come into play here as surely as on assignments from a city desk.

The opportunities are greater than ever before, as are the possibilities for training.

---

[17] "Media Research 'Not Honest,'" *Editor & Publisher*, June 10, 1961, p. 26.

# Part Three

# *The editorial side*

*Chapter 9*

---

# Free lancing
# for magazines

Happiness, to a free-lance writer, is having all the time he wants in
which to write, several electric typewriters, a copying machine, services of a private secretary as well as of a researcher whenever needed,
assignments coming in steadily from editors eager for his copy, and
checks for from $1,000 to $5,000 arriving for his accepted work every
week or so, after which he receives letters from Hollywood or his
agent seeking book, cinema, and television rights.

This description may be of a free lancer's dream of paradise, but
the realities of the situation portray a different picture. It is indeed
an attractive if selfish life for the few writers who live more or less in
the way just described. But most free lancers do not exist so pleasantly;
in fact, those who even approximate that life of fantasy can be counted
by the tens rather than the hundreds. Perhaps actually there are none
at all, for by the time the free lancer reaches the point where he has
all the help he wants and all the requests for copy he can desire, he
still must work so hard living up to his reputation and maintaining
his pace that sometimes he wishes he were not so successful, like the
one who complained because he received so much fan mail to answer.

Most free-lance writers, as a matter of fact, have other jobs. For
the typical free lance gives only a part of his energy and writing talent
to this type of writing; otherwise he could not maintain himself and a
family. Many leading novelists and short story or article writers who
contribute to magazines are university English teachers, housewives,

staff members of publications or book companies, lawyers, doctors, or largely engaged in some other occupation or profession than writing itself.

A few, such as the famous Johns of modern American writing—O'Hara, Cheever, Steinbeck, Gunther, Hersey, and Updike—are so industrious and prolific that they can live on their earnings, but they are the exceptions rather than the rule. More typical are Bernard Malamud, Bennington College professor who won the Pulitzer Prize in 1967 and whose short stories appear in various magazines; Joyce Oates, another story writer, who teaches at the University of Windsor; Lillian Ross, article as well as short story writer and a member of the staff of *The New Yorker;* and Wallace Stegner, poet and English professor at Stanford since 1945.

All this does not mean that writers who wish to contribute to magazines cannot hope some day to reach the point where they do no other work. But it is difficult to make writing a full-time occupation, especially in the realm of fiction, for not only is competition heavy but also the market for the short story, novelette, and novel is not as great among magazines as it was before the 1950's. Today there is more chance for the non-fiction writer—the author of articles, humorous essays, and other factual rather than imagined material.

Traditionally, it was the newspaper reporter who supplied the free-lance copy—a way of earning money in his spare time. If he was at all successful at it he dreamed of shifting over to full time, sometimes giving up his job, as did Irving S. Cobb. But usually he failed to make a go of it—Cobb was an exception—and returned to the staff of his publication, if he could.

The newsman tried free lancing when he tired of the too rapid tempo of his job. He had heard of independent men and women who once occupied desks in the city room who now wrote a dozen pieces of copy a year and earned two or three times as much money as before. He decided that he wouldn't mind doing that, too, as who would not.

When the free lancer, on the other hand, tires of the too slow tempo and need for self-discipline of *his* job, he thinks seriously of returning to the magazine, radio or television station, newspaper, or advertising agency, with its routine and its relative security. He remembers the days when he had time at home with the family, was not constantly concerned about returned manuscripts the mailman might be delivering, and did not care much that *Pleasure* magazine, one of his markets, was overstocked for six months.

The other fellow's job always looks better than one's own until one really understands what the other fellow's is like. Each has its advantages and disadvantages. The greatest advantage on either side is proving that one can be independent and professionally competent. The successful free-lance writer's work seems to be a sinecure. But what the dreamer forgets is that to become successful, free lancers served apprenticeships that were as boring, ill paid, and insecure as an occupation can be. Like the would-be novelist who has not yet written the first page but dreams of book club selection and Hollywood contracts, the dreamer about free lancing sees only the end of the road, not the ruts, road blocks, and washouts on the way. The journalist who aspires to be a free-lance writer (or artist or photographer) should take a look at the entire career, not unrealistically fix his eyes only on the days of affluence following success.

### Free lancer and magazine

A free lancer is an unattached specialist, commonly associated with journalism and cartooning, but not restricted to those occupations. For there are free-lance editors, photographers, illustrators. Even baby-sitting is a free-lance job, for the sitter does the work on her own terms. She is her own boss, works only if she wishes to, makes her own collections, and assumes full responsibility. Originally, the free lancer was associated with military life, being a knight who sold his fighting power to kings or military commanders. But in our time he is unattached and usually unauthorized, and generally a writer for magazines. Although newspapers occasionally buy free-lance materials, they are issued too frequently to rely upon random or occasional contributions. Dailies, especially, must have regular and dependable coverage; a free lancer who provides it is invited, sometimes, to join the staff as a regular.

Magazines, carrying a wider variety of material and being national and even international in distribution, would find it prohibitively expensive to employ regularly the many writers required to supply their columns. Because of the speed with which news events occur, the newsmagazines must maintain scores of correspondents posted around the world. But most magazines do not need and cannot afford this service.

The free lancer, willing to assume the cost of preparing copy that is not requested or may not be satisfactory when it has been, becomes an important element in the operation of a magazine editorial department. Despite his unofficial relationship, he is a recognized and important member of the editorial personnel. His work has a share in magazine history. There probably never has been an editor whose mail was not in large part the unasked for poems, essays, sermons, and stories of a writer seeking publication in a magazine whose office he never has visited and whose editors are total strangers to him. Exceptions are extremely specialized magazines of business or science, but even they receive, now and then, manuscripts mistakenly addressed to them as though they were periodicals of general material.

Unattached experts also work for the commercial art firms that service magazines and are departments of publishing houses as well as for the picture editors. Many a featured photo story in *Life* or *Ebony* has been the work of a free lancer (see Chapter 13). The connections of free lancers with editorial departments may be as specialized as consultants and translators.

A large national magazine receives as many as one hundred thousand unsolicited manuscripts a year from eager free lancers. The percentage of accepted material is discouragingly small. It is estimated, nevertheless, that about twenty-five thousand persons in the United States seriously attempt free-lance writing, as a part- or full-time occupation. These writers, it appears, are not easily discouraged. Most magazines buy only one or two per cent of unsolicited material brought to their desks by the mailman. They would buy more if they could obtain copy of the desired quality. Elaborate systems for handling this inflow of material are set up. These are so expensive to maintain that some magazines have considered refusing to examine unassigned copy; for a time the Curtis publications did so during an economy wave. So little usable material arrives that the investment in servicing is not worth the trouble and expense. It continues, however, because it builds good will and now and then turns up copy that reveals a new talent worth developing.

These outside writers supply magazines with all types of copy: articles, short stories, novels, editorials, department content, fillers, puzzles and games, and even ideas in the raw, which also are paid for. Restricted magazines, such as the more specialized trade and technical publications, can afford to disregard the free lancer more than others, for he usually knows so little about their specialties he cannot provide them with usable material in any case. Periodicals that cannot or will not pay for contributions—little literary magazines, most company publications, and smaller periodicals of religion, education, the arts, and other such interests—are grateful for and print contributions, if a free subscription or ten copies of the issue containing the material is acceptable payment. Nor should the beginning free lance spurn such a suggestion: it is a way to break in and it is a service to the field of the publication.

## Free lancers in action

Among stories that inspire daydreaming are these:

Lawrence and Sylvia Martin's by-lines, separately or together, have appeared in *The Reader's Digest, Cosmopolitan, Holiday, This Week, Harper's,* and many other magazines, as well as on a half-dozen book covers. They write travel articles, pieces about conditions in many areas of the world, and descriptions of little known places. They send their friends colorful postcards from all over the world, but most often from Mexico where they have made their headquarters and home in Cuernavaca. Here, a few hours by automobile south of Mexico City, the Martins spend part of each year. (Two sales a year to the *Digest* can pay their Mexico expenses, for the cost of living, while rising constantly, is comparatively low there.) They play tennis, entertain friends, and write. Mexico provides raw material—Sylvia's book, *You'll See Them in Mexico,* is based on life in Cuernavaca and illustrated with photographs taken in the streets and shops. But most of their subjects and ideas come from travels elsewhere in Latin America or in Europe. Their writing reflects in its style the enjoyment of their type of life.

This pleasant independence was not always theirs. Lawrence Martin grew up in Chicago; in his college days he sold a few short stories to the pulps. While he was working on small newspapers he wrote articles for minor magazines. As an English teacher he contributed to scholarly journals. His teaching brought him into contact with editors, especially after he began teaching journalism rather than English. His big break came one day at a banquet when he sat beside Arnold Gingrich, then editor of *Esquire* and *Coronet,* later publisher of *Esquire.* Gingrich remarked that he had liked very much a little essay Martin had contributed to a university magazine.

"You should have sent that to us," he said.

"Send it to you! That's just what I did, and you turned it down," was Lawrence's reply.

Because a manuscript reader, not the editor, had rejected this essay, Martin was asked to send Gingrich other manuscripts. He did so, began to appear often in the pages of both magazines, and after a time was added to the staff, playing an important part in the founding of the short-lived magazine, *Ken.* Finally Martin left the academic world to practice journalism full time again. After a few years in staff work he moved to Mexico for free lancing.

The Martins at first did it the hard way—without a specialty. Later they settled on travel as their special field, as have Richard Joseph, Robert S. Kane, Horace Sutton, and many others. They are reporters, with clever styles and keen eyes for the unusual. But the free lancer who wishes to contribute to magazines as an occupation usually finds the job easier if he concentrates on one or a few subjects, as did the late Beulah S. France. She did it with a specialty, since she was a registered nurse, with post-graduate training at Columbia University, George Peabody College, and Pratt Institute. Supervisor of nurses for the Metropolitan Life Insurance Company for five years, she also had done medical publicity writing for the New York City Health Department and one of the large drug supply firms.

Against this background it was not difficult for Mrs. France to give weekly radio health talks, to edit *American Baby* and serve on *Country Gentleman,* and to contribute free-lance articles to almost fifty magazines, including *Good Housekeeping, Parents', McCall's, American Home, Better Homes,* and *This Week* as well as to technical journals of her field, such as *American Journal of Nursing, Research Quarterly, Public Health Nursing, Childhood Activities,* and *Medical Economics.*

Subject matter is not the only specialty, however; another might be style. That is more the specialty of the fiction than of the non-fiction free lance. Many a short story writer or novelist is valued by editors because of his way of writing, a way which may so please readers that they will read this particular author no matter what carries his by-line, just as some persons go to see movies with certain actors regardless of the picture.

One of the most successful all-around free lancers is Richard Gehman, who sometimes is called a one-man manuscript factory because he turns out such an enormous amount of copy. He writes for such a varied group of magazines as *True, Cosmopolitan, Saturday Review, TV Guide, Ladies' Home Journal, The New Yorker, Esquire, Argosy,* and the little literary magazines.

Author of four novels, five non-fiction books, several dozen short stories, and hundreds of articles, he hails from Lancaster, Pa., whose West End Junior High School paper published his first writing. He then edited the senior high magazine. His first professional journalism was a weekly column for a Lancaster throwaway newspaper. Next he got a job on the regular Sunday paper in town and continued newspaper work while in school or on vacations, covering various beats.

As time went on, Gehman did a variety of writing in New York City: publicity, radio commercials and scripts, booklets, short stories, articles and humor. Finally he turned to full-time free lancing. In his book, *How To Write and Sell Magazine Articles,* he advises would-be writers to: (1) read, (2) get some sort of education, (3) waste time (by which he means gain experience of all kinds), (4) practice, (5) develop a point of view, and (6) be disciplined.

The stories that most free lancers tell about their careers are not, however, always as pleasant as these. There was, for instance, the anonymous contributor to *World's Press News* who read one day that a hard working free lancer can make from eighty to one hundred pounds a month (then about $350 to $450).

"Some free lances may *earn* the gratifying incomes . . . but they are more than ordinarily fortunate if they *receive* them," he remarked cynically. He explained that he had been free lancing for twenty years; during the second decade writing was his sole occupation. Contributor to more than a hundred different publications, he also was the anonymous author of a best-selling book to which he had sold the copyright because of a pressing need for money. He wrote under six pen names, turning out novels as well as scientific treatises.

"Even so," he said, "I am constantly in financial difficulties, not through extravagance; but simply because money does not come in sufficiently regular amounts to permit of my getting, and keeping, straight."

A New York free lancer, using the assumed name of M. Scott Kenyon, has described what happened when he gave up a $125-a-week job to free lance. For three years before relinquishing his regular check he had had fiction published regularly in magazines, receiving as much as a thousand dollars for a story. Starting with savings of $1,200, he and his wife thought he could sell enough stories to provide a three hundred dollar a month income.

"It sounded like a good plan, but several factors kept it from working out." These factors were strong competition, changing editorial needs, and the effect of being entirely independent on making writing pay. Stories of a type once easily sold began to come back; formulas were changing. Kenyon then borrowed money and set out to write only to make money. Because he was not sincerely interested in writing, the manuscripts were inferior and rejected.

When the first year of free lancing was over and Kenyon had earned almost nothing, he took to hack work. He wrote book reviews, which he called "the worst paying occupation on earth." Four or five months elapsed before the reviews were printed; he received $12.50 for a five-hundred-word criticism. He was paid six dollars for one that took four days to prepare. Ghost-writing was more than he could stomach because it required him to espouse views he did not honestly hold. Finally he turned to teaching, ironically being hired to instruct others in what he had failed at: writing. "Today," he concludes, "I am still free lancing, and I am still in debt."[1]

### As a sideline

The ambitious free lancer should consider his work as a sideline unless he is willing to risk undergoing the experiences of innumerable M. Scott Kenyons. It must remain an extracurricular activity at least while he devotes years to becoming expert in a specialized area of human knowledge. Even after gaining a reputation he will find it necessary to retain permanent connections with institutions in his special field to provide a backing for his work. Most writers depend upon their main occupation not only for their major income but also as a source of facts and ideas. Free lancers cannot function in a vacuum; they must expose themselves to impressions and experiences. Everything they see and do has possibilities for copy.

One day as a writer was riding on an elevated train in Chicago he noticed a young man across from him reading a book, no ordinary book, but a dictionary. The lad was mouthing the words silently and reading down the columns slowly but steadily. The writer moved to sit beside him and watch more closely, observing that the reader was in the middle of the A's. Interested, but thinking little further about it, he left the train at a Loop station.

Later that morning he passed a tobacco store window in which was a stack of dictionaries and encyclopedias at 49 cents, 69 cents, and 89 cents. Not long after, as he paid his bill in a drugstore, he noticed ink bottles to which small dictionaries were attached as premiums. Each incident remained separate until, on the trip home, he glimpsed on a picture house marquee the announcement in electric lights of a volume of an encyclopedia obtainable by exchange for a dime and a coupon being printed in Chicago newspapers.

After further observations, thinking, and speculation on the possibilities in all this ready access to words and facts, this free lancer prepared an article called "The Menace of Words," and sold it to *Coronet*.

If a writer can discover ideas so casually as this from ordinary experiences, he surely can find many from his regular work. Ability to write about one's occupation or special area of expertness explains the same by-lines signed to different articles or stories in given fields on similar themes. For some years Howard Whitman and Paul DeKruif were depended upon for sound articles on medicine, health, or related subjects. Robert L. Heilbroner and John Kenneth Galbraith treat economics, finance, and public affairs; Morton Hunt is

---

[1] M. Scott Kenyon, "Free-Lance Writing Is Risky," *Tomorrow*, January, 1949, p. 20.

© 1966 by Chicago Tribune-N.Y. News Synd., Inc. 9-29
® World Rights Reserved

"She doesn't believe you're a writer...go ahead, Sheldon... show her your rejection slip!..."

looked to for biography; Martin Marty for pieces dealing with religion; Alton L. Blakeslee and Walter Sullivan for articles about science; Ken W. Purdy for motoring and auto pieces; and Erma Bombeck and Art Buchwald for humorous essays on their own experiences.

## Setting up in business

Whether the magazine free lancer practices full time or only part time, he must be set up to function methodically. Free lancing is risky enough without being further complicated by careless handling of manuscripts, inadequate records, and faulty source materials.

Because most free lancing is done after hours, we shall examine the working plan of a writer who makes most of his living other ways, a typical instance. Fred Welch has a full-time job as writer and editor for a publication issued by a major industry. This work keeps him busy daytimes writing or rewriting news copy, preparing headlines, verifying statements, obtaining approval from the top brass, reading proofs, pasting dummies, and following similar routines.

Some evenings, over weekends, and on holidays, when he is neither too lazy nor too tired, he writes articles for business and other specialized magazines. Before writing most of his longer pieces, he completes the arrangement with an editor; he gambles on the shorter ones.

Two typewriters (one a portable), a file cabinet, manila folders, four or five small file boxes, several box files, hundreds of 3 x 5 white file cards, high quality stationery by the ream, packs of carbon paper and second sheets, supplies of several sizes of envelopes, extra typewriter ribbons, and two cameras with such auxiliary equipment as a tripod constitute his main working tools.

One manila folder is labeled "Ideas." Into it are dropped slips of notepaper, discarded envelopes, and old letters on which he has scribbled possibilities for articles he has thought of at the office, en route to the building where he works, or while munching lunch. He has found it wise to capture ideas in words before they escape; they can disappear as fast as ice cream melts on a hot day.

A certain idea, let us say, stays with him. He has long been interested in bells. His own work has some relationship to them, but he has read their history and from here and there has a small accumulation of materials on them. He searches out the expert on bells in the community, interviews him, taking pictures of that man's private collection, and visits a museum to study its holdings. He also writes to the firms that make various types. He asks the editors of their company magazines for pictures, explaining his hope to market an article on bells and requesting certain data about their manufacture here and abroad. While waiting for materials to arrive, he examines trade and technical publications for more clues, having been led to them at the library by indexes of such publications.

Facts and photographs gradually accumulate. To them Fred adds his notes, made on labeled file cards, with headings representing various topical breakdowns or subdivisions. He studies this raw material, sorts and arranges it, prepares an outline, and queries one or more editors. To query is to try out the idea on an editor, to see if he is interested. Guided by the suggestions of an editor who responds favorably to the query, he now embarks on his first draft. He then rewrites portions, adds new data, rearranges, and edits carefully. Another draft is produced; the procedure is repeated until he is satisfied or must stop in any case.

He makes a carbon copy of the final draft and puts it, his notes, and other materials in a folder bearing the article title. Off to the interested editor goes the ribbon copy. On a 3 x 5 record card he has entered the title, length, number of pictures, and places to which he might offer it. If the manuscript makes several trips out and back, these are entered. When finally sold or retired, that fact is noted.

If a free lancer of fact materials does not live near a public or some other accessible general library, he needs a collection of reference books. In addition he requires volumes dealing with the specialty upon which he writes. Fred Welch's small reference collection includes:

| | |
|---|---|
| *Webster's Biographical Dictionary* | *Punctuate It Right!* |
| *Webster's New World Dictionary* | *English Grammar Simplified* |
| *University of Chicago Manual of Style* | *Encyclopedia of Concert Music* |
| | *The Columbia Encyclopedia* |
| *Fowler's Modern English Usage* | *The Writer's Market* |
| *Roget's Thesaurus* | *The Writer's Handbook* |
| *Webster's Dictionary of Synonyms* | *The Literary Market Place* |
| *Familiar Quotations* | *The World Almanac* |
| *The Holy Bible (RSV and King James)* | *An Encyclopedia of World History* |
| | *Goode's School Atlas* |
| *Dictionary of American Slang* | *Abbreviations Dictionary* |
| | *Writers and Artists Year Book* |

Into the box letter files and file cabinets go correspondence and folders containing carbon copies and used materials; into the small boxes go cards representing completed work. One holds cards for articles that are "alive," that is, in transit or still worth trying to publish; another, the ones representing articles placed but not yet printed; another, the cards for published articles, showing publication date, volume, and page numbers, for later bibliographical or other use; the fourth, cards for articles retired because outdated, so often rejected that he has lost interest in them, or lost. At all times this free lancer knows the exact status of any given piece of writing.

This system is only one of several in common use. It is adaptable to fiction, poetry, or any other writing form, and is suitable to keeping records on the books one writes as well. A variation is to keep the records in a notebook, a page allotted to each magazine to which the free lancer sells. This type is more practical for one who sells regularly to the same markets than for a writer who has many outlets. Some authors keep classified folders or note cards for their ideas as well as for finished work. Free lancers must beware, however, of becoming so engrossed in their record keeping that they have little time to write.

Fred Welch does a big postal business. When he queries an editor he sends a stamped, addressed envelope to expedite the answer. When he finally mails a script and its accompanying photographs, drawings, or other illustrations, he includes an envelope slightly smaller than the cover, also stamped and self-addressed. The material does not weigh so much on the return (if there is one, as usually there is) since there is then only one envelope. Fred always notes the mailing cost on his record card, so that if the material is shipped out again he need not reweigh it or trot to the post office each time. Since all materials must be sent first class both directions, with some exceptions that can go under the educational materials rate, the postage item mounts quickly and is to be considered in making out his income tax reports.

Even after a manuscript is placed, Fred has business with the post office. He may receive proofs; these must be read and returned. Although the magazine company will send him at least one copy of the issue carrying his work, he usually asks for extras, paying for them when necessary, so as to be able to show them to future journalistic employers, to reprint, or to use as book chapters. Fred, being a conscientious writer, likes to check the printed article against his carbon copy, to see what changes were made by the magazine editor. On the printed version he circles or underscores changed or added words, and learns about editors and editing from the process.

Fred Welch has the practice of keeping various denominations of postage stamps on hand, since the post office is not near. He also has acquired a set of rubber stamps which absorb some of the routine motions. One carries his name and address, another the words *First Class* and another *Please Do Not Bend or Fold,* the latter needed to protect his pictures even when sent between pieces of cardboard. Gummed tape is on hand for reinforcing envelopes.

### Sources of ideas

Where does a free lancer find ideas? We have seen how some are born. But not everyone would have noticed the youth reading a dictionary or the widespread sale of word books of different types. Lawrence Martin, seeing one of the curbstone mailboxes set so a motorist could mail letters without leaving his car, used it as a springboard for an article about the ways in which Americans live in their automobiles and the social effects of such motorized life. An unobservant and thoughtless person might have taken the situation for granted and overlooked the possibilities.

One of the textbooks for free lancers tells the story of Jack Robinson, a mythical character, who notices the peculiar architecture of a house he is passing. He inquires, obtains details about the origin and virtues of the house, and sells an article about it to a shelter magazine. But the authors of the text do not explain that Jack was able to detect the peculiarity because he is a night-school student of architecture. Fred Welch, who cannot tell Georgian from Byzantine, would pass by this article idea, but he is something of an expert on philately and can smell out an article while looking at an old stamp collection. If Jack Robinson is not up on stamps, he must concede this subject to Fred Welch.

Ideas for articles, stories, and other types of magazine copy come from events heard about, documents, letters, and already published book and periodical materials, and if used always give credit. Fred Welch, for example, when his accumulated ideas do not strike fire in him, leafs through one of his market guides for writers and rereads what certain magazines seek. In the light of their demands, some recent experience may serve as the nub of an article. Human experiences, after all, come first as a source of ideas, for they are more likely to be original and to be written of with feeling and conviction.

Thus ideas may come from anywhere. Subjects are to be found on all sides. The limitations that exist are with the writer. The quicker his mind, the more alert and observant he is, the more capable of making associations and seeking relationships; the more cold knowledge he possesses, the more likely he is to generate ideas for stories and articles. Professional free lancers seldom complain about lacking ideas; they groan because they do not have enough time and energy to convert all their ideas into copy, to travel, to revise and revise and revise the many manuscripts they could turn out.

### Sources of information

His idea being clear (and writing it out helps to clarify it), where does the writer obtain his background information? Here his kinship with the newspaper or magazine reporter is obvious; he uses many of the same sources. He turns to government offices, from village to international. He may appeal to any of countless organizations: chambers of commerce, educational societies, social clubs, fraternal societies, luncheon clubs, alumni associations, and hosts of conferences and conventions. Publications other than those for which he writes are vital sources. So are libraries, syndicates, museums. All the knowledge gathered by organized society is accessible to the free lancer and is essential for either fiction or non-fiction.

If he knows his own and nearby communities, the free lancer does not lack sources of information. What cannot be obtained at firsthand may be obtained by mail or telephone. Publicity releases, surveys, photographs, and other prepared material are his for the asking. He needs to know what he wants and where to find it, no small order in the complex society which is the United States. But there are directories and guidebooks aplenty, even reference books about reference books, such as Winchell's *Guide to Reference Books* and Shore's *Basic Reference Books*. As the free lancer works into his specialty, he builds into his mind and his files his most often used sources of information and taps them as necessary.

### Marketing his work

His idea having been developed into an article or fictional work, the free lancer must know where to send his material. The professional does little writing before he knows the probable disposition

of his finished manuscript. He has studied the markets and sounded
out editors, especially if he writes factual material.

Big-time free lancers usually are presented by authors' representatives, also known as literary agents. Most writers do their own
marketing until fairly well established and regularly productive.
Only a writer who can command high prices and turns out a substantial volume of copy can earn the aid of a representative. An exception is the beginner who engages a combination critic-agent to
coach him and market his work at the same time. Ordinary free
lancers, who write only in spare time, prefer to market their writings
themselves. If so, they are most effective when they read regularly
the magazines to which they seek entrance, equip themselves with
market lists, and consult writers' magazines for changes in publication
addresses, personnel, and needs.

Once a free lancer is fully professional and sells frequently, agents
are eager to handle his work. Magazine fiction writers have more
need of aid than do writers of non-fiction. Subsidiary rights are more
important to authors of short stories, novelettes, novels, plays, and
other obviously creative material; their copy is more likely to be
reprinted and to be sought for stage, radio, motion pictures, or television. Agents charge a 10 per cent fee. In return they share their
knowledge of specific editorial needs, legal technicalities, and literary
opportunities and work to make the writer's output more lucrative,
inasmuch as they benefit from his success. A representative long
associated with a particular writer becomes virtually a business
manager, close friend, and legal adviser.

From the magazine editor's standpoint, a dependable agent is
almost a staff member. He (often as not women are agents, too)
watches for material that meets the magazine's seasonal requirements.
He introduces promising new writers who will, it is hoped, build a
following for themselves and the magazine at the same time. The
writers on his string are reliable, require a minimum of checking and
rewriting, and can produce copy quickly. Fully half the material used
by large national magazines reaches them via representatives because
the free lancer who does his own marketing generally sends copy that
is technically below par, untimely, or misdirected. Editors find too
often that the ordinary free lancer depends upon intuition instead
of precise knowledge.

### Magazine writing style

*Style* has two meanings in journalism. The first is the manner
or way of writing; the second is the body of rules relating to grammar, capitalization, punctuation, and typography. The second is
considered in Chapter 12.

Because there are scores of books and hundreds of articles on
the general subject of style as a manner of writing, it would serve

no purpose to go over that well-handled subject here. You will find agreeable and sensible treatment of it in the famous writings on style: Sir Arthur Quiller-Couch's book, *On the Art of Writing,* numerous passages in Somerset Maugham's *The Summing Up* and in Vera Brittain's *On Being an Author* (both worth reading in entirety if a writer seeks a career), the sections on style in *Structure and Style,* edited by Gerda Okerlund and Esther Vinson, and the delightful little book, *Elements of Style,* by William Strunk and E. B. White.

"Splendid words properly strung together are the foundations of style," W. A. S. Douglas, a newspaperman, magazine free lancer, and author, once said. The words *splendid* and *properly* should be noted. They explain why most beginners, while they possess some kind of writing style, usually do not display one of any distinction. Few splendid words appear in the clumsy, tortured, misspelled, vague writing typical of classroom papers. The far from splendid words have not been strung together properly. With coaching, new writers learn to assemble the dull words properly but they have a dull effect, nevertheless. As talent and training assert themselves the splendid words begin to become evident.

In the experience of the author of this book, style is related to the personality of a new writer. When novice becomes craftsman he can alter his style. He no longer transfers his personality to paper, unless he desires to do so. Henry F. Pringle, recalling his acquaintance with H. L. Mencken in the early days of *The American Mercury,* said that the editor's manner belied his belligerent style. Certainly one would expect Mencken, as seen through idol-breaking and *schimpfing* writings, to be a martinet if not a Bismarck. Instead, as his friends often reported, he was kindly and meek. His biographers point out, however, that he was not always so; in his youth he was brash and explosive. Experience tempered him if not his style.

An excitable and emotional sophomore is likely to turn in impulsively written copy, full of expletives, exclamations, unproved generalizations, underscored words, and zeal. A non-stop talker, with a storytelling gift, probably submits rambling but amusing articles and stories, with a thread of narrative in fiction and apt use of incidents, in non-fiction, that keep one reading. That quiet young man so full of concern for the fate of the world likely will hand to a teacher or mail to an editor a thoroughly documented and thoroughly drab treatise produced by combining research for a political science course and steady reading of *The Nation* and *The New Republic.*

Style, it has been said, is the man, but this is true only of the novice. If you change the man you change the style perhaps, but not if the man is a competent craftsman who like Max Beerbohm could write in the styles of Wells, Shaw, Galsworthy, Kipling, Chesterton, and a dozen others. Some great writers had varying personalities in one lifetime but their styles remained individualistically the same.

In their writing styles, magazinists differ from other journalists
in but one respect: they are more versatile. The newspaper writer,
unless he is one of the few columnists with free rein, must make
his style conform to the patterns of the newspaper. Consequently, all
accident stories sound more or less alike; a divorce case is written
about much the same way in Providence, Rhode Island, as in Pasadena, California; an obituary is an obituary, whether printed in
Tucson, Arizona, or Utica, New York.

But magazines, even the specialized, are more varied in writing
style than newspapers, and more willing to allow writers some lati-
tude in style. All is by-lined but the news, which alone avoids individual expression. Also, magazine fiction is personal writing and having a place in the general magazine, it projects the author's style
much as does the novel or short story in a book. A periodical that
carries poetry, essays, various types of articles, columns, editorials,
and departments, all signed by their authors, has none of the newspaper's anonymity. So great is the variety that it is difficult to single
out any particular writing style as typical of the magazine.

In general, however, the free lancer, whatever type of material he
chooses to prepare, may assume that his readers possess a larger
vocabulary than newspaper readers (within the limits of the type of
magazine he has in mind), that they are more sensitive to refinements
of writing and will appreciate, for example, use of striking phrases
and careful avoidance of the cliché. Magazines have learned through
readership studies that the educational level of their readers is
mounting, that increasing numbers of them have high school and
college educations, and that a better response to complex words and
ideas can be presumed than newspapers or radio and television stations could count upon.

# Chapter 10

---

# Fiction in magazines

T HERE is a knock on the door.

"Come in."

The door is opened slowly. There stands a young woman who might just have come off the entertainment circuit in Denmark, Finland, or Sweden. She is a real yellow blonde and has light blue eyes, and she is dressed for skiing.

"I'm Elsa Tullisaari," she says. "I'm one of your advisees. Can I talk to you about my program? I know these aren't your office hours, but . . . "

The instructor resists being pedantic and saying that she *can* but that it is more a matter of *may*.

Having only recently visited Scandinavia the adviser is interested in knowing if this student might be from that part of the world. Surely, she looks it. She's no Greta Garbo or Ingrid Bergman, but with that head of hair and that name she must at least be second generation.

It turns out to be Finland. Yes, second generation. Her parents came over in the thirties, settled in Pennsylvania, and are in the dairy business.

From there on, however, Elsa is like dozens of other college freshmen at universities, be they young men or young women, planning to enter a school of journalism. When you ask them why they are interested in journalism the majority say (most a little bashfully and a few with much self-confidence) that they want to be "creative writers."

"Creative writer?" You ask what Elsa, Bill, Janet, Peg, Jon, or Ron means by that and you get a vague answer. But it boils down to the students wanting, at some indefinite time, to be authors of novels, poems, plays, short stories, and other literary work.

They consider journalism, it turns out, merely a path to success in creative writing. There is little interest in journalism itself. These beginners think of it chiefly as a practical necessity for them to know in a country that does not guarantee a living for more than a few of its novelists, playwrights, and other conventionally creative writers.

"But," one usually asks the Elsas, "how do you know you have ability to be a creative writer? What makes you think you can write?"

Shyly she answers that her high school English teacher told her so, that she got A in all her English courses, that she "loves" to write and to read. Almost always she says she is "interested" and "loves" it.

And of course Elsa plans to major in English. Why not, for she already is making high marks in her English course, although there is not enough writing in it to suit her.

So her freshman program is planned, including an introductory course in journalism, with a lecture weekly and one period devoted to trying a hand at some of the practical aspects, like newswriting, copy editing, copywriting, and script writing. And there's a lot of talking about what journalism is and some of the problems facing publishers.

Then, about halfway through the semester, the dean's office sends along several deficiency notices. One turns out to be for Elsa T. The deficient advisees are called in for interviews.

After discussing the charming styles of Danish furniture and the designs on Finland's chinaware, Elsa's troubles are faced.

"Oh, yes, I'm doing well in English. It's the math. I never should have taken it. And,"—here she hesitates but finally comes out with it—"and the journalism."

She is completely lost in the math course. Too abstract. Can't make head or tail of what the teacher talks about. Perhaps she should just take an F. But what really makes Elsa unhappy, she says, is the journalism. That should be her strong subject. She was so sure she would "love" it.

"And I like Mr. Finch," she insists. "He tries to help us all. But it's . . . well, it's so *different*. We don't write anything *creative*. Just those dull news stories about unimportant meetings and dead people, and all that correcting of other people's mistakes. I'm an artist. Frankly, I didn't come here to learn to write all this dull stuff."

While this excited speech was going on, the instructor looked again at the delinquency report. Under "Other comments" Mr. Finch had written:

"This student cannot spell even simple words correctly. She is not accurate about names and other basic facts. And she obviously isn't studying the text. She has failed to submit some assignments; several others have been late and so also were automatic F. She is pleasant and friendly and I believe wants to be cooperative, but she has little self-discipline; seems not to have learned how to study systematically yet."

The report also shows that Elsa had failed six of the seven current events quizzes. The adviser decided this might be the place to start discussing her work.

"I just can't get interested in the news," she says. "I know I should—my citizenship teacher says the same thing. But I don't seem to be able to."

Does she look at a newspaper every day? No. No papers on her dorm floor.

Does she listen to a radio or watch a tv newscast regularly? No. The set is downstairs; she has no radio; some of the other girls do but they listen to music. The tv set always has some western or soap opera on it. She might get a little transistor radio for Christmas and try to listen to news. But that won't do her any good until next semester.

Does she read one of the newsmagazines or other news periodicals? No, no newsmagazine. Now and then she looks at *Seventeen* and *Mademoiselle*.

Does she suppose that she and her roommate might discuss news every day and try to find a newspaper or radio?

"Joannie listen to news! Heavens no. Joannie is an art major. She has even less interest in news than I do. And she doesn't have to, for *her* courses."

Well, Elsa would try. And she'd get a notebook and outline the textbook chapters. And get her work in on time hereafter. And buy a small dictionary and look up the words that might be wrong—if she can tell if they are. And take fuller notes in class. But as for math—this stumped both the adviser and Elsa. It was left that she would see her math instructor and meantime the adviser would discuss her problem with him, also.

Just as Elsa rose to tighten her big, floppy overshoes the adviser said:

"How's your creative writing coming along?"

"I like my English class," Elsa said somewhat irrelevantly. "Mrs. Bandy's a wonderful teacher. But I wish we'd write more than those little essays."

"But if you want to do creative writing, why aren't you writing poems and short stories on your own?" the adviser asked.

Elsa sat down again and was silent.

"And how about that novel we talked about? Have you started it yet?"

Elsa now looked hurt.

"When would I have time for creative writing? All this mathematics and journalism and religion and civics and English and, and . . . "

"But don't you think that a writer writes no matter what else happens? You said you love it, that it is your life. . . ."

"I do and it is! But I have so much else to do."

It was suggested that she might write a story and enter it in the *Literary Review* contest. This took Elsa off the hook. She brightened at once and said she would try.

A month later, when the deadline was passed, she met her adviser on the campus one afternoon.

"Get your short story in on time for the contest?" he asked, after preliminaries.

"Contest?" she repeated vaguely. "Oh that. No. I had an idea one day but when I tried it out on some of the kids down at the Cinders none of them liked it, so I gave it up." She knew the adviser was disappointed, and quickly added, "Maybe next semester I can try again."

Elsa never tried again. And after awhile she forgot all about "creative writing" and became an education major, because this would give her a sure way to earn her living when she left college. She liked children, too.

What has just been narrated is based on fact and is fictional only in that names have been changed. Elsa T. is a combination of numerous students who said and did more or less what she says and does. The reader may think the intention is to say that most students who want to write fiction and other creative material have no talent and certainly not the slightest idea of the discipline of a writing career. And such a reader would be entirely right.

Few students are realistic, but even more unrealistic are people of any age who long to spend their lives as writers of fiction or non-fiction. At the other extreme from the Elsas are the older men and women, often retired from business or widows or widowers, who hope to make extra money writing what they call stories or perhaps articles about a trip to Japan taken thirty years ago.

To some extent they are better off than Elsa because they do at times have something to say, although it may not be original enough to see print. But they have had experiences and should be able to illuminate some corners of life. They believe, however, that all one needs in writing fiction is to sit before a pad with a pencil and the words will pour forth. Somehow, they believe, these words will fall into proper position. The idea that they need to study the market horrifies them; to some this is crass commerce, to others a land of mystery. Most are defeated by the necessity to study techniques: how to handle dialogue, how to describe characters, how to provide motivation for the action, and the many other problems that confront the fiction writer.

All this is not an attempt to discourage writers of magazine fiction. It is in the interest of giving the aspiring author a realistic point of view. Now and then one finds an Elsa T. who has talent, who works almost like a slave to perfect her writing, who writes and writes and writes, sends out her poems and stories and keeps on sending them out, takes courses, does much intelligent study of writing on her own, lives richly in life and thinks about it, and has something to say. And, once in a while at a writers' conference, one comes upon a mature person who similarly is able and willing to devote the many hours needed to develop himself into a writer of fiction, who like the successful Elsas, after years of practicing and trying and failing and then having a little success, develops a style and a technique all his or her own and above all has something in his heart and has learned to say it with beauty and originality.

And then there are the in-betweeners who flood magazine offices with copy. These are the would-be writers of any age between high school and retirement who long for the television appearances, the authors' teas, and the best-seller listings. Most of them, also, are untalented and lazy, but now and then a hard worker strides forth and is able to produce dependably.

For all but the most gifted writers, writing is grinding, hard work requiring great self-discipline. Editors of magazines who receive free-lance copy complain that many would-be writers have not the slightest idea of what is involved. The editors find copy messy and inaccurate, stories completely unsuited to their type of magazine, failure of the writer to study the publication's content before sending it a manuscript, and amateurish and unprofessional stories. Such complaints explain why so little of the free lance material sent to magazines is used.

The newcomer to fiction writing also must overcome the idea that he can write his stories by staying home. For a time this practice may work, if he writes only about his own experiences and environment. But there comes a day when this source runs dry and the material becomes repetitious. The fully creative writer, if we must use this artificial distinction, is not independent of reality. If a story is historical, the writer must put in considerable time checking on how his characters might have dressed in those days, what they ate, how they spoke, what tools they used, and what they hung on their walls. This aspect of fiction writing is one of the most taxing and tiring, requiring hours in libraries, burrowing among old letters in historical societies, and talking to old timers who lived in the days described, if the period is recent enough.

## *Fiction is not journalism*

Even though printed between magazine covers, fiction is not journalism. Writers of it use the research methods of the journalist, but what they produce is only remotely connected with journalism.

Journalism is concerned with facts, truth, what really happened. Sometimes the action in a short story or novel is based on reality, but it need not be, and details usually are invented. The fiction writer mixes a product of the imagination with facts and the result is untrustworthy as history. Journalism, which commonly is considered a record of contemporary history, cannot afford to be confused with unreality. Fiction is a fabrication. Journalism never should be.

Ordinarily the reader who sees the word *fiction* thinks of a story, a tale of some sort. Depending upon his experience, he may have in mind science fiction, a mystery story in a drugstore rental rack, or a classic catching dust in a bookcase at home.

But fiction is more than a tale. According to Webster's *Dictionary of Synonyms,* which makes a careful distinction between *fiction, figment, fabrication,* and *fable,* it "so strongly implies the use of the imagination that it serves as the class name for all prose or poetic writings which deal with imagined characters and situations (or with actual characters or situations with less concern for the historicity of the details than for the telling of an interesting, coherent story)."

"All prose or poetic writings" include not only the short story or novel but also verse, anecdotes, plays, yarns, tales, and anything that qualifies as a created piece of writing. Because the short story and novel appear in modern magazines, they are little dealt with in this chapter. Less than one-fourth the editorial content of many general magazines is fictional, consisting of short stories of various length, portions of a continued story, a few short poems, and a modicum of other fiction. A few specialized periodicals of the theatre and of literature reproduce the texts of plays, motion picture scenarios, or radio and television scripts. Most mass circulation magazines never print plays; that was why the *Saturday Evening Post's* publication of Arthur Miller's "After the Fall" in 1964 was so unusual. It is legitimate, as a reflection of established practice, to use *fiction* as a designation of the invented materials in modern magazines.

## *Fiction's changing place*

Although its place is smaller than before, fiction still is prominent in today's magazines. Its original domination of them was no accident but the result of public demand. Early in American journalistic history both newspapers and magazines considered fiction of all types as important as news stories and editorials. As newspapers surrendered the bulk of fiction to magazines and books, finding it more profitable to emphasize news and opinion-forming functions, the public turned expectantly to the periodical for work of new writers and new work of established authors. A century ago it was usual to find the best work of leading fiction writers in the popular periodicals (see Chapter 2). Before the advent of the popular mass magazine late in the nineteenth century the magazine publisher rivaled the book publisher in presenting the finest literature. William Dean Howells, novelist, editor of the *Atlantic,* and leading literary figure of the latter half of that century, once said that "In belles-lettres at least most of the best literature now sees the light in the magazines and most of the second best appears in book form."

Although it is still true that much of the best fiction appears first in the magazines, it must be noted that the quantity is less than ever before. Until the years immediately following World War II, serious, literary fiction was pushed out of the popular general periodicals into the quality and literary periodicals. *Harper's* and the *Atlantic,* once the popular general magazines of the country, were the only two survivors of a group that had long prided itself on being hospitable to high quality fiction as well as to intelligent writing on public affairs. *The Century, The Forum, Scribner's,* and *The American Mercury* (under Mencken), all influential in periodical fiction publication, merged, disappeared, or changed their emphasis.

Replacing the literary or artistic story and novel in the general American magazine for a time was the commercial story, published to give readers momentary amusement or escape into a dreamland in contrast with everyday activities. Only the most hard minded were able to dwell on tales of disappointment and human misery brought about by economic maladjustment and war. The level of public education had not risen to the point where magazine readers sought solution of their problems through fiction.

The motion picture helped perpetuate the idea that the tale is a means of escape from reality and no more. Later, television took over the role. In view of these trends, writers found it more profitable to write stories for the mass audience than for the limited group, by now represented largely in the little literary magazines.

During the inter-war years the literary writer found only the little magazines and a few surviving quality periodicals interested in what he had to say and his particular way of saying it. Experimental trends in fiction made the severance from the mass magazines all the more certain. Gertrude Stein, James Joyce, Henry Miller, Anais Nin, and other writers of their school would not have been understood by readers of *Good Housekeeping* or the *Saturday Evening Post* even if their editors had been willing to publish their work. The writing of scores of new authors in the period between wars was not always acceptable even to their friends: when not puzzlingly non-communicative their stories were endless reminiscences of childhood impressions. Aspiring writers of magazine fiction had themselves to blame as well as undeveloped public taste if the popular, commercial story held sway.

After World War II, greater participation by the United States in world affairs, increase in public education, and the growing realization that in an atomic and space age life is a serious business (not to be escaped before television sets, in movie palaces, and in sports arenas) restored the literary story to the popular magazine, if not to the prominent place of the previous century. Writers of psychological fiction, character stories, and situation novels were occasionally welcomed. Witness the incident story of *The New Yorker, Harper's Bazaar, Town and Country, Cosmopolitan, Esquire,* and *Mademoiselle,* and, now and then, even of the mass circulation women's service magazines. Some continued to publish escape fiction, but mixed with it were artistic stories, often portraying life far different from that of the readers.

The short story somewhat regained its place, but the serial story became less popular because the twentieth century is one of speed. Readers are too impatient to wait a month for the next installment; they have too much else to distract them. Some writers object to forcing their stories into measured portions with suspense endings to tease readers on for the sake of circulation. Short tales are a congenial part of magazine editorial content since unlike the newspaper, but like a book, the magazine can be saved for occasional picking up. Also, the story is not as suitable, collected with others, as book content as is the novel. Only collections of tales by standard authors are commercially successful. In the popular magazine the story for decades has been concerned with topical and comparatively transient events, ideas, and experiences. It is more quickly dated and outmoded than the novel, which uses a broader canvas and deeper background.

### Fiction in specialized magazines

The novel and the short story, by the third quarter of the century, had regained their prominence in general magazines, with some change in quality, obviously downward. In any substantial degree, however, fiction had not yet found its way into specialized periodicals with two exceptions: the religious and the education magazines.

Occasionally a business periodical, an educational magazine, or some other devoted to a special field has published a piece of fiction. Its plot has had to do with the business or trade; its characters have been shoe retailers, merchant princes, or teachers, as the case demanded. But as fiction such copy has received—and usually merited—no serious attention. Readers of specialized magazines do not look to them for escape material; the more devoted to his occupation the businessman, the more engrossed in his work the chemist, the less patience either has with the trivia he considers fiction to be. He may read a fantastic tale or a who-done-it to rest his mind, but the magazine or book that contained it he tosses aside as of no more importance than the rind of the melon he ate for breakfast. Editors of specialized magazines that do not customarily use fiction buy it now and then as a means of varying content, but few experts in technical fields are competent to provide acceptable fiction copy (note the efforts, for instance, of Bertrand Russell); and fiction writers are not interested in either the appropriate subjects or the relatively low rates available from this market.

For a century and a half fiction in the religious periodical has been an exception, although much of the time of dubious quality. In the early days after the Revolution the religious magazine was on a par with the general publication. It was the magazine of ideas and the purveyor of two types of literature: poetry and essays (see Chapter 20).

Poetry, for example, was the principal feature of the *Episcopal Watchman,* issued in the 1820's and 1830's. Book reviews were printed in most religious journals. The religious storytelling, largely for children, was highly moralistic. Tassin, examining the religious magazines of the eighteenth and nineteenth centuries, found that the general magazines of the early period were "as much religious as literary." When the religious magazine later began to emerge "it was for a long time as much literary as religious," as he put. it.[1]

A review of the religious magazine's content since the Civil War, to be obtained from Mott's detailed histories and examination of the periodicals' files, reveals that essays, poems, book reviews, short stories, and serial stories became regular fare. The moralistic tone of the stories persisted but became more subtle by the middle years of this century. Essays, poetry, and criticism remained in most of the religious journals, but stories were confined to two types: the general religious periodical and the magazine for children and young people.

The non-church-published educational magazine for primary school teachers carries much fiction which such educators may use in the classroom. Thus the magazines for children themselves are by no means the only outlet for stories, poems, and plays, as the content of *The Instructor* and the *Grade Teacher* shows.

### Fiction in the magazine routine

Most poetry that reaches magazines comes from free lancers, although a staff member occasionally contributes it to his own publication. Short stories and other tales come "over the transom" and on order. Editors of adventure, science fiction, romance, and crime story

---

[1] Algernon Tassin, *The Magazine in America* (New York: Dodd, Mead & Co., 1916), p. 257.

magazines are able to order much of their copy, since it is produced in machine-like fashion. The more literary or artistic a periodical, the more dependent it is upon the creative urges of the writer.

The editorial office records the manuscript when it is received, sends it on the rounds of the readers or to one specializing in judging fiction, rejects or accepts it, and generally processes it in the manner of all copy. There are a few differences. Non-fiction may be accompanied by photographs or consist of them almost entirely. They require retouching, cropping, integration with the typescript, and other handling. Because of these photographs, the article may be accepted or rejected; in any case if accepted the script is dummied differently than a short story. Since fiction, except in confession and fan magazines, is illustrated by drawings and paintings rather than photos, an illustrator must be engaged or assigned to this work. The layout differs from that of the article, being highly individualized; in the largest magazines text often is subordinated to paintings accompanying it.

Fiction writers are paid more than article writers. Higher rates go to the fictioneers because their bigger and more regular followings are important to circulation. Better pay prevents their being bought away by other publishers. Writers with devoted readers command for many years rates matched only by a few celebrated article writers, and in most instances the latter are not professional authors so much as widely known statesmen or military leaders. The literary work and rewards earned in his day by Winston Churchill are an example. *McCall's* pays $2,500 for a first short story and $3,000 for the second. a novelette in *Redbook* brings $7,500. Even the best standard rate for an article is half these sums.

*Chapter 11*

---

# Writing articles
# and other non-fiction

An idea that authors of articles and other non-fiction resent is that they are not creative writers.

Often people who daydream about literary careers assume that writing the article, the criticism, the editorial, and the essay is not creative work. They are unaware of the creative process that occurs when a journalist is seized with an idea for an article, let us say one so practical as a piece on a type of modern ship, the hydrofoil. The writer starts with nothing more than the nugget of an idea: that an attractive and useful article might be composed around the hydrofoil, telling how it differs from other vessels, how it operates, what a trip on it is like, and what such transportation means for the future of travel by water.

Is it not creative, says the article writer, to assemble the facts, experience the sensations of being on a hydrofoil and put the reactions down in words, do research in nautical history, and mold the whole into a coherent, logical, and orderly piece of writing? How is this procedure any less creative, he asks, than molding a figure from clay? Where there was shapelessness there now is shape; where there were just scattered, unrelated facts and ideas there now is form.

In one sense, the fact writer is more creative than the fiction writer, for he must work within the limits of reality. If relationships between the parts of what he is using in his construction are not there he must find them without inventing them, as the story writer may do without the slightest adverse criticism.

Fred Welch, the free-lance writer we met in another chapter, one day sat in a friend's home listening to phonograph records. His friend handed him the newest edition of an encyclopedia of phonograph recordings. As Fred leafed through it he noted a paragraph, beneath a listing of "The Bee," which stated that this composition usually is attributed erroneously to Franz Peter Schubert, whereas it actually was written by another Franz Schubert, of Dresden, years after the more famous musician died.

At the time this isolated fact meant little to the writer. It was a curiosity in a collection of historical comments about music. But a few weeks later at an art cinema theater he saw a movie short about Franz Peter Schubert in which the composer is shown going to the piano to play "The Bee," which according to the encyclopedia had not yet been composed.

This incident set Fred to wondering what other such musical confusions there might be. He began scouring Grove's *Dictionary of Music and Musicians,* Hughes, Taylor, and Kerr's *Music Lovers' Encyclopedia,* the biographies of various musicians, especially the multitudinous Bachs, and his own file of accounts of hoaxes and fakes in case any dealt with the musical world. He found other reports, one of which served neatly as a news peg: violinist Fritz Kreisler's admission that he wrote much of the music he played in the early days of his career but credited it to minor French composers, out of a proper modesty. Interviews with musicians in the community, including the dean of the school of music at a nearby university, provided other data. All this material, when put together with a theme, made an acceptable article for *The Etude.* Fred knew nothing about music technically. He could neither read it nor play an instrument; he was an appreciator. But he designed the article from the grain of an idea and as a result had a sense of creative achievement.

Perhaps the term, *non-fiction,* is somewhat to blame for the notion that fact writing is not creative writing. The word is subject to much misunderstanding. Newcomers to journalism sometimes speak of *non-fiction articles,* or of *fiction articles,* or *non-fiction stories. Fiction,* as it is used here, refers to imagined, invented, created stories, that is, narratives published in a magazine. *Non-fiction* (meaning not fiction) is real, neither imagined nor invented, and may or may not be presented in narrative form. An article is not fiction. It is not invented or imagined; it is rooted in fact. To use *non-fiction article* is redundant; if it is an article it automatically is non-fiction. Its use assumes that there are *fiction articles,* a contradiction, although it is true that there are *fictionized* articles. These are presentations of facts that include also imagined scenes and characters to provide the illusion of fiction and greater readability. *Non-fiction stories* also is confusing because *story* implies an imagined account, a tale, a yarn. Newspaper people talk about news stories, a dubious term, since many readers think a story is fabricated, as literally it is.

All magazine non-fiction, with the exception of games and puzzles, carries the quality of factualness.

## Defining the article

In the family of journalistic writing the article is most like the literary form known as the essay. But it is not an essay, usually being less personal and less limited in scope. It is a written composition of variable length intended to convey ideas and facts for the purpose of convincing, instructing, or entertaining.

Akin to the magazine article is the newspaper feature, which is more like it than is the essay. Features customarily appear in newspapers; articles in magazines. Inasmuch as the Sunday supplements —*This Week,* the *New York Times Magazine,* and the scores issued for local consumption only, are examples—and the special pages of both weekly and daily newspapers increasingly print both articles and features, the distinction between them by place of publication has little reality.

More fixed are differences in length, form, and content. The newspaper feature generally is short, a few hundred words at most. The type called *human interest* runs but a few paragraphs; only in exceptional instances does the interview or biographical feature exceed more than two thousand words. The feature borrows much in tone from the news account, sometimes beginning with the summary lead or conveying the essence of the news, admittedly minor, in the first few paragraphs. Patterns, popular in all newspaper writing because they permit speedy production, give features similarity in form. Finally, the feature is more or less timely, generally stemming from a news event not long past; it emphasizes facts rather than opinion; little stress is placed on its authorship.

The magazine article is the opposite of the newspaper feature: whereas it varies in length it generally runs from one thousand to about six thousand and usually hovers around two thousand words; it may be constructed in any one of many different fashions, not being bound by any rigid pattern; it may be seasonal or timeless; because it ordinarily is signed by its writer it tends to be more personal; opinion may be expressed freely in it, although it must be documented.

Certain of these differences are pointed up by comparison of the following excerpts from a newspaper feature and a magazine article:

ATLANTA, Aug. 18 (UPI)—Delta Air Lines flight 743 was en route from Chicago to Atlanta. The stewardess informed the pilot a woman passenger was ill with strong symptoms of an appendicitis attack. The pilot sent an immediate radio request to Atlanta and a doctor met the flight at the airport.

After a twenty-three-minute delay because of the emergency, the flight took off again for Miami and the physician filed his report. The woman's girdle was too tight.[1]

### By Julie McDonald

"Billy is having a lot of trouble with schoolwork, but his class is so big the teacher just can't find time to give him the help he needs!"

The speaker is a pretty young mother with a worried expression, and her problem is all too common in this day of crowded schools and overworked teachers. Even children who do well in school could do better if space and teachers could be multiplied, but it takes time to build bigger schools and train more teachers.

All over the country, parents and educators, looking for a stopgap solution to this problem, are investigating the use of teacher aides to relieve educators of time-consuming "housekeeping" chores and allow them to concentrate on teaching.

Bay City, Mich., was the first to try such a plan. A grant from the Ford Foundation financed a job analysis and time study of teachers' routines which showed that non-teaching duties consumed 21 to 69 percent of their time.

Instead of instructing children, they were watering plants, cleaning blackboards and policing playgrounds. On the strength of these findings, nonprofessional aides were hired to perform such tasks. . . .[2]

The newspaper feature, it will be noted, begins with specific facts: the airline's name, the route, even the flight number. The tone is matter of fact, so that the surprise ending can be all the more effective.

The magazine article, which receives a by-line, begins with a quotation and emphasizes a general situation. The first three paragraphs of the original are timeless; within limits set by unchanging conditions, they could have been printed a decade earlier or they may be applicable a decade hence. Not until the fourth paragraph does the article become specific; then it gives facts about a certain school in a particular locality and from there relates what is happening in several other parts of the nation. The time element is broad; it is in terms of a year.

### Types of articles

While not absolutely standardized, article types are simple in classification. The commonest are biographical, personal experience, autobiographical, historical, adventure, argumentative, explanatory, how-to-do-it, and discussion. These often overlap or are known by names different than the ones used here. Magazine editors do not

---

[1] "Air Liner Emergency," United Press International, Aug. 18, 1959 as published in the New York *Herald Tribune*.

[2] Julie McDonald, "Help For Our Teachers," *Family Weekly*, Sept. 20, 1959.

demand that writers adhere to these classifications; the distinctions sometimes are ignored. But they provide a general working system by which magazine journalists recognize the construction and purpose of an article. Gathering and filing of material is facilitated and article possibilities are suggested.

Bird, in his book, uses a classification terminology that further clarifies types: personality sketches, first person narratives, third person narratives, confessions, interviews, essays and argumentatives, processes, and collectives. [3] Only the last two may need further explanation. The process article corresponds to the more common how-to-do-it; collectives are articles made up of related examples, such as one that brings together seasonal menus or hints to homemakers. In his book, Schoenfeld adds a few new categories: research, point of view, and news features. [4] The first is the article based on the findings of study and investigation, the second is the discussion, argumentative, or opinion article, and the last the orthodox little newspaper feature, such as the airline story reprinted here.

The free use in non-fiction of such fiction devices as invented conversation, imagined characters, and dramatic presentation is reflected in the narrative article. The core is fact, but the reader is to be warned that scenes and incidents are fabricated for the sake of readability. Even invented scenes and incidents are likely to be typical and probable; at least this in the allegation. This type is not for the beginning article writers who, likely to be shy on facts in any case, should avoid temptation to let imagination supply what leg work or research should produce.

### Articles in the magazines

Whatever the type, virtually all magazines use articles, for the periodical publishing fiction only is rare. Almost no publication offers only one type of content, by form. Magazines of poetry sandwich in critical articles on trends in the world of verse or book reviews, some of which are so extended they actually are articles. Even confession and romantic story magazines, generally considered solid-packed with fiction, carry a few short factual pieces, usually relating to some adventure in the same mood as the fictional content. Most consumer magazines are dominated by articles or other non-fiction, such as editorials and essays. Cooking, charm, and fashion departments weigh the balance in favor of the article because their content is composed of articles with departmental headings.

Magazines depend upon the article form to attract readers unin-

---

[3] George L. Bird, *Article Writing and Marketing* (New York: Rinehart, 1956), p. 239.

[4] Clarence A. Schoenfeld, *Effective Feature Writing* (New York: Harper & Brothers, 1960), pp. 59–63.

terested in fiction, the men or women who turn to periodical literature for understanding of current events, or for information about
parts of the world or occupations from which they are remote. The
article writer who writes for a March or April issue about a new way
to solve income tax problems or can suggest for an April or May
number simple and original gardening shortcuts endears himself to
editors. The writer well informed on international affairs is welcomed
by magazines whose readers are concerned about world events; he
may contribute continously for many years, as study of contents pages
reveals.

Editors obtain articles from strange or unknown free lancers, by
assigning topics to their own staffers, through authors' representatives,
from government or private agencies interested in presenting their
stories, and from non-professional experts in some area of knowledge.
Not all these writers have the same facility in article writing. Staff
writers, experienced free lancers, and clients of recognized literary
agencies are likely to produce acceptable copy needing relatively little
revision. Others usually are more interested in content than in form,
but editors are willing to undertake revision for the sake of information they can provide.

### Sources of ideas and subjects

What has been said in general in the preceding chapters about
the free lance writer's sources of ideas and subjects applies equally to
the article writer, be he independent or a staffer. His knowledge, his
powers of observation, his ability to see relationships between facts
and ideas, and his capacity to probe human and documentary storehouses are his primary resources.

Since article writers draw precisely upon reality and must have
extraordinary concern for accuracy, they find books, organizations, reports, official records, and other verifiable sources particularly necessary to their work. Everything experienced article writers do is potential material, although much of it would produce only trivial or
profitless results. The professional learns to conserve his time and
energy for work that advances his purpose, which may be to earn
money, to influence others, or to express himself.

A bromide of the literary world is that there are no bad subjects,
only bad writers. The skill with which magazine staff members rewrite poorly handled but fundamentally useful contributions lends
strength to this generalization. A biographical sketch is received; it
is a dull rehash of a *Who's Who in America* entry. But the man
about whom it is written is in the news. His personality is inherently
attractive. The writer simply has failed to catch his essential character in words. A more competent journalist is put on the article; he
visits the subject's former communities, from the man's associates
gathers stories revealing habits and characteristics, observes man-

nerisms and notes facts about the man's appearance, tastes and preferences in eating, dressing, and reading. The result is a *New Yorker* Profile or a penetrating sketch in *Harper's* or *Fortune*. The first writer did not see his goal, did not study a similar finished article to see what it contained, did not know sources to consult for lacking information. The second writer knew what comprises a successful biographical sketch and lost no time going to the sources.

Walter Pitkin, who made popular the idea that life begins at forty and also taught writing courses at Columbia University for many years, contended successfully that a writer may open an almanac to any page and find an idea or subject. He demonstrated his method in one of his books. Fred Welch, the free lancer whose experiences have been touched upon, once wrote an article about an article of his that was published without payment by an unscrupulous magazine. He sold the account of the experience to one of the writers' magazines and made up some of his loss, at the same time warning other writers. Pitkin made the most out of the commonplace, and Welch out of the exceptional.

A member of an article-writing class one day told the instructor that she had chosen to write a series of three articles about religion. Her plan seemed sensible, although the teacher had no knowledge of her religious background. The first paper was a melange of prejudices and misinformation. Instead of planning it, the student had merely set down the notions she had gathered from a little miscellaneous reading and church attendance restricted to her childhood. When the teacher probed into her life history, he learned that she was a buyer in the floor-coverings department of a large mail-order house. He suggested that she prepare three articles on floor coverings, with one of the shelter magazines in mind as her market.

Aiming at *Better Homes and Gardens,* she wrote, "How To Buy Hard Surface," "How To Buy Wools," and "Styling Your Linoleum," and sent them off to Des Moines. Shortly afterward one of the editors invited her to lunch, discussed the articles with her, suggested minor revisions—and bought all three. Then Ethel Brostrom wrote the instructor:

"Before you read any further, sit down. The impossible has happened. I clicked—with not one, not two but three articles. I might add there is also a possibility of two resales plus three other articles to be written. . . . Thus endeth Chapter 1 in the Horatio Alger series—more will be forthcoming, I hope."

A few years later, after she had become a regular contributor, *Better Homes* invited her to its staff as an assistant editor. She shifted somewhat reluctantly from merchandising to magazine journalism, entering a magazine editorial career that took her eventually to *Mademoiselle* in New York. She soon published her first book, one on home decorating, and several more followed.

No one should derive from this account the idea that writing articles on religion is of less importance than writing them on floor coverings. But the writer had nothing whatsoever to contribute about religion; she wrote out of ignorance. She did know her own field. By considerable study and use of the article-writing techniques she was taught she could have become a writer on religion, no doubt.

In somewhat the same way another novice article writer who knew something about religion but nothing about home decorating, food preparation, or housekeeping was dissuaded from turning out vague and unoriginal scripts dealing with dieting in favor of articles on religious subjects that she could handle effectively because of sincere conviction and firsthand experience and training.

These two persons had about equal ability. Each did better with the other's first choice of type of subject than with her own. Each was a poor writer on a subject about which she knew little; each was a capable writer on a subject she understood.

### Other non-fiction

Virtually all large magazines offer the reader one or more of three departments: letters, humor, and news. Other divisions are characteristic of groups of periodicals. The women's service magazines all set aside a given amount of space monthly for material on fashions, cooking, household equipment, child care, house furnishings, shoppers' service, current events analysis, movies, books, records, music, broadcasting, and theatre. Trade and technical magazines divide portions of their issues into departments pertaining to their special fields. *Editor & Publisher,* which deals with all phases of newspaper work and some related fields, for example, presents regular departments on advertising, circulation, promotion, production, photography, law, and syndicates.

A magazine department is an organized section regularly offering material in a particular field of information. It may occupy a column of type, an entire page, or a group of pages each issue, or at more or less regular intervals. It enables the publisher to gain and hold attention of readers deeply interested in certain areas. Ask any magazine reader why he likes a particular periodical and he is likely to name departments or writers whose work appears in departments from which he gets facts or enjoyment. These attractions may not be sufficient to hold the reader, although they may have more influence with him that he realizes. He may mention policy, general appearance, fiction, or even quality of paper stock as an attraction, but the chances are that he is an amateur gardener and likes the human interest approach of a columnist who mixes a little humor with his gardening advice. Or, if the reader is a woman, she may take special pleasure in learning about new household gadgets, made known through the shopping service of her favorite magazine.

**TABLE 11.1.** *Common Types of Departmental Copy in Four Kinds of Magazines*

| Consumer | Business | Company | Religious |
|---|---|---|---|
| Letters | Letters | . . . . . . . . . . . | Letters |
| Humor | Humor | Humor | Humor |
| Fashions | . . . . . . . . . . . . . . | Fashions | . . . . . . . . . . . . . . |
| Sports | . . . . . . . . . . . . . . | Sports | . . . . . . . . . . . . . . |
| Cooking and foods | . . . . . . . . . . . . . . | Cooking and foods | . . . . . . . . . . . . . . |
| Arts* | Books | . . . . . . . . . . . | Books |
| Child care | . . . . . . . . . . . . . . | . . . . . . . . . . . . . . | . . . . . . . . . . . . . . |
| Foreign correspondence | Foreign correspondence | . . . . . . . . . . . | Foreign correspondence |
| Shoppers' service | . . . . . . . . . . . . . . | . . . . . . . . . . . . . . | . . . . . . . . . . . . . . |
| Contributors | Contributors | . . . . . . . . . . . | Contributors |
| Poetry | . . . . . . . . . . . . . . | . . . . . . . . . . . | Poetry |
| News | News | News | News |
| Furnishings | . . . . . . . . . . . . . . | . . . . . . . . . . . | . . . . . . . . . . . . . . |
| Equipment | Equipment | . . . . . . . . . . . | . . . . . . . . . . . . . . |
| Games and puzzles | . . . . . . . . . . . . . . | Games and puzzles | . . . . . . . . . . . . . . |
| Gardening | . . . . . . . . . . . . . . | . . . . . . . . . . . | . . . . . . . . . . . . . . |
| Decorating | . . . . . . . . . . . . . . | . . . . . . . . . . . | . . . . . . . . . . . . . . |
| . . . . . . . . . . . . . . | Free literature | . . . . . . . . . . . | . . . . . . . . . . . . . . |
| . . . . . . . . . . . . . . | Advertisers' index | . . . . . . . . . . . | . . . . . . . . . . . . . . |
| . . . . . . . . . . . . . . | Looking backward | . . . . . . . . . . . | Looking backward |
| . . . . . . . . . . . . . . | Vital statistics | Vital statistics | Vital statistics |
| . . . . . . . . . . . . . . | Field subjects† | . . . . . . . . . . . | . . . . . . . . . . . . . . |

* Books, films, radio, television, the dance, painting, music, theater, records.
† One on advertising, for instance, may include advertisers, agencies, marketing, etc.

Departments assist the magazine in fulfilling its function as a storehouse. They provide miscellany, short, practical materials that vary the pace from the long story, lengthy article, and smashing, four-color paintings. They also provide a personal touch that the main features lack. In the production of the periodical they permit a measure of flexibility inasmuch as an issue can be expanded or contracted by addition or omission of minor departments or by shortening or lengthening of certain ones, if they consist of independent short units, paragraph comments, or jokes, for instance.

The writer who realizes the place of the department in today's magazines can more readily write for such sections. Superficially, since by-lines appear with most departments, they seem to be the private areas of name writers. But close examination reveals that their authors or editors seek contributions from others, ranging from the satirical pieces in Martin Levin's "Phoenix Nest" in *Saturday Review* to the recipes and verse in Marilyn Brake's "From One Woman to Others" department in *Michigan Farmer*.

### Editorials, fillers, miscellany

While fiction, articles, and departments account for almost all the space in a given magazine issue, some is left for editorials, columns, fillers, cutlines, and other identification material as well as for calendars, games and puzzles, and similar miscellany. These types of content are supplied by both free lancers and staffers.

*Editorials* are short essays, similar to the persuasive opinion or argumentative article except that they are shorter and simpler in construction. Their place in magazines is not as vital as in newspapers, although their long-run effect may be important. Also, the editorial in the consumer magazines has little resemblance, except in form, to that in the business magazine or technical journal. A daily or weekly newspaper editorial or radio-television news commentary is, in the time sense, on a par with the news and in position to offer comment of immediate, short-term interest. But even weekly magazines, because of slowness of production and wider distribution, suffer from a time lag (overcome only by a few newsmagazines at great expense), tend to take the long view, dealing with long range problems or developments in current affairs or with seasonal or human interest topics. Most Americans look to general magazines for entertainment and information rather than guidance in opinion; only a minority reads reviews that concentrate on opinion, as noted in Chapter 17.

In trade and technical periodicals, however, readers expect prompt comment on trends and events in the general field with which the public deals. To meet this expectation some specialized journals include late inserts, in the form of newsletters or departments, or send newsletters between issues.

Magazine editorials conform to the standard editorial pattern in

American journalism: they generally do not exceed one thousand or fifteen hundred words in length, are constructed like essays, seek to make a single point, and ordinarily are anonymous, although magazines more often than newspapers carry the signature of the author, who is likely to be the periodical's editor or publisher.

Columns, once they appear regularly, generally in the same position and using the same amount of space, actually are departments. Their content embraces all the many types of journalistic writing: articles, stories, tabulations, reminiscences, jokes, editorials, interpretation, and humor. For the reader they are journalistic grab-bags. As do newspapers, magazines provide varieties of columns, in hope that their authors will acquire personal followings. Some readers never miss "The Editor's Easy Chair" in *Harper's;* others would not think of skipping John Ciardi's "Manner of Speaking" in *Saturday Review.*

*The New Yorker* and *The Reader's Digest* have made *fillers* famous. In the former they range from clippings so pointed that they need little editorial comment to regular contributions for "Our Own Business Directory," "Dept. of Understatement," "Words of One Syllable Dept." and "What Page of the————D'ya Read?" In the *Digest* they are called "Campus Comedy," "Laughter," "Patter," "Personal Glimpses," and "Toward More Picturesque Speech." Both magazines, and their imitators in this respect, buy such material from free lancers. Because fillers offer would-be contributors of longer material a comparatively easy entrée, they have given some writers their start. Their purpose is to offer the reader a resting place mentally, a bit of relief from the succession of longer pieces, and to provide the editor with short copy of various lengths to fill out a page or section in making up the periodical.

*Cutlines, underlines, captions,* and *overlines* are terms variously and confusingly used. They are the dressing for illustrations. Because they are the work chiefly of editors they are explained fully in Chapter 12.

*Calendars* are records of forthcoming events compiled by the editorial staff from publicity sources and official notices as well as by direct reporting. They appear as dated and chronologically arranged items, headed baldly as "Calendar," "Coming Events," or "What's Going On." In *Time, Holiday, Dance, The New Yorker, Cue,* and several score regional magazines they list what is to be shown within a given period at motion picture and legitimate theatre playhouses and museums, what sports events are scheduled, and a mass of more or less static bodies of information, such as names of hotels, churches, and public buildings. Regional magazines in some instances consist of little more than such data. Specialized magazines serve as important sources of such information. The largest calendar-type magazine is *TV Guide,* since it sells twelve million copies a week.

*Games and puzzles* represent the odds-and-ends type of magazine content. Having been invented, or at least designed out of facts in some instances, they are closer to fiction than fact. More commonly to be found in magazines for children and youth, they also have a place in magazines for more sophisticated readers: crossword puzzles in *The Nation* and Double-Crostics in *Saturday Review,* for instance. A few magazines are filled with such material.

## News in magazines

News is nothing new in magazines. It was a part of the earliest, with their reports of distant wars and nearby legislative action. In those days it was not timely information, as there were no radio, wireless, or cable dispatches, no world-encircling news-gathering syndicates and associations, and no professional journalists stationed at news-distributing points around the globe. News came in letters or was cribbed from other publications, both arriving on this continent by boat after months en route.

A typical pre-Civil War magazine news account read like this:

> South Carolina has been peculiarly unfortunate in the loss of eminent men, who represent her state sovereignty in the national councils. The death of the immortal Calhoun, on the 31st March, 1850, was followed by the appointment of the Hon. Franklin H. Elmore, to fill the vacancy. His credentials were presented on the 17th April, but his career only reached the 27th May, when he died at Washington, at the age of 60 years.
>
> The Hon. Franklin H. Elmore was a native of South Carolina, and . . .[5]

When newspapers quickened their pace, few magazines sought to continue printing spot news, for the "spot" now was much closer to the place of publication. The Civil War moved newspaper editors to unheard-of enterprise in gathering news speedily. Hybrid magazines like *Frank Leslie's Illustrated Weekly* did not surrender the news function but after the war were changed into vehicles of opinion and interpretation. Improvements in printing enriched the magazines from the turn of the century on. They appeared in colored inks and offered excellent photographic reproductions. The consequent stimulation of elaborate advertising led to slower production, by comparison

---

[5] "Miscellany," *The United States Magazine and Democratic Review,* July, 1850, p. 86.

with the newspaper, for circulations began to reach such proportions—among the national periodicals at least—that long press runs became necessary. Higher-speed presses enable large magazines to produce and distribute their mounting circulations, but did not permit them, with the exception of the newsmagazines, to compete with newspapers. The advent of radio and television, with their capacity for instantaneous news reporting, put general magazines and even newspapers almost completely out of spot news competition.

News in magazines now is:

1. Originally reported and written material not covered by regular newspapers and broadcast media. Although small in volume, it often is important and found primarily, when general information, in newsmagazines.

2. Rehashed, rewritten accounts of major events of a preceding period, interspersed with timeless features. This type occurs in various general magazines.

3. Straight news of a special group within education, industry, science, religion, or some other distinctive field of human activity. This is important spot news but so specialized in interest that general newspapers, wire services, and newsmagazines omit all but that which is thought to have general significance.

4. The behind-the-scenes, now-it-can-be-told, inside-dope type of news copy appearing in a few general periodicals, a number of trade publications, and a smattering of other specialized magazines. For the sake of timeliness these brief items are inserted in the last form and often are printed on paper of different color from the body of the magazine and in type that makes them look like newsletters of the Kiplinger style.

Magazines approach news in their own way. Since much of the time they cannot tell it first, they seek to do what newspapers and radio-television newscasts cannot do well: explain it and give it depth and background. They provide the meaning of the news and give the reader perspective on it. *The Reporter*, a bi-weekly founded in 1949, devoted itself largely to this function. Max Ascoli, its publisher, announced:

> We are publishing *The Reporter* because we think there is room in the United States for a type of reporting free from obsession with headline "news" and from the conceit of "opinions." We believe that the national and international facts which affect the lives of the American people can be gathered, selected, and interpreted with a sense of their causes, inter-relation, and possible outcome. We believe that they can be reported in the perspective of what they mean to the American people and what the American people can do about them.[6]

---

[6] Prospectus for *The Reporter*, New York, 1949.

## *Writing news for magazines*

The form of news in magazines does not differ markedly from that for news in the older medium, the newspaper. If it is spot news, as it may be occasionally, it follows the conventional 5-W form so long associated with newspapers and news agency dispatches, answering in its opening few paragraphs the questions Who? What? When? Where? and Why? If the news is important the newspaper usually unwinds it all over again, elaborating on the opening, called the *lead*. If the news is being interpreted, because already known and now requiring explanation, the magazine writer attempts, just as does the newspaperman, to present the background and indicate the significance of the event to the reader.

Straight news stories appearing in most magazines except for one element—time—could have been printed just as appropriately in a newspaper. All the specialized pages of newspapers and specialized magazines illustrate this. Comparing the financial and business pages of newspapers with the business magazines such as *Business Week* and *Forbes* can supply examples. Publicity news writers are so aware of the similarities that they can send their releases to both newspapers and magazines with the expectation that the article will appear in both media, changed only in the time reference and perhaps in the amount of the copy used.

These two news items are much alike in the arrangement of the facts, but one is from a magazine and the other from a newspaper:

Atlanta Civic Ballet, the country's oldest regional ballet, celebrates its 35th anniversary April 17–18.

One of its most novel works will be "Prologue," in which a different section has been assigned to each of the company's four directors.

Premiers for the gala are "Llanto del Pueblo" and "Danzon" by Carl Ratcliff and "Valse" by Robert Barnett.

A matinee will feature the Atlanta Civic Ballet's second company in Merrilee Smith's "Madeline and the Gypsies."

"Evenings of Dance" will be presented at the New York State Pavillion at the World's Fair on May 3 and 4.

The performances will be given by groups and companies that are connected through sponsorship with the Lexington Avenue Young Men's and Young Women's Hebrew Association, the Clark Center of the Young Women's Christian Association or the McBurney Young Men's Christian Association.

The modern dance companies scheduled to appear are headed by [names of dancers and dance companies follow].

The programs, which will be free to the public, are being arranged by Marian Horosko.

The first is from *Dance* magazine; the second from the New York *Times*.

In some subjects vocabulary, rather than either subject matter or form, is different. Science is an example, as is any technical or scientific subject with its own language.

The considerable similarity between news writing for the magazine and the newspaper (or news service) should explain why persons planning to do such writing for magazines are expected to study and practice news reporting alongside those who expect to be on the staffs of newspapers and wire services.

museum of oddities, including the opera hat Rudolph Valentino is
said to have worn the night of his death.[3] Russell Maloney, writing a
Profile (*The New Yorker* has registered the word) of the magazine, re-
peats what is probably the most famous of the classic tales about the
publication: the one in which James Thurber hauls a telephone booth
to the middle of the reception room, places it with the open side up,
and lies down in it, face white with powder and in some versions, with
a lily in his hand as well.[4] No teller of this tale has ever explained
what Thurber did with the wires.

Such pastimes, and the friendly cooperativeness more characteristic of magazine editorial departments, are part of a scene that is typical
of the human side of American business life. The department is one
of a standard group, all needed for efficient and effective production,
and each with a staff and procedure of its own.

With a few exceptions, physically speaking, magazine editorial
departments are even less inspiring sights than newspaper newsrooms,
which, despite the aura put around them by movies, novels, and television tales, are only slightly more cluttered than business offices. The
visitor to a magazine company's headquarters is likely to confront a
series of small offices, although the lobby or foyer giving access to them
may be not unlike Hollywood's streamlined version of a reception
room. The palatial quarters of several big national magazine publishers are impressive but not typical.

Because editorial is historically the premier department, its head
may have more splendid furnishing than any other executive except
the publisher or owner. But the small offices around his, as time goes
on, look much like those used by the staff members in other businesses.

Magazine editorial offices are places in which to correspond with
writers, negotiate with publishers, buy supplies, and handle copy.
They provide the backdrop for processing typescripts and illustrations; except for the art department there is little to give the setting
either garishness or romance. The artists may hang on the walls of
their rooms originals of paintings used for covers and photographers
may paper their rooms with glossy prints. But the editors do not have
even that much to divert them; they are systematic and orderly
workers. They must be, if they are to coordinate minds and skills and
bring the publication out on time.

### Staff organization

Although a magazine editorial staff labors in a more or less standardized type of office, the organization of personnel is not fixed. Two

---

[3] Allen Churchill, "Ross of The New Yorker," *The American Mercury*, August,
1948, p. 155.

[4] Russell Maloney, "A Profile of *The New Yorker* Magazine," *The Saturday Review of Literature*, Aug. 30, 1947, p. 7.

staffs never have precisely the same structure except in offices where one person does all the work or where a magazine is one of a group with standardized operations. The chief variation is in distribution of duties.

Many titles appear on magazine mastheads. But staffers with identical titles may do entirely different work on different magazines. Variations are wide, not only between kinds of magazines—the business

**TABLE 12.1.** *Comparison of Typical Editorial Staffs*

| Consumer Magazine* | Scholarly Journal† |
|---|---|
| Editorial Chairman | Editor |
| Editor in Chief | Associate Editor |
| Editor | Department Editors (4) |
| Art Director | Editorial Board (30) |
| Managing Editors | |
| Assistant Managing Editor | |
| Picture Editor | **Religious Monthly** |
| Modern Living Editor | |
| Foreign Editor | Editor |
| Special Editorial Adviser | Associate Editor |
| Senior Copy Editor | Assistant to the Editor |
| Senior Editors | Editorial Associate |
| Assistant Editors (3) | Contributing Editors (4) |
| Editorial Managers, Branches (5) | |
| Editorial Research (14) | |
| Editoral Production Manager | **Business Magazine** |
| Editorial Business Manager | |
| | Advisory Editor |
| | Editor |
| **Literary Magazine** | Contributing Editors (6) |
| | Managing Editor |
| Editor | Associate Editor |
| Associate Editor | Editorial Advisory Board (18) |
| Contributing Editor | |

\* On this and other magazines here listed photographers and artists are omitted.
† The editorial staff is largely unpaid; the work is a contribution to the field.

magazine pattern is not like the consumer book pattern—but even between magazines of like function and objective.

Practically the only standardization is in the general staff organization, built around functions rather than titles. At the head is the editor; beneath him is the managing or executive editor, to whom report a series of associate, assistant, or special editors, with editorial assistants and clerical help undergirding the entire structure. Cooperating with them, as partial staff members, are artists, photographers, correspondents, and consultants, who may serve other departments equally.

On typical staffs such as those shown in Table 12.1 most technical work is performed by a few persons. The associate, departmental, advisory, or contributing editors of a specialized magazine rarely are in the editorial offices. If in charge of departments, they conduct their business by mail, sending copy in before an agreed deadline. If they serve as consultants, they help form policy, cooperate on plans for editorial campaigns, or judge particular contributions, meeting as a group perhaps once or twice a year, if at all. Much work is done by remote control. Their most valuable contribution may be the use of their names and titles to lend authority to the magazine.

### Functions and titles

All persons named on the masthead of a big consumer magazine, as well as those not so announced, usually are full-time employes with specific duties. *Time* has about one hundred, not counting the stringers (part-time correspondents) throughout the world, on its editorial staff.

Although Henry Jones is called managing editor, the managing editor's duties on a periodical actually may be performed by Thomas Smith, executive editor, who has proved to be a better administrative officer than Jones. To the managing editor, then, goes a share of the speech making and policy forming so important as parts of the editor-in-chief's post. Duties and functions, then, are not standardized by title.

Unionism has had little impact, thus far in magazine journalism's history, upon staffs, whereas it is unionism which has standardized duties on metropolitan dailies, wire services, and radio-television stations. By contrast the duties of particular positions on these media are set forth specifically, for all departments covered. But this is true with only a few dozen magazine offices. Duties on magazine staffs are not regularized by titles and may never be, since editorial work is individual and creative. The publisher is more interested in what a staff member produces than in what he is called. High-sounding editorial

*Fig. 12.1.* The art directors at a specialized magazine check the dummy of an issue. *(Photo by Audrey Heaney)*

designations have become so numerous and widely used as substitutes for more tangible rewards that they are not taken much more seriously than titles of advertising agency or bank vice-presidents.

A staff member's work is more significant than his title, especially to the new magazine journalist, although the newcomer may at first sacrifice much for an impressive place on the masthead. It is not at all uncommon for a man or woman who has a big title on one staff to move to another publication where his rank appears to be comparatively low. The experienced magazinist knows that titles often are only a facade.

Whatever the relationship between honorific and functions, the personnel of the editorial department must be organized for editing the book. If organization is illogical or faulty, inefficiency results. It may lead to intrastaff discontent, conflict in authority, unnecessary duplication in handling materials, failure to meet schedules, and inadequate record keeping.

### *The editor*

Central figure and motive power of the staff—that is the editor. He is director, commander, captain, master. All the traditions of headship reside with him. The advertising department director may earn more but he does not have the prestige of the editorial head. Only the publisher or owner outclasses the chief editor and often that absent, almost legendary, figure plays little active part.

American magazine journalism has a tradition of great editors, a tradition however that is being forgotten as magazining becomes more a business than a mission or a calling. In earlier chapters we have noted some of the leading literary figures like the poets and novelists Lowell, Poe, and Howells. To them can be added Abbott of *The Outlook,* Mencken of the *Mercury,* Edward Bok of the *Ladies' Home Journal,* Godkin and Villard of *The Nation,* Lorimer of the *Post,* Mary Mapes Dodge of *St. Nicholas,* Hamilton Holt of *The Independent,* Page of the *Atlantic,* John Brisben Walker of *Cosmopolitan,* McClure of the magazine bearing his name, Norman Hapgood of *Collier's,* Ray Stannard Baker of the *American,* Frederick Lewis Allen of *Harper's,* Bruce Bliven of *The New Republic,* Ben Hibbs of the *Post,* Harold Ross of *The New Yorker,* Carmel Snow of *Harper's Bazaar,* Edna Woolman Chase of *Vogue,* Henry R. Luce of Time Inc., Herbert R. Mayes of *McCall's,* and Frank Crowninshield of *Vanity Fair.*

In the days when these magazinists and the creative geniuses preceding them were at work, a magazine editor was more of a public figure than he is today. He was treated as something of a revered leader. But a literary glow rarely lasts around a magazine editor these days; he not only is less literary and austere but also younger and more businesslike. The personality is less evident. Only a few stand forth in the early 1970's midcentury: Osborn Elliott, *Newsweek;* Norman Cousins, formerly of *Saturday Review;* John Mack Carter, *Ladies' Home Journal;* William Shawn, *The New Yorker;* Carey McWilliams, *The Nation;* DeWitt and Lila Wallace, *The Reader's Digest;* Joseph J. Thorndike, *Horizon;* Betsy Talbot Blackwell, formerly of *Mademoiselle;* and Wade H. Nichols, *Good Housekeeping.*

Today's consumer magazine editor's administrative duties rarely allow him time or energy for writing. He must leave much to the executive or managing editor. Around the turn of the century, however, the editor whose own books of fiction or non-fiction were not published was an exception. Today the one who writes books is the rarity. And in the specialized magazine area, with some notable exceptions, such as Gerard Piel at *Scientific American,* the editor as writer hardly functions at all.

There was a time when the subscriber could name the editor of his magazine. In the years between World Wars I and II the cynical voice of Mencken was heard through *The American Mercury,* and people knew who was talking. Today, however, if a magazine has a voice it is institutional rather than individual. The editor now is businesslike, devoting much time to policy making, supporting outside groups that bolster policy, and seeking to improve the image of his magazine as well as of the magazine industry as a whole. He must give more thought to the circulation than to the classics, to readership studies than realism versus naturalism, to advertising revenue rather than article writing, and to subscriptions instead of scholarship. Caution, not crusading, is the vogue in a time when costs are enormous. A century ago magazines consisted mostly of pages of eye-straining, unrelieved type. That day is past. All editors now must have some understanding of production because even specialized magazines use art work, photographs in many patterns, elaborate display headings, and colored inks. Today's big-time editor is a combination editorial executive, businessman, and graphic artist. His expertise is in management rather than in writing or editing.

## The editor's duties

The work done by the editor varies by magazine. Staffs differ in size, as we have seen, but not in basic functions, all of which must be performed whatever the magazine's circulation or physical dimensions. An editor may be responsible for only one phase, if he works on a large publication, or for all of them, if he is the one man of a one-man periodical. An examination of all the usual duties is needed next. The description is in terms of the consumer magazine, since everything its editor does, while on a more elaborate scale, must be done by the rest.

Editorial functions may be divided into five: **a.** commercial or financial, **b.** public opinion, **c.** directive, **d.** writing, and **e.** public relations.

When he buys or authorizes the purchase of manuscripts, art work, photographs, syndicated copy, reader interest survey reports, or other materials, the editor performs a *commercial* function. He continues to do so when he sets and adjusts salaries, or payment for part-time employes. On small magazines he also may solicit and accept subscriptions or sales for single copies; another apparently extracurricular activity is selling advertising space. On virtually any magazine he signs subscription solicitation letters prepared by the promotion or circulation department. Because he is the one held responsible for content, he has an influence with the reader other executives cannot exploit. The editor also deals with book publishers, other magazine executives, and any agencies that request permission to reprint content

or make other further use of it. Similarly he negotiates with authors'
and artists' agents. So many are the demands upon editors to be business rather than editorial executives that some of the leading ones in
1963 formed the American Society of Magazine Editors, a subdivision
of the Magazine Publishers Association. Ted Patrick, late editor of
*Holiday* and first ASME chairman, said the group would "fight and
die for editorial integrity" and that the members intend to be disdain-
ful of advertising.[5]

His *public opinion* functions are discharged in two directions—toward the authors he publishes and toward readers. The first is done by
reading widely in books and magazines to discover what contem-
poraries publish. He must know current literature intimately enough
to understand trends, especially among writers who do not cater to
public demand. Pressure from the financial side makes it difficult for
all but literary magazine editors to carry out this part of the public
opinion function. To obtain perspective on the writing of their own
time, the most diligent also reread established works of non-fiction or
fiction, depending upon their interests and the nature of their magazines. The editor seeks to gauge the public opinion of the consumer
group by watching circulation of his own and other magazines to
learn what they indicate about public taste. As a more responsible
type of barometer he supervises or employs others to conduct reader
interest and readability studies. These, and content analyses, he examines as carefully as any businessman studies production reports from
branch factories. At the same time, the editor resists being too much
influenced by such findings.

Nor does he neglect an older clue to public opinion: his correspondence from readers. A letter like this, sent to a national literary
magazine by a teacher in a church-maintained college, may give him
pause:

> Sir:
> I regret the necessity of canceling our subscription. Obviously this
> periodical, excellent from a literary standpoint, is intended for, shall
> we say, "broadminded adults." No doubt the editors themselves would
> hesitate to put it in the hands of young girls of good families, entrusted
> to our care for Christian and moral, as well as secular education. We
> try to keep them as unsophisticated as possible in a world teeming with
> problems of adult life.

Naturally an editor is deeply interested in editorial comment on
his own publication. He rightly believes that requests for reprints of
material and letters asking permission to reproduce what he has published indicate effective editorial work.

---

[5] "ASME Born; Pledges Fight for Integrity," *Editor & Publisher*, Sept. 21, 1963,
p. 13.

His direction of the magazine (function c) begins with the determination or carrying out of its formula or pattern. He contributes ideas for content, both written and illustrative, or suggests, if not orders, methods of treatment. Alone or with others on the staff as a sort of executive committee, he determines policy, that is, the positions the magazine is to take on public questions or the attitude it is to assume about internal technical problems. Some of his time is spent on examining and judging suggestions of superiors, subordinates, and outsiders about the conduct of the magazine or the nature of its content.

The editor ultimately is responsible for technical operations in his department—a central and traditional part of the directive function. He directs others in performing these operations, does them himself, or shares them. The larger the magazine the fewer the technical operations performed by the editor unless he is a dictator or retains them as being of most importance. Such retention, however, is not typical of big magazine editorial philosophy today.

What are these technical operations? Editing copy, selecting, cropping, and sizing pictures and other art work, writing captions and cutlines, planning and maintaining schedules, layout and dummying, reading proofs, and other detailed production except typesetting and such print shop work.

The editor's function as a writer (d), although carried out far less than ever in periodical history, must be carried out on the small magazine. Even on the largest, he may write an occasional editorial or use a first draft of one from an assistant as a basis for his own. His contribution to the small one may be a personal column. In the specialized field, particularly the little magazine world, many a periodical is founded and edited by a writer seeking an outlet for his views. His material may be too unorthodox for standard publications; in some instances it is technically below par and in others the ideas are too far out for the usual consumer. So he buys himself a soapbox and freedom of self-expression—so long as he can pay for them. He can continue to do so only if his magazine is well promoted and attracts a sufficient number of readers and advertisers to remain solvent.

Writing *for* the magazine is paralleled by writing *about* it: promotion letters, advertising copy, text for posters, articles for professional publications outlining editorial methods or needs of the periodical, news stories about extraordinary content or internal changes of possible public interest.

Editors always have done a measure of public relations work (function e) even when most of their time was spent composing essays or negotiating with writers for contributions. Not until recent years, however, has this work been consciously directed at improving the relations of the magazine (its image, as publicists like to say) with one or more of the various publics with which it deals. Virtually everything an editor does affects public relations.

Andrew Bradford, pioneer publisher, sold more than his magazine from his store while he was editor of the *American Weekly Mercury* in Philadelphia early in the eighteenth century. He put up for sale molasses, whalebone, corks, chocolate, goose feathers, snuff, and other goods accepted as payment for the magazines, thus supplementing his editing and publishing business. This trade was helpful in building public relations, as well as financing the print shop.

A century later Park Benjamin, once editor of the *New-England Magazine* of Boston, sought to control the public relations of his second periodical, the *American Monthly* of New York, by putting it successively behind one cause after the other—the American Lyceum, the Whig Party, an international copyright law, to name the more conspicuous. For a time each improved the magazine's relations with the reading public.

Fortunate in public relations, not all of which were planned and controlled, was Sarah Josepha Hale, of *Godey's Lady's Book,* a dynamic and aggressive editor, especially for one of her sex in her time. Through her magazine directly and by organizing committees in Boston and taking part in civic activities, she exerted remarkable influence. She helped organize Vassar, the first college for women; she founded a society, possibly the first, to improve wages and working conditions of women and children; she organized the first day nursery and founded the Seaman's Aid; she raised money for monuments and the preservation of national memorials. Also, she conducted campaigns in support of unpopular causes of the nineteenth century: equal education for women in grade schools and in higher education, employment of women as teachers in public schools, retention of property rights by married women, creation of public playgrounds, and acceptance of women medical missionaries. [6]

Bradford, Benjamin, and Mrs. Hale did not, of course, define the activity that became explicit by the midyears of the twentieth century as public relations. It has been defined as "the creation and carrying out of broad policies that will be reflected in favorable public opinion."[7] They created and carried out policies because this action is inherent in editing.

In our time, editors do public relations work more consciously, fitting a later definition by Lesly: "All activities and attitudes intended to judge, adjust to, influence, and direct the opinion of any

---

[6] Ruth E. Finley, *The Lady of Godey's* (Philadelphia: J. B. Lippincott Co., 1931), p. 17.

[7] Philip Lesly (ed.), *Public Relations Handbook* (New York: Prentice-Hall, Inc., 1950), p. 22.

group or groups of persons in the interest of any individual, group, or institution." [8]

The editors now make speeches before local, state, national, and international groups of journalists, of leaders in the field in which they are most concerned because these are the areas of their magazine content, or of persons active in public affairs. They serve on countless committees, both in and out of their profession. These duties may or may not be directly related to their magazines or their own work; their image building is more broadly effective with outside brotherhoods, associations, and conferences. Whatever their activity, it is important in dealing with their publics.

## *The editor's routines*

An editor's routines depend upon his responsibilities. If he does editorial work, circulation, advertising, research, promotion, all in one, as in small offices, routines are many and varied. In an average-size editorial department, on a business magazine, say, each of the four or five staffers has his own routine, although each is expected to handle other work in an emergency or when it is vacation time.

The editor-in-chief, associate editors, and other sub-editors follow routines or systems to provide smooth coordination of their work with that of colleagues. Three elements comprise such systems: copy, staff, and editorial tools, both physical and mental.

The editorial department obtains copy of all sorts and must be equipped to process it through both human and mechanical means. If this work is to be done efficiently, there must be a systematic plan, developed around various editorial functions and talents of the available personnel. In the business world this planning is done through job analyses. A study of this type was made of a successful business magazine, producing a set of typical routines for the staff of an editorial department. Routines here are called functions. It should be noted that routines for several editors include duties lying outside direct processing or other magazine procedures.

### Functions of the Editor[9]

1. To fix editorial policy, on consultation with publisher.
2. To supervise the work of the editorial staff.
3. To determine, each month, and to plan well in advance, the editorial content.
4. To read and/or approve all copy, photographs and art work used editorially.
5. To write editorials, feature articles and news items.

---

[8] *Ibid.*, 1962 Edition, p. 861.
[9] Prepared for staff use by Albert G. Ryden while editor of *The Boys' Outfitter.*

6. By constant study and research to become and remain highly informed in two fields:
   a) In all matters relating specifically to the boys' business—including market and store problems, prices, fashion, etc.
   b) In the broad field of economic developments, so that boys' industry trends may be correctly related to general business trends.
7. To be chief representative of the magazine at business functions.
8. To interview those coming to the offices for information and counsel.
9. To serve as secretary of the association serving the field.

### Functions of the First Associate Editor

1. To be in charge of editorial routine—routing of copy to printer, pictures, deadlines, etc.
2. To be in charge of editorial make-up, including page layout, typography, use of photographs, art work, color, etc.
3. To read *all* copy.
4. To dummy or supervise the dummying of all editorial pages.
5. To be chief proofreader.
6. To assist in the writing of news items.
7. To set up and keep up to date a style book.
8. To help in the preparation of the annual directory.
9. To serve as alternate to the other associate editor.

### Functions of the Second Associate Editor

1. To write feature articles, either upon assignment from the editor, or based upon original ideas okayed by the editor.
2. To be in charge of taking fashion photographs, including monthly covers.
3. To be chief reporter, and to represent the magazine at business functions not attended by the editor.
4. To assist in the writing of news items, with the special responsibility of stimulating retail news, and making certain that all boys' department personnel changes are reported.
5. To serve as substitute for the editor in interviewing those coming to the office for information and counsel.
6. To assist the editor in research.
7. To be chief writer of picture captions and to assist in dummying and proofreading.
8. To be office photographer and to take editorial photographs, from time to time, at business functions.
9. To serve as alternate to the first associate editor.

### Functions of the Assistant to Editor

1. To be secretary to the editor and to do secretarial work for the associate editors.
2. To be keeper of the records for the editorial department.
3. To dummy the news and personals pages.
4. To assist in proofreading, copyreading, and in the writing of news items and picture captions.
5. To assist the editor in research.
6. To be assistant office photographer.
7. To help in the preparation of the directory.

*Fig. 12.2.* Three editorial staffers at the *Parke-Davis Review* pitch in to paste galley and engraver's proofs in position on pages. *(Parke-Davis Review Photo)*

8. To be secretary to the secretary of the trade association, in emergencies.
9. To serve as alternate, when necessary, for the associate editors.

### In general

All members of the staff are responsible for familiarizing themselves, in a general way, with the work of all other staffers, so that during the absence of one or more the department may function with maximum efficiency.

In some offices editorial routines have developed into complex systems. In most, however, since the majority of magazines are small, the plan is easy to understand.

Typically, a secretary opens the mail and routes the manuscripts and editorial correspondence to the two or three editorial people who

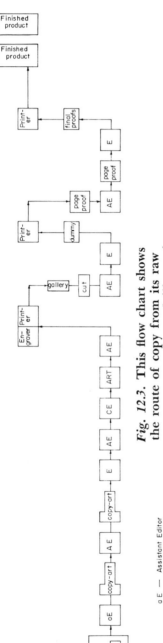

*Fig. 12.3.* This flow chart shows the route of copy from its raw state as typescript and illustrations to its appearance in finished magazines. It moves from editors of different grades for okay; then to copy editor and art editor for processing for reproduction; to engraver and printer, who transmute it into engravings and type; then in proof form back to the editorial department, which prepares a dummy. This dummy is sent to the printer. He returns page proofs to the editors who check these and return them to the printer, who, when all is corrected, produces a finished product. This flow assumes a letterpress publication.

aE — Assistant Editor
AE — Associate Editor
E — Editor
CE — Copy Editor

are expected to handle it. She makes no judgment of the quality of the submissions. The subordinate editors pass upon what they received and consult the editor-in-chief, at regular sessions sometimes but more often individually, about the plans for their sections of the magazine. In some offices these same editors process the copy; in others, if the volume is great enough, staff specialists prepare it, be it art work or photographs or manuscript. When they have finished it goes to the editor-in-chief for final approval, and then is sent, after being recorded, with working dummies, layout sheets, and other guides to the printer. It is sent in segments, as completed and as coordinated with the general plan for the future issue. Copy for several issues is sent when available, since the offices work from one to three issues ahead.

The sub-editors who handle the copy, either as specialists in the procedure or in behalf of their own sections of the book, usually design the page make-up, in consultation with the artists, but on some groups of small magazines, this type of planning is done for all and the editorial department of each periodical has a consultant relationship and must approve what has been done before it is carried out by the production department.

When proofs of script and illustrations are returned, first in galley form and then in various stages of pages, the double check on the printers and engravers is undertaken in the editorial offices, often by assistant editors or editorial assistants, who are encouraged only to make it conform and report suggested changes to a superior.

A general principle holds on most: the routine work is left to subordinates; the making of major judgments falls to top editors. This practice is not ideal, but often the work cannot be handled otherwise by small staffs. This routine stems from policies set by the publisher, owner, and editors.

John Fischer, describing the relatively simple operation policies of the *Harper's* editorial department, told a group of advertising executives that the magazine, at the time of his speech, had seven editors and six assistants and secretaries, few enough so that staff meetings were held in one office. Readership polls were not taken because he is skeptical "about the theory that a readership poll can tell you what readers like." Such a poll can tell what they preferred at some earlier time but they are likely to be interested in something else for the future, Mr. Fischer believes.

About 20,000 manuscripts are received annually; every one accepted is discussed thoroughly before publication. About two hundred are used, or only 1 per cent. Around 8,000 letters are received in a year, some suggesting articles.

Another policy, he explained, is to give preference to a competent article or story by an unknown instead of a mediocre one by a name writer. Staff-written material is in the minority, no particular social or political opinion is followed, and control of the editorial content is entirely in the hands of editors.

In explaining this, Mr. Fischer observed that "On a number of magazines the basic editorial decisions—including the hiring and firing of editors is made by people on the business side," a mistaken policy, he believes. A final policy is avoidance of formulas, which he thinks are dangerous because they provide no element of newness for readers. [10]

Contrast such policies and routines with those of a little literary and opinion magazine lasting, typically, for only three years. *New Horizons* had a staff of three: two owners, who were co-editors, and an associate editor, all giving their time and even paying a subsidy. The two hundred manuscripts received each week were listed in a dime-store notebook by the associate editor, who accepted or rejected, submitted tentative acceptances to the editors, and was consulted by them on content of future issues. The associate editor handled the copy from final acceptance until the printer received it for conversion into type. He planned the issue and pasted proofs into a rough dummy on the carcass of a former issue. Advertising was minor, affecting editorial plans almost not at all.

### Copy sources

A magazine is made of materials coming from many sources. This statement does not refer to paper, ink, and metal used in physical production but to the origin of manuscripts, facts, ideas, illustrations, and all the other units that constitute copy in the editorial department.

Sources are internal and external:

*Internal:* Owners; editors; staff writers, photographers, illustrators; consultants; advertisers; correspondents.

*External:* Free lance writers, illustrators, photographers; tipsters; syndicates; readers; industrial publicity offices and other publicity sources; government offices and bureaus at all levels; public institutions, such as libraries, museums, colleges; clipping bureaus; map and chart companies; other magazines for reprint and digest material; newspapers and other media, especially books; authors' and artists' representatives; miscellaneous documentary sources, such as isolated pamphlets.

Only one of these is peculiar to magazine journalism: the authors' and artists' representatives or agents. Newspapers use all the other sources, albeit some more than others. Services of a world news-gathering agency, such as United Press International, are employed by a few magazines but many newspapers. Free lancers are a vital source of magazine material and by comparison do little work for newspapers.

---

[10] John Fischer, *op. cit.*, pp. 9–11.

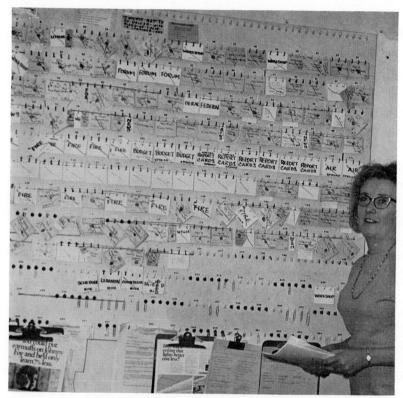

*Fig. 12.4* A planning board used by the Management Publishing group of Greenwich, Conn., which issues *School Management, College Management,* and other specialized magazines. *(Management Publishing Group Photo)*

Knowing how to tap sources is part of the editorial task. Internal ones offer no problem; external are more difficult. Free-lance copy arrives unsolicited but most of it is unusable. Editors learn which independent writers are dependable and occasionally feed them assignments. They also make their wants known through writers' magazines, clubs, and conferences. Tipsters sell news or ideas for magazine material for development by staff or assigned writers. Syndicates are listed and classified in directories such as the annual supplement about them to *Editor & Publisher* but are of little importance to general magazines. Readers provide letters, ideas for articles or stories, and miscellaneous contributions but cannot be depended upon regularly. Publicity materials, like free-lance copy, come unsolicited, and often are useless as prepared but can be a source of ideas and directly usable copy to business and other specialized periodicals. Publicity departments are helpful for checking manuscripts, providing pictures, and supplying other illustrations. Government bureaus, like publicity offices, are able to provide some significant, official materials for direct or background use. Editors soon discover which of these offices are more valuable sources than others.

Universities, churches, and other public institutions constantly are probed by magazines particularly for non-fiction ideas and materials. In New York City, heart of the magazine publishing world, editorial assistants troop in and out of the lion-guarded public library at Fifth Avenue and Forty-second Street. The general magazine, with the widest scope of any periodical, depends greatly on such reservoirs of knowledge. Even ordinary specialized magazines cannot maintain libraries sufficiently elaborate to meet all needs and must reach into special collections, such as the John Crerar and the Newberry in Chicago.

Authors' representatives bring material unbidden if they believe a periodical will pay well and promptly for copy; they, too, are listed in directories, such as *Literary Market Place*. Newspapers and magazines are received by exchange and subscriptions. Alert editors watch the competition carefully and also examine magazines for new ideas in subjects and display techniques.

Several references have been made to directories listing persons and firms from which material may be obtained. Well-equipped magazine offices have them on hand and purchase each new edition regularly. The membership list of the Society of Magazine Writers is a valuable clue to first-class free lancers.

### Planning the magazine

No matter how well an editor knows his sources, he still must tap them with a purpose. He no more orders and buys without some idea of the use he intends to make of the material than a housewife enters a supermarket and spends a thousand dollars according to the moment's fancy. Experienced cooks buy supplies with specific recipes and planned meals in mind. So it is with carefully edited magazines.

No matter how scientifically planned, however, a magazine's content is not approved by all readers. Here is a bit of doggerel known in many magazine offices:

SPEAKETH THE EDITOR [11]

Getting out a magazine is no picnic.
If we publish original matter, they say we lack variety.
If we print jokes folks say we are silly.
If we don't they say we are too serious.

---

[11] Reprinted by *The Writer's Monthly,* January, 1947, from *Catholic Opinion.*

If we publish things from other papers, we are lazy.
If we are out rustling news, we are wasting time.
If we are not rustling news, we are not attending to business.
If we don't print contributions, we lack appreciation.
If we do print them, the paper is full of junk.
Like as not some fellow will say we swiped this from some
    other paper—So we did!

Working from three months to a year ahead helps avoid some of these accusations. That there can be long-range preparation is an advantage of magazine journalism. The less dependent the publication upon news trends, the more feasible the long-distance planning.

National magazines manage to work far ahead by holding regular planning sessions of department members in which various trends are noted and discussed. If, as in the case of a service publication, the climate of opinion and national economy indicates emphasis on frugality in housekeeping, projected issues will include articles, picture stories, and departments stressing money-saving devices and inexpensive commodities. Small magazines, limited to planning by a staff of a few augmented by consultants, sometimes titled advisory or consulting editors, are not often so systematic because of the difficulty of meeting. The need for these consultants accounts, in part, for names of prominent specialists on mastheads of magazines put out by two or three persons on a small budget. They are unsalaried advisers.

## Departmental problems

The best of plans cannot anticipate all problems, although their number and severity can be reduced. The editor whose plans for an issue seven months hence include an extra article, extra short features, and other reserve material is in a position to meet the problem created if a contributor is unable to prepare a promised article, or the typescript, almost too late in any case, is lost en route.

Editorial department problems are numerous enough to require an entire book devoted to their solution. Julien Elfenbein, a business magazine editorial executive, did in fact use most of the space in a 422-page book on the problems of this special group of periodicals. Some idea of the nature of the questions editorial departments must answer may be gained from noting some that are typical; they are handled differently by various magazines but each must be confronted:

1. What shall be the division of content for a given issue or group of issues?
2. Shall the staff be experienced or trained on the spot?
3. How shall controversial material be presented without loss of objectivity or independence?

4.  How can editors avoid printing material that competing publica-
    tions issue first?
5.  How can editors pick topics, months ahead, that will be of deep
    public interest when the material on them appears?
6.  How can editors avoid excess inventories?
7.  How can editors avoid rewriting manuscripts but, when neces-
    sary, improve them without molesting the writer's style?
8.  How can editors help specialists who are not professional writers
    prepare material for the magazine?
9.  How can editors find out whether the vocabulary used by con-
    tributors is suitable to most readers?
10. How can editors check and verify articles without running up
    excess expense?

### *The copy editors*

All who write for magazines, whether free lancers or staff members, are pushers of pens and pencils, but the ones who push the
writing tools the hardest are the *copy editors,* a term now used in
both newspaper and magazine offices, and gradually replacing *copyreader.*

Writers depend upon typewriters for their finished work but
editors still rely on slim cylinders of wood and lead, rarely blue, and
increasingly on ball-point pens, a doubtful practice since erasing
lead pencil marks is easier than removing inky ones. No one has
learned to edit on a typewriter, although a standing wisecrack about
authors who are too generous with hand corrections is that they
write their scripts longhand and correct them  by machine.

Pencil-pushing in the editorial department means copy editing,
rewriting, preparing headings, scheduling material, and other technical editorial duties. On the small magazine one or two persons
are responsible; on the large one, specialists perform each major
operation.

The pencil-pen pushers usually are editorial assistants, assistant
editors, or associate editors. If no one else is available, the chief
editor himself may do the work. A ratio holds here: the bigger the
magazine, the less technical editing is done by the head of the department, and vice versa.

Time Inc., has developed an elaborate system of copy checking
in an effort to provide an almost foolproof procedure for *Time* and
*Life.* That no system can assure error-free results is proved by the
faults in every issue of any magazine, as can be shown by reading
the letters columns. But a newsmagazine, like a newspaper, must
be especially on guard because it deals with hastily obtained, rapidly
changing information supposedly factual. It cannot afford too many
ribbings such as that by Walter Winchell:

"*Time* Mag, the other issue, scolded colymist John McClain for
being rooked on a story that swindled editors all over the land.

" 'If,' heckled *Time's* press editor, 'Big City Columnist McClain of the *World-Telegram-Sun* had bothered to check. . . '

"If *Time* had bothered to check, it would have put McClain on the right newspaper—The N.Y. *Journal-American.*"[12]

Neither *Time* nor any other magazine can have the attitude of the son of an editor who scolded him for not studying harder in school.

"You must go every day and study hard," the father said. "Otherwise you can never be an editor. What would you do, for instance, if your magazine came out full of mistakes?"

"That's easy, dad," the lad replied. "I'd blame the printer."

Many an editor shifts the blame to the printer when talking over his mistakes with the rest of the staff but he does not often confide that opinion to the men in the printing plant. He finds it better to use his energy to set up systems to prevent occurrence of errors. Such defense, not perfect as we know, has been set up as part of *Time's* research plan. Researchers at Time Inc. are young women who develop article ideas, report routine stories, dig up background at libraries, run errands, check spelling, and perform dozens of similar editorial duties.

Under this system, modifications of which also are used at *Horizon* and other magazine offices, the researcher does the documentation while the writer plans his approach to the assignment. The researcher consults materials in the reference library. She gives the best of the material, in memoranda, to the writer. This information, to the best of her knowledge, is dependable. At least six persons work on each major story: managing editor, senior editor, senior researcher, writer, special researcher, and copy editor. The researcher checks after the managing and senior editors have gone over the material. Here *Time's* famous red and black dot system is used. The researcher puts a black dot above each word for which there is a secondary source, a red dot above each for which there is a primary source.

Additional checking is done by others. The completed article goes to the copy desk for retyping and for review of spelling, punctuation, style, slips, and inconsistencies. When errors still occur, *Time* readers are likely to report them to the editorial offices, which leads to further research and verification. Only well-manned staffs can take such pains.

Sometimes, despite many readings by several editors, errors creep into copy. The *Saturday Evening Post,* in its Nov. 17, 1960 issue, faced up to one this way:

> We don't make nearly as many errors as the LETTERS columns seem to indicate. In fact, our accuracy average is quite high, and most of the errors we do commit are not serious. But once in a while we pull a goof that is, in the memorable designation of the late F. H. LaGuardia, a beaut. On Page 92 of last week's issue we advertised that this week's issue would contain AMERICA MUST GROW, an article by Walter Lipp-

---

[12] Walter Winchell's column, Syracuse *Herald-Journal,* Nov. 28, 1950, p. 21.

mann. In truth, the Lippmann article had been published in the November 5 issue. The four editors who let the error slip past them were
beheaded, of course.

## Characteristics of copy editors

Every editorial staff needs persons with the ability to do detailed
work patiently and the imagination to provide dramatic ideas. Since
these virtues rarely are found in combination, editors are obliged to
seek and are fortunate when they can find staffers who possess one
or the other in any notable degree.

The patient, painstaking person may be a comma chaser, but
comma chasers are necessary in journalism. The young women who
place red and black dots over words must understand their work and
be convinced of its importance. Many an occupation is equally concerned with detail. A telephone operator must be accurate about
digits. An airline clerk must place the correct flight numbers on
each part of a ticket and corresponding numbers on control sheets
for the right date. A surgeon must make an incision in exactly the
right spot. The importance of exactness in the physical sciences needs
no argument. Journalism has long been criticized for its proneness to
inaccuracy.

But many human beings are impatient with details. They may
be imaginative people able to see large problems, to generate significant ideas, or to exercise wise judgment. Brilliant theoreticians sometimes are highly impractical, as witness the eminent physicist who
helped harness atomic energy but could not repair a leaky kitchen
faucet. Editorial staffs need these minds, also. An associate editor
who detects social trends and sees relationships in events that lead
to important article ideas is as vital to the publication's success as
the comma chaser. He should be left free of burdensome detail so
he can produce ideas springing from comprehension of large areas
of human activity. An associate editor who understands human
nature and historical trends is as rare as one with an encyclopedic
mind who makes no more than one mistake an issue.

By the time a person has lived two decades he or his associates
should be able to categorize him as an editorial worker, although
not all persons fall entirely into either the comma-chaser or idea-man
class. A similar allotment of talents exists on newspapers as on magazines. Some newsmen are first-class reporters, being remarkably
successful in gathering information. Their sources open up, they
make fruitful contacts and uncover unusual information, and they
work speedily. But they cannot write effectively about what they
learn. When they approach the typewriter, they become self-
conscious and stiff, do not know how to plan their writing, and their
copy is poorly organized and wooden in style.

Other newsmen, however, write with facility. They tell a story charmingly; features seem to roll from their typewriters. They toy with their readers, knowing exactly how to make them smile or cry. They can take a pageful of notes and turn out a column of type without using telephone, encyclopedia, or reference files. But send them down to city hall, and they cannot find out if the mayor is in town. Assign one of them to interview a newly arrived family, and these citizens will find out more about the reporter than he does about them.

Even the most elementary attempt at editing helps any aspiring magazinist to discover his potentialities. He will learn whether he is a slow or fast thinker, can condense over-written material, clarify obscure writing, catch the high point of interest in a piece of copy and translate it into title or headline, grasp patterns of magazine pages, improve another person's writing without destroying style and individuality of expression and do it deftly in pencil, instead of having to retype. Anyone who meets these tests will know that he has certain skills welcomed in magazine editorial offices. He also may have others that are revealed if he is allowed to help plan content, deal with authors, and react to ideas presented by other staffers. But the path to these responsibilities is via the editorial desk.

Schools of journalism offer many services unknown to or not valued by the man or woman on the desk who did not study journalism in college. One such service is that of testing capabilities of young people before they accept responsibility on the job. Journalism education is obligated to discourage those unfit for journalism while helping them discover their bent and to encourage the fit in developing their capacities as revealed in the classroom. Many a journalism teacher has had the experience of finding that a particular student who does excellent work at home at his own convenience and pace sometimes goes to pieces under conditions that duplicate a practical situation similar to one which he would encounter when working. He may not recover from the experience, or he may, and develop into a competent craftsman able to stand the pressures of everyday editorial life.

Journalism laboratory conditions reveal one's ability to work carefully only when there is no time pressure or to be a meticulous craftsman even when deadlines are pressing. A magazine editing class has brought self-revelation to many a student when lecture courses have left undisclosed his basic work habits. Usually he has time to shift to another field or change his practices, if necessary, but in any case he has been put on his guard by learning his strengths and weaknesses before he takes up that editorial job.

### The copy editor's tools

Whatever their distinctive traits, the pen or pencil pushers, like all skilled workmen, need tools. Some are physical, others mental.

The physical tools are commonplace but important: typewriter,

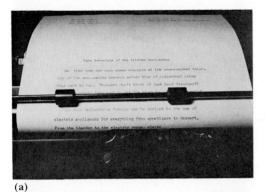

(a)

(b)

(c)

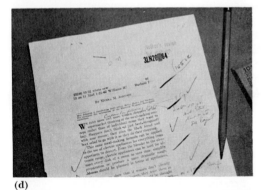

(d)

*Fig. 12.5.* "From copy to printed page" describes this record of the life of an article prepared for a specialized magazine in the field of home economics. (a) The raw copy; note the ample spacing. (b) An editor marks it for typesetting. (c) Now retyped line for line to fit the magazine's column measure, another editor typestyles it and copyedits it further. (d) Galley proof, with further typographic instructions added and additional line editing (for instance, a five-letter word deletion has been replaced with another word of the same length). (e) Page proof with certain elements, such as the identification of the author, now placed to conform with a page layout (not illustrated). (f) The issue of *What's New in Home Economics* opened to the page carrying the printed article. *(Photographs Courtesy Magazine Publishing Division, The Reuben H. Donnelly Corp.)*

(e)

(f)

pens and pencils, pastepot, shears, books, rubber stamps, and the other bric-a-brac of the editorial desk. If properly made and used, these improve operations in any editorial office. The mental tools are such qualities as sound judgment, retentive memory, knowledge of policy, and grasp of a system of processing copy. These tools cannot be bought at the nearest stationer's; they need analysis and explanation.

Sound judgment is based on experience and possession of information which gives the editorial worker perspective and background. These enable him to solve problems that would puzzle the tyro and of which the beginner would not even be aware. Take, for example, the procedure copy editors follow when they encounter libel in a script. The novice, not recognizing the legal offense, might allow it to stand. The more experienced desk person judges it in relation to the law itself, actual legal cases of which he knows, and previous incidents in which his magazine has been involved.

Memory is a physical endowment. Some persons are better endowed than others; those with poor memories can hope to improve them. A faulty memory handicaps any journalist, although in the magazine world it is less of a detriment than in the rushed journalism of newspapers and wire services. Modern psychology has thrown considerable light on memory training. This mental tool is sharpened if one is capable of complete concentration on the work at hand. Concentration can be developed through practice, and for the most careful work it is absolutely necessary. How, for example, can a desk worker edit intelligently the sixth page of a manuscript if he cannot recall what was on the second? In that case any number of contradictions, repetitions, and inconsistencies may be missed. Sometimes noise or the absence of it affects concentration. Whatever the cause, failure at this point opens loopholes through which inferior work reaches the printed page.

Knowledge of policy comes, of course, through familiarity with the magazine. A person who is to begin work on a certain periodical tomorrow morning cannot be expected to know its policy thoroughly. He is a better beginning staff member, however, if he has been reading the publication and in general is aware of whether it is neutral, pro, or anti something or other. Anyone who handles manuscripts and illustrations should become informed about editorial policies as soon as possible.

Grasp of a system of copy processing is easy to obtain. Every magazine has its own. Basically they are the same, varying in details only. The aim of all is to communicate rapidly and accurately to the printers and engravers the exact intentions of the editorial department as to conversion of the copy into type and engravings. They all rest upon knowledge of typography and printing and a set of symbols. To operate his magazine's system efficiently, the editorial worker on a letterpress printed publication should know:

1. What types are available from his printer. This information can be obtained from the printer's type specimen book or a set of proofs of samples of type in stock (or in the shops of the printers to whom work may be subcontracted).

2. What typographical dress pattern his magazine follows. The personality of a publication is determined to a great extent by this pattern. Compare a magazine of 1925 with an issue of today. From the standpoint of newsstand display, for example, the *Atlantic* was drab in that year, but four decades later it was brightened by increase in page size, use of color and art work on its cover, and emphasis on selected articles, stories, or authors. The part played in any magazine's history by knowledge of typography justifies study of the graphic arts as recommended in college to aspiring journalists.

3. Precisely how to use certain symbols in giving instructions. These signals fall into two groups: the copy editor's and the proofreader's. They should not be confused or used interchangeably because a few are held in common.

### Prerequisites to copy editing

Copy editing does not begin with the writing of a caption and continue with cursory reading of typescript. It begins with an understanding of the aim and scope of editing.

The editor's purpose is to prepare material for publication, which means that he must mark it for printer or engraver, correct errors of statement, grammar, spelling, and the like, make it conform to style and policy, see that it is in good taste, and be certain that it fits the space assigned to it.

The scope of his work differs according to the place where he is employed. It is not possible to say, categorically, that editorial offices never change an author's work, except to eliminate absurdities, or that they rewrite practically all copy. Some copy is left unchanged, most is altered a little, some is edited drastically. Magazines sometimes buy ideas only or a manuscript is bought with the understanding that it will be used as the basis for new copy to be written by someone else. Editors differ in the strength of their ethical sense as well as in the amount of their energy. Time is a factor, complicated by the fact that editing is only one of numerous duties shouldered by the editor. A given manuscript may call for complete revamping, but if it is thought that few readers would be able to appreciate the result, it is allowed to go through with only minor changes. Staff members soon learn how severely they may use the editorial pencil, for the editor generally makes his wishes known.

The writer prefers—and correctly—that he be consulted if changes are needed and that he make them or have the chance to approve or disapprove them. Well-edited magazines operate in that fashion.

## *Magazine English*

This subheading is used to make a chapter division point, not to label a type of English. There is no magazine English, any more than there is book or pamphlet English. Language usages of newspapers have been described in books and articles on journalistic English, thus creating the impression that the magazine may employ a special kind of English in its pages.

A single type of English would be impracticable because magazines are highly diversified in both appeal and content. The language of the *Journal of Applied Psychology* is not the language of *Pageant*. The short stories in *Epoch* have little in common with those in *True Story* except the letters of the alphabet. To provide a common language would mean to resort to Basic English, which might be suitable for the simpler publications but hardly for those presenting complex, abstract ideas. For efficient and rapid communication technical language must be used in many specialized magazines. Enough is employed even by such publications as *Oil and Gas Journal* or *Popular Electronics* to affect word choice and style of every writer and editor associated with them. As has been said, magazines print all types of fiction and non-fiction; newspapers, on the other hand, are confined mainly to non-fiction. They deliberately avoid technicalities, since most of them are for the general reader.

Effective English may be defined as English that communicates successfully. Success is achieved through clarity, simplicity, accuracy, and originality. Although these qualities can be imparted to the language used in any type of writing, the quality of English in American magazines is uneven. That in many confessions and adventure magazines is trite and banal; in the comics, slangy; in business journals, often wordy and colorless; in company magazines, frequently colloquial and routine. The fault of the majority of specialized magazines of science, education, labor, the arts, and other segments of knowledge is that they are written in vague, highly decorative, hopelessly roundabout, or abstract English. Chiefly in the general, literary, and opinion publications do we find an effort to refine phrases and select exact words to express meaning plainly and accurately, and not in all of these, by any means.

The quality of English varies because readers do not repudiate a magazine guilty of shoddiness. They should not always insist upon merely grammatically correct language; sometimes clarity is achieved by breaking rather than observing a rule, as in the instance of the split infinitive and the use of personal pronouns. "To neatly replace" is clearer to some readers than is "to replace neatly," and "it is me" is more readily understood than is "it is I." But readers should become impatient with periodicals that cover themselves with stereotyped language (samples: "frank and fearless," "widespread discussion," "narrowly escaped," "hunger for salvation," "planned for the near future") or use twenty words where thirteen would do ("Alex Alexander, who narrowly escaped a dreadful death in a huge avalanche back in 1958, lives in Canada today" might be "Alex Alexander, who nearly died in an avalanche in 1958, lives in Canada").

Carefully edited magazines do not necessarily command the highest circulations. Literary and opinion publications are uniformly low in distribution; confessions, sex, and comic magazines far outsell them. Those that deal with ideas and information of limited public interest cannot make their appeal on language alone. Beauty and originality of style do not sell many magazines; in fact, they may even discourage sales because the public as a whole has not yet developed a taste for them. The public will read what is of interest to it; if, in addition to communicating, the language is intrinsically beautiful, well and good, but first it must convey meaning clearly.

Pencil-pushers know the language limitations of various magazines and of the reader groups to which they appeal. With these limitations in mind, they work constantly to communicate accurately and clearly. They seek help by studying semantics, elementary grammar and rhetoric, and readability reports.

### Magazine style

Literary style already has been examined in Chapter 9. In the strictly editorial sense, style is a body of rules followed by editors to obtain uniformity in presentation. It governs abbreviation, capitalization, punctuation, use of names, titles, numerals, and such special forms as sports tabulations. Associated with it are rules for copy preparation, copy editor's and proofreader's symbols, common grammatical faults, spelling errors, and legal pitfalls.

Magazine style resembles book more than it does newspaper style. Few special rule books have been issued for copy editors on periodical desks. For many years standard guides for both magazines and books have been the United States Government Printing Office *Style Manual* and the University of Chicago's *A Manual of Style;* others, including the more recent *Words Into Type,* have found their way into some magazine offices. A few business, technical, religious, and other specialized magazines have their own style books, necessary because of their special vocabularies or strict policies. But there are few magazine booklets and leaflets of the type long issued by such newspapers as the Milwaukee *Journal,* New York *Times,* and *Christian Science Monitor,* as guides to reporters, desk editors, and correspondents. The more elaborate of these newspaper manuals are used by magazines that use many news stories and wish to present them in newspaper form.

Magazine style resembles book style because magazine and book printing have been associated and conditions of printing are similar.

In the book and magazine, page size is small and column width greater than in the newspaper. Both are more formal publications. Both also are read more carefully and under better conditions. Further, magazine style has resulted from adaptation of copy editing marks or symbols used by book publishers and newspaper copy editors. Newspaper desk men employ, on local copy, a more or less uniform set of about two dozen symbols understood by the operators in the composing room, either those setting type on machines or those cutting tape to be fed into such machines. Book houses use about the same number, many of them duplicating newspaper practice. The magazine adaptation extends beyond the choice of copy markings to include such practices as spelling in full rather than abbreviating, writing out numbers in words rather than using figures, and capitalizing and using punctuation more liberally than newspapers.

Reports from copy editors show that magazine desks commonly employ the symbols in Fig. 12.6. For guidance in spelling they depend upon Webster's *New International,* the *American College,* Webster's *Collegiate,* Webster's *New World,* Funk & Wagnall's *College,* and the *New Century* dictionaries. For other points they rely on the *Style Manual, A Manual of Style,* or *Words Into Type.* Sometimes magazines have house rules of their own, the editor or the editorial staff making exceptions to the general practice to suit local conditions or special opinions.

Contributors prepare their copy in one form, usually in pages of about twenty-five lines of ten or twelve words to the line, typewritten and double spaced. After editing it, editorial staffers often prepare it in another form. They have it retyped with lines containing only the number of words or characters that the magazine's column width will accept in a given type face. Specially prepared paper sometimes is used to facilitate this recasting.

In most magazine offices the writer's copy is sent to the printer with editing symbols and type instructions added by an editor. Highly organized magazines, however, process copy to such an extent that it is more economical to retype it than to delay the printer with hand corrections. They also require extra copies for examination by legal advisers or supervisory editors.

If the space-measuring system calls for it, ruled paper is used. It may be divided into 85 units, in groups of five starting from a left-hand margin of one inch. The editor needs merely to count the number of 85-unit lines to gauge the total length. Material also is measured in picas, the printer's unit of measurement, for expressing width and depth of columns and the size of margins. A pica corresponds to twelve points, about one-sixth of an inch. The length of the typewritten line marked into columns by picas instead of typewritten letters thus is immediately translated into the printer's unit of measurement. Editors find it convenient to restrict the length of the typewritten line to the number of letters and other characters and number

**Fig. 12.6.** The symbols used by magazine copy editors. Do not confuse these with proofreader's marks.

of spaces accommodated in one line of type of the style to be used. Underlines for pictures similarly are measured in advance of setting into type so that they will fit the space allowed. Exact procedures in copy control are set forth in many readily available pamphlets and books, such as Edmund C. Arnold's *Ink on Paper*.

Satisfactory control of copy depends partly on the condition in which it is sent to the printer. The copy editor has to juggle copy, type, and space to achieve what he envisions. He must be able to imagine how a typescript will look when it has been transformed into printed pages and when related to illustrations and advertising.

Dr. Robert Root outlined briefly the three major steps which, under ideal conditions, the copy editor of a magazine follows when dealing with a piece of copy.

"First he glances over the whole piece to get the general picture," Dr. Root wrote. "Second, he goes through it to eliminate errors and tighten up the language. If it seems necessary, he may go over it again to check libel, taste, and policy. Next, he will normally write the headings and add any necessary instructions for the printer. The copy is now ready to go, but he may finally, especially if it is important, look over the whole to see that the headings and edited copy fit together into a workmanlike unit."[13]

Dr. Root then qualified this description realistically, by saying that this is the model procedure and perhaps the ideal to be sought, and explaining that in actuality the editor does not usually divide the process up so neatly. He corrects misspellings as he sees them, not being able to resist the correcting during the first reading. And if as he reads for sense he also gets an idea for a suitable title he notes that at the same time as he reads.

## Rewriting copy

A manuscript can be improved by complete recasting as well as by meticulous editing. Although as much editing as possible should be done by the pencil, there comes a time when an entirely new version is desirable. Time permitting, the author is asked to do any extensive revising and recasting; otherwise he is consulted by telephone or telegram, and later shown the new manuscript, and then proofs of it.

Almost any editorial staff member may do this work, although in a large department certain subordinate editors handle the bulk of it. Magazine offices have more time for rewriting than do other media, and therefore can be expected to do it. In fact, the reputation for high quality workmanship possessed by the magazine in the United States has come in part from insistence upon painstaking revision and rewriting. The fact, also, that magazines are carefully planned and

[13] Robert Root, "Copyeditor at Work," *Editor's Notebook*, March–April, 1963, pp. 7–8.

assembled makes rewriting possible and important for them. Furthermore, periodicals are held responsible for the views of writers who sign the material, whereas newspapers, except in editorials, can by-pass criticism by saying, "Can't blame us for that. We didn't say it, we merely reported it. We print all the news, we don't make it." Only the general magazines attempt to remain detached or are indifferent to strong criticism; all others hold positions, whether by accident or design. That the position generally is conservative socially and politically is beside the point here; to maintain it the copy editor must be on guard. Rewriting sometimes is the only way to maintain policy or avoid misrepresentation and misunderstanding.

The purposes of magazine rewriting are to:

1. Make copy fit a designated space.
2. Make it conform to policy.
3. Improve its literary features, such as structure, vocabulary, use of anecdotes and illustrations.
4. Supply missing material or add more recent information.

Rewriting involves changing copy, including signed material. How much may a copy editor alter it? Only one in authority should venture to do more than correct spelling, improve grammar, remove redundancies, and change factual statements known to be incorrect. Major textual alterations, involving omission of large blocks of material, addition of new matter, complete rephrasing for achievement of different effects, or presentation of another point of view require authorization by a superior. They may be suggested by a subordinate, proposed by the editor in charge to the author, or authorized by him and later submitted for approval.

Under realistic conditions, magazine editors assume varying degrees of freedom to rewrite copy. Some antagonize careful authors by their ruthlessness, like the editor who printed an article criticizing another magazine for inserting material but who did precisely that to an article by a writer for his own magazine, adding sixteen lines at the end without consulting the author. Other editors, being timid or overly thoughtful, allow copy of questionable merit to go through unchanged. The majority do whatever is the less trouble: they are determined with writers who are pliant or do not care so long as they are paid; they are discreet with those who are sensitive and particular.

Deft editors accomplish considerable revision without authors realizing what has happened to their copy. Once when Ben Kartman was associate editor of *Coronet* he received a manuscript which was one-fifth longer than the space which had been allotted to it. By judicious editing and rewriting of certain parts he eliminated the excess. When the author saw proofs of the final version she did not detect the changes, for she had checked only against her recollection, not the original copy. She was astonished when told what had been done, and she approved.

The better edited a magazine, the higher its literary standards; the more sensitive it is about author-editor relationships, the less it tampers with contributed material. This statement may sound paradoxical, but it is not. High standards, usually, go hand in hand with respect for the author's rights. Consequently, cheaply managed magazines of sensational appeal pay little attention to the literary niceties and are ruthless with copy because neither authors nor readers have standards that demand any other treatment.

A compromise is to buy copy with the understanding that the material it contains will be rewritten and the revision published as a collaboration by two authors. *Harper's,* for example, at one time followed the policy of attaching the name "George C. Clark" to articles that were rewritten. There was no such person; it was merely an office name. Large magazines commonly assign a staffer to such rewrites and unite his name in the by-line with that of the original writer. An editor is within his rights if the author signs his check with that understanding.

Editors make fewer changes in fiction than non-fiction because it demands a higher degree of creative work by the author. It is nearer to being an individual work of art and a personal expression, in which loss of style through editorial changes would be more serious than in non-fiction. Also, the best fiction is more difficult to obtain; it brings a higher price and its authors are more in demand. But note that this fact is true only of the best. An editor who pays a high rate for copy by a popular author is not given to offending him by changing his copy severely. Finally, writers of non-fiction often are one-time newspaper people accustomed to having their copy high-handedly altered at the desk.

Editors of hobby, popularized science, and trade magazines have a particularly acute rewriting problem to face. Clifford Hicks, special projects editor of *Popular Mechanics* and formerly its chief editor, once explained in a letter to the author: "A sizable share of our stuff must be rewritten from scratch. Many free-lance features come in, built around a sound idea and with good photos. The facts are there, too. But the copy either is poor or doesn't conform to our style. In many cases such articles are well worth a rewrite job, a task that naturally falls to one of the editors. . . ."

The need for such extensive rewriting comes because writers on technical subjects, although well informed on their topics, are not often highly competent writers. Scientists and mechanics must spend too long learning their own fields to find time for study of journalism.

Ultimately, rewriting of magazine copy means that the rewriter himself must be a capable craftsman who can treat another person's work as source material, add or subtract information, and produce a new piece of copy of higher literary quality that more nearly meets the magazine's standards or rules.

Whether he does patchwork or turns out a completely new article or story, the editor aims at achieving almost impossible goals: to preserve so much of the original style and content that the author is not conscious of the full extent of the revision and instead appreciates the new result as an improvement, and to see that the new version is of the greatest possible interest and benefit to the reader.

### Fitting copy to space

If all magazines had a production editor, the other editors could leave to him or her the procedure known as copyfitting, which actually is more in the realm of graphic arts than editorial practice. But on most publications this work is left to one or more of the regular editors, the production editor being a staff member hired mainly by large firms publishing consumer magazines, or publishing companies that have groups of small magazines, or companies that, while issuing only a small book, perhaps see the importance of a production expert who also has other duties.

The complex arrangements of material on a magazine page, especially of the consumer variety, occur with careful planning, of which copyfitting is an important part. If a page, a pair of opposite pages, or a sequence of pages containing related material, such as a picture story or a long, illustrated article, is to have a distinctive treatment and personality every element must be planned precisely. Such planning includes determining the exact amount of type in relation to headings, illustrations, folio lines, advertising matter, and white space. The process of figuring out how much manuscript will occupy a selected area on a page, in a designated type size and style, is called copyfitting.

On many small magazines with simple layouts, the editors merely count words and estimate the amount of space they will fill. Various quick rules of thumb are followed in the rough systems of this sort. One is that a manuscript page with one-inch margins, in elite type, 25 lines to the page, carries about 325 words; that same material in pica type will run about 275 words to the page. But this method overlooks the differences in lengths of words (*to* is a word; so is *transmogrification*).

Genuinely scientific methods of copyfitting, however, are far more complex and to be preferred. They are slower, but they may, in the long run, prove to be more economical, for they avoid resetting of material, waste from oversetting, or extra charges for settings to fill space unaccounted for by rough estimates.

Even on small periodicals trouble can be avoided by having all copy retyped, line for line and character for character, to correspond to the basic body type being used. The more varied the sizes and styles of body types, either within a given manuscript or between succeeding pieces of copy, the greater the need for copyfitting techniques.

Mechanical aids are available to speed up the process of counting characters, such as flat gauges to be placed on typewritten lines or gauges mounted on small wheels and run down the center of manuscript pages as in measuring mileage on a map with a similar gadget. Such devices are no more nearly accurate than word counting. Also, it must be remembered that in recent years many varieties of typewriter type sizes and styles have been introduced and the assumption that any typewritten character of a stated size corresponds in width, say, to that of the type face of the same size selected for it may be incorrect.

Edmund C. Arnold makes copyfitting relatively uncomplex yet scientific as he explains it. He defines it as "establishing ratios between typescript and type" and recommends the character-per-pica system. In this method the editor determines average line length in the copy by counting characters. He then determines the average number of lines on each page. The next step is to multiply the number of lines by the characters on each line. The result is the number of characters on each page of typescript. This figure then is multiplied by the number of pages, giving the total of characters in the copy.[14]

## *Preparing headings*

No other regularly issued product of the press uses the wide variety of headings to be found in modern magazines. Sometimes within the covers of one issue a magazine displays all the principal types of heading material: headlines, titles, subheads, blurbs, editorial notes, and captions. It should be emphasized that the word *heading* applies to all these elements and is not a synonym for *headline,* which is essentially a newspaper term.

The differences between the six types lie in appearance and use. In general, magazine headings are smaller than those of newspapers, although they appear more prominent because they often are printed in colored inks, always on smaller pages, and usually with greater contrast. They also are simpler in design. A metropolitan paper may have from forty to fifty different sizes and styles of headlines and half as many other headings, such as column titles, that remain the same

---

[14] Edmund C. Arnold, *Ink on Paper* (New York: Harper & Row, 1963), pp. 65–66. For explanations of other methods of copyfitting see: Rowena Ferguson, *Editing the Small Magazine* (New York: Columbia University Press, 1958), pp. 134–38; Russell N. Baird and Arthur T. Turnbull, *Industrial and Business Journalism* (Philadelphia: Chilton Co., 1961), pp. 152–60; *Copy Fitting Method* (Brooklyn, N.Y.: Mergenthaler Linotype Co.), a pamphlet; Robert Root, *Modern Magazine Editing* (Dubuque: Brown, 1966), pp. 109–14.

from issue to issue. A typical magazine collection of headings consists of about a half-dozen different styles of headlines and confines titles to two or three type families in varying sizes. A few large magazines in addition use a wide variety of hand-lettered titles for special effect.

The six types of heading material, headline, title, caption, blurb, editorial note, and subhead, are defined as follows:

**The headline.** This is a unit of one or more (usually more) lines of type that is larger than the body type of the publication and placed above or in some other dominating relation to the article, story, or other type of copy to which it refers. A typical magazine headline reads:

## *Imported Panels Portray*
## *Life of Gustav Vigeland*

The headline's function is to attract the reader, to dress up the reading matter, to summarize its content, and to permit speedy reading. It is a complete sentence containing a complete idea.

**The title.** Usually this is a one- or two-line heading primarily intended to whet the reader's interest rather than to summarize the content of reading matter above or beside which it stands. Ordinarily it contains no more than four or five words, whereas the headline, especially when imitative of newspapers, uses from six to a dozen or more. It is typographically larger than the headline: the fewer the words, the shorter the title but the larger the type in compensation. The Vigeland article might carry this title:

## A SCULPTOR'S LIFE

The title is not, ordinarily, a complete idea or sentence but ideally a somewhat provocative and puzzling label, like "Adding Insult to Burglary." In routinely edited magazines label titles often are used, such as "Report on Manadan Conference." This treatment should be avoided because it fails to arouse interest except among those deeply concerned with the conference.

**The caption.** This can be either a heading or an explanatory legend accompanying an illustration. The meaning of the word is badly confused. Accurately it means an overline, i.e., a headline placed over a map, photograph, drawing, or other illustration. Through careless use it has come to mean the lines below or beside an illustration (which are correctly known as *underlines* or *cutlines*) that explain it to the reader. Captions above elements are used less as more magazines bleed their illustrations. Example of a caption (a cutline) placed under the picture of a machine:

> The "Onset" electronographic press prints without pressure, the paper only contacting the plate. Ink migration is accomplished by electrostatic force.

**The blurb.** This is a subordinate type of heading. It is additional material about the content of an article or story, set in larger than body type and cut into the body of the copy or placed near the main heading. Its purpose is to arouse further interest in the reading matter, to make the entire article or story tempt the reader, a device more necessary with the title than with the headline, since the title is fragmentary, whereas the headline is complete. A blurb for the Vigeland article might read:

*The amazing story of the Scandinavian sculptor, little known in America, whose life-like and life-size figures are at the center of a never-ending debate in Norway.*

Blurbs run from a few words to some sentences in length; they are a convenience for editors who lack illustrations with which to break up type pages.

**The editorial note.** Rowena Ferguson distinguishes the editorial note from the blurb by pointing out that it is longer, sometimes a substantial paragraph, "and provides supplementary information about the article, which the editor addresses to the reader. Often in his note the editor makes the article more intelligible and more relevant to the reader and so increases reader interest. . . . When a piece carries an editorial note, it is not just an appendage to the copy; it is one of the elements of the page design."[15] To this description can be added a further distinction from the blurb: the editorial note contains less sales talk and more amplification of the content of the manuscript.

**The subhead.** This is also a subordinate heading type, and is of two kinds. One, known in some editorial offices as a *subtitle,* is a secondary headline or line that reads out from a title or headline but is not set close enough to the main heading to be considered part of it. It is

---

[15] Rowena Ferguson, *op. cit.,* pp. 149–50.

a favorite of departmental editors. For example, below a department labelled Trends appeared this subhead, in smaller, contrasting type:

## $T$RENDS

### What's Behind What's Happening

The other kind of subhead is comprised of a line or two set in the body of the reading matter at regular points breaking up masses of un-relieved type. Usually slightly larger than the body type or set in bold-face or italics, these lines are intended chiefly to make the type matter visually more attractive, but they also guide the reader through the substance of the material. Usually this type of subhead is used with non-fiction; since fiction is marred by them, editors choose to employ large initial letters, spaces, and asterisks, at regular intervals, to achieve the same optical effect. Here is an example of a subhead as it appeared in non-fiction copy:

> Now before I tell you how we at *Time, Life,* and *Fortune* try to use direct mail to get results and to win friends and in-fluence people, too, I think I had better admit that there are two main schools of thought about direct mail advertising.
>
> **Two Main Schools**
> The first is what we might call the formula school. This group maintains that there are basic rules of direct mail
> . . .

Closely related to heads are by-lines, the name of the author of a manuscript or of the artist who drew the illustrations or the name of the photographer or studio that provided the photographs.

Headings can be as dangerous, if they are faulty, as other content. Libel and other offenses have been committed in their wording. An error involving *The Reporter* magazine illustrates the point. More than 100,000 copies of the Jan. 10, 1957 issue of that bi-weekly of pub-lic affairs had been mailed to subscribers when a typographical error was found in a title on the cover.

The line was intended to read, "Our Gentle Diplomacy." It had been transmitted over the telephone from New York to the printing plant then used in Dayton, Ohio, and set in type. Proofs of the cover were not received in New York until the issue was off the press, mailed, and distributed to newsstands; this was extraordinary and came about because of holiday mail schedules, for ordinarily such proofs were read before distribution began. When the magazine was received by readers, the line read: "Our Gentile Diplomacy." The 25,000 newsstand copies were recalled and the heading deleted. A letter of apology was sent to the 100,000 subscribers.[16]

## Writing the headings

Editors write headings for each article or story separately, keying each to the related reading matter, but group them according to style of type before sending the copy to the printer. Some editors vary the practice; they write the heading directly on the manuscript, at the top of the first sheet, marking it for type style. Others, influenced by newspaper practical experience, set up each head on a small sheet, sending that to the printer with the main copy.

These headings are not always prepared in advance of sending copy to be set. To avoid using rush time for this work, copy is sent to the printer with the letters "HTK" or "HTC" (Head To Come) or without any indication as to what is to be done about the heading. A copy editor writes the title or headline later from galley proof. This delay is not serious in magazine offices except close to the final deadline, for usually there is time for such slow production. It has the advantage of allowing editors to change their minds about dressing the copy; if sufficient material is on hand they can practically remake the magazine while dummying.

Well-run editorial offices retain carbon copies of articles or stories sent to be set. Editors then are able to write headings while the live manuscript is being reproduced and to send head copy along later, before proofs are returned. These delayed procedures are not practical in high speed newspaper, newsmagazine, or opinion magazine offices, where much simultaneous production is necessary if deadlines are to be met.

The physical form of heading material, like that of reading matter, may be set forth in the contract with the printer, who may refuse to accept hand-written copy of any sort. Even if the printer is not insistent, the more efficient method is to work out headings in pencil on scratch paper and then to type the final draft.

Whether heading copy is marked for type size and style depends upon the understanding with the printer and whether the heading is a title, headline, or one of the other kinds. If a magazine uses repeatedly five styles of heads, samples are set by the printer and mounted, several sets of them being prepared for production and editorial department guidance. These headings are numbered or coded by letters. Whenever text for one of them is prepared, the corresponding number is placed on the copy to indicate its form.

Title styles, however, are either not used repeatedly or are few in

---

[16] "Magazine Explains Error in Headline," The New York *Times,* Jan. 1, 1957.

number, simpler, and shorter than the headline. It is as efficient, therefore, to note the size and style of type on the copy for each one as it would be to use the samples and codes. The writer writes beside the title copy some such instruction as "36 pt. Gar 2 col. bf u and lc." Other headings may be in the same type but in 24 or 48 point, otherwise the procedure is similar.

Captions sometimes are more difficult to write than headlines or titles. That part appearing over an illustration is relatively simple. The form of caption known as underline or cutline is troublesome when precision is demanded. To produce neat pages sub-editors must count the characters in each line to assure that the lines are square at both sides, i.e., that the last word reaches the right-hand margin. Failure to do this spoils the appearance of a picture story or any group of pictures in which ragged ends are quickly noted by the reader. To achieve regularity, caption writers use specially ruled paper, divide allotted space into lines, note the number of type characters in each line, and rework the wording until it fits. This mechanical perfection must be achieved without lessening the effectiveness of the underline; it still must describe, explain, or identify the illustration, relate it to the text of the article, and arouse the reader's interest.

Not all editors, however, are so careful. Most of them type out the legends to whatever length they happen to reach, then send the copy to the printer, and later paste the proofs into proper position, jumping more reading matter to the back of the book if necessary to make room for cutlines. Such loose procedure is feasible for single pictures but is likely to produce irregular and disorderly looking pages if there are many illustrations. Caption material is marked for the printer as is any other copy.

Usually an agreement with the printer specifies that underlines are always to be set in certain size and style type. Common usages require italics or boldface and the first few words of the underline always set in caps or some other variation. To set them off, these lines are indented either one-half em or one em on each side. Conventionally, they should not be set more than two standard columns wide; if a picture is as much as six or eight inches wide, the lines are doubled up, that is, set three inches (36 picas) in width and run in columns side by side. Often lines are run in odd positions, that is, set into a space cut out of the engraving. A few commercial magazines, such as *Esquire* and *McCall's*, seeking typographic novelty, break these general rules for the sake of the over-all effect, which often is dramatic, even if not particularly readable.

Subheads are written along with copy for the main heading. If large enough and in distinctive type, they are grouped on separate sheets. Those placed between paragraphs generally are inserted by hand before the copy finally is retyped or are written in on final copy. These must be marked for style if there is no standing agreement with the printer. They are no wider than half the magazine's column if they are to be centered in the column and not more than three-fourths if they are to run flush-left or flush-right (to one margin, with white space at the other).

Blurbs are placed on separate sheets, marked for their special typographical characteristics, and keyed to their article or story by some such guide as "With Red Moon." Blurbs and editorial notes, therefore, also are elements of copy. They involve little writing but as factors in page layout are able to spoil or improve page appearance. Credit lines are kept inconspicuous, because they can intrude on pages, but they are important in allocating responsibility and meeting commercial requirements of credit for work done.

## Counting headlines

Counting a headline is part of the procedure followed in producing headlines and captions intended to fit allotted space. Primarily a newspaper practice, it is a simple device on which the new magazine staffer constantly relies until he is able to think in terms of letters, numerals, punctuation, and spaces.

Any heading that is to fit exactly a given amount of space must, like reading matter copy, be measured precisely. Counting units, which makes this possible, is done more often in writing headlines and captions than in preparing titles, which are more flexible.

In the headings schedule used by any magazine each headline takes up a predetermined amount of space, either in picas, inches, or columns. For example, a headline designated as *B* may consist of two lines arranged in step fashion, thus:

In the size of type used in the sample provided by the printer this headline is to fit into a two-inch column. The full width of the column, in the given type style and size, may be twenty units, that is, twenty letters, spaces, numerals, and punctuation. But the heading is more pleasant to the eye if it does not occupy all the space but leaves two spaces blank at the end of the first line and the beginning of the second (or at the right end of both lines, in the case of a flush-left head). Therefore the editorial department lays down the rule that this heading is to consist of two lines of eighteen units each. The copy editor writes it so that it does not exceed this length and for neat appearance and symmetry preferably does not fall below seventeen units.

Headlines are used not only above news copy but also throughout magazines that seek a newspaper appearance, as does *Variety*. Magazine publishers have borrowed from newspapers the typical news headline, but have limited their selections to a few specimens. Since the rules of preparation are those of the newspaper, newspaper copy desk experience is valuable to the magazine editor.

## *Preparing titles*

The title that appears on an article, story, or other piece of copy when it arrives rarely can be used as it is by the magazine's title writer. It probably will not fit, since the author did not know the publication's rules on titles or the eventual choice of size or style for his particular piece. Also, most authors do not know how to produce effective titles. Like headline writing, this takes skill of a certain kind. Authors should continue titling their own material, however, not only because the editor then has a convenient reference to the story or or article, but also because he is given a start on preparation of a final heading. In numerous editorial offices busy or lazy sub-editors use the author's title even if defective or choose a type style and size so as to be able to use it without more labor on their part.

Although in most offices headlines are strictly confined to a limited number of styles, having been designed according to certain generally understood patterns, such as two or three stepped lines, pyramided lines, or flush-left, titles are restricted to a few variations of the same type or allowed to run wild, following neither order nor pattern. Lacking a distinct model and being fragmentary, a title is harder to write than a headline. A title is expected to be more creative, to possess more originality, than a headline. It does not rest so much on the function of imparting information; it must lure the reader by cleverness and spirited language, especially if it is used with fiction.

Titles are counted out but are mechanically easier to produce than headlines. This mechanical simplicity makes up somewhat for the greater creative effort required. Bird has analyzed titles used in magazines and found a dozen types: striking statement, provocative statement, label, paraphrase, declarative sentence, how-why-what, rhyme and alliteration, question, direct address, quotation, exclamation, and balance and contrast.[17] These are non-fiction titles only. Titles over fiction cannot be categorized thus, for each expresses the nature and mood of the tale. "Speedy William" is short and itself speedy, to reflect the tone of the story, for example.

---

[17] George L. Bird, *Article Writing and Marketing* (New York: Rinehart, 1956), p. 163.

Usually titles serve as headings over departments, although small headlines may accompany them to show content changes from issue to issue; in fact, this policy is advisable to keep the department from seeming the same from one issue to the next. The department heading itself may stand unchanged, consisting of hardly more than a label used for identification purposes, but an additional and varying headline is needed to tell the reader what topics are covered in the current issue. All these headlines, of whatever type, are written as if they were to be used over independent copy, and may be thrown in with assembled copy or run-of-the-magazine headings or attached to the department editor's copy for the given issue.

## Handling pictures and layouts

Picture handling is part of the editorial staffer's work. To put this operation in its proper setting, it has been described in the next chapter, which deals with magazine art and photography. Preparing layouts, making up, and dummying the magazine also are operations in which the magazine editorial department plays an important part. These have been dealt with in Chapter 6.

## Keeping schedules

Airlines and bus companies would not attempt to operate without schedules that keep the public and their employes aware of when and where transportation is available. Industry depends upon production schedules almost as much as upon raw materials, because failure to meet them denies the product to others that need it. So it is with the magazine, which like any well-ordered business sets up routines for continually repeated operations and schedules to assure that all parts of magazine production are completed by the required time.

In the journalistic world schedules play an especially important part because the objective of most routines is to complete work by pre-arranged, stated deadlines upon which many departments depend. The production manager may have on his office wall a Productrol, originally intended for use in factories that produce such consumer commodities as refrigerators and shoes. By advancing colored pegs across the board he can tell at a glance the production status of each magazine or procedure involved in publishing. This control board pegs off when copy for future issues has gone to the printer, when photographs were dispatched to the engraver, when color cover copy was sent for reproduction, when these materials were returned with proofs, when dummies have been dispatched, layouts requested and received, printing schedules fulfilled, different signatures or forms completed, and when binding work is underway.

At another extreme is a small specialized magazine such as a

(a)

(b)

the fisheye lens. The art director accompanies the photographer to supervise what is done, since he is aware of the total page size, the logo, and the cover words. Helland and Shapiro make the final selection.

(c) An art assistant strips in the logo and cover words, the contact print having been developed and set up for a key line.

(d) Shapiro (right) and Helland check proofs for positioning of the various elements and to verify color fidelity. About ten days are needed between the operations in Figs. 12.7a and 12.7c. The plates then are shipped from the engraver to the *Professional Builder*'s printer, and the covers and entire issue are run off.

(c)

(d)

*Fig. 12.7.* (a) This sequence relating to magazine cover copy preparation begins with a shot of Dick Helland, art director of *Professional Builder,* a Cahners Publishing Company magazine, sketching on an acetate sheet on which the *Practical Builder* (now *Professional Builder*) magazine logo is imprinted. He discusses with James J. Shapiro, executive editor of the magazine, which stories lend themselves to cover treatment and makes several different sketches at this stage. In this instance, some type of fisheye lens photograph will be used to capture a usual subject in an unusual way.

(b) Helland selects four or five of the best photographs from a group of about one hundred shots taken by an outside professional cameraman who has such special equipment as

# Practical Builder

THE BUSINESS MAGAZINE OF PROFESSIONAL BUILDERS/DEVELOPERS          A CAHNERS PUBLICATION/MARCH 1967

You've got to look at
# TOWN HOUSES
differently

Special: Brilliant Selling in a Boggy Market

Building the Instant Campus

(e)

(e) The cover in its finished form. The basic color is dark brown, the fence is dark gray, the houses are in three shades—blue, brown, and gray —and the grass is a light, wintry green. *(All Photos From Professional Builder)*

243

company publication. The editor merely types lists of what is sent to the printer and the engraver and checks these against the proofs when they arrive. Since only one issue is produced at a time, few items need to be recorded or watched in progress.

Between these extremes is the typical situation in which a magazine depends upon several basic types of schedules for control of its editorial operations, which depend upon other departments. The larger the staff and the more operations it performs, the greater the need for schedules. The most common schedules found in editorial offices are:

1. The *inventory,* a bookkeeping system to keep track of all unused copy on hand.
2. The *copy schedule* or assignment sheet, a specific list of all types of material to be used in a forthcoming issue, whether on hand or to be assigned.
3. The *issue schedule* (sometimes combined with the copy schedule), a list, maintained by the managing editor or whoever is in charge, of what has been sent to the engraver and printer for a particular issue. Somewhat like the preceding schedule, it reflects with a greater degree of accuracy the status of copy after editing.

Conscientious scheduling makes it possible to handle such a situation as one described by the managing editor of a farm magazine:

"I had left a four-page signature open for late stories and musts. Before I had finished my second morning cigarette, a full page ad, originally scheduled for November, was dropped in our lap for the current issue. That meant I had three pages for late stories and musts. I dummied in only the most important ones." [18]

---

[18] Letter to the author from Robert Williams, managing editor, *Pennsylvania Farmer.*

# Chapter 13

# Photojournalism and art

John Adams Thayer, once advertising manager of the *Ladies' Home Journal* and *The Delineator* and later publisher of *Everybody's*, tells in his autobiography the story of the origin of a certain cover. The whole *Everybody's* staff was unable to think of a design idea to accompany an article by Thomas W. Lawson, a financier who crusaded against unethical financial practices. Mr. Thayer telephoned Ralph Tilton, an artist, who shortly after produced a suggestion over a luncheon table.

"You say your Lawson article treats of stock market operations. To me that suggests bulls and lambs," the artist said. "Why not go to a toy store and get a bull's head and a little lamb on wheels? Arrange them artistically, with a suitable background, and you will have a good cover." He penciled on the tablecloth a rough sketch, which Mr. Thayer describes as "not only appropriate but highly striking."[1]

Art work in big circulation magazines nowadays rarely depends in that way upon impulse and expediency. Photography now matches art work in importance, especially for covers. Production of magazines has become so systematized that a large national publication leaves little to chance or inspiration. Now and then, of course, emer-

---

[1] John Adams Thayer, *Astir: A Publisher's Life Story* (Boston: Small, Maynard & Co., 1910), pp. 243–44.

gencies occur, but illustrative content is as carefully prepared as reading and advertising matter.

Typical of today's cover work was the preparation of one for
*Fortune*. When that magazine's art director learned that an issue
would carry as its major article one about Sears, Roebuck and Co.,
emphasizing its interest in high fashion, he saw this as an opportunity
to use a model for the first time on *Fortune*'s cover, and a high fashion
one at that.

Walter Allner, the director, decided to put the model in the
middle of a collection of materials from the Sears catalog. He and
Sue Considine, an artist in his department, sketched a tentative cover,
using fifteen items from the giant Sears catalog, which includes 170,-
000. They took the cover items, including a huge tractor tire and a
television set, to a New York City photo studio to set them up for the
picture cover. By coincidence, a popular high fashion model, Suzy
Parker, was in the studio working in another setup.

Miss Parker was selected at once to be in the cover picture with
a Sears fur, diamond, and blue jeans, flanked by the tire, television
set, a stove, a guitar, and a painting. About forty different shots were
taken.

### Photography's new importance

In the years when *Everybody's* was a leading magazine, art work
usually illustrated consumer magazines. Generally it had been used
up to then to decorate pages or to portray scenes in the fiction. Even
the business and other specialized magazines made some use of fussy
borders around text pages or to ornament the advertising. Photographs were subordinated to art and to text; groups of pictures were
common enough but picture stories were little known. As periodicals
were looked to more for news and less for entertainment photojournalism came into its own.

Although it has subsided somewhat from its complete dominance
in the period from about 1940 to 1955, stimulated as it was by wars
and recessions, photography still is more important than art work;
particularly since magazine fiction is not as popular as it once was.
Articles, and the other non-fiction now in such great demand from
magazines, being factual, naturally call for the realism of the camera. Reportorial photography is identified with the modern magazine.

Rhode and McCall have traced the rise of reportorial pictures in
the post World War II period to the influence of *Life* and *Look*. This
influence, they say, "has spread not only to other publications, including newspapers, but through the ranks of amateur photographers.
The dramatic success of the news picture magazines before the war
ushered in a new era of emphasis on not just photos but on photo-

journalism. The photographic coverage of the war greatly reinforced the trend."[2]

Present-day magazines of virtually all types (this naturally excludes most of the scholarly and literary) not only publish more reportorial photography but also more pictures in general, print them in large sizes, ask cameramen to try for inherently more attractive composition and to avoid the monotony of certain standard poses. They also make room for picture stories occupying from a few pages to at times almost entire issues. Particularly responsive to the value of pictures have been the thousands of magazines in the industrial or company category.

Another effect of the vogue for more and better pictures in magazines has been upon magazine photographers themselves, who have achieved new importance. They now have several organizations of their own. One, particularly active in the periodical world, is the American Society of Magazine Photographers. The full-time free lancers, and this includes some of the outstanding photographic artists, have the help of representatives, just as writers have their agents. Such picture agencies, known by credits reading Magnum, Globe, and Black Star, sell pictures, obtain assignments, and protect rights.

These photographers, at least when working for the larger consumer magazines, are able to command high prices, since there now is a broader market for their prints. They are able to sell them several times over. Donald Feitel, in a book for the photographic free lance, tells of the experience of Frank Gilhoon, who operates his own agency. Having taken four panoramic views of New York he set out one day to sell them to a postcard maker and disposed of the one he considered his best for $10.

"On the way back to the office," Feitel relates, "he happened to stop in at a magazine office he hadn't called on in weeks. Turned out he had just the picture they were looking for and they bought one of the three remaining for $1,000."[3]

A study of the market guides shows that most big magazines pay about $150 a page for black and white and $200 a page for color, as well as some part of the expenses. Pictures for covers bring more than those for inside pages, especially if in color, and cost the publisher anywhere from $400 to $2,000. Usually the publisher retains all rights.

Another effect of the photo boom is the encouragement to photog-

---

[2] Robert B. Rhode and Floyd H. McCall, *Press Photography* (New York: Macmillan Co., 1961), p. 28.

[3] Donald Feitel, *Secrets of Successful Free Lancing* (Philadelphia: Chilton Co., 1958), p. 109.

raphers to shoot much film. Picture editors of big magazines want a wide choice and know that with the taking of many pictures sometimes unusual and unplanned results are obtained. A. J. Liebling, the late gadfly of smug editors and publishers, once said that if he could shoot thousands of pictures on one assignment he too could produce extraordinary results. For it is true that the large magazines permit a photographer to take hundreds of pictures, of which only four or five are used. Since the supplies are provided by the magazine, for a staffer, the camerman has no reluctance to make the most of this liberal attitude, and shoots ten times more than he would for a small magazine too poor to put perfect results ahead of costs.

Not only are magazines in general more hospitable than ever to picture copy, but entire magazines are published consisting of little but photographs. The large popular photo magazine was the rage for a time, and we saw titles such as *Pic, Foto, Quick, Hue,* and *Photo-History.* The survivors are led by *Life* and *Ebony,* to which can be added *Sports Illustrated, Sepia,* and a few others that contain more pictures than reading matter. The supplements to Sunday newspapers come into this category as well, and like the conventional picture magazines are discussed in later chapters. They bear such names as *Sunday, Parade, Family Weekly, Tuesday, Tuesday at Home,* and *Weekend.*

Not even the magazines of photography—*Travel and Leisure, Popular Photography, Modern Photography,* and the like—are without text. As *Life* had to learn, they need words to say what it would take too many pictures to portray.

### *Departmental organization*

In the largest magazine companies, art or photographic work has achieved the status of a department on a plane with editorial, advertising, and circulation. In the majority, art directors, art and picture editors exist aplenty, but most do other tasks as well and have such small staffs that their work is performed through a department subdivision called an art or picture office, division, section, or department.

The few full-fledged departments are to be found in big publishing firms that issue large-circulation magazines. The *National Geographic's* photo department is headed by a director and staffed by one associate director, a chief and an assistant chief of film review, a chief of photographic equipment, a chief of photographic research, and a chief and associate chief of photographic laboratories. The magazine has an illustration editor, with an associate editor, and two assistant editors, a layout and production chief, two senior picture editors, two researchers, and a librarian. On this periodical photography is separate from the illustration staff; there are thirteen photographers and a lab staff of about thirty.

*Life* places its titled photographic staff high in the echelons. Among them are such noted photographers as Yale Joel, and Carl Mydans. The twenty staff photographers are supplemented by film editors, picture bureau members, picture librarians, and heads of the laboratory. A director of photography supervises the department.

It is economical for those companies that publish more than one magazine to have large staffs of artists and photographers occupying studios and laboratories equipped with cameras, enlarging machines, drawing boards, stocks of photographs, airbrushes, and other paraphernalia necessary for production of paintings, drawings, and photographs. Some firms expect one department to serve all others, meeting art and photo needs of advertising, editorial, and promotion departments. Others have found that matters run more smoothly if each operating department has its own crews.

Small magazines organize such work in several ways. They may depend entirely upon free-lance artists and photographers who take assignments; they may hire commercial firms; they may entrust this function to the printer or engraver, who is perhaps able to provide such auxiliary services as part of his contract. Few magazine offices use any of these four plans exclusively. The publisher who has his own art and photo departments often buys sketches or pictures from free lancers if their output meets some particular need. The firm that depends mainly on commercial studios usually is not averse, unless it signs an exclusive contract, to have on the string an imaginative person who can carry out difficult assignments quickly.

## Products and procedure

Included in the output of the art department, when strictly interpreted as the staff of non-photographic artists, are cartoons and other line or wash drawings, paintings, maps, charts, graphs, tables, hand-lettered text, an uncountable variety of decorations such as spot sketches and ornaments, and advertising and editorial layouts. The photography staff's contribution to "art" comprises single photographs of innumerable types and sizes, picture stories, and the treatment of pictures, sometimes with cooperation by the art department, into montages and other groupings.

The philosophy of artists and cameramen on magazines has been well phrased in a letter to the author by Lawrence Martin, free-lance magazine writer and former associate editor of *Esquire* and other magazines:

> It was the Chinese who said everything first, who laid it down that one picture equals ten thousand words. But it was the Americans, who do everything first and do it most, that did something about it. It was the Chinese, for a further matter of fact, who invented movable types

long before Gutenberg, but it was the Americans who brought out newspapers for the masses. Here are two landmarks in the history of civilization—the invention of the popular newspaper, and the discovery that the world loves nothing so much as a picture.

That the world does desire pictures is clear from the popularity of picture magazines, commercial cinema, comics, gravure supplements to newspapers, illustrations in all publications, picture books, amateur movies, the camera craze, television, cartoons, and old and new stereoscopes.

The magazine is only one of the media meeting this demand, but it has done so to the limit of its capacity. The number of magazines depending almost wholly upon photography for conveying their messages has increased and the quantity of pictures in the magazines in general never has been so large. And periodicals consisting mostly of cartoons have been popular for well more than a century, reaching their apex in the comic magazines of our own time.

The ways in which photographs are used in magazines have been classified by two editors, one later becoming editor of *Look:*

1. As illustrations for text, i.e., illustrating and decorating articles and departments.
2. Picture-text combinations. In this use pictures are arranged in continuity and related to the text, with the text subordinated to the pictures and consisting mainly of captions. Writer, photographer, and layout artist combine their efforts to produce these.
3. Pure picture stories. These are sequences of pictures that do not require text at all, although they may carry a little for decorative effect. Such stories are the result of careful planning, the details of which the authors present, with full illustration, in their book.
4. Picture stories with text stories. Here is a combination of text illustrations and picture-text combinations or of text illustrations and pure picture stories.[4]

This analysis could be applied to art work; actually pictures are replacing it and supplementing it so as to do what paintings and drawings once did exclusively. A primary purpose of art was to illustrate text, and it survives as the main form of illustration for fiction except in certain confession, mystery, fan, and novels-in-pictures magazines that use photographs to point up the narrative's realism. The comic magazine is a literal picture-text combination. The picture story or the picture-and-text story is not new, but it generally has been used with humorous rather than serious subjects.

A suggestion of the principles on which art work should be used

---

[4] Daniel D. Mich and Edwin Eberman, *The Technique of the Picture-Story* (New York: McGraw-Hill, 1945).

*Fig. 13.1.* An editor of a small magazine goes over pictures and galley proofs with an assistant art director. *(Photo by Audrey Heaney)*

has been set down by George W. Leech, former art editor of the *Strand,* a famous monthly in London now gone after fifty years during which it printed the first Sherlock Holmes stories and much of the work, for the first time, of Rudyard Kipling and H. G. Wells. Leech wrote, in one of the few books in any language on magazines and the art work:

> In the first place an illustration should *illustrate* the author's text. Not in a narrow, finicky way that is only concerned with detail, but in the broader appreciation of essentials.
> Secondly, it should *decorate* the page or pages it occupies. In these days of competitive publishing, a magazine is largely bought on its attractive appearance at first sight.
> Thirdly, the illustration should *reproduce* well and be treated in such a manner as to suit the particular conditions and limitations of the magazine for which it is done.[5]

Procedures in both photography and art divisions are similar. The person in charge, called art director or manager if he oversees the art work of several departments, or art editor if he is responsible chiefly for the editorial department's use of illustrative materials, is expected to be familiar with the text for which art is being prepared. He, or a subordinate, to use an editorial department instance, reads through an article or story for its gist. Another reading is made for selection of incident or reference to be illustrated. What subjects and how many are to be illustrated vary with the place of art work in the magazine as a whole. An art editor whose practice is to use a three-quarter double spread (that much of two facing pages) and jump most of the reading matter from that plus one more unillustrated page to the back of the book will call for one large painting only. But the editor who runs an article or story on successive pages may decide on at least one picture or drawing for every other page or about every two thousand words.

The editor, rather than the artist or photographer, selects the subjects and sizes because he knows the totals of art content of the issue and is more likely to choose what is needed rather than what is easy to produce. He makes assignments to artists and photographers according to their specialties or particular abilities. Roughs (unfinished sketches) are submitted by artists or prints by photographers; these craftsmen also are supposed to have read the copy they are to illustrate. The preliminary sketches approved, the artist presents the final drawing. The photographer is finished when he turns in his prints unless workmanship or selection is unsatisfactory even after the editor has seen negatives or contact prints. From final

---

[5] George W. Leech, *Magazine Illustration* (London: Pitman, 1939), p. 54.

drawings or approved prints the production process proceeds, line cuts and engravings being the final result.

## Photography and production

An operation involving photography that is relatively new in magazine offices is preparing pages to be photographed for use in offset lithography, a printing process increasingly used by small circulation periodicals (see Chapter 6).

The production editor or an art department staff member is given this responsibility. He has a dummy which the editorial and art departments collaborate upon, showing the relationship of the major elements on the page: type, photographs, and art work. The type is represented by corrected proofs of both body type and headings, the photos are finished prints (unless they are not being used in the same size), the art work is finished. If the latter two are not to size, windows must be left for later insertion in proper dimensions.

These elements must be assembled to correspond to the original design for the page, carefully squared off to fit the page size, and cleaned of all visible pen or pencil markings. It then is photographed in the plant where this type of printing is supplied. Such camera copy, as it is called, must be pasted up for every page in the magazine.

Another application of photography to production is in the use of machines that assemble characters by photography on film to be transferred then to a printing plate.

## Third-dimension photography

A technique for photographing and, through printing, mass reproducing of pictures that appear to have depth, or a third dimension, was announced in 1964 by *Look*. The result reminded those old enough to remember them of the stereopticon viewing of early in the century, the photo slides that come from the double image of the stereopticon camera, and the 3-D motion pictures at which one had to look with special glasses.

The three companies involved in the production presented their invention in the Feb. 25, 1964 issue of *Look* via an article about Thomas A. Edison and his various discoveries. Printed with it was a photograph, inserted at the gutter, showing a bust of Edison surrounded with several of his inventions. In black and white, 4¾" x 4", it appeared fuzzy and blurred, but when moved slightly the illusion of depth was created. A new type of camera and new photographic techniques were worked out, with Arthur Rothstein, then *Look's* technical director of photography, collaborating. Xograph, a project of Cowles Communications, Inc., now produces 3-D pictures in four colors; they are used on magazine covers, in direct mail and other advertising, and in packaging.

As early as 1961 a similar process was used by Hallmark Cards, Incorporated, producer of greeting cards. Another method, achieving results much like those of the Cowles example bound into this book, has been worked out by Hallmark with the P.I.D. Corporation. This other process also has been used for magazine illustration, direct mail advertising, and greeting cards.

Among the periodicals using Xographs was *Venture . . . The Traveler's World,* a monthly published by Cowles until its recent discontinuance, which attached one to the cover of each issue. *Elle,* the French monthly for women, uses one on its cover occasionally; *Graphic Arts Buyer, Product Engineering,* and other specialized magazines have

*Fig. 13.2.* Arthur Rothstein, while technical director of photography for *Look,* with the 3-D camera which he helped to develop. This equipment provides two-dimensional photographs that appear to have a third dimension; they were used on *Venture* magazine covers and still are seen in advertising and on book covers. *(Look Magazine Photo)*

used them now and then; numerous advertisers have affixed one to their displays in *Advertising Age* and other publications.

The third-dimension photograph is not new, however. The theory of it goes back beyond the turn of the century; one of the early experimenters was Frederick E. Ives, generally thought to be the inventor of the half-tone engraving process now commonly used. Some years before Cowles used its first 3-D Xograph, Hallmark experimented with it for greeting cards. Although the end result is the same, the processes used by Cowles and Hallmark differ.

Various smaller firms have produced such simulated third-dimension photographs but only Cowles did so for mass magazine use. For a time, Cowles was experimenting with a process by which the Xograph and the printed matter for a magazine page could be produced in one operation. It also was reducing the size of its camera (two tons of equipment and three men originally needed to use the equipment) and expected to achieve one about the size of an attaché case; many of the operations now done in the field would be performed in the studio. But when *Venture* was killed and soon thereafter all other Cowles magazines were sold or folded, interest in the technique lapsed.

## Magazine photography

Famous artists have had a part in the history of the magazine for more than a century. Nathaniel Currier and James Merritt Ives, noted lithographers still famed for their prints, elevated the artistic level of magazines in the last half of the nineteenth century. In the same period, periodicals reproduced work by such prominent artists as Winslow Homer, contributor to *Harper's Weekly;* F. O. C. Darley, illustrator of Irving's *Legend of Sleepy Hollow* and *Rip Van Winkle;* and Timothy Cole who drew for both *The Century* and *Scribner's.* Later in the same period Frederick Remington produced his famous western paintings for *Collier's.* Maxfield Parrish and Charles Dana Gibson contributed to many magazines. In this century other names became common signatures on magazine art work: Neysa McMein, Art McDougall, Norman Rockwell, N. C. Wyeth, J. C. Leyendecker, Helen Hokinson, Rea Irvin, Gardner Rea, Gluyas Williams, John Held, Jr., Peter Arno, Charles Addams, Charles Schulz.

But fame came to magazine photographers much later than to illustrators, largely because only simple photo-mechanical processes were used during the early years, whereas finished art work was being reproduced by means of woodcuts. The first magazine halftone reproduction of a photograph appeared as late as 1881, in *The Philadelphia Photographer,* a year after reproduction in a newspaper. Magazines were slow to exploit the process, only such larger ones as *Harper's Monthly* and *The Century* availing themselves of the possibilities in any quantity.

As Robert Taft shows in his study, *Photography and the Ameri-*

*can Scene,* magazines began by 1900 to use more photographs as illustrations. Within ten years those heretofore illustrated chiefly by woodcuts were using five to ten times as many photos as other kinds of
illustrations.

The trend developed until photographs became the dominant
type of "art" in all magazines except a handful of consumer books
that use paintings for covers and as accompaniments for fiction. The
career of magazine photographer attracts many young people who
have seen the effective work of Margaret Bourke-White, Robert Capa,
Frank Scherschel, Gjon Mili, "Weegee," Pete Martin, Frank Bauman,
Fritz Henle, Arthur Rothstein, Gordon Parks, William Garrett, Cornell Capa, Eliot Elisofon, Carl Mydans, Alfred Eisenstaedt, and numerous others. It is difficult, however, to make publication distinctions, for photographers who create for one see their work reproduced in several others, also. A shot taken for newspaper use may
be published in a magazine after it has been presented as background
for a television news program and sent by wire across the continent.

The major techniques used by magazine photographers are those
of all who handle cameras. Magazines retain more interest in pic-
torials (feature pictures, as of scenery) than do newspapers. The picture story, which takes time and money to plan and execute, is more
practical for the magazine than another type of publication. But the
skilled photographer can adjust to differences. With the photo no
longer merely an adjunct to writing but an end in itself, the cameraman is enthusiastic over his professional objective. Mary Ellen Slate,
an editor of a book issued by a group of magazine photographers,
characterizes the magazine photographer this way:

". . . intense visual imagination, ability to dramatize editorial
ideas and to bring back exciting picture stories . . . is a new kind of
communicator . . . who takes his place with the reporter, the writer,
and the painter . . . he is an amalgamation of the three: he records
facts, spins fancies, and portrays beauty."[6]

## *Cameras*

The 35mm or miniature camera is in common use by magazine
photojournalists. They were the first to see the merits of this small
but effective camera and put it in their kits soon after World War I.

It has more advantages than disadvantages. In its favor: availability of fast films making flash guns unnecessary, numerous expo-
sures (20 to 36), simple and speedy operation, extraordinarily fast
lenses, including several quickly interchangeable ones, easy portability, inconspicuousness, small size, and light weight. Its disadvan-

[6] American Society of Magazine Photographers, *Photographic 1949* (New York:
Whittlesey House, 1948), p. 11.

tages: coarseness of grain and other flaws are easily visible when large prints are made from its negatives, especially in blow-ups, and comparative slowness of processing.

Root, in his substantial chapter on the subject in *Modern Magazine Editing*, lists "Five Pointers on Pictures" that are valuable to note. (1) select a few good pictures; (2) display pictures in large sizes; (3) crop pictures for impact; (4) use bleeding for a purpose; (5) tell a story. These points are worth recalling when editing prints.

## Handling pictures

The taking of photographs, creation of paintings and drawings, and developing and printing of film have been described in many guidebooks for journalists. The editing of photographs from the magazine point of view also deserves a book some day.

An art or picture editor's handling of pictures includes performing or having staff members perform these duties:

1. Buying from syndicates, free-lance photographers, or other publications, to meet specific needs.
2. Directing a photographer who, as a staff man or woman, is expected to take what is needed.
3. Cropping and scaling prints.
4. Preparing captions and underlines.
5. Planning picture stories, montages, and other layouts.
6. Following through on proofs from the engravers to see that specifications have been met accurately; reordering when necessary.
7. Returning or filing used pictures.

Cropping is the process of removing portions of a photograph that detract from its message. Professionals experiment by covering portions of the print with their hands, pieces of paper, or cardboard. When the areas to be used are determined, scaling takes place. This process is one of proportioning a picture so that it will fit an allotted space. When these proportions are settled the print is marked on the reverse side, at the edges only, to avoid damaging the photograph, covered with an overlay of tissue on which the dimensions have been outlined, or marked with marginal lines on the front of the print.

Behind cropping and sizing, the preparation of picture stories, montages, and other assemblies of prints, and the selection of single prints are judgment, experience, and an artistic sense which cannot be learned from textbooks.

Magazine art and photo editors are concerned over fidelity of reproduction of prints they select, and they ask for careful retouching and a wide variety of pictures from which to select those finally to be used. It is commonplace, therefore, for an editor on a well-to-do magazine to comb through several hundreds of photographs in searching for two or three that are suitable.

Office floors frequently are the working tables for photo editors for the obvious reason that usually no other flat surface is wide enough to accommodate dozens of prints for simultaneous examination and comprehension. Next most popular are wall racks into which prints can be slipped. The process of picture selection is one of slow experiment, of trial and error in arrangements. For not only must the editor keep an eye on each picture's qualities but he also must remember the material which the prints are to illustrate, if they are not picture stories or some other independent units.

# Part Four

## *Types of magazines*

*Chapter 14*

# Consumer magazines /
## *Digests, fans, comics, sports*

ONE MORNING, as the writer was pondering his notes for this chapter, trying to decide whether to begin with a definition of consumer magazines or with facts about their number, a long-distance telephone call came from the office of one of these magazines. The caller was a former student, on the staff of one of the largest slicks for women. She was arranging a short story contest to be conducted by the magazine among college students. Being relatively new in the work and shy about asking her superiors, she felt free to appeal to one of her journalism teachers.

Fresh from college, this young woman was able to point out to her editor-in-chief that the magazine, despite its circulation in the millions, was not reaching a group who might develop into lifelong subscribers. Other magazines were attempting it, with their Prix de Paris and College Board competitions serving as important promotions, but they had much less to gain than did any general magazine for women. One was a high fashion book that many of the girls could not afford after college. The other was a young girls' periodical that they would outgrow. A contest among college girls, to bring them into the general women's magazine fold, was a sound idea.

The mass *(consumer* and *general* are alternate names for them) magazines' place can be understood readily by this incident. In its purest form such a magazine appeals to all persons, men and women alike, regardless of occupation, age, or state of health. Those called *Glamour, Family Circle, Ladies' Home Journal, Good Housekeeping,* and *Mademoiselle,* to name some of the more popular, find it profitable to appeal to women as women. Although no single magazine is bought or even read by all the literate inhabitants of the United States, total reading remains a goal. The fact that *The Reader's Digest* has achieved a readership of approximately one hundred million, more than twice that of any other periodical or newspaper, encourages all publishers of general magazines.

Consumer magazines can be defined, then, as those that have broad appeal and are aimed at the whole people, as distinguished from specialized magazines, which deliberately are produced for a group whose chief interests are not those of the majority. Among the consumer magazines are the general periodicals and the ever growing apparently specialized publications of wide appeal, such as the women's, men's, picture, news, digest, fan, cheesecake, comic, and confessions magazines. With exceptions, these are consumer or mass magazines in two senses: they appeal to what constitutes the masses and they have mass circulations.

To some people the only true colleges are those in the Ivy League, the only true churches those of certain denominational names, and the only true magazines those ordinarily called consumer. We shall not argue about the colleges and the churches, but the idea that the consumer magazine is the only true one should be challenged.

As we have seen from the definition of magazine, the basic concept of a periodical is that it is a storehouse. That the storehouse must contain merchandise of only general appeal, however, is not in the formula.

Perhaps the only justification for thinking the consumer or general magazine to be the true magazine is that it offers itself to the world and therefore is thought to serve all the public rather than a segment of it, as do the specialized publications. Or, that the readers of general magazines are genuine consumers—men, women, and children, of all ages and backgrounds and at all economic levels.

That the industry is itself confused is shown in the fact that the proponents of the consumer magazine—the associations and the publishers themselves—are not agreed about the number in this country.

The disagreement is as wide as the figure 250 used by Arnold Gingrich, publisher of *Esquire,*[1] and the 971, reported by Standard Rate & Data Service.[2]

---

[1] "The Facts of Life and Death in the Magazine World," address by Arnold Gingrich before the Association for Education in Journalism, Aug. 28, 1963.

[2] In July, 1971.

It is the consumer himself, however, who is more undecided and vague even than the professional counters. Like as not he thinks that magazines are limited to the handful he sees held up as symbols: the few of general appeal, the women's, men's, sports, and perhaps popularized science.

Strictly speaking, there are not a dozen consumer magazines left in the United States, for the number of those making genuine consumer, mass, or general appeal has been reduced in recent years. A women's magazine, no matter how large its circulation, after all does not appeal to all readers, nor do men's, sports, travel, or other special interest publications.

For practical purposes, therefore, included in the consumer magazine category as a core should be the magazines of no specialization (like *The Reader's Digest* and the new *Saturday Evening Post)* and around that center those of appeal to a wide segment or section of the consumer audience *(McCall's, Redbook, Sports Illustrated,* and *Seventeen,* for instance).

## The American masses

Unlike most countries, the United States has no masses in the usual sense of a huge group of economically underprivileged and educationally undeveloped people. That is not to say that Americans are all wealthy and well educated. By comparison with certain less fortunate nations we have far fewer ignorant and poverty-stricken citizens, but we still have a large number. The American masses are middle-class citizens, of moderate income and at least grade school education. These form the great central group to which magazines of general circulation appeal.

Americans aged twenty-five and over, according to the Bureau of the Census, in 1962 had completed 11.4 years of school. Women averaged about one-half year more than men. Neither, therefore, on the average, had completed high school. This figure may seem low, but it is the highest in the nation's history and will be higher, since enrollments in schools and colleges mount annually.

The appeal to the group that has had little schooling or has made no effort to teach itself obviously can be accomplished only through pictures and drawings. Appeal to those of varying amounts of grade school education also must be heavily pictorial, with simple words and sentences, short length materials, and approach to basic emotions. It must not demand great specialized knowledge except in each person's particular working or hobby fields.

Other sociological facts must be taken into account by publishers of consumer magazines. For example, the nature of the relatively unschooled person's daily work conditions him for kinds of reading different from that of the white-collar worker. A person who labors outdoors at physically tiring work may find it difficult to settle down to brain-straining reading. Power to concentrate on the printed page among unschooled, little-schooled, and well-schooled persons differs widely.

General magazines therefore are aimed at the largest segment of our population with reading habits different from those of the persons sometimes called intellectuals. Within this middle-class group are the mass magazines of mainly emotional appeal: adventure, confessions, fan, crime and detection, sex, and comics. At the same time the middle class supports the women's, men's, and others aimed at those of medium education. Almost all are simple enough to be of interest and use to practically everyone.

### The slicks

The more physically pretentious and financially successful of the consumer magazines are known as the slicks, in contrast to the old pulps and because of the shiny paper on which they are printed. These are directed to the economically better off, middle-class Americans—the dominant group in this country, either by income or by interests. They are aimed at the people who exemplify American ambitions to be one's own boss, own one's own home, have a family, a car, a boat, and a backyard swimming pool, give all members of the family comfort and security, live and dress attractively, and be socially-minded at least when prodded by the Cancer Crusade or the United Fund.

These particular Americans are solid, independent people in many ways and sufficiently eager for success to respond to the appeal of well-printed, colorful, but not too serious magazines like the *National Geographic* and *Life,* the leading periodicals for women of all ages, newspaper magazine supplements, shelter, and family magazines, to name the more popular types.

Sprawling circulations are characteristic of these magazines for the American bourgeoisie; several dozen exceed one million, and a score go beyond two million. They have what Robert Fuoss, one-time editor of the *Saturday Evening Post,* called "a reverence for bigness." Addressing an advertising club in Detroit he said:

> It is this reverence for bigness, for example, that makes a newspaper devote more space to the World Series than to the Inaugural Address and to make Roger Maris's sixtieth home run only slightly less important than The Second Coming. It is why the statistics on Marilyn Monroe are far better known than those on the annual budget. . . .
> I believe we editors have fallen victims of the American reverence for bigness. I believe we have been sold a bill of goods. And I believe that radio and television were the sellers—and you (the advertisers) the acquiescent partners.[3]

---

[3] *Changing Times,* May, 1962, p. 40.

Cheerfulness and optimism also mark the slicks. Whereas the worship of bigness continues, however, there are signs that the Pollyanna attitude is diminishing. Fundamentally these publications reflect faith in the nation and confidence in the future, for the nation if not the world. Editorial opinion is not expressed directly so much as by selection of the points of view of others to be emphasized.

Another dominant attitude is social conservatism, a natural position considering that publishing is a business enterprise. The conservative wants to leave matters more or less as they are—literally to conserve. The reactionary wants to go back to the good old days. The radical, as we commonly misuse the word in the United States, wants to change the present conditions drastically, trying some social scheme not yet tested by practice. Actually, if he lives up to his label, he wants to go to the root of matters. The conservative is cautious about exploring new ideas and the radical may believe in being even more exploratory; the reactionary attacks the ideas. Because mass circulation magazines seek the response of the largest possible number of the literate populace, they cannot afford to be either reactionary or radical, i.e., extremist. Therefore they must be conservative because the American middle class as a whole is conservative.

The slicks move slowly in introducing strange or new ideas to their readers. At times they ignore or gloss over them, by-passing certain facts altogether. If, for example, the unrest among the Negro and other racial or religious minorities in the United States in recent years came as a surprise to the white population it was because of the failure of most of the press, including the slick magazines, to take much interest in the problems of the underprivileged.

The big slicks are changing in this respect, however, under the impact of greater need to be realistic, for now usually there are several articles a week or a month on important public questions in each. They are indicating that their editors realize the nature of the world around them. Failure to have done so earlier was a factor in the disappearance of *Woman's Home Companion, American,* and others in the 1950's and the failure of *Look* and several smaller magazines in the 1960's and early 1970's.

No doubt exists, however, about the usefulness of the slicks in helping their readers solve their personal problems. Most, especially those for women, display this characteristic lavishly. They offer many articles and departments on how to make simple objects, on how to run a household, on where to buy new products (especially if advertised), and on the latest medical advice. Such practicality endears them to their readers. The philosophy behind this policy is explained by *Mademoiselle* in its history:

"*Mademoiselle* tries to be a completely rounded 'guide, philosopher, and friend' to intelligent young women. To bring good taste—good taste in fashion, in cosmetics, in decorating, in every aspect of

living—to 'smart young women' everywhere, is the main plank in
*Mademoiselle's* editorial platform."[4]

The application is made by providing career articles, offering
specific information about vocational fields open to young women,
printing news about positions, recipes, fashions, advice on clothing
care, and fiction by leading authors. In recent years this fiction has
been somewhat *avant-garde;* the magazine also has been non-con-
formist in its articles on controversial social problems, such as conscientious objectors to war.

Another characteristic of the slicks is technical excellence un-
reached by any other large group of magazines. Certain members—
*Town and Country* and *Holiday* are examples—are as handsome
but they do not appeal to the bulk of the population, nor are
there as many in the classification. *McCall's, Ladies' Home Journal,*
and *Life,* with their striking color photography, extraordinarily
original art work, accurate and original printing and designing, smart
page layouts, efficient and successful organization of staff—these and
other technical qualities are extraordinarily superior to the bulk of
American magazines. This achievement is possible only when the
general consumer magazine is a successful business operation.

Technical perfection—American know-how—is associated with
the final dominant characteristic to be listed: commercialism.

Any self-supporting magazine must to some extent be commercial. The more successful the more commercial. Frederick Lewis
Allen, while editor of *Harper's,* put it this way in a speech:

". . . the magazine must be able to pay its bills and live in a
commercial world. Nor is this an unhealthy objective. The commercial test—the necessity of operating at a profit—provides a stimulus
without which many a subsidized journal desiccates. It necessitates
in the editors a healthy respect for their readers."[5]

The extent to which the mass magazines have become commercial is brought out by examining their financial progress, with net
annual profits running into millions of dollars, as we have shown in
Part II. But these big publications must be seen at close hand, not
lumped together merely as slicks, but as separate groups—those for
men, those for women, the shelter books, the news and the picture
magazines.

### Digest and pocket magazines

Sydney J. Harris, a syndicated columnist, once announced
his intention to start a new magazine, *Digest Digest.* On second
thought, he decided that his title was too long: it should be *Dgst*

---

[4] *A Short History of* Mademoiselle (New York: Street & Smith, undated, revised),
p. 9.

[5] Frederick L. Allen, *The Function of a Magazine in America* (Columbia, Mo.:
University of Missouri Bulletin), Vol. 46, No. 23, p. 3.

*Dgst.* As a heading for his department that day he used "Hrrs Strts Dgst Mgzn."

A British writer on American journalism commented that the reader of *The Reader's Digest* need only put its articles "into a glass of water and when they are dissolved, drink them quickly and he gets a dose of culture."

The digests and their cousins, the pocket-size magazines, have had to put up with such joshing since this handy form of periodical came into popularity with the American middle class in the 1930's. The severest attacks have been upon *The Reader's Digest* and its principal editor, DeWitt Wallace. Wallace and his fantastically successful monthly have been the subject of several books and scores of articles.

S. Claude Bartley, writing in the *Christian Science Monitor* magazine, has tried to account for the digests' popularity. He traces the magazine use of *digest* to James Boswell and Joseph Addison, and insists that the prototype is not that issued from Pleasantville, N.Y., but *The Living Age,* which was almost a century old when it died in 1942. That magazine gave its readers summaries of articles much in the digest manner, although generally it selected material dealing with public affairs.

The success of the digest type of magazine has been achieved by satisfying certain reader desires and requirements. Mr. Bartley points out that there is a common impulse to pass on to others what has been enjoyed in magazine as well as in other reading. Many persons who have this impulse content themselves with underlining or clipping material and keeping scrapbooks. The publishers seek to gratify this urge for its own sake, but they also wish to make money out of the hobby of clipping, filing, and pasting into books favorite passages or pictures.

Another cause of the success is the portability of the magazines. They can be read while the reader is in transit. Just as the tabloid newspaper has solved the problem of reading in crowded bus, suburban railway, and subway by providing the reader with a paper that he can fold small, so the pocket-size digest magazine enables him also to read magazines comfortably. Women can carry it in their purses; men can poke it into side pockets.

Readers also wish to keep up (or to seem to be keeping up) with what is appearing in many different magazines without needing to cull them. Reading a wide assortment is difficult in view of the large numbers that crowd the newsstands. Subscribers to *Science Digest, Negro Digest, Family Digest,* and others in even more specialized fields, such as *Education Digest* and *Automotive Service Digest,* at least have wider coverage than if they kept to a few publications.

Not all digests are pocket-size. Nor are all pocket-size magazines digests. Usually those that carry condensed materials are small, but

Combat, Paris

***Fig. 14.1.* Sorry, sir, I sell only digests.**

several small-size ones take pride in printing short but complete material. Nor are any of these magazines to be confused with paperback books, condensed or complete, for the latter are books in the standard sense: full-sized novels, biographies, cartoon collections, and histories.

*The Reader's Digest* is largest of all, with circulation in the United States exceeding seventeen million and more than thirty overseas editions adding another eleven million. It is one of the few true digests remaining from a group of general circulation magazines of its type which once included such large ones as *Magazine Digest* and *Everybody's Digest.* The periodical of usual content treatment but small physical size is not a true digest. *Pageant, Youth,* and *The Link,* for example, publish short material aplenty, but the copy is written for their pages and is not the result of bowdlerizing a longer piece.

### Criticisms of digests

The common objections to a true digest include these:

1. Condensation harms the original manuscript. The author, and not an editor, should decide what, if anything, may be omitted from an article or book to be condensed for republication.

2. The digests give their readers the impression that they have the essence or major points of what an author has written, but actually readers have lost the chance to examine all the evidence or study

minor points and re-evaluate them as possible major arguments or ideas.

3. Articles actually are not always reprinted from other magazines, but are "planted" in advance. This practice is identified in particular with *The Reader's Digest*. The objectors declare that this increases monopoly, since contracts give that magazine first choice. Editors of other magazines, therefore, keep an eye out for what might attract the *Digest,* thus spreading the latter's policies. Since 1944 *The New Yorker* has refused to let that magazine reprint its material, and so notified its contributors, saying that it objected to "the *Digest's* indirect creative function, which is a threat to the free flow of ideas and to the independent spirit."[6]

4. *The Reader's Digest,* especially, is accused of being politically and socially reactionary, a charge made at one time or another against most popular and commercially successful magazines but particularly outspoken in respect to the *Digest*.

### In rebuttal

Defenders of the digests declare in rebuttal that condensation often improves rather than damages articles, and cite authors who praise the editing of their manuscripts. They add that in the instance of *The Reader's Digest,* the magazine from which the article or other material is drawn and the author receive rewards far beyond those obtainable elsewhere. On one occasion a staff writer for *Printers' Ink* was paid $200 for the right to reprint an article of a few hundred words written as part of his job.

The defense made of the social and personal philosophies presented in the digests is that philosophies of that character are as legitimate as others.

"Planting," while not so named by the "planters," is defended as justified because neither free-lance contributions nor run-of-the-mill published materials available permit an editorial staff responsible for a monthly of gigantic circulation to keep a proper balance between subjects or treatment of ideas. When *The Reader's Digest* is challenged on its social position it has told protesters that it receives as many hundreds of letters praising its stand as condemning it. As even its bitterest foes must admit, under the American concept of freedom of the press, it has a right to its viewpoint, whatever it be.

Whether any magazine should omit important facts from articles, consistently select for reprint only such materials as reinforce its social position, and avoid printing a letters-to-the-editor department is not so easily defended. In a nation with so many magazines expressing varied viewpoints, however, it is possible for the reader to find argu-

---

[6] "New Yorker Ends Its Agreement for Reprints in Reader's Digest," The New York *Times,* Feb. 12, 1944.

ments on all sides of a question. Whether he has access to those other publications is another matter.

## The Reader's Digest's *founder*

The career of *The Reader's Digest* is parallel with that of its co-chairmen, DeWitt and Lila Acheson Wallace. They developed this publication to the point where only one other is as widely read in the United States: the Bible.

A Greenwich Village basement storeroom was the scene of its beginning. Its staff consisted of the Wallaces. It came about this way. After attending both Macalester College and the University of California, Wallace worked for a St. Paul, Minn., book and magazine publisher and for a novelties firm. Wounded during the Verdun offensive of World War I, he was hospitalized. Looking through many magazines during convalescence the idea for the *Digest* occurred to him and he passed the time by experimenting with condensations. After the war he did publicity work until the depression of 1920 cost him his job and drove him to think once more about his magazine idea. When no publishing firm would finance the publication he borrowed $600 from relatives and $5,000 from other persons, and with Mrs. Wallace founded the magazine.

They prepared promotion circulars before going on their wedding trip; when they returned they found enough advance subscriptions to justify bringing out the first issue of the *Digest* in February, 1922, printing 5,000 copies. Within a year they had 7,000 subscribers and had moved into a Pleasantville, N.Y., garage. In three more years they had added two persons to the staff and reached 20,000 circulation. Their formula continued to work, circulation rose into many millions, foreign editions were founded, book and record clubs were begun, and the garage was replaced by palatial offices.

### Confession magazines

The confessions carry such names as *True Confessions, Exciting Romances, True Experience, Jive, Real Story, Secrets,* and *Revealing Romances.* At any one time a dozen large ones can be found in this group, with *True Story* as the circulation leader, having about 2,485,000; *True Confessions* is second, with 465,800. *True Story* has led since its founding in 1919. Its philosophy is typical of this whole group, and is followed by its rivals. It gives its readers realistic fiction, even to the point of illustrating stories with photographs instead of drawings. In recent years it has ventured into the general women's type of material, with more and more non-fiction on the personal affairs of women, particularly on courtship, personality, popularity, health, charm, dress design, children, beauty secrets, and marriage.

The business of providing confession magazines has become a big one, which any mass circulation publication must be. Aimed chiefly at women, these publications are issued by a few large companies, controlling from one to four each. Confessions are somewhat alike in appearance and format: they use shocker titles, print posed photographs as illustrations, and provide a mixture of fiction, articles, and many departments. Sometimes the fiction is in the first person to build the tone of reality but is the work of professional writers. Advertising is distinctly feminine. National ads frequently are sold to the entire group. Offset printing is used for some signatures and gravure is common for entire publications.

Small as they are in number comparatively, the confessions are an important group of magazines, for they influence women on personal problems largely at the emotional level.

## Fan magazines

Closely related to and often coming from the same editorial offices as the confessions are the fan magazines. They are similar in format— roughly 8 x 11—with color covers that feature television, stage, or movie stars currently in the public eye. A long-time member of the group of about fifteen usually available is *Photoplay*, with more than 1,500,000 circulation. Other typical titles are *Movieland, Modern Screen, Screenland plus TV Land, Screen Stories,* and *Motion Picture.* Several are issued by the confessions' publishers.

Content, aside from usual departments like letters and picture or program reviews (in some instances remarkably candid), is intended to gratify the intense personal interest of the millions who go to the movies and the many more millions who listen to radio and watch the television screen.

Fiction here is not unlike that in the confessions in its general tone, but it is less realistic and not so often written in first person. The non-fiction consists of descriptions of the home life, hobbies, or other activities of stars and, increasingly, scandal stories or gossip about Hollywood's or New York's married couples and bachelors. Picture stories in color are popular. Outside the rating departments, no serious consideration is given to the movie or to broadcasting as an art form. Such an expression as "art form" would not be understood by many readers. They consider movie, radio, and television a chance for escape from reality.

The radio and television fan magazine is on a somewhat higher educational level than the one devoted to motion pictures, because broadcast programs contain a larger quantity of material of interest to persons of higher education, such as news, documentaries, and special events programs. This situation comes about because the magazine, as an instrument, may be directed at a single group of readers but radio and television, in any operating period of up to 20 or

22 hours, must have some content of interest to a variety of listeners. There also is the government regulation about material in the public interest—educational and religious programs, for example. A radio receiver or television set may be in any kind of home. The advertiser and the station owner both hope to interest everyone.

Physically similar to the confessions, fan magazines are no older than the particular area of entertainment they serve; television books are newest and movie magazines oldest. Confession and fan magazine circulations are comparable.

Nations that still have royal families provide their people with human objects of worship and respect. Republics like the United States offer no such opportunity. So the people compensate by their adoration of stars of screen, radio, video, and sports. Fan magazines provide an outlet for hero worship and play their part, along with motion picture and television, in establishing popularity of certain fashions, manners, and modes of speech.

### Girlie magazines

The girlie, cheesecake, or sex magazines in their turn are kin to the confessions and fan. An undetermined number of readers buy the latter two types because of sex frustration or loneliness. They feel closer to the celebrities of the entertainment world through reading about them and seeing their pictures. Recall the pinups in military quarters and college dormitories, and the stranger who tried to see Greta Garbo to propose marriage and did will her his money.

These magazines are more appealing to their readers than outright fiction would be because they know that the current hero or heroine of the screen, be it in a theatre or on a home television set, really exists. The reader group for the cheesecake magazines is small in number, mostly male, and a steadily changing one; the American public quickly tires of nudity for nudity's sake. The sex magazines range from a few huge financial enterprises like *Playboy* and its closest imitators to mainly small circulation collections of jokes and cartoons with a sex angle. Most of this group are filled with specially posed pictures or drawings.

Cheesecake publications received their nickname from their many pictures of sparsely-clad young females; the name was borrowed from news photography. A few of their publishers are the same group firms that produce the confessions and the fan books, but the majority are issued by small, one-shot firms. Only a few companies make a specialty of this type of periodical.

Pictures of unclothed human beings are not in themselves necessarily lewd, sexy, or indecent, although they can be, any more than the nude persons themselves are immoral merely because undressed. Many critics of the sex magazines rest their objections on the fact that the publishers combine pictures which inherently are harmless with jokes, stories, and other content that sometimes is prurient and intended only to stimulate sex impulses.

Campaigns to rid newsstands of the supposedly objectionable magazines of this character often are conducted by well-intentioned persons who call for special legislation to meet the problem, not realizing that such legislation could be used, eventually, to censor other types of publications on political bases.

## Sports periodicals

Although the people of the United States are tremendously interested in and active about sports and recreation, they do not read magazines in corresponding numbers. A half million people attend the World Series baseball games, and twenty million all told patronize those of the two major leagues during the season. It is common for from fifty thousand to seventy thousand to attend one football game, either professional or collegiate. More than thirty million persons bowl in a year. One would expect that several magazines covering these and the many other sports so popular in this country would have circulations equal to that of *TV Guide,* which is around fifteen million, or at least of *Farm Journal,* with almost three million. But the leaders, *Outdoor Life,* 1,750,484, and *Field and Stream,* 1,685,365, are not general sports magazines, but are aimed at hunters, fishermen, campers, and boaters. Not far behind is *Sports Illustrated,* over two million and a quarter in circulation; it covers all sports, but makes a somewhat literary appeal and goes in for listing sports records and reporting news, being a weekly.

Fans are supplied, generously, by radio and television, by daily and weekly general newspaper coverage, and by special newspapers, such as *The Sporting News.* They also have available a wide assortment of extremely specialized sports magazines, such as *Archery World, Lakeland Boating, Skier,* and *The Woman Bowler.* None has achieved a large circulation. And it also is reasonable to think that people treat sports purely as entertainment and, except for the adolescent or female hero worshippers, are not inclined to read in depth about it or do more than gaze at pictures relating to their favorite form of it. That much the specialized magazines, sports papers, and sports pages can satisfy.

Motor car magazines, such as *Hot Rod, Motorcyclist, Motor Trend, Rod and Custom,* and *Road and Track,* come into the sports category, and have burgeoned, in the 1960's, into large publications for this field. Several have achieved from a half million to nearly one million circulation. These combine the how-to-do-it mechanical and science magazine appeal with the fan appeal.

Possibly the distinctively sports magazine that tells most about mass periodical publishing problems is *Sports Illustrated,* which appeared in 1954 as a new member of the family of Time Inc. Handsomely printed, with color, it first contained articles and picture stories dealing with such unlikely sports topics as the latest in children's clothes in use in Florida, polo, and yachting. The standard sports subjects also appeared, but the diversity was great. This policy was deliberate, the publishers believing that coverage of sports news, especially in a weekly, where timeliness is expected, would be extremely difficult in view of the heavy coverage by other media. Early predictions by some experts were gloomy, but within a few years the circulation department was able to report 70 per cent renewals of subscriptions and the editors were paying high prices for copy by William Faulkner and other leading American literary figures. Advertising response, slow at first, finally kept pace.

The success was achieved by careful planning, which took more than a year, and by the ability of the mother company to pour literally millions of dollars into promotion. A member of the *Sports Illustrated* staff, describing the launching, explained that "one stringent criterion" was set for the magazine: "it must be fun to read. We put it this way; 'a pleasurable magazine in a world receiving less than its full measure of joy.' "[7]

Other steps taken were these: the market was surveyed to see if there would be enough readers, an assistant managing editor of *Life* was appointed managing editor of the new magazine, the formula was worked out, a net paid circulation of 450,000 was set as the goal for the first issue, to be divided between 350,000 subscriptions and 100,000 newsstand sales. Advertising staff and branch offices were set up, the advertising rate was pegged at $3,150. Several dummies were designed before the final version appeared on Aug. 16, 1954. The circulation goal was passed in two months.

### The comics

Whether the comics really are magazines can be argued, but they are more so than not, for they look like, are sold as, and are read as if they were magazines. They are lumped by the public with the newspaper comic strips, logically enough because many of the same characters appear in the comic books, as they also are called.

No magazines have stimulated so much serious writing and study, at least no group which appears so unconcerned about being taken seriously. In recent years the comics have become the subjects of several books and since they began their rise to popularity in the 1940's have been examined in numerous articles in serious journals of religion, psychology, sociology, and education, as well as in popular

---

[7] "How *Sports Illustrated* Was Launched," address by Bob Hughes before the Advertising Federation of America, 1954.

periodicals. They have been probed as factors in juvenile delinquency, used as educational tools along with textbooks, and served as
sources of amusement for adults as well as their intended juvenile
readers.

The first comic publications, although not magazines, have been
traced to 1858. In their present form they were begun in the mid-
1930's, the first founded in 1935. Within four years there were 27; by
1941 they had reached 32, all more or less alike and all selling for a
nickel or a dime. By 1950 they had increased by 1,000 per cent, for
350 were on the market, but still similar in appearance and published
by about fifty different firms. In four more years they had passed the
four hundred figure. But by then, also, the effect of television was beginning to set in, and within a year—by 1955—the number of titles
dropped back to 335.

Not only did the animated cartoons on the television screen
start the slide downward but also the organized efforts of certain religionists, sociologists, and some other persons appalled at the steady
diet of horror, crime, monsters, obscenity, and brutality included in
many also began to tell. In an attempt to elevate the industry a group
of publishers approved a code. It effectively halted most abuses but
also put numerous publishers out of the business.

Another way of meeting the problem was publication of "good
comics," and adoption of the comic magazine form to other purposes,
such as telling the story of "Adventures in Jet Propulsion" and the
picturing, in a pamphlet that looked like a comic magazine, of *The
Races of Mankind* with the title, "There Are No Master Races."

Comics as purveyors of advertising naturally became of interest
when their aggregate circulation reached eight hundred million, as it
did during the peak years. Soon manufacturers of guns, batteries,
breakfast foods, and other commodities of interest to youngsters
bought space. Another development was to encourage publishers by
giving awards for publication of what were considered acceptable
comics.

By the early 1960's the comic magazine industry had settled
down. The annual total circulation dropped to about three hundred
and fifty million, the number of publishers to one-fourth of what it
had been, and advertising had largely passed into television. The
comics publishers began diversifying by distributing paperback books.

During the entire period of wide distribution the comics of all
qualities, perhaps more than any other type of American publication,
found their way abroad, first in the hands of military personnel overseas and then to meet the demands of an eager market of persons of
low reading ability who enjoyed picture stories.

Capitalizing on the adult appeal of the comics, a group of publishers during the late 1950's added several of satirical humor dressed

up as comics. The leader is *Mad,* which grew out of the offices of a successful horror-humor comics publishing firm and evolved an original formula which numerous imitators have sought to reproduce. The magazine not only has an estimated circulation of almost two million copies for each of its eight issues a year but also does a good business selling *Mad* T-shirts, miniature china busts of Alfred E. Neuman, the magazine's toothy mascot, collecting royalties from three foreign language editions, and issuing collections of *Mad* content in book form. *Mad* and its imitators do not carry advertising and, in fact, delight in needling the industry as well as many other American institutions, personalities, and practices.

### *The new pulps*

Although the old pulp magazines of the 1920's and 1930's are gone, remembered as providing what Marcus Duffield called day-dreams for the masses, there are successors to this tempestuous fiction in garish covers and printed on cheap paper. These are the men's ad-venture, crime, and sex exploit magazines, such as *Man's Conquest, Target, Real West, Man's Adventure,* and *Man's Daring Adventure.* Mr. Duffield also called the old pulps "part of the underworld of literature" and "lineal descendants of the old-time dime novels."[8]

The publishers and the authors of the action-laden stories in the new versions would contest the first but willingly accept the second characterization, for both functionally and physically they follow in the Dead-eye Dick and Jesse James story tradition, with a dash of sex added. The accusation of literary underworldness would be refuted in part by the point that not all the modern style pulps are alike. Some concentrate on brutality and violence or sex. Others print science-fiction, stories of the supernatural, travel and adventure tales, and narratives of fantasy, sometimes by gifted and skilled writers and read by persons of education and taste.

The old pulps were so called because of the low-quality, coarse, thick paper on which they were printed. The present-day versions use somewhat higher quality paper, and are therefore able to offer more effective art work; they are not limited, as were many of the original pulps, to line drawings.

Circulations of these magazines today are moderate, considering their mass appeal. Their publishers own more than one and sell space for the group simultaneously, so as to command higher rates and provide wider readership guarantees. Records reveal these pub-lishers to be the groups responsible as well for certain of the confes-sions, fans, cheesecakes, and comics. *Cavalier,* a cross between a pulp

---

[8] Marcus Duffield, "The Pulps: Day Dreams for the Masses," *Vanity Fair,* June, 1933, p. 26.

and the sophisticated men's magazine, has hit four hundred thousand circulation at times, and leads the field.

The early pulps have an historical interest for the magazine journalist, for they encouraged many new writers. H. L. Mencken and George Jean Nathan dabbled in this field when they issued *La Parisienne* and *Saucy Stories*. H. P. Lovecraft, a skillful writer of supernatural stories, is almost as important as Poe in the history of the short tale. Edgar Rice Burroughs, best remembered for Tarzan, wrote for the old pulps constantly. August Derleth, one of the most prolific serious writers of regional novels, a poet, short story writer, and science fictioneer, as well as specialized book publisher, contributed to the pulps tales in the tradition of the Gothic novelists and of H. G. Wells in his "The Time Machine" period. Other names of distinction once found on covers in the pulp past are those of E. Phillips Oppenheim, Walter Havighurst, Talbot Mundy, Theodore Dreiser, Booth Tarkington, Rupert Hughes, Fannie Hurst, Bill Nye, A. Conan Doyle, Rudyard Kipling, Frank Norris, and Edith Wharton. Among the artists were Norman Rockwell, Howard Chandler Christy, and James Montgomery Flagg.

## Science fiction magazines

Reality having caught up with the fantastic stories of a half-century ago, there has developed a small group of magazines with loyal readers who find in them literature of high quality at times and also extraordinary insight into the direction of civilization. These are the science fiction publications—*Analog Science Fact Fiction* is the puzzling title of one (around 90,000 circulation) issued by the same firm that publishes the far more romantic *Vogue, Glamour,* and *Mademoiselle.* It carries "stories of the future told for scientifically trained, technically employed adults." Their central theme, the editors explain, usually is concerned with problems "of an ordinary technician employed 50 to 50,000 years hence."

Others, carrying more fantasy, more fiction, and perhaps less science, are named *Weirdbook, If, Fantasy and Science Fiction,* or *Galaxy,* and have between 60,000 and 75,000 circulation each. Often garish in appearance, their stories can tempt the citizen from television tales more effectively than other magazines. Both free-lance and staff written, they remain hospitable to the writers for the old pulps, at least appreciating the spirit of those unattached dreamers. Most of the authors are men and, as with the pulpies, use of pseudonyms is common. But there is little room for editorial staffers.

*Chapter 15*

---

# Consumer magazines/
## *News and picture*

$T$HE THEORY behind publication of both the news and the picture magazines is that the news has become so complex and voluminous that the reader of daily newspapers and the listener to broadcasts is confused and overwhelmed by it all. He needs, therefore, a publication that reports the news in a different perspective. Such a magazine takes the stories reported one by one in dailies and broadcasts, boils them down, and tells what they mean. The picture magazine, its editors hope, will portray the news and convey it as only the camera can.

In its first issue—March 3, 1923—*Time* indicated that it was intended for "the man who wants the facts, the man who wants to do his own thinking after he has the facts [and] the busy man." In a later statement, after the magazine was well established, *Time* denied that it was a magazine but said it was an invention "to use the printing press to do a regular job of getting all the most interesting news of the world into the minds of an intelligent man or woman." [1]

The newsmagazine, as *Time* calls itself and thus has provided a name for its two rivals (although *Newsweek* prefers *news weekly*), is supposed to supplement the newspaper, not replace it. It cannot be used as a substitute because its news is virtually all national or in-

---

[1] *The Story of* Time (Chicago: Time Inc., undated), p. 3.

ternational; local happenings cannot be covered. But the three leaders—*Time, Newsweek,* and *U.S. News and World Report*—are important because of the perspective they offer and because at times they attend to news omitted by newspapers or broadcasters by reasons of lack of space or time, policy, presumed lack of reader interest, insufficient initiative, or editorial indifference.

News, however, no longer is the chief fare of these magazines. Even before it was published, *Time* paved the way for expansion of its formula by printing in one of its 1922 promotion pieces, a specimen issue, a line in Latin that the magazine was to be "concerning all things known and various other things." The "various other things" have come to an important place. Restating the old news and reporting what the other media may have missed or avoided, no matter how attractively, was not enough. The "take-out," a backgrounding, long article, similar to an extensive newspaper feature or a full-blown general magazine piece, is only one of the "various things" now. Others are check lists of books, theaters, television programs, criticism of the arts, and opinion articles. Injected into the news reports, also, are a point of view and angling. *Time* has gone far beyond summaries of the news, with or without opinion. The invention is of a method more than a function.

For many years prior to the first newsmagazine as we know it, *Review of Reviews, World's Work, Current History,* and *The Literary Digest* dealt with news, summarizing, explaining, and evaluating it. All, plus small and less successful imitators, attempted interpretation of events, in a somewhat academic manner, to be sure. Usually they were monthlies. They missed much news, or confused news with opinion, or carried more opinions than news itself. They were not written simply enough to be widely appealing, nor did they personalize events as do the present newsmagazines whenever possible. Also, news in the early 1900's was neither as complex as now nor were the people as much interested as today in world news.

What do present magazines of this character do, then, that their predecessors and the newspapers overlook or cannot attempt in presentation of the news? They departmentalize, print short condensations, concentrate on one big story each issue, maintain no direct, stated editorial policy, reduce writing to a single style and tone, winnow out duplications, repetition, and what are considered unnecessary details, take time to provide historical background, use many photographs and other types of illustration, draw special charts to make complex material clear, play up letters to the editor, delve into news areas neglected by newspapers and broadcasters, such as the arts, the sciences, journalism, and education, and tap sources throughout the world sometimes untouched even by the wire services.

All newsmagazines have a general pattern for their presentation of events with the exception of *U.S. News and World Report,* and a few of the specialized members of the group. It is much like that of newspapers in principle except that papers usually are too rushed or understaffed to follow theirs precisely. Like the papers, the magazines give facts, but fewer of the detailed ones. They try to understand their readers' backgrounds, making elaborate surveys to find out. By learning from continuous study who reads the newsmagazines the editors know what mold of interest, what experience, what background and feeling to write toward. In this sense these magazines are service publications.

Once style was a distinguishing characteristic, especially of *Time,* but little of its eccentricity survives. It combined words *(Brisbanalities, radiorator, sophomoron),* employed distinctive phrases; one which is classic: "Death came, as it must to all men. . . ." It made free use of personal descriptive words ("bald, bashful, nervous Treasury Secretary So-and-So"), and still uses carefully such rhetorical devices as repetition, puns, and literary allusions ("Alas, poor Gottschalk").

More important is that all newsmagazines frequently use the narrative form in news telling, unlike general newspapers, which for the most part continue the inverted pyramid structure. This form makes reading slow, ordinarily, but by conciseness and effective selection of detail, especially in imparting the human touch, the newsmagazine leads the reader into an account he might ordinarily not read. The sort of detail that attracts readers is the dropping into a report what some public figure ate or drank or smoked on the occasion of a certain banquet.

Among the big three *U.S. News and World Report* confines itself to its function, which on its cover it has declared to be to devote itself "entirely to reporting . . . interpreting and forecasting the news of national affairs." It has no interest in style for its own sake but is content with straightforward writing. Most of its articles of importance are longer and more thorough than *Time's* or *Newsweek's,* as well as fewer. And, as a further distinction in content, it makes some effort to summarize press opinion and to provide special, interpretative full-length articles on news subjects with a view to pointing up trends; it also runs opinion pieces and the full texts of important documents.

At their best, the general newsmagazines provide more interpretation of news than daily or weekly newspapers and offer the reader a handy summary of the big stories. Their existence has stimulated newspapers to more news analysis, especially in Sunday roundups, and given rise to a newspaper using a somewhat similar formula, the *National Observer,* which in its advertising equates itself with the newsmagazines.

Newsmagazines are much discussed, far out of proportion to

their number. It is a rare symposium on modern journalism that does not include attention to them. Like the voluminous writing about them, these discussions often as not are uncomplimentary.

## Pros and cons

*Time* has drawn most of the barbs. Among the more serious charges against it has been that it uses unproved generalizations. An instance occurred in 1958, when the magazine reported the merger of International News Service with the United Press Associations by saying: " . . . on a coronation story, editors could rely on the Associated Press for the dimensions of the cathedral, the United Press for the mood of the ceremony, and the International News Service (sometimes) for an interview with the barmaid across the way." *Time* also called International News Service's work "splash and dash journalism." These comments brought outraged replies from INS officials and staff members.

*Time* has also been accused of resorting to innuendoes to support editorial policy. In an article on the National Committee for a Sane Nuclear Policy, familiarly known as SANE, in 1958, the writers described the committee as "well-heeled." It listed the members, who included Lewis Mumford, the author; Norman Cousins, the editor; the late Harry Emerson Fosdick, the minister; Paul Tillich, the theologian; Elmo Roper, the poll conductor; David Reisman, the sociologist; Oscar Hammerstein, II, the librettist; James G. Patton, head of the National Farmers Union; and Linus C. Pauling, the scientist. But when Patton was identified it was done this way: "James G. Patton (who runs N.C.S.N.P. material free in N.F.U. publications)." And Dr. Pauling was described as " . . . the committee's scientific anchor man, Caltech's busy chemist and busy politician. . . longtime supporter of Communist-line fronts. . ." There followed a footnote reading: " 'Professor Pauling,' reported the House Committee on Un-American Activities in 1951, 'has not deviated a hairbreadth from the pattern of loyalty to the Communist cause since 1946.' " The article also implied that SANE was ready to surrender the U.S.A. to its opponents. [2]

After Mr. Cousins published a protesting editorial in the *Saturday Review,* Henry R. Luce, then editor-in-chief of the magazine, wrote to Mr. Cousins that he had not intended to question the intelligence or patriotism of those mentioned in the article. A title like "How Sane the SANE?" would seem to question their sanity directly. A precise study of this practice in *Time* appeared in the Aug. 15, 1959 issue of *New Republic* in an article by Jigs Gardner, which he called "Time, The Weekly Fiction Magazine."

---

[2] "The Atom. How Sane the SANE?" *Time,* April 21, 1958, p. 13.

Except for the printing of letters stating such criticisms, publication of denials that *Time* ever has pretended to be objective, and occasional speeches by its executives, the magazine has made little reply to these attacks. It relies possibly on the record of success of the company, for the firm has had a net annual profit in recent years of between seven and ten million dollars, and the fact that the circulation of *Time*, in particular, has passed 4,250,000 a week in domestic sales and 1,350,000 in foreign.

*Newsweek* has evoked few of the bitter attacks that have befallen *Time*, although it has been included in general criticisms of the newsmagazines that appear now and then. These deal with such points as the impossible task the magazines have set themselves, in presuming to cover all the important news of the world, and the inclination to emphasize human interest over hard news for the sake of readability. Since it changed hands in 1961, when it became the property of the firm that also publishes the Washington *Post*, its style has become more sophisticated. It has 2,600,000 domestic and 1,250,000 foreign circulation.

The arguments that revolve around *U.S. News and World Report* are based on its persistently conservative political and social position rather than on its journalistic techniques, but as in the instance of *The Reader's Digest* this contention comes from those who do not welcome the conservative position no matter how honestly held. Several studies have shown *U.S. News and World Report* to be more careful about presenting different viewpoints fairly than its rivals, especially *Time*. It stands third in circulation, with about 1,900,000.

### *Origins of the Big Three*

The three leaders had different origins and have come through somewhat different experiences on the way to stability and acceptance.

*Time* was founded in 1923 by Henry R. Luce and Briton Hadden, who were Yale friends, after each had worked briefly on newspapers. They had difficulty raising capital for their venture. The first issue was drab, by comparison with the colorful book now being produced, and reader as well as advertising reaction was mild. It took three years, with only tiny profits, for *Time* to begin taking hold. But once it succeeded it became the core of a firm that now publishes three other magazines in this country *(Life, Fortune, Sports Illustrated)* and is joint publisher of others in Japan *(President)* and Argentina *(Panorama)* as well as publisher of overseas editions of several *(Life International, Life en Español,* and Asian, Atlantic, and other versions of *Time)*. Time Inc. also engages in printing experimentation and book publishing.

*Newsweek* came on the journalistic scene exactly a decade after *Time*, on the edge of an economic depression. Its founder was T. J. C. Martyn, an Englishman who had been on the New York *Times* and

*Time* and brought long experience in both U.S. and British news work. He called the magazine *News-Week* and made it a weekly news summary. Almost from the beginning its format was similar to *Time*'s. It avoided the anonymity or group journalism formula, i.e., a system whereby many different writers and editors collaborate to produce an unsigned article. In 1937 it was merged with *Today*, a magazine of public affairs. Malcolm Muir, who became publisher that year, changed its name to *Newsweek: The Magazine of News Significance*. He went in heavily for forecasting the news as well as interpreting it, spreading this function for a time to many departments.

In its early years *Time* struggled minus an angel, or at least without a big one; but *Newsweek*, when the Harriman and Astor families helped and *Today* was joined to it, was pulled out of its financial troubles by big angels indeed, for they have been among the wealthiest families in the nation. After *Newsweek* was placed on sale in the early 1960's, the Astor Foundation sold its controlling shares to Philip L. Graham for nearly $9,000,000. Graham, already owner of the Washington *Post*, died in 1963 and the magazine remained in his widow's control.

*U.S. News and World Report*, although also the result of a merger, had an even more nerve-testing start than *Time*. It grew out of an idea held firmly by David Lawrence, the dominant personality on it since its beginning. He began *U.S. News*, in Washington, the same year *News-Week* was born, basing the magazine on the idea of a newspaper he called *United States Daily* and later *United States Weekly*. This publication was to report Washington and the nation fully with complete texts of important speeches and documents. Thirteen years later he started *World Report*, to do for international news what the *U.S. News* magazine did for national. Neither was strong, in either circulation or advertising. Lawrence merged them in 1948, and on his definite formula and social policies he has steadily built it.

These three have withstood all imitators or varieties of competition. Among the losers were *Pathfinder, Fortnight, U.S.A.-1,* and *World*.

*Pathfinder* had been a rural area weekly founded in 1894. Stimulated by the success of *Time* and *Newsweek*, it became more departmentalized and reached a circulation of about one million by 1947, by which year it had changed its name to *Town Journal*. It declined under the competition of the older newsmagazines and its identification with the farm press, whose general appeal content also could not hold out against the slicks.

All three current newsmagazines pride themselves on their large staffs and the original news coverage such staffs provide at home and abroad. They exceed, in number, the personnel of most newspapers, go in heavily for photojournalism, and especially in the case of *Time*, maintain extensive editorial operations for writing, rewriting, and verifying material. Their offices have been populated by numbers of prominent writers, a few of whom have pictured their experiences in novels or plays. *Time* has been the ostensible setting for *The Big Wheel*, by John Brooks; *The Great Ones*, by Ralph Ingersoll, once publisher of *Time*; *That Winter*, by Merle Miller; and *The Death of Kings*, by Charles Wertenbaker.

The newsmagazines are alluring to many young men and women seeking careers in journalism. They rely on them as shortcuts to the news and therefore are familiar with their content and methods. Their newspaper-office fast pace attracts those young people who think news work is exciting and they anticipate the discipline which staff work can provide for them. They are not so aware, however, of the considerable effort that goes into writing that never sees print because of space limitations, the anonymity of the work, the loss of individual style.

To these aspirants, as well as to the general public, it appears that there are only three American newsmagazines. But the consumer type is only that seen on newsstands. Others use the formula in the specialized fields. Perhaps the best known are *Business Week*, much like *Time* or *Newsweek* in pattern and *Sports Illustrated*.

### Picture magazines

Picture and illustrated magazines may seem to be alike, but technically they are not, because not all illustrations are pictures. And if we accept the loose use of the word *picture* as a synonym for *photograph* we must make a clear distinction. A true picture periodical depends upon photographic pictures to present its content. Thus the *National Geographic* is an illustrated magazine; *Life* is a picture magazine. The former has considerable text and various non-photographic illustrations; the latter is dominated by photographs, with text and other types of illustrations secondary.

The periodical using illustrations can be traced back to Revolutionary War years. *The Royal American*, published by Isaiah Thomas in 1774, was illustrated with engravings, some executed by Paul Revere, better known today for a certain horseback ride. As new methods of reproduction were devised and as photography was improved, illustrations became cheaper and more common.

The picture magazine of our own time was developed from the picture-text periodical when it was realized by publishers that photographs can convey a message more clearly and dramatically than type. European journalism was quick to use the technique and numbers of famous magazines resulted, including the *Illustrated London News*, founded in 1842 as a weekly and still flourishing; *L'Illustration* in Paris and *Illustrierte Zeitung* in Leipzig, both founded soon after.

The London publication, whose first issue of sixteen pages carried thirty wood block cuts, bears considerable responsibility for picture magazine growth in the United States. A wood engraver of whom we already have read, christened Henry Carter but later better known under his assumed name of Frank Leslie, left his post of superintendent of the English weekly's engraving department to come to the United States. Here he helped produce *Gleason's Pictorial Drawing-Room Companion,* whose sixteen pages contained many woodcuts and in appearance resembled the *London Illustrated News.*

In 1855 Leslie brought out his own sensational and speedily produced *Frank Leslie's Illustrated Newspaper,* whose changes already have been noted. A year later the Harper brothers, publishers of *Harper's Monthly,* put a similar publication on the market, *Harper's Weekly.* It, too, relied heavily on woodcuts. On its staff was Thomas Nast, later to become one of America's most effective political cartoonists. The *Weekly* went down in American history for its coverage of the Civil War; pen and pencil drawings of war scenes were timely because they were engraved rapidly, for that era. In later years of the war, Matthew Brady's photographs were used. Mention must be made also of the hand-colored fashion plates and elaborate black and white drawings of *Godey's Lady's Book* so much admired in the latter half of the century.

Photography was used increasingly for copy as well as a method of producing engravings. Common in all popular magazines, only the highly specialized were slow to use it. Some periodicals still use none or little, for reasons of high cost, editorial inexperience, or lack of necessity.

Publication of New York tabloid newspapers during the first half of this century and the success of rotogravure supplements introduced by newspapers toward the end of the nineteenth century encouraged greater use of pictures by both newspapers and magazines. *The Mid-Week Pictorial,* founded by the New York *Times* in 1914, was an immediate predecessor of the picture magazine of today.

The original such publication, in the modern sense, was *Life,* first published in November, 1936, by Time Inc., which paid $85,000 for a weekly, merely for its name, *Life.* The old *Life* had been a provocative humor magazine for sophisticates, but was on the wane. The new *Life* owners experimented for a long time before publishing. They had no idea their product would be so sensationally popular at once. After several try-out versions, called *Dummy* and *Rehearsal,* the picture weekly was launched. Enough copies were printed to meet the demand of the nearly one-quarter million charter subscribers and the expected curiosity sale of about the same number. Circulation shot to a million a week within six months, bringing an advertising loss of a million dollars because circulation guarantees were exceeded. More than three decades later the circulation had hit 8,500,000 but twice since has been reduced by the firm and in 1972 was set at 5,500,000.

At first *Life* sought to cover news pictorially, attempting to do with pictures what its companion, *Time,* did with type. As advertising accumulated—and *Life* went close to the top in volume and revenue—this became impossible because there was neither time nor space. Gradually it took on more of the characteristics of the general magazine of text. It added time copy, that is, features that might be printed at almost any time, and editorials. Text remained essentially subordinate to pictures, however.

As are all outstanding magazine successes, *Life* was followed by many imitators. One, sometimes considered an imitator but almost simultaneously issued, was *Look, Life*'s closest rival. It had been projected a decade earlier than *Life,* however, but did not become a reality until two months after *Life* was out. This biweekly, issued by a firm until then closely identified with the newspaper publishing business, also quickly achieved high circulation. From its beginning, however, *Look* was less like *Life* than seemed apparent. It published much more general magazine material, such as interviews, personality sketches, quiz games, health articles, humor, and articles in considerable depth on public issues. Its circulation also reached 7,750,000 every other week, not weekly, before it was cut deliberately to 6,500,000. But it still was too high when advertising revenue fell early in the 1970's.

A third entry in the field is *Ebony,* directed at a special audience, the black people. With many of *Life's* physical characteristics, it is the flagship publication of its publishing house, and has more than 1,200,000 circulation once a month. Somewhat similar in appearance and formula is *Sepia,* with a circulation not yet reaching 100,000.

A number of attempts to rival these have failed, some after reaching as much as a million circulation: *Click, See, Pix, Pic, Flash, Foto, Focus, Photo-History, Friday,* and *Peek* were among them. Several of these imitators modified the pattern, either by reducing the size or asking the readers to flip pages to produce an effect of movies.

The magazines that supplement newspapers, usually on Sunday, have been influenced by the successful picture magazines and one of them, *Parade,* is a full-fledged picture magazine in content, now ranking as the largest of these supplements. Various newspapers distribute not only it, but also *Family Weekly* and other national rivals. Scores have their own consisting of little but pictures.

Some have developed into well-printed periodicals, commanding the work of leading writers and offering national advertising. Outstanding in the quality of its editorial copy is the *New York Times Magazine,* with a circulation of 1,500,000 each Sunday. In 400 other cities are supplements appearing with consumer advertising but localized copy (the latter a boon to the free-lance writers and photographers of the area).

The circulation leaders are the syndicated supplements: *Parade,* with approximately 16,000,000; and *Family Weekly,* with about 8,000,000. *Sunday,* a group of supplements containing localized copy and syndicated advertising, has about 20,000,000 aggregate circulation.

Even the magazines that seek to popularize mechanics and science might well qualify for admission to the picture magazine family. When Henry Haven Windsor, Sr., founded *Popular Mechanics* in 1902 he issued a pronouncement of policy which said: "Most magazines use illustrated articles. We do not. We use described pictures." Such has become the policy of *Popular Mechanics'* competitors as well. Mr. Windsor's analysis applies to all picture magazines:

> The general run of the contents of this magazine is based entirely upon the pictures. If the picture does not rise right up out of the page and hit the reader in the eye, then we regard it as a failure. In other words, the picture must not only be of something the reader has never seen, but it must be of such a nature as to arouse his interest and curiosity at least sufficiently to induce him to read the article accompanying it.[3]

Rivals of the news as well as of the picture magazines for a time were a cluster variously called midget, dwarf, and pocket magazines, with brief names to match; *Hue, People, Jet,* and *Quick* were the leaders. Their tiny size was adopted to achieve printing economies and to attain the ultimate in portability, not a virtue of *Life, Look, Click,* and the other oversize books. Sold almost entirely on newsstands, their price was kept low, to ten cents. Only *Jet,* intended for Negro readers, survives. They condensed news to capsule size, barely more than a sentence, departmentalized it, and printed many pictures. Several hung on for a few years, achieving a half million circulation. *Quick,* a 1949 venture of the Cowles firm, later publisher of *Look* and *Family Circle,* was the most widely read. Failure of the group as a whole, *Jet* excepted, can be explained by the inability of an editor to present news pictures effectively in such small space and the reluctance of advertisers to duplicate their space in these magazines or prepare special plates for them.

But another group in this area has gone on successfully. These are certain of the many, inspired by the success of *Sports Illustrated* and of many in other parts of the world that put *illustrated* in their names, who followed a formula of some text and numerous pictures. Examples are *Mechanix Illustrated, Soul! Illustrated, Man's Illustrated,* and *Electronics Illustrated.*

---

[3] "A Guide for the Editorial Staff," an undated memorandum issued by *Popular Mechanics* and signed R.M.G. (Roderick M. Grant, then editor of the magazine).

Probably one of the least known U.S. periodicals in the U.S. itself
but one of the most influential is *America Illustrated,* issued by the
Department of State in Russian and Polish language editions for sale
in those countries. Consisting largely of articles illustrated with photographs and of picture stories of American life, each is the size of *Life*
or *Ebony* and eagerly received abroad. Russia, in turn, distributes
*Soviet Life,* in this country, by agreement. It too uses many photographs and drawings, much color printing, and is about evenly divided
between text and illustration. Similar to it is *Poland,* an illustrated
magazine in English for distribution in the United States.

So great has become the vogue of the picture and illustrated
magazine that *Cosmopolitan* once carried on its cover the line: "The
Magazine for People Who Can Read."

Robert Taft, Daniel Mich, and other writers on today's pictorial
journalism like to quote a Wordsworth sonnet published as an indict-
ment of the picture press four years after the relatively austere
*Illustrated London News* appeared. This sonnet's complaints would
most certainly be intensified if the poet could see the picture journalism of today, existing in a world of visual images conveyed by motion
picture and television. He wrote:

> Discourse was deemed Man's noblest attribute,
> And written words the glory of his hand;
> Then followed Printing with enlarged command
> For thought—dominion vast and absolute
> For spreading truth, and making love expand.
> Now prose and verse sunk into disrepute
> Must lacquey a dumb Art that best can suit
> The taste of this once-intellectual Land.
> A backward movement surely have we here,
> From manhood,—back to childhood; for the age—
> Back towards caverned life's first rude career.
> Avaunt this vile abuse of pictured page!
> Must eyes be all in all, the tongue and ear
> Nothing? Heaven keep us from a lower stage![4]

[4] William Wordsworth, *The Complete Poetical Works of William Wordsworth*
(Boston: Houghton Mifflin, 1919), p. 246.

## Chapter 16

# Consumer magazines /
## *For men, for women*

W OMEN PROVED that they would buy magazines aimed at them long
before men responded with comparable enthusiasm to their exclusive
periodicals. But the males' interest never has equalled that of the
females. Women's patronage of their magazines has given six of them,
including three well over a half-century old, from five to eight million
circulation. And three more have several million each. Perhaps this
imbalance comes about because women had an earlier opportunity to
patronize their own magazines, for the first appeared in 1792, *Lady's
Magazine.* Except for periodicals about masculine activities, such as
hunting and fishing, man's own magazines did not begin to appear in
force until the 1930's, when *Esquire, True, Argosy,* and a few others
began to boom. Several explanations further explain this difference
in response, for it has persisted.

Women, being the traditional homemakers, have more time for
reading than do men; they read more fiction than men, and women's
magazines have carried it for many years; the early men's magazines
were concerned largely with adventure or sex and these topics alone
were not enough to interest extraordinarily large numbers of males in
magazines; the more modern magazine for men includes serious ideas
as well as amusement. Furthermore, more American men have become
sophisticated, better educated, and more widely traveled than ever
before, and demand more from their magazines.

## For the males

Just what is a man's magazine? Is not one like *Popular Mechanics,* which is read largely by men, a man's magazine? But a definition including it, hunting, fishing, baseball, and other magazines of men's interests would be too broad. More reliable as a definition is to say that a man's magazine is one that makes its appeal to man's maleness; similarly, a woman's magazine is one appealing to woman as a woman. By using such distinctions possibly we can bring some order out of the newsstand welter of publications for each sex.

**Adventure.** One of the oldest groups, it goes back to the days of the pulps. Early in the century scores of cheaply printed magazines carried articles and stories, illustrated by pen-and-ink sketches, telling of exploration and adventure, usually on other continents. The work of some of the nation's most popular writers appeared in them, such as Jack London and Robert W. Service; among the foreign writers was Joseph Conrad. As science fiction and the realities of the atomic and space age made the reading of ordinary adventure tales tame, a sex element was introduced. A few of large circulation, while still surrounded with the aura of daring and courage, go in for topics that come close to those in the sports magazines: racing cars, guns, and science.

**Detective.** Although more and more women are finding jobs on police forces and in crime detection laboratories, such risky work still is largely male. And a battery of magazines is issued every month or two to give male readers the vicarious experience of being sleuths. Closely related to mystery magazines, they emphasize drama and action; many a police reporter makes a little money on the side writing up famous old crime cases as well as crimes that have just occurred. Sex appeal has entered some of these pages, also. A bimonthly called *Confidential Detective Cases,* for example, prefers, it tells writers, "true crime cases . . . that will appeal to a male audience. Cases must involve a woman principal, either victim or killer."

**Sophisticated.** Much of the place on the newsstands of the *Captain Billy's Whizbang* type of publication has been taken over by *Playboy* and its satellites and imitators. Early in the century, particularly during World War I, various pocket-size publications provided men with sex-theme cartoons, jokes, anecdotes, and what then passed for pin-up pictures of more- or less-dressed women. These often were coarse rather than clever, of greater interest to boys than men. After them came the sophisticated sex-appeal magazines which achieved high popularity in the 1940's. Best known of that early group and now a member of a different category, was *Esquire,* which soon after it grew out of being a men's clothing magazine, stimulated a series of imitators bearing such names as *Sir, Mr.,* and *Ringmaster.* Its formula in the early 1930's was much like that of the present *Playboy;*

in fact, Hugh Hefner, publisher of *Playboy*, once was an *Esquire* staff member. He became disgruntled over salary, quit, and started his own magazine. Meantime *Esquire* saw a new market: the sophisticated young intellectual, especially in college towns, as well as the man-about-town type who finds what have been called "the lusty, busty magazines" to be on the juvenile side.

Park Honan, analyzing *Playboy* in *New City*, offers an interpretation that explains most publications in this category: they offer sexual escape; they confer sexual prowess on readers who lack it; they give the reader an illusion of being a sophisticate. Also, as *True* was told by Ernest Dichter, a motivational research expert, the average man "is suffering from a fear of losing his male superiority" and a man's magazine protects him.

**Physical culture.** Perhaps the only realistic appeal to man's maleness is made by a small group of periodicals which feature man at his most muscular. They bear titles like *Tomorrow's Man,* and belong just as much in the health or self-help category, for they concentrate on articles and pictures dealing with the bulging physiques of college athletes and professional strong men.

### *The* Playboy *phenomenon*

Although *Playboy's* formula is not original, by means of clever promotion, the force of its publisher's personality, and the seriousness with which it has been taken by theologians and writers on current topics it has become a phenomenon of journalism. Contributing to this position of apparent importance for what is essentially a magazine appealing to the hedonistic side of men has been a two-year-long series of editorials by Hefner on "The Playboy Philosophy," discussing in detail various aspects of censorship, the magazine's credo, the arguments of its opponents, American puritanism, religious freedom, pornography, and many other subjects.

This series and the magazine itself, during the early 1960's were widely discussed in lectures and written about, articles appearing in such widely different publications as *Cosmopolitan, U.S. Camera, Time, Christianity and Crisis, New City, Newsweek, motive,* and *The Nation.* The burden of the world-wide argument against it applies as well to the dozen or so that are like *Playboy.* But those called *Dude, Cavalier, Escapade, Male, Fling, Nugget,* and *Impact* (a lesson in titles, showing the addiction to the one-worder) have been able, because they cannot command the advertising revenue of the leader, to obtain manuscripts from few writers as famous as those who appear in *Playboy.* That monthly pays $3,000 for the lead short story and $1,500 for others. The imitators are prone to the sensational type of article, such as "I Took Dope To Cure Myself."

The most sophisticated argument against these magazines is of the type that came from Dr. Harvey G. Cox, associate professor of church and society, Harvard. It was his article, coupled with general discussion of *Playboy,* that moved Publisher Hefner to launch his philosophical disquisitions. Dr. Cox avoided the position taken in most religious publications when discussing magazines of this type.

"Moralistic criticisms of *Playboy* fail," he wrote, "because its anti-moralism is one of the few places in which *Playboy* is right."

A theological attack on the magazine that focuses on its "lewdness" will misfire completely, Dr. Cox said, adding: *"Playboy* and its imitators are not 'sex magazines' at all. They are basically anti-sexual. They dilute and dissipate authentic sexuality by reducing it to an accessory, by keeping it at a safe distance.

"It is precisely because these magazines are anti-sexual that they deserve the most searching kind of theological criticism. They foster a heretical doctrine of man, one at radical variance with the biblical view. For *Playboy*'s man, others—especially women—are *for* him. They are his leisure accessories, his playthings. For the Bible, man only becomes fully man by being for the other." [1]

### In the women's world

Wrote a reader to one of the multimillion circulation magazines for women:

> I think women's magazines in general are making a mistake in continuing to confine their scope to the traditional women's concerns. True, these are a part of our life, but only a *part.* . . . I would like to see many more articles dealing with political subjects (women are not *apolitical),* with such serious domestic problems as desegregation, with international problems, such as disarmament. But most of all, I would like to see all subjects dealt with not from the so-called "women's point of view" . . . but just from the human point of view. We are no longer living the lives of women, but of active citizens. . . .

Through the pounds of analytical articles on women's magazines and the several books devoted partly or fully to them, this idea has run since the days of Sarah Hale. It has appeared in the speeches of the defenders of women's rights just as persistently. Some women want to be treated as people, not as beings set apart and called women. But the plaint seems to come from a minority, as do all causes at their outset. Every noble attempt to give women a magazine of the sort described by the letter writer above has failed consistently, remained at low circulation, or required the subsidy of associations, clubs, and churches to maintain it for a relatively small internal group of readers.

---

[1] Harvey Cox, *"Playboy*'s Doctrine of Male," *Christianity and Crisis,* April 7, 1961, p. 60.

The chief reasons that women do not get the sort of magazine the letter writer suggests are that most American women do not want such a publication and are satisfied with what they now have, and also that women who wish the type of reading matter she requests are able to turn to the discussion and opinion publications such as the *New Leader* or *The Nation*. A woman reader can find what the letter writer wants elsewhere if she really desires it enough.

The problem of the women's magazine publisher, therefore, is to continue to hold the millions who are satisfied with the present menu of a few serious articles, varied fiction, and numerous service departments offering recipes, fashion hints, beauty guides, and advice about love life. Magazines that have built up circulations of five to ten millions and correspondingly heavy advertising schedules do not alter their formulas lightly. Yet publishers know that they must make changes, so as to keep pace with their readers' changing interests. It is like a racing car streaking along a track, with others like it beside it or now falling back or running ahead. A wrong move and the car can go spinning into the rail. We have seen several such disasters in the past few decades: *Today's Woman,* which died with advertising billings of $7,000,000 a year and more than 1,200,000 circulation; *Everywoman's,* the magazine sold in supermarkets, taken over by *Family Circle; Woman's Home Companion,* the victim of costly competition with other leaders but also administrative difficulties; *Flair,* Fleur Cowles' dream magazine that was too costly to print in view of its failure to draw enough advertising; *Charm,* lost when its publisher sold a group of his magazines to another firm with a similar publication; *Household,* tied to farm women but lost when they found general magazines for women useful enough in the new-style farm life; smaller ones upset were *Woman's World, The Woman, American Lady.*

### The present field

Using again our measuring stick to determine a woman's magazine: one that appeals to woman as a woman, and not alone to her extracurricular interests, we find several classifications.

**Brides.** Not a large field, and occupied over the years by only three or four at a time, it is a successful one. By comparison with giants like *McCall's,* the members of this group have modest circulations, ranging from 290,000 for *Bride's,* with *Modern Bride* exceeding 307,000. They sell considerable advertising space. In contrast to the well-being of these magazines is the experience of Esquire, Inc., which attempted to bring out a male counterpart, *Bridegroom.* It failed.

**Mothers.** Indubitably an exclusively women's group, it also is small in number of publications, around half a dozen at any one time, but

much larger in circulation though smaller in advertising volume than the ones for brides. *Mother-to-be—American Baby* has 1,083,000 controlled and *Baby Talk* about 910,000.

These serve a changing market, for women do not remain either brides or young mothers all their lives. But the market goes steadily on, as do marriage and motherhood; it is merely that the cast of characters changes.

**Girls.** Several large and influential magazines appear in this group. Whereas the men's field takes in boys, magazines aimed directly at the male youngster have decreased until today there is only one magazine of general appeal to them, *Boy's Life,* sponsored by the Boy Scouts of America, with well over two million circulation. But young girls, like their mothers, respond more enthusiastically to magazines and not only read any of those intended for women in general but also their own: *American Girl* (the Girl Scouts' equivalent of *Boy's Life*), *Seventeen, Ingénue, 'Teen,* and *Coed,* not to overlook another dozen issued by various religious groups, such as *Catholic Miss. Seventeen* is the circulation leader, having passed 1,400,300. The nearest competitor has half that amount (see Chapter 20).

From the exclusively female magazines we move into the large group aimed at women to trade on their interests: the service, shelter, beauty, cooking, fashion, and other subjects.

**Service.** Two types of women's magazines come to mind when any is called a service publication: the big three (*McCall's, Ladies' Home Journal,* and *Good Housekeeping*) and the big two *(Family Circle* and *Woman's Day).* These are the survivors of groups which once included other giants. Strictly speaking, however, the ones that should be included out of the five are the two inexpensive periodicals of huge circulation that women generally pick up at the check-out counter in supermarkets: *Woman's Day* and *Family Circle.* Both are among the first ten in magazine circulation in the United States, *Family Circle* exceeding 7,000,000 and *Woman's Day* having passed 6,900,000. These two concentrate on practical help to women by providing articles on cleaning methods, ways to improve a house's interior appearance, recipes, patterns, and family problems. They minimize fiction, current affairs articles, and other such fare of the big three general rivals for advertising and circulation, boasting of their useful rather than entertainment value. Also deserving to be classified as service magazines but not usually included because of their high specialization, are several such as *The Workbasket,* for women who sew, bought by more than 1,400,000 every month, and the newer *Hair-Do & Beauty,* whose service should be obvious from its title and which is taken by more than half a million, the outgrowth of the increased availability of home hair-treatment equipment.

**Shelter.** Men are deeply interested in shelter, and one would think even more so than women, since they are the providers for and guardians of the family. But shelter, in this sense, means not only houses but also what goes into and around them—furnishings, interior decorating, gardening, maintenance. A handful of revered magazines, two born just before or just after the turn of the century and others in the 1920's, has held forth in this field and in both circulation and advertising revenue rank among the largest. *Better Homes and Gardens,* with more than 7,780,000, stands among the nation's top ten; *American Home,* second to it with 3,500,000; *House and Garden,* 1,030,000 is next; *House Beautiful* has about 860,000. They are not precisely competitors; the concept of *home* is not exactly the same among them. *Better Homes* and *American Home* are pitched to readers who live in middle-class homes; the others are aimed at residents of expensive houses, comparatively. In the same area, more from the advertising aspect than from the reader's point of view, are *Flower and Garden, Flower Grower,* and *Popular Gardening.*

*Sunset,* similar to the standard shelter magazines but with a West Coast orientation, commands well over 980,000 readers in a time when the large regional magazine has had difficulties, as seen in the death of *Holland's.* In any case, women are the principal readers.

**Fashion.** Just as there are two kinds of shelter magazines, for the low- and high-cost home owners, so there are two devoted to helping women with fashion. On the one side are the two so-called high fashion books, which have dominated the field for half a century: *Harper's Bazaar* and *Vogue.* On the other are *Glamour* and *Mademoiselle,* which cater to the business girl and college woman, and emphasize the moderate-priced fashions. Although none has an extraordinarily high circulation by comparison with the three general magazines for women, *Glamour* is at the top with 1,442,920 and *Harper's Bazaar* last with 428,000. Their advertising is substantial in volume although not lucrative enough at times for such expensively printed periodicals.

Still more practical than these are the pattern magazines that qualify more by format than by content: *Simplicity Fashion Magazine* is largest, with about 835,000, followed by *McCall's Patterns and Fashions* and *Vogue Pattern Book.*

**Beauty.** Helping women become or remain beautiful has for years been one of the chief functions of most magazines for women, especially those of general appeal. Nevertheless there are available several of a specialized type that go beyond the apparently sufficient advice and help in the big publications. If concerned about taking care of her hair a woman has access to *HairDo & Beauty;* if it is her rouge, lipstick, or face powder she needs advice about there is *Beauty Fair.*

The pitch to women takes place along other lines; not on newsstands are, *M.D.'s Wife, Modern Secretary, New Lady,* and *Essence,* the latter two for black women readers.

## Centers of contention

The general and fashion groups of women's magazines have pro-
voked certain writers since the post-World War II years, when the first
serious dissatisfactions with them gained national attention. Elizabeth
Bancroft Schlesinger, for instance, reported a survey of women's
magazines covering issues between October, 1944 and March, 1945, the
period during which Dumbarton Oaks, Bretton Woods, and the Yalta
meetings were constantly in the news. A presidential campaign and
an Office of Price Administration battle with shortages and rationing
were among the other important national issues confronting the American people. Mrs. Schlesinger found that neither *Ladies' Home
Journal, Woman's Home Companion,* nor *McCall's* even mentioned
the meetings or made any reference to "the part women could play in
bringing about international cooperation for future peace." [2]

Articles on war, she found, were confined largely to its emotional
impact on people, especially the individual. At the same time, these
magazines had a circulation together of ten million copies; in the six
months covered they therefore totalled sixty million (and she could
have assumed 240,000,000 readers in the same period). Yet three fundamentally important plans and actions to settle some of the world's
turmoil were ignored.

The temper of the criticism of the dominant women's magazines
can be judged from some of the articles published since Mrs.
Schlesinger's attack. Under the tame title, "The Magazines Women
Read," another woman writer observed that those of the late 1940's
"are all slick, illustrated, middlebrow and prosperous; and they are
all, or nearly all, composed of the same four ingredients: (1) advertisements, (2) social and household hints, (3) 'serious' articles, and (4)
fiction." [3]

Soon thereafter, Mary McCarthy, short story writer and novelist
*(The Group),* spread her reaction in a two-part article in the course of
which she dissected the content and social philosophy of the big
magazines for women being published about 1950, including not only
the ones mentioned already in this chapter but also one now gone to
rest in the graveyard with *Charm* and *Woman's Home Companion:
Junior Bazaar.*[4]

Marya Mannes, who has leveled many a blast at American editors
and publishers of certain types of newspapers and magazines, went to
work next, in 1953. She invented an editor, "Constance Maybie," who

---

[2] Elizabeth Bancroft Schlesinger, "The Women's Magazines," *The New Republic,* March 11, 1946, pp. 345–47.
[3] Ann Griffith, "The Magazines Women Read," *American Mercury,* March,
1949, p. 273.
[4] Mary McCarthy, "Up the Ladder From Charm to Vogue," *The Reporter,* July
18 and Aug. 1, 1950.

did not take the advice she ladled out so readily to the millions of readers of her *Woman's Hour*.[5]

Two years later the men stepped in with their hatchets. David Cort, an amusing and sharp critic of the social scene, examined the togetherness slogan that *McCall's* then boasted, found little of this element in the magazine's content, and then went on to cast doubt that American women really were responding to the conventional appeals of their magazines.[6] But the most sarcastic male attack on togetherness and the magazines came from Philip Wylie, author of the ire-stirring book, *Generation of Vipers*. He took off on them in a *True* magazine article (a magazine for men), in which he wrote: "Togetherness, being woman-oriented, is headlessness, mindlessness; it is anti-thought and pro-body. It concerns what we call 'creature comforts' exclusively. It so serves great and admirable goals of women, which are not, however, the normal goals of mature men. Togetherness rejects those goals entirely."[7]

And thus it went. Two pieces in *Playboy* attacked the women's magazines as being the truly pornographic ones, not the men's periodicals. They were the "pious pornographers." The publication of a book by Helen Woodward, an experienced magazinist, apparently stimulated further assaults on the women's magazines; she said that she disliked their "pretense that the publication is a lofty, kindly, noble enterprise" when she knew that "it is simply a business."[8] Along came new pieces in *Harper's, America, Nieman Reports, Time, New York Times Book Review,* and others, all in addition to numerous extensive ones in the trade press reporting the bitter fight then going on in the early 1960's for circulation between the rivals. The magazines came in for satirizing in *Mad* and belaboring by newspaper columnists, such as Inez Robb. And when the autobiographies of two of the most famous editors, Edna Woolman Chase of *Vogue* and Carmel White Snow of *Harper's Bazaar,* were published, both books drew in the magazines of opinion reviews reflecting many of the viewpoints noted here, as did the anthologies of *Vogue*'s content.

Another center of contention in the women's magazine group is *Cosmopolitan,* an old lady among American periodicals, since it was founded in 1886, but acting like a giddy teen-ager these days. For many years it often offered fiction of high quality, Ernest Hemingway being among its contributors, and non-fiction that was stimulating. At different times it was a news interpreter, a muckraking crusader, and a nondescript monthly of popular fiction only. During its early years it

---

[5] Marya Mannes, "Any Resemblance . . . Lady Editor," *The Reporter,* Nov. 10, 1953, p. 32.

[6] David Cort, "Together in a Sea of Soap," *The Nation,* Sept. 15, 1956, p. 217.

[7] Philip Wylie, "To Hell With Togetherness," *True,* May 1958, p. 92.

[8] Helen Woodward, *The Lady Persuaders* (New York: Obolensky, 1960), p. 188.

had as editors several of the nation's leading magazinists—John Brisben Walker, Ray Long, Harry Payne Burton, and for a short time Herbert R. Mayes, later to become famous for his rise to power at *McCall's.*

In trouble through lack of advertising in 1965, *Cosmopolitan's* owners—since 1905 the Hearst Magazines, Inc.—chose a new editor, a woman who never had been connected with the magazine world but was known for her writing. This was Helen Gurley Brown. Up to then Mrs. Brown was best known for her books, *Sex and the Single Girl* and *Sex and the Office.* She revived the magazine with a formula often likened to *Playboy's* in its catering with complete faithfulness to its readers' interests. She reorganized the book both physically and in content, adding come-on titles to the cover and articles and departments about personal problems of women. Both circulation and advertising zoomed, the fare about catching or keeping your man and portraying in all possible ways that woman is first of all a sex object attracting just the right readers for the advertising appeal. As late as April, 1967, *Cosmopolitan* ran an article entitled "Sex and the Japanese Single Girl"; since there are at least 136 sovereign nations, the formula could be carried through 1978.

In response to the criticisms, perhaps, there have been attempts to issue magazines free of the faults held up by Miss McCarthy, Miss Mannes, and the others. None has succeeded. One was named *Realm.* It lasted for one 1963 issue. It had described itself as *"for* and *about* successful women in business, the professions, government, and the arts." *Realm* promised to "introduce women to women . . . recognize their talents . . . report their achievements." The second issue was printed but not distributed, because of lack of advertising support. The support was not forthcoming because advertisers thought they could reach such readers through existing magazines aimed at businesswomen.

Two more were brought out in the early 1970's: *New Woman,* subtitled "The Magazine for Women Who Think," and *MS,* an advocate of the women's liberation movement and edited by Gloria Steinem, formerly associate editor of *New York* magazine.

# Chapter 17

# Specialized magazines / Opinion, black, literary, humor

Frank P. Walsh, newspaper and magazine journalist, once wrote an article on railroads for *The Nation,* which had a circulation then of 27,000. He also published a series of articles on the same subject in the Hearst papers, which at the same time had an aggregate of ten million. Never, Walsh later reported, had he met a man who had read his Hearst syndicated articles, but the day *The Nation* went on Washington's newsstands his telephone began ringing. Calling him were senators, editors, lobbyists, reformers, and other influential persons. [1]

This incident typifies a fundamental difference between the philosophies behind the magazines of opinion (also called class and grouped with others) and the consumer magazines. The publishers of opinion periodicals believe that the educationally and economically higher or upper-income citizens have more influence in the long run. Although many editors before him had followed the second philosophy, its leading exponent was Edwin L. Godkin, founder and first editor of *The Nation,* still an important journal of ideas and comment on current affairs and the arts. The representative of the mass philosophy was William Randolph Hearst, Sr., who carried it out in both magazines and newspapers.

---

[1] Lewis Gannett, "Villard and His *Nation,*" *The Nation,* July 22, 1950, p. 80.

The term *class,* used in the magazine industry, is a dubious one in a democracy that prides itself on being a classless society. It means appeal to readers who are above average in education and income, but not necessarily so in intelligence.

The magazines variously classified as quality, opinion, discussion, idea, controversy, and interpretation are all in this specialized family. Their circulations are low compared with those of the consumer group. Usually the volume of their advertising is likewise small, even smaller than circulation. Physically they are varied, ranging from the bland look of the butcher-paper weeklies, as *The New Republic, Commonweal, The Nation,* and others are described because of their stock, to the physically more attractive *America* and *National Review.* Between them are the physically substantial *Atlantic, Harper's, Yale Review, Saturday Review, Virginia Quarterly Review,* and a few of the larger and more artistically planned little literary magazines.

### The black magazines

Magazines in this area of journalism divide into three main groups: consumer, religious, and scholarly. Rough estimates indicate about 140 publications other than newspapers, some of them among the oldest periodicals in the United States.

The dominant organization is the Johnson Publishing Company of Chicago, which issues *Ebony,* a picture monthly with more than 1,250,000 circulation; *Jet,* a weekly photo-news review; *Black Stars,* about entertainers; *Black World,* a serious monthly of general discussion articles on various aspects of black life. Johnson also publishes books.

Another important firm is Good Publishing Company of Fort Worth, Texas, which also has four magazines, all monthlies and distributed nationally. Its leader is *Sepia,* a competitor of under 100,000 circulation for *Ebony; Hep, Bronze Thrills,* and *Jive* are concerned largely with the entertainment and sports worlds and black figures in them, and running confession articles by and about women.

Also important is *Tuesday,* a monthly magazine supplement to white newspapers with circulations in black neighborhoods. Its circulation has passed the 2,250,000 mark. It alternates with a sister publication, *Tuesday at Home.* Because of its distribution system (about twenty papers in major cities) *Tuesday* has the largest circulation of any black publication. Various religious and scholarly magazines, some noted in other parts of this book, gain attention; travel, business, public affairs, literary, and technical magazines for black readers also are issued.

Black magazine journalism is lively, segments of it are militant about social problems, other parts are concerned more with homogenizing their readers. It is a changing press and perhaps, as the black people attain first-class citizenship, will become economically more secure and influential.

## *The quality group*

At the century's turn four magazines constituted the quality group: *Atlantic, Century, Harper's,* and *Scribner's.* Earlier they had been magazines for the middle classes, with travel articles, photographs, jokes, and sketches, but in the early 1900's they gradually rose to a more frigid atmosphere of intellectuality. Their fiction became less popular in appeal and more frankly highbrow; photographs disappeared in favor of line drawings; travel accounts gave way to political analyses; and jokes were replaced by the work of leading poets.

The term *quality* was introduced for advertising purposes, for their appeal was to persons of considerable intellectual capacity and fairly high incomes. Because their readers, in other words, were persons of quality, an advertising department could make the point that they liked dependable workmanship in products offered, had good taste in eating and clothing selection, enjoyed dependable incomes, understood poetry, liked to go to the theatres and concert halls, dabbled in philosophy and other abstractions, and were persons of sound personal habits.

Having less prestige but more literary importance than some of the big four, in the first quarter of the century, were *The American Mercury* as it existed under Mencken's editorship, the *Virginia Quarterly Review, The Bookman, The Forum,* and the *Yale Review.* Inasmuch as these never had been general magazines, no sharp shift in personality was required. In advertising volume only one or two ever joined the big four, for which, indeed, advertising never was plentiful, anyway.

Only two of the big four survive, *Atlantic* and *Harper's,* and they have joined their business departments for more economical operation. As a consequence they are in a stronger economic position than at any time in their long histories. From the satellite group the *Virginia Quarterly* and *Yale Review* still carry on. Sometimes the *Saturday Review* is joined with the *Atlantic* and *Harper's* as a modern quality magazine, especially since it broadened its base by dropping *of Literature* from its title.

The quality magazine field is not highly lucrative because it is dependent upon a relatively small reader group with fixed and heav-

*Fig. 17.1.* The chief editors in recent years of the *Atlantic,* one of two survivors of the quality group of the last century: Mrs. Emily Flint, managing editor; the late Charles W. Morton, associate editor (standing); and the editor in chief, Robert Manning. *(Newsweek— James F. Coyne Photo)*

ily taxed incomes whose purchases are much the same as those of consumer magazine readers. The biggest advertisers, such as manufacturers of detergents, are convinced that they can reach the quality magazine readers through the general magazines, radio, and television; they continue to buy space mainly in the slicks.

This group of specialized magazines, because it deals heavily in uncommon facts and esoteric ideas, with emphasis on the former, fails to attract the typical middle-class reader, who turns to magazines for escape, personal guidance, or entertainment, and not for education, intellectual stimulation, or front-rank fiction.

### The opinion magazines

If reluctance to think is a barrier to popular support of the quality periodicals, it keeps most of the idea, opinion, discussion, and controversy journals in constant search of subsidy or at the bare survival level. These magazines—the better known are *The Progressive, The New Leader, The New Republic, The National Review, Liberation, The Nation, Ramparts, Congress Bi-Weekly, VISTA, Monthly Review, Focus/Midwest,* and *Commonweal*—antedate in purpose and type those aimed at the so-called people of quality. They can be traced to the religious magazines of the early nineteenth century, when those pious periodicals played major roles in molding public opinion. The religious press, in fact, still includes potent magazines of ideas and opinion stemming from the application of religious principles to modern problems: *Christian Century, United Church Herald, The Lutheran, Christianity and Crisis, Christianity Today, Commentary,* and *Catholic World* are among the more widely known (see Chapter 20).

Opinion magazines are so called because of the space allotted to expression of viewpoints about current problems and because they are somewhat less objective than the quality group and consumer publications. Most do not intend to be debating societies but are openly committed to causes. But the two groups—quality and opinion —are similar in sources of manuscripts, readers, and advertising. The majority of the opinion books are weeklies that seek to comment swiftly on events. Physically most of them are unimpressive, depending upon drawings and a few halftones for illustrations, rarely use color, and are printed on ordinary quality stock. Their circulations are under 50,000, with the exception of *The New Republic, Ramparts,* and *National Review.*

Yet their influence has been extraordinary if one considers their circulation size and, from the popular viewpoint, essential dullness. Their impress upon American life is related in such books as C. C. Regier's *The Era of the Muckrakers,* Louis Filler's *Crusaders for American Liberalism,* and the memoirs and autobiographies of Villard, Godkin, Robert Morss Lovett, Norman Thomas, and Michael Williams.

Other indications of influence, at least of individual periodicals of ideas and opinions, come from a study made in the mid-sixties by Professor John H. Schacht of the University of Illinois College of Journalism and Communications.

In his report, issued as the result of a grant from the Magazine Publishers Association, Professor Schacht noted some indirect and direct influence in instances such as these:[2]

1. *Survey* magazine's influence in the McNamara brothers case in 1911 in Los Angeles. The magazine proposed establishment of a Federal Commission on Industrial Relations, which President Taft accepted.

2. Richard Rovere's article in 1964 in *Encounter,* the British monthly, discussing Senator Barry Goldwater's political views, which is thought, by the many follow-ups of it, to have been influential in his nomination by the Republicans.

3. Others were articles that appeared in *America* on air-raid shelters; about the Oberammergau passion play, in *Commentary;* the sugar lobby, in *The Reporter;* the film, "The Miracle," in *Commonweal;* one by Milovan Djilas, one time Jugoslav vice-president, in *The New Leader;* and several more from *The Nation.*

The influence of magazines was dramatized during 1966 and 1967 by the sensational results achieved by the then almost unknown *Ramparts.* This periodical, begun originally as a literary quarterly in 1961 by Roman Catholic laymen, developed into a nationally circulated monthly of about 200,000 circulation. It added a book publishing firm, a bi-weekly Sunday paper (for a time), and was planning radio and television ventures.

Once departed from its literary and religious type of content, *Ramparts* engaged in progressively stronger exposés. "The Menace of

---

[2] John H. Schacht, *The Journals of Opinion and Reportage* (New York: Magazine Publishers Association, 1966), pp. 40–49, 66–67.

Barbie Dolls" was one of the earlier subjects. Soon it began running copy that reminded older students of American magazine journalism of the muckraking days of McClure and Steffens. The first piece to attract genuinely nationwide attention was an attack in early 1966 on training programs in South Vietnam conducted by Michigan State University. The editors accused the university officials of harboring a spy operation by allowing agents of the Central Intelligence Agency to be part of the program, which, it charged, actually was engaged not in university work, but counterintelligence. The charges were found to be true, at least in part, although the university officials denied that they knew the program was being so utilized.

The CIA itself came fully into the limelight in 1967, and the influence of the magazine was dramatized when its charges led President Johnson to order reforms in the agency. *Ramparts* asserted that the National Student Association, American Newspaper Guild, and dozens of other groups, including numerous foundations, had knowingly or unknowingly accepted financial support from the CIA to carry on, in a cloak and dagger manner, activities which made political instruments of Americans attending meetings and other activities abroad. Subsequently, *Ramparts* won a George Polk Memorial Award in journalism from Long Island University.

The formulas of the opinion magazines were summarized by Walter Lippmann, a founder of *The New Republic,* at the magazine's fiftieth anniversary dinner in 1964:

> The point of all this is that the paper was meant to be what it now is—the organ of no party, of no faction, of no sect, and of no cause, concerned not with liberalism and progressivism and conservatism as ideologies, but with all of them in the perspective of the tradition of civility in our Western society. This is not the only kind of journalism by any means. There is need and there is room for advocacy and for causes and for parties and for ideologies. But this particular kind of journalism, of which the touchstone is the civilized tradition itself, is an interesting kind of journalism for the journalist, and, one must hope, for the readers.[3]

### *Godkin and* The Nation

Edwin Godkin bequeathed to journalism an unusual philosophy. His view, as phrased by Willard G. Bleyer, pioneer journalism educator and a leading historian of the press, was that a publication should "appeal to the thinking classes rather than to the unthinking masses."

The holder of this unorthodox philosophy was born in Ireland of English parents in 1831. Godkin studied law for a time, then wrote his first book, *History of Hungary,* when he was only twenty-two. He then became a London *Daily News* war correspondent in the Crimea

---

[3] "Remarks on the Occasion of This Journal's 50th Year," Walter Lippmann, Bill Mauldin, *et al., The New Republic,* March 21, 1964, p. 14.

and an editorial writer for the *Northern Whig*. In 1857 he came to the United States, and here he decided to remain. In that same year he resumed study of the law and was admitted to the New York bar in 1858. He re-entered journalism in 1861 as a New York *Times* editorial writer. Henry J. Raymond, the paper's founder, soon offered him a part ownership which he refused.

During the Civil War he became ambitious to establish a high-grade weekly journal of politics and literary criticism, like the famous English periodicals, the *Spectator* and the *Saturday Review*. By 1865 with the help of friends he had raised one hundred thousand dollars from literary men and teachers at Harvard and Yale and in the big eastern cities. A stock company was set up with forty shareholders and *The Nation* was founded. Godkin was made editor and Wendell Phillips Garrison the literary editor.

Godkin, a follower of Jeremy Bentham, the English philosopher, believed in utilitarianism, i.e., that the happiness of the individual depends upon the happiness of the greatest number, or enlightened self-interest. This viewpoint recurs throughout Godkin's life. Bleyer wrote that the editor believed in "peace, retrenchment, and reform" or a Victorian English liberalism.

During his sixteen years as editor of the magazine and his later editorship of the New York *Evening Post* (then a full-sized, dignified daily), Godkin stood for complete reconciliation with the South, tariff reduction, civil service reform, sound currency, a laissez-faire economy, and the highest possible standards for public officials.

His views brought him into opposition with two other noted American journalists, Horace Greeley and Charles A. Dana. Although Greeley likewise was an idealist, Godkin opposed him for President because of his belief in protectionism. His opposition to Dana was more personal; he considered him an opportunist.

Godkin gained full control of *The Nation* within a year after its founding, when he fell into disagreement with some stockholders. He served as editor from 1865 to 1881, when he sold it to Henry Villard, a financier and one-time reporter. Godkin became co-editor of the New York *Evening Post,* also just acquired by Villard, and his career became that of a newspaperman rather than a magazinist. Toward the end of the century he returned to England somewhat disillusioned and believing that democracy, the Great American Experiment, had failed. He died in 1902, with many encomiums by leading American writers, scholars, editors, and public figures.

## The Nation *goes on*

When Godkin sold the magazine, it became a weekly edition of the *Post* and remained so for thirty years. Its contributors continued to be distinguished: Gamaliel Bradford, William Roscoe Thayer, George Lyman Kittredge, Edward Eggleston, and Joel Chandler Harris being among them. Wendell Garrison took over the editorship and remained in it until his death in 1907. He was a meticulous, wise, and high-minded editor who kept the magazine in the Godkin tradition, but as he lacked that editor's force and originality the circulation suffered.

Successive, short-term editors were Hammond Lamont, Paul Elmer More, and Harold deWolf Fuller, all former university professors. More fiction was published under them. Contributors included such noted critics as Stuart P. Sherman, Norman Foerster, Frank Jewett Mather, Carl Van Doren, and W. P. Trent. Theodore Dreiser's early novels were sympathetically reviewed, in contrast to their reception elsewhere.

The magazine's second most famous editor came to the post in 1918 during a controversy over its attitude toward war. He was Oswald Garrison Villard, grandson of William Lloyd Garrison, the abolitionist editor. Villard, who died in 1949, was, like Godkin, vigorous, bold, and independent. The magazine, after a temporary slump, was reinvigorated. An attempt to suppress it because of its antiwar stand only called attention to it in 1917. H. L. Mencken said then that it succeeded because it "began breaking heads."

Villard remained editor until 1933, when he handed the post to Ernest Gruening, later governor and then U.S. senator from Alaska; next was Freda Kirchwey, the only woman to run the magazine; after her came Henry Hazlitt, who resigned shortly to join *Newsweek,* and Joseph Wood Krutch, Columbia drama professor. Raymond Gram Swing and Max Lerner became co-editors when Gruening and Hazlitt departed. Villard remained as owner until 1935 and until 1940 as contributing editor. He severed connections in disagreement over the magazine's war policy, which now had changed from opposition to support.

Other disagreements developed with the new owner, Maurice Wertheim, founder of the Theatre Guild, banker, and philanthropist, and in 1937 the Wertheim Foundation sold it to Miss Kirchwey. By then it had reached a 43,000 circulation, the largest since its founding. In those years it was carrying the by-lines of Heywood Broun, John Chamberlain, Allen Tate, Norman Thomas, H. L. Mencken, Katherine Anne Porter, John Haynes Holmes, Louis Adamic, Stuart Chase, Reinhold Neibuhr, and Carl Sandburg.

World War II having weakened the magazine financially (it never has obtained much advertising), Miss Kirchwey sought new support. In the early 1940's a non-profit corporation, the Nation Associates, was set up with an endowment of several hundred thousand dollars. Miss Kirchwey resigned as editor and publisher in 1955 and was succeeded in the first post by Carey McWilliams and in the second by George G. Kirstein. James J. Storrow, Jr., became publisher in 1966. Circulation has remained small, around 30,000.

*The Nation,* in 1967 obtained by merger the circulation of *Frontier,* a 17-year-old Pacific Coast monthly not unlike itself in point of view. The magazine also thus acquired a West Coast office. This merger was the first in its more than a century of history.

## The critics speak up

So much detail is presented about *The Nation* because it is a leading example of the influential magazine of small circulation that stands in a separate group from the conventional concept of the magazine as primarily a business venture. Such a publication, dealing as it does with controversial ideas, is likely to invite criticism, usually adverse. The quality magazines are rarely chided for their content or their conduct. But the magazines of firm opinions are not so much taken for granted.

*The Nation* and *The New Republic* have received the greatest publicity. Both have been called "confused and confusing" in their political roles.[4] Both have been criticized for their writing. "By and large these magazines are badly and erratically written," wrote another critic, who at the same time admitted that he prefers them and their companions to the consumer magazines.[5] Extremists damn them as being either too radical or too conservative. When Henry Wallace, formerly Secretary of Agriculture and later Vice President, became editor of *The New Republic* in 1947 the weekly was denounced widely for accepting his leadership, even after he had resigned from the staff in view of his activities as a Progressive Party presidential candidate.

Far more troublesome was the banning of *The Nation* from high school libraries in New York City in 1948. The action was taken by the New York City Board of Superintendents, which voted to cut it from the approved list because of a series of articles on the Roman Catholic church by Paul Blanshard. The ban was renewed in 1949 and 1950, and continued for more than another decade. The American Civil Liberties Union and other groups protested to the Board, and the magazine took its case to the Supreme Court. During the same period it was ruled out of libraries in Newark, N.J., and removed by extra-legal means (with *The New Republic*) from the library shelves of Bartlesville, Okla. Not until 1963 was *The Nation* again permitted in the New York high school libraries. Thus both the magazine's religious and political views brought opposition. These incidents had no appreciable effect upon circulation, which remained about at the usual level, but the staff had to give considerable time and attention to the cases.

Physically more attractive than its liberal-doctrine competitors, the

---

[4] Lillian Symes, "Our Liberal Weeklies," *The Modern Monthly,* October, 1936, p. 7.

[5] Robert Lekachman, "Now at Your Newsstand, As Usual," *Columbia University Forum,* Summer, 1962, pp. 2, 3.

*National Review,* in the late 1950's and in all the 1960's, rose as a new conservative voice among the opinion magazines. Built on a formula somewhat like that of the by then departed *Plain Talk* and the early version of *The Freeman* of the Albert Jay Nock and Suzanne LaFollette days, it was begun by William F. Buckley, Jr., a young man of means who had become known for a book, *God and Man at Yale.* A man of broad ambitions (he later ran on the Conservative Party ticket for mayor of New York, wrote a widely syndicated newspaper column, and was the central figure in a television series), Buckley at first was unable to obtain sufficient advertising and support to push the magazine's income and circulation high enough to avoid deficits.

*National Review* was launched in 1955 with about $300,000 supplied by Buckley and his friends. He and they have bailed it out whenever necessary, although in the early 1970's its circulation rose to about 100,000, far outstripping most of the liberal organs; and it began receiving advertising support from such conservative business champions as the Schick Razor Company and right-wing book firms.

A factor in its greater acceptance was the attractive typography, use of photographs, avoidance of the butcher-paper stock, and a few cartoons. With the aid of prominent conservative voices like those of John Chamberlain, Russell Kirk, James Burnham, Henry Hazlitt, and William Henry Chamberlin, it has taken positions in content on the opposite sides of public questions from *New Republic, The Nation,* and the others in the liberal camp. The conservative viewpoint seemed at last to have found a consistent and not ill-natured voice in *National Review.*

Despite their ideological differences, in 1969 the *National Review* and *The New Republic* began selling general advertisers space at a reduced rate if bought in both magazines.

### Opinions at extremes

East is east and west is west, depending upon where one is standing. Opinion magazines similarly are judged to be extreme in their views depending upon from what premise one begins.

On the one hand are magazines, some superficially like newspapers, coming from groups at what was termed the extreme political and social right during the early 1960's. They come from the National States Rights Party, the Christian Education Association, the John Birch Society, and Christian Faith, Inc. Among their publications are *The Thunderbolt,* bearing the subtitle, "The White Man's View"; *Review of the News; American Mercury,* but not the one made famous by H. L. Mencken and George Jean Nathan; and *American Opinion.* Examination of these and others in the group show a predominance of anti-black, anti-Jewish, anti-Cuba and Chile, anti-Catholic, anti-Communist, anti-organized labor, anti-United Nations, and anti-National Council of Churches of Christ content. By their methods of journalism—distortion, assigning guilt by association, and outright publication of opinion as news and fact—they have come to be classified as hate publications.

On the other hand are the hate periodicals of the extreme left. Not as numerous, their opinions often are as vitriolic and unfair. Their targets are the business world and its organizations, usually both major parties and all the minority political bodies opposed to their own, churches of all types, the press, radio and television, and the groups at the other extreme. Their positions differ from the rightists', for they defend the minority groups' campaigns for civil rights, side with the rank and file if not the leaders of organized labor, and defend the United Nations. The publications cannot exactly be equated with those of the right in aims as much as in journalistic methods. Typical of them is *New World Review*. The failure to criticize communism, never to find fault with it, is an accepted policy of these and others in the group.

## The underground press

Although most of the publications known by the vague expression "the underground press" are of newspaper format, their content is heavily that of magazines, particularly those of opinion.

A phenomenon of the hippie period, estimates of the number published by 1972 have run as high as six thousand, depending upon whether off-campus college publications are included. Mention of this press calls to mind usually such city papers as the *East Village Other,* the Los Angeles *Free Press,* and magazines like *The Realist, Rolling Stone,* and *Crawdaddy.* For a time most of them were politically militant, prone to breaking the conventions of language as well as journalism and typography, but in time various of the leaders became so successful that they became more like the established publications, gathering considerable revenue from advertising. In general they have been carelessly written and edited, faddy, and without any consistent program either journalistically or socially. The more sedate and constructive now prefer to be known as the alternate press. The movements for a cleaner environment and communal living also produced their own magazines, such as *Earth*.

## The literary magazines

The literary magazines of the United States have been pushed into the journalistic background by the commercial publications, which have all the permanent and prominent places on the newsstands, sell the most advertising space, and have the greatest number of subscribers. A century ago the literary magazine was an important publication in the nation's life. Today it is no longer in the public eye. While still needed as a place of nurture for the new writers and as a record in creative writing of our time, it lives a life more or less of its own.

It exists in two forms: the small circulation periodical that has been published for a decade or more and has acquired substantial backing from a university or college is one form; the other is the little literary magazine which ventures into the world like a young bird and probably will be gone in a year or two.

The first, the purely literary magazine, has become so entwined with the little magazine that it is difficult to separate them. The lines of difference are perhaps only artificial and no more than length of life. Certainly they are irrelevant to literary quality. The "big little" magazines, as the better established literary magazines have been called, usually are physically more precisely edited and produced (a logical consequence of their greater financial support) and are issued with more dependability than the "little literary" periodicals.

There was a time, also, when both groups were more remote than they are today from the commercial magazines. But the greater hospitality to *avant-garde* or at least non-conventional fiction by *Mademoiselle, The New Yorker, Esquire, Cosmopolitan,* and *Redbook,* for example, has shortened the distance between them.

As the new, young serious writer looks around him, seeking a place to publish, he naturally is puzzled. So few of the literary magazines of any size are on newsstands or in libraries that he is in the dark about most of them. Which publish the writing he wishes to produce? For a time there was a clue, *The International Guide,* but lack of support ended its two-year life, much as if it had been a little magazine itself.

Although it does not flourish, the magazine of outstanding literary content continues at least numerically strong, thanks largely to academic support and the sacrifice of its editors and owners. Among those extant at this writing that perhaps rank higher than little magazines, which have a vagabond or gypsy reputation, are the *Massachusetts Review, Contact, Poetry, Quarterly Review of Literature, Epoch, New American Review, Tri-Quarterly, Hudson Review, The Literary Review, Texas Quarterly, Odyssey, The Sewanee Review, South Atlantic Quarterly, Prairie Schooner, San Francisco Review, Evergreen,* and *Partisan Review.*

In the quality group, *Harper's* and the others, literature, in the sense of being creative, imaginative writing, has for some years been subordinated to non-fiction. This situation, as we have seen, also exists in the purely commercial magazines that make room for serious fiction.

As we shall see when we come to the little littles, it is perhaps just as well that the new writer turns to them ahead of the larger and more stable ones, for the reception is friendlier. The literary magazine in the United States today has become addicted to schools. That is, in one group, *San Francisco Review* and *Evergreen,* for example, we find that the avant-garde group of writers is welcome. In another group—*The Literary Review* and the *South Atlantic Quarterly*—the hospitality is to the more conventional writer. And within these groups are others in subdivisions based on form.

A big division is poetry, which is almost the entire content of a number: *Poetry, Blue Grass, Approach, Metamorphosis, Descant, American Bard, Blue Guitar, The Lyric, Poetry Northwest, Poet and Critic, Sonnet Sequences.* A few others emphasize plays, as does the *Tulane Drama Review.* Still others emphasize regional literature: *Kansas Magazine, New Mexico Quarterly, The Prairie Schooner,* and *Georgia Review* are a few examples. They do not exclude other material.

Attempting to achieve more economic independence, a group of sixteen literary magazines in 1961 formed the Association of Literary Magazines of America (ALMA). The aim, it declared, was "to increase the usefulness and the prestige of the literary magazines of the United States and Canada." They organized "to secure outside financial help for the magazines from individuals, foundations, and other organizations; it will undertake to meet collectively the grave problem of distribution and promotion which the magazines face. . . ."

At a second meeting the next year the group was doubled in size, adding such veterans of the struggle as *Poetry* and *Hudson Review.* By then a few small grants had been obtained from foundations and a little success had been achieved in soliciting advertising contracts for all at one time. In 1966 the Coordinating Council of Literary Magazines was formed to work more intensively on the financial problem. By 1970 it had obtained grants amounting to $150,000.

## The little little magazines

The National Foundation of the Arts and Humanities in 1966 granted $55,000 for publication of an anthology of the work of little magazines. Payments of $500 to $1,000 were to go to the writers as well as to the editors of the magazines represented in the book, an astonishing windfall for an author who probably received nothing but extra copies for his poem or story.

Reporting the drawing by lot, from a dozen names of firms, for the publisher to produce the book, the New York *Times* described "all the heads of the companies present expressing their doubt about the sales potential of the projected book."

Why this dubiety? It rests in the history of these magazines, all poor cousins in an affluent family. Their origins are a clue:

> With some friends I started *Advance;* you've probably never heard of it, have you, it isn't much mentioned in the family. It was appallingly juvenile as all such little magazines were, but it had some good things in it. I particularly remember one thing we did. We were

proud of our masthead, young men who start magazines always are; we were always at the press making sure that our names were spelled right, and that the type hadn't gotten old and the names indistinct. And when we looked at the proof of a new issue, wet off the forms, smelling of damp butcher-paper and printer's ink, what do you think was the first thing we read? The article we had wangled out of the prominent novelist? Certainly not; we read the masthead first. There they were, big and black, the names, our names, the living testament of our rebellion and independence. I sent a gratuitous subscription to *Advance* to my father at his office, and another to my Aunt Julia, who I considered to be in need of it.[6]

So does a character in a modern novel about magazine life describe what he obviously considers an early journalistic indiscretion. But this fictional *Advance* displayed characteristics of the typical little magazine, the windmill tilter, the one-man magazine, as it also has been called.

The little magazine is tiny in circulation, deeply interested in politics, literature, social problems, and the arts, generally unorthodox, usually sophisticated, experimental, and non-commercial. Because it is low in circulation as well as small in format it may be confused with pocket magazines or digests, which are small only physically. Truer cousins of the little magazines are the better established quarterlies and monthlies already noted, several of which began as little magazines. A typical quarterly leaves the little magazine classification when it achieves a five thousand circulation.

About one hundred of the littles have been in existence in any year during the decades since the 1930's, when they reached their peak. Their death rate is great, because they are established usually by inexperienced magazinists and have limited support. At least one writer on them, Gorham Munson, is optimistic about the mortality. He believes that the little magazine can do its work in two or three years and need not survive longer.

Circulations often go no higher than a few hundred copies. Because they are operated at a financial loss, their owners must keep them modest in size and physical quality, with some exceptions. They range from pocket size to flat, but the small format is usual. Quarterly or just now-and-then are the favorite frequencies. Subscription prices are high by comparison with the giants of the magazine world, for they range from two to ten dollars a year; single copies usually cost from fifty cents to two dollars. Numerous little magazines of the present are published under college or university auspices, by a group of dissenting, *avant-garde*, or struggling writers and artists, or by the politically and socially rebellious.

Some of the better known littles published in the United States in earlier years had titles that signify their artiness, defiance of the

---

[6] John Brooks, *The Big Wheel* (New York: Harper & Brothers, 1949), p. 140.

world, or aspirations: *Retort, Imagi, The Golden Goose, Circle, Accent, The Tiger's Eye, Approach, Decade, Neurotica, Illiterati, Line, Furioso, New Horizons, Portfolio, Matrix, Experiment, Gale, Compass.* Several notable magazines of the type from overseas had influence in American literary circles: *Botteghe Oscure* (Italy), *Horizon* (England), *Meanjin* (Australia), *Quixote* (Spain); some were sponsored by American writers.

So fragile are their lives that to list those available in the 1970's is dangerous, but they need to be lifted a bit from obscurity and lack of place in most directories. We find among scores available *Zero, Epoch, Kulchur, Wormwood Review, Origin, Dissent, Audience, Shenandoah, Chelsea, Mutiny, Free Lance, Dryad, Mandola, Umbra, ManRoot, Nexus, Gnosis, Intrepid, The Smith, Discovery,* and *North American Review,* the last of special interest as an attempt at a revival of the famous monthly of the nineteenth century. Tomorrow, some of these may vanish to be replaced by still other littles. Others, having to do with film, broadcasting, politics, homosexuality, and other non-literary subjects, also are found in the few bookshops that handle the littles. All these must be added to the ALMA members.

The short-lived but influential magazine edited by Emerson, Thoreau, and Margaret Fuller, *The Dial,* is a candidate as the first of the modern type of little magazine in the United States. It was born out of a revolt against the judgments of British critics that Americans had no literary accomplishments and sought to give this country's authors an outlet of their own.

"A little magazine," as defined by the historians, "is a magazine designed to print artistic work which for reasons of commercial expediency is not acceptable to the money-minded periodicals or presses."[7] That aim motivated the successors to *The Dial*—Louise Imogen Guiney's Boston magazine, *The Knight-Errant;* in San Francisco, *The Lark;* and in Chicago, *The Chap Book.* When Harriet Monroe founded *Poetry* in 1912, in Chicago, she was continuing the interest of the poets, who have gone on establishing and sacrificing for the little magazines since the *Dial* days.

In 1914 another Chicago author, Margaret Anderson, founded *The Little Review,* now remembered because its editor was the only one willing to print James Joyce's *Ulysses,* not without opposition from postal authorities. During the dozen years of its life, a long one for such a magazine, the *Review* also published the writing of others destined to fame: T. S. Eliot, Ezra Pound, and Wyndham Lewis. At that time most littles, not yet labeled *avant-garde,* considered themselves liberal in politics or literature.

Another that lasted a dozen years was *The Midland,* issued in

---

[7] Frederick J. Hoffman, *et al., The Little Magazine* (Princeton, N.J.: Princeton University Press, 1946), p. 2.

Iowa City. This one inspired *The Prairie Schooner* and *The Frontier,* later combined and still published at the University of Nebraska as practically a quality periodical.

· World War I stimulated the publication of the littles. The disillusionment following that war and the increase in unemployment were expressed in New York and Paris by American writers with opinions not welcomed by conventional periodicals. *Transatlantic Review, Secession, Broom, Glebe, Transition,* and *This Quarter* gained international attention.

One day in 1930, Edward J. O'Brien, later widely known as editor, author, and short-story anthologist, received from Tennessee a magazine produced on a duplicating machine. None of the names of the contributors to *The Gyroscope* was familiar to him. He decided to examine its pages for stories that he might include in his annual collection of the best. Three of the then obscure writers impressed him: Katherine Anne Porter, Janet Lewis, and Caroline Gordon. He not only reprinted some of the stories but also in his anthology suggested that other literary groups imitate the methods of *The Gyroscope.*

This proposal was taken seriously by Whit Burnett and Martha Foley; in 1931 their *Story* was born. Editing it in their spare time, this man and wife team of foreign correspondents in Austria kept it going although they lost their jobs and moved to the Spanish island of Majorca, where living was less expensive. They put all their extra money into *Story,* printing it on a seventeenth-century hand press, sending to other parts of Europe for types (especially for the *w,* which is not used in Spain). The circulation during the first year was only six hundred, but among contributors were Manuel Komroff and Kay Boyle. Soon the editors took it to the United States, where it was published until 1949, when it was temporarily suspended, but revived again as a bimonthly and was later issued under the name *Story and Play,* but it ceased in 1964. It was revived again in 1967 by a large firm, Scholastic Magazines with Whit Burnett as advisory editor and Hallie Burnett, who joined him in editing the later *Story* in the United States, as consulting editor. George Dickerson became editor of the new version, which had a *Ramparts* format but not content. It soon was converted into an anthology of college writing. During its early years it carried original work by Ernest Hemingway, William Faulkner, Erskine Caldwell, Ludwig Bemelmans, and William Saroyan.

### The interwar years

The flurry of interest in the littles that had begun before World War I continued until the second in 1939. During this interwar period, in the historians' judgment, these periodicals were responsible for the introduction of at least 95 per cent of the post-1912 poets. Scores of magazines were founded. As the newly discovered writers received more ready acceptance in commercial magazines and as

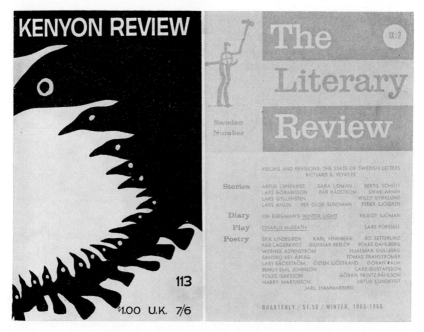

*Fig. 17.2.* Two literary magazines which have received international attention are those of Fairleigh Dickinson University and Kenyon College; the former emphasizes the work of foreign writers; the latter introduced many poets during its life from 1939 to 1970.

these magazines themselves, under prodding by anthologists and critics, proved more hospitable to new writers, the function of the little magazine became more one of criticism than of original publication. The 1940's found them engrossed in critical theory and political maneuverings, and sharply divided over the publication of orthodox, realistic writing as against non-commercial material variously called surrealistic, dadaistic, or by the name of some other departure.

Evidence may be given readily that the credit to little magazines for the discovery and encouragement of new writers is deserved. *Poetry,* now considered more substantial than a little magazine, was the first to publish the work of Vachel Lindsay, Carl Sandburg, T. S. Eliot, Edgar Lee Masters, Robert Frost, Elinor Wylie, Sara Teasdale, Marianne Moore, Sherwood Anderson, John Gould Fletcher, Amy Lowell, Hart Crane, George Dillon, Archibald MacLeish, Robert Penn Warren, Louise Bogan, Countee Cullen, and Jessie Stuart.

Ernest Hemingway, who was both novelist and journalist, was a famous discovery of one of the littles. A virtually unknown periodical, *The Double Dealer,* first published one of his stories. After several littles used others, he published his first book, *Three Stories and Ten Poems,* issued in Paris by a non-commercial press. This thin collection of little magazine material came to the attention of Scribner's, a prominent and old New York publishing house. In 1926 it issued Hemingway's first novel, *The Sun Also Rises,* and a notable literary career, encouraged by little magazines at the start, was under way.

Other now prominent writers thus encouraged include D. H. Lawrence, Richard Aldington, Aldous Huxley, Ruth Suckow, Alfred Kreymborg, Saul Bellow, Ralph Ellison, Robert Lowry, Robert Lowell, William Carlos Williams, Truman Capote, Henry Miller, Nelson Algren, Louis MacNeice, Dylan Thomas, Richard Wright, Lionel Trilling, Langston Hughes, Lucia Trent, Conrad Aiken, E. E. Cummings, and Willard Motley.

And if one now examines the various book collections of outstanding short stories one is sure to find that a large proportion of the writers had first appeared in little magazines or quarterlies.

### Explaining their obscurity

Despite this service to the worlds of ideas and literature, most magazine readers in any country know nothing about the littles. They are obscure because even in the United States their owners cannot afford wide newsstand distribution and elaborate promotion campaigns. But this limitation is true of other types as well: religious, educational, and labor. A more important reason is that the general public is not interested in the content of the little magazine. Perhaps if they could be seen on more newsstands a little of this indifference could be overcome, but any substantial support rests on public acceptance, which cannot be expected until Americans as a whole are a better educated people.

The magazines also remain obscure because they are such small operations. One or two persons generally do all the work except printing and the bulk of the writing, illustrating, or photography. Some have been hand-set, hand-printed, and hand-bound—*Decade of Short Stories, The Phoenix,* and *Retort,* for example.

*New Horizons,* issued from 1938 to 1941 in Chicago, offers a typical picture of how a little magazine is brought out. Begun by a young couple, Robert and Margaret Williams, it was called *Creative Writing* at first. Produced on a duplicating machine, it was theoretically a monthly but actually issued whenever the young owners could pay the printer. It was rechristened *New Horizons,* announcements were sent to writers' magazines saying it was interested in manuscripts of many sorts, and a post office box was rented. An associate editor collected an average of two hundred manuscripts weekly, recorded and sifted them, and submitted the possibilities for publication to the Williams, who finally accepted or rejected.

Only the printer and the post office were paid. The former de-livered the copies to the editors' home, from where they were addressed to subscribers or shipped in bundles to a few large city bookstores. Advertising, comprising about 5 per cent of the content, came chiefly from other little magazines (with no cash exchange), Chicago shops, and well-wishing friends. Although at one time the circulation reached nearly three thousand, the revenue was insufficient to pay past and current bills. Promotion consisted largely of postcard notices, news stories to Chicago literary editors, and word-of-mouth campaigns by the three editors. *New Horizons* ceased publication in 1941 when its war-and-peace policy conflicted with the national temper. After the war the Williams started a camp for children in Massachusetts; be-ginning in the late 1950's they began issuing *Rockolog*, containing literary and artistic work of their campers and visiting speakers.

Increasing printing costs, a source of trouble for all magazines, big or little, have hurt the little ones. A few turned to cheaper print-ing methods, such as offset, but the hardy group that survived wars and depressions found the support of angels (*Paris Review* was sus-tained by the Aga Khan, for example) or of colleges necessary.

Fleeting as these magazines are, they have had, since 1952, a small magazine devoted in part to keeping track of them and offering a forum for discussion of their problems. This periodical is *Trace*, printed in England and edited in this country.

## Their purposes

The content of most littles is too esoteric for the American middle class, with its limited background for understanding what these maga-zines strive to do.

Showing contempt for commercialism, the ephemeral littles have collectively protested against security and against the smugness that they believe accompanies such security. They claim originality, in-tellectual honesty, and literary influence as their reward in place of solvency, national circulation, and fame. In the mid-thirties, when Robert Cantwell examined more than fifty for an article, he dis-covered such statements of purpose as these:

"We want to reach the unknowns." "We want to encourage the young writers." "Our task is to combat stark leftism in proletarian literature." ". . . agencies through which writers, with something more in them than a dubious ability to write advertising copy dis-guised as fiction, could establish themselves."[8]

Three decades later more of the group have become the organs of people with social causes, the principal cause being that of break-ing social rather than literary conventions and traditions, although

---

[8] Robert Cantwell, "The Little Magazines," *The New Republic*, July 25, 1934, p. 295.

for a time in the 1950's, through such magazines as *Big Table,* there was considerable desire to shock with naturalistic writing.

The little magazines, being free in spirit if not independent financially, often have given room to freakish ideas, to ridiculous experimentation, and to defiance for its own sake—or at least so it seems to those who may not understand their writing. Poor work also creeps in under the guise of experiment; this, however, is one of the prices of freedom of expression.

## Magazines for sophisticates

Certain magazines for sophisticated elements in the American population come close to the literary group. Precise classification is impossible in the instances of *The New Yorker, Audience, Esquire, Holiday, Réalités, Town and Country, Gourmet, Travel and Leisure,* and others read by persons of sophistication, considerable means, or a consuming interest in living fastidiously, fashionably, or just cleverly.

*The New Yorker* forbids exact pigeonholing because it is sophisticated yet possessed of a social conscience, humorous yet hospitable to the finest reportage and to an individualistic concept of what is literary. Superficially *Gourmet* is no more than a magazine for people who like rich foods, but it conveys other ideas just the same.

The sophisticated magazine, despite the diversity of those in the group, is more nearly a true member of the so-called class magazine group than of any other type dealt with in this book, although *Harper's Bazaar* and *Vogue* belong just as much in the women's department.

Appealing to the economically "upper class," the sophisticated magazine also has "class" itself. It is the epitome of technical perfection. Its appeal is to what is known as "the international set," a social aggregation who do what they do because it is the thing to be done; it is "smart." If they are to be interested in hotels, the "perfect appointments" must be mentioned; if a restaurant is to tempt them, it must have "a fabulous cuisine." The sophisticate moves in an air of decadence that touches his magazines, lightly in the case of *The New Yorker,* somewhat more pervasively in *Town and Country.*

At no time has this genuine class magazine group been large. Its first member probably was *Harper's Bazaar,* founded in 1867 by the Harper brothers (see Chapter 2). It was intended to be "A Repository of Fashion, Pleasure, and Instruction." The Harpers spelled it Bazar, as did the German periodical, *Der Bazar,* which had suggested the new one; but thirteen years after the Hearst magazines took it over they added the extra *a.* In the sense in which the Oriental people use it, a bazaar is a place where rare silks, soft velvets, costly jewels, and other beautiful and pleasure-giving objects are sold, having been brought from all over the earth. Not a smelly, ugly marketplace, it is itself a spot of beauty.

From its first days *Harper's Bazaar* reflected this tone, although not so lushly as now. Its fashion plates were brought from Europe. It gave space to articles on the arrangement of house interiors. Being a weekly until the end of the century, it offered many departments and features, including a "Facetiae" page to which the principal contributor was the popular humorist, John Kendrick Bangs.

Aimed at women from the start, it had several distinguished journalists among its early editors, notably Margaret Sangster and Elizabeth Jordan. When Hearst bought it in 1913 he added to its tone of sophistication and smartness. Henry Blackman Sell, later to leave journalism for success in the canned food business and to reenter it as editor of *Town and Country,* was the first of a series of editors successful in maintaining its recherché and mannered style. He was succeeded by Charles Hanson Towne, Arthur H. Samuels, and Carmel White Snow. Mid-century saw its pages dominated by advertisements and pictures of cosmetics and clothes. During its earlier years its contributors had included such notable writers as Arnold Bennett, W. L. George, Robert Hichens, William Dean Howells, and Mary E. Wilkins, but fiction and essays have had little place in its pages in recent years because today sophisticates are more interested in sports—especially yachting, cruising, and hunting—than in literary or artistic trends.

Yet the change in emphasis seems to have been advisable, for the magazines that clung to satire, the arts, and highbrow literary work have disappeared: *The Smart Set, Vanity Fair,* the original *Life, Sportsman, The Spur,* and *Judge,* to note only the most outstanding.

## The vogue for **Vogue**

A companion to *Harper's Bazaar,* only in the sense that it serves the same field, including the operators of dress shops and the studios of dress designers, is *Vogue.* They are anything but companionable, for the competition is sharp. Originally *Vogue* also was a weekly. Founded in 1892 as a snob-appeal magazine of the New York City social set, it went into the hands of the firm that still owns it in 1909, when Condé Nast purchased it. In a half century it rose from 22,000 circulation a week to more than half a million.

Peterson points out that Nast believed that a magazine for people who could afford luxuries was the most economical for an advertiser of such merchandise to use because there would be so little waste. He sought a selective, not a large, circulation.[9]

This philosophy of publishing turned out to be sound, not only for *Vogue,* but also for other publishers later, as demonstrated by *The New Yorker, Sports Illustrated, Cue, Holiday, American Heritage,*

---

[9] Theodore Peterson, *Magazines in the Twentieth Century* (Urbana: University of Illinois Press, 1956), p. 254.

and *Horizon,* among others. In the case of the latter two the theory works about circulation only, since there is no advertising.

Not only did *Vogue* grow in circulation and advertising but it also became international in scope, because of editions issued in France and England.

## *The* New Yorker *bridge*

As a bridge between the sophisticated and the humor magazines is *The New Yorker,* for it is both. This magazine has broken most of the conventional rules of magazine making but carries on because it has built a solid place for itself in both places.

It gained it because during its first three decades it was led by a strong editor, Harold Ross, whose successor, William Shawn, has maintained its traditions. It has managed to couple sophisticated fiction and cartoons with meticulously accurate directories of what is going on at the city's motion picture houses, theatres, concert halls, museums, sports stadia, ice rinks, and art galleries. Its memorable cartoons—often anthologized and reprinted elsewhere—seem to offset its storyless short stories, its gigantic paragraphs, its eye-straining body type, and its occasional sniping at its own advertisers. It appears to be casual and purposeless; the devil-take-it tone has dominated it since its founding in 1925.

Saul Pett, an Associated Press writer, once interviewed Harold W. Ross, the founder. The occasion was the magazine's 25th anniversary. When asked if his concept of the magazine had changed over those years, the editor said he did not know. "You just run a magazine by instinct, not doping things out in advance," he said. This lack of aim has left room for a wide variety of contributions—humor in word and drawing, criticism of an authoritative order, short fiction, essays, poems, sketches, errors clipped from other publications, the distinctive biographical-personality articles behind the registered name "Profile," satire, shopping advice, long studies of institutions and human activities, correspondence from overseas, and short features, anecdotes, and editorials jammed into an opening section called "Talk of the Town."

No other important modern magazine was so much the reflection of its first editor as *The New Yorker.* Ross, who was called "charmingly churlish" and "a lovable old volcano," has been the subject of two books, a play, and dozens of articles in eminent periodicals. Yet he wrote almost nothing for his magazine, instead supervising it with meticulous care about all fine points, being responsible for its extraordinary record of accuracy and originality.

A one-time newspaperman and former editor of *Stars and Stripes,* the A.E.F. paper, Ross broke into magazine work as editor of the *American Legion* magazine, serving from 1919 to 1924. He then shifted to editing *Judge,* a weekly that for years had held a high place as a repository for satire and humor, but by 1924 was suffering from the impatience and cynicism of the American people following the war. Among Ross's friends from *Stars and Stripes* days were Franklin P. Adams, newspaper columnist later to become more widely known still as an "Information Please" expert, and Alexander Woollcott, critic and raconteur. They introduced Ross to Robert Benchley, Gardner Rea, Dorothy Parker, George S. Kaufman, Alice Duer Miller, Rea Irvin, Marc Connelly, and other sophisticated artists and writers who were to become frequent by-liners of *The New Yorker*'s early years.

Ross, himself, according to Henry F. Pringle,[10] put up $20,000 and Raoul H. F. Fleischmann invested $25,000. Within six weeks early in 1925 these sums were gone, and Fleischmann and others added nearly $300,000 more. This sum, too, in a few years needed replenishing and another $390,000 came mainly from Mr. and Mrs. Fleischmann, illustrating the drain on resources the launching of a new national magazine could be even then. But by 1927 the book had entered the financial black, not, however, until it had been kept alive by a total capital injection of nearly three-fourths of a million. At one time early in its years the capitalizers agreed, at a dinner, to kill it but the step was not taken before a new issue was out; the reception for that issue (on the strength of one article) was so encouraging that the group decided to stick it out a little longer.

The sophistication of the original concept is symbolized by the portrait drawn by Rea Irvin for a cover that is repeated each February on the anniversary of the first issue. Its subject is a mythical gentleman known at the office as Eustace Tilley. This foppish figure is examining a butterfly through a monocle. On his head is a beaver hat and around his neck a high stock. A further indication of intention to be sophisticated was the early announcement that the magazine was not intended for "the old lady from Dubuque."

The old lady would rarely be offended, but she might be puzzled, especially if she read the short stories, which are famous for their pointlessness or their resemblance to straight factual writing. On finding a reference to the local smart set of New York as "dudes," the old lady might wonder at this defiance of traditional sophistication. On reading the criticisms she might conclude that nothing ever pleases the magazine's blasé critics. But she would not be puzzled when reading the "Talk of the Town," where memorable essays on social problems have appeared and where some of our time's most effective and sensitive use of English may be found. Each year more than a score of books of short stories, biographical sketches, essays, cartoons, and articles, all of which originally appeared in *The New Yorker*, are issued by a variety of publishers.

[10] Henry F. Pringle, "Ross of *The New Yorker*," *'48—The Magazine of the Year*, March, 1948, p. 15.

### *Other humor magazines*

The variety of periodicals containing humor is so great in the United States that it is dangerous to settle them in any one chapter. They are as disparate as humor itself, which can be slapstick or subtle, sophisticated or simple, satirical or sexy. In magazines it ranges from that of *The New Yorker* or *National Lampoon*—satirical and subtle— to that of *Jest, Joker,* or *Laugh In*—obvious and slapstick.

With the disappearance because of war, depression, rising costs, the effect of motion pictures, radio, and television, of the leaders, such as the old *Life, Judge, Ballyhoo, Vanity Fair,* and their various and many imitators, the magazine totally devoted to humor has been reduced to two types. One is a group of small joke and cartoon books of minor circulation and quality and the other the humor magazines in comic book form—*Mad* and its satellites.

Whether *The New Yorker* should still be considered a magazine of humor is arguable, for it contains much serious material. Yet many persons, misled by its cartoons, so categorize it. Others so misjudged are *Esquire, Playboy,* and *Penthouse* (and their companions in the men's field), which have considerably more serious fiction and articles than the overlay of cartoons seems to indicate.

Of them all, however, *The New Yorker* has been the most influential and unusual in its formula as it developed from an Americanized *Punch* to its present unique place in the magazine world.

# Chapter 18

# Specialized magazines/
*Business*

I F WE TAKE in all categories, the magazines of business are unques-
tionably the largest single group in the magazine world. Of the approximately 20,000 periodicals of all types issued in the United States,
in excess of 10,000 are for or about the business world. This figure
has two main parts: the approximately 2,600 business magazines
(known also as trade or technical magazines and business papers) and
the roughly 8,000 company magazines (also called industrial publications and house organs).

Examination of these publications brings us, also, face to face
with the first clearly specialized group, aimed at a distinctly unified,
special interest public.

To examine in detail the component parts of the specialized
world is beyond the needs or the scope of this book, especially since
the range is limited only by the number of possible subjects. Few
are the interests not served by at least one periodical. Magazines exist
for cat fanciers, glider flyers, plumbers, stamp collectors, jail prisoners,
ballet dancers, and teachers of journalism in universities, in colleges,
in public high schools, in Catholic high schools. Physicists, physicians,
psychologists, and photographers all have many magazines of their own.

The specialized magazine exists because the general periodical
cannot possibly find space to gratify such varied and intense interests.
It also serves as a builder of loyalty, a propaganda organ, a means of
making money for a publisher, and a news medium.

First to use the specialized magazine was the world of business. In the United States the business and industrial publication has led the specialized magazine field in number and technical quality, but has left to the religious, philosophical, educational, scientific, and labor magazines the dissemination of broad ideas and the challenging of existing standards, practices, and viewpoints.

If newsmagazines are cousins of newspapers, magazines of business and industry are at least second cousins. But news weeklies are few, whereas business periodicals number in the thousands. News and news interpretations are prime content of business magazines. General newspapers and consumer magazines cannot be expected to report and to analyze detailed news of particular businesses or industries, for example. Neither space nor reader interest would permit. Hence the existence of such magazines as *Industry Week, Traffic World,* and the *Boot and Shoe Recorder,* each with from three to a dozen competitors. Hence also the existence of the company publication for employes, customers, dealers, stockholders, or distributors. There are more than five times as many business magazines as general daily papers.

### Types of business magazines

Julien Elfenbein, at one time editorial director of the house furnishings group of magazines issued by the Haire Publishing Corporation and author of the first comprehensive book on the business press, argues that all varieties of publications issued for the world of business should be known as *businesspapers,* since the use of many labels is confusing. Inasmuch, however, as the majority of publications are not newspapers but magazines, a case can be made for the combination word businessmagazine.

However labelled, these periodicals generally are issued weekly or monthly. Stanley A. Knisely, while executive vice-president of Associated Business Publications, Inc., an organization of such magazines as well as newspapers, distinguished these periodicals from other forms of journalism. He defined the type thus: "A business paper is a highly specialized publication which disseminates current information to a special group of business people who need this information to help them do a better job and, hence, make a better living."[1] Four classifications have been clarified by ABP:

1. Industrial or technical magazines read by persons in industry— foremen, department heads, superintendents, engineers, managers *(Modern Manufacturing* and *Railway Age).*
2. Institutional magazines read by men and women employed in colleges, clubs, schools, hotels, hospitals *(Hotel and Motel Review).*

---

[1] Stanley A. Knisely, in an address on "The Practice of Business Paper Publishing" in a series sponsored by New York University in 1947.

3. Merchandising magazines read by dealers, jobbers, wholesalers, and their supervisory staffs *(Hardware Retailer)*.
4. Professional magazines used by sales and advertising people, physicians, surgeons, architects, lawyers, and scientists *(Advertising Age, Progressive Architecture)*.

## The nine functions

Elfenbein notes nine functions for the four types: (1) Adult education, providing advanced knowledge for persons in industry; (2) News, gathering and writing information; (3) Editorial, crusading for higher standards and "safeguarding the competitive character of private profit enterprise"; (4) Integrating, interpreting news; (5) Forum, providing a place for exchange of opinions; (6) Advertising, acting as middleman; (7) Research, providing, among others, data about readers and markets and about production and distribution processes; (8) Public utility, living up to the responsibility provided by the guarantee of the freedom of the press; and (9) Public relations, giving information to its various "publics."[2]

Not all business magazines fulfill all of them, but all fulfill some of these functions. Although corner newsstands do not sell the publications, copies enter most communities, for retail merchants subscribe, public libraries attempt to carry those of greatest local interest, and factories, garages, repair shops, and other such businesses receive them, either by subscription or controlled distribution.

Their value is illustrated by a businessman whose comparatively small electrical products firm receives at the time fifteen. The list shows their variety, for it included *Home Appliance Builder, House and Home, Harvard Business Review, Electric Heating Journal, Appliance Manufacturer, Metal Products Manufacturing, Electricity in Building, Electrical Construction & Maintenance, Electrical Wholesaling, Electric Heating & Air Conditioning, Contractors Electrical Equipment, Electrical South, New England Electrical News,* and *Electrical West.*

When asked what purpose each serves, he replied that it helps him:

1. Keep abreast of what our customers are thinking and what their problems are—builders, contractors, utilities, distributors.
2. Work much more intelligently with people, and gain their confidence, when talking to them about *their* problems.
3. Handle our approach to the distributors if I know and understand their problems in business—their profit structures, their selling, their inventory problems, etc.
4. Keep abreast of competition—new product developments, leading articles, outstanding personnel.

---

[2] Julien Elfenbein, *Business Journalism* (New York: Harper & Brothers, 1960), pp. 14–15.

5. Keep abreast of my own market potential, i.e., gives me marketing statistics.[3]

In fulfilling its functions, the business magazine serves specialists as surely as do publications for scientists, religionists, and educators. Being one of the earliest and financially most successful of specialized journals, the business magazine not only is largest in number but reaches a high level of technical perfection as well. Some are among the handsomest journalistic products of the press, employing four-color printing, expensive paper, and numbers of specially prepared photographs, diagrams, charts, and graphs. *Fortune, Business Week, Nation's Business,* and most of the periodicals of the printing, architecture, housing, paint, and certain other industries or professions are high in technical quality.

But these magazines resemble only slightly the early business publications, such as the numerous *Price-Currents* of the eighteenth century commonly accepted as forerunners of the modern business publication.

Possibly *Hunt's Merchants' Magazine,* founded in 1839, was the first national business periodical.[4] Railway publications survive as the oldest. *The American Railroad Journal,* now called *Railway Locomotion and Cars,* was founded in 1832.

## Pioneer editors and publishers

Transit publications are closely connected with the early history of this type of magazine not only because they were among the first published but also because several of the leading business magazinists began their work with transportation publications in this type of journalism. The foremost name among business journalists in the United States is that of James H. McGraw.

McGraw started in journalism on the weekly in his home town, Chautauqua, N.Y. He wrote school news. He also joined his school principal in a side venture, writing a column and selling subscriptions for a monthly, *The Countryside.* After high school he attended a normal school. His former superior and journalistic partner by this time had gone with a friend to New York City to engage further in journalistic work, making a connection with a new industrial publishing scheme. The men started the *Street Railway Journal* and the *American Journal of Railway Appliances.* They also bought *Steam,* renaming it *Power,* the title it still bears. In 1884 McGraw joined them as a subscription salesman on commission. Soon he was earning

---

[3] Letter to Miss Joan Piper from Richard C. Piper, vice-president in charge of sales, Markel Electric Products Inc., Buffalo, New York.

[4] David P. Forsyth, *The Business Press in America* (Philadelphia: Chilton Co., 1964), p. 71.

$40 a week, a large sum in those days and far more than he could hope to be paid as a teacher.

"I was committed to teach another year for $700, but when the year was over I hastened back to New York and joined the American Railway Publishing Company."[5]

This firm was the one begun by his friends. When it fell upon bad times, McGraw raised money to buy a part interest and keep it afloat. In time he became owner. He went on to develop one of the giant magazine publishing empires: the McGraw-Hill Company. This firm now publishes about sixty magazines, and is part of a unit which has a related company to publish business and technical books.

James McGraw's name is associated with that of another business journalist with an interest in transportation, John A. Hill. But Hill, unlike McGraw, had practical experience in railroading, which he left to acquire a group of five publications, including *Coal Age, Engineering News, American Machinist, Engineering and Mining Journal,* and *Power*. These were united with the McGraw publications after his death in 1915.

Like McGraw, E. A. Simmons knew nothing about transportation when, in 1889, he began reading exchanges for the *Railway Age-Gazette* in Chicago. This $5-a-week job developed into managership of the office by 1892, when his weekly salary was $12. Ten years later, when it was $20, he had become an advertising salesman. When *American Engineer* offered him $40 he reported this to W. H. Boardman, his publisher, who enabled him to buy into the business. Today the firm, known as Simmons-Boardman Company, is one of the largest in business journalism.

Another schoolteacher-to-be, Horace M. Swetland, became prominent in the business magazine world; among still others who brought to their publications preparation in fields other than transportation were James H. McGraw, Jr., M. N. Forney, and Samuel O. Dunn.

While it is possible without technical experience to attain a position of importance and influence in business journalism, most notable editors and publishers have possessed technical backgrounds. Among them was Roy V. Wright, editor of *American Engineer,* graduate of two engineering schools, and former employe of two railroad companies. James Wright Brown, for many years editor and publisher of the magazine for newspaper journalists, *Editor & Publisher,* worked on big dailies in Detroit, Chicago, and Louisville and was general manager of a daily and of another magazine of journalism before becoming proprietor of *Editor & Publisher*.

Edmund Wade Fairchild, who began what is now one of the leading firms, emphasized the gathering of business news. The com-

[5] G. D. Crain, Jr. (ed.), *Teacher of Business: The Publishing Philosophy of James H. McGraw* (Chicago: Advertising Publications, 1944), p. 26.

pany, still bearing his name, issues eight publications, two of them magazines and several of them dailies *(Women's Wear Daily, Daily News Record, Home Furnishings Daily)*. Fairchild, in the 1890's, began by supplying news for a grocery store trade paper in Chicago, then acquired a men's wear publication. With his brother, Louis E. Fairchild, he built a firm which still is run by their descendants.

Another pair of brothers who founded a prominent business publishing firm was Andrew J. Haire and Alphonsus P. Haire, sons of a merchant family. They organized the Haire Publishing Company in 1910. Two of Andrew Haire's sons succeeded their father in the firm.

Although many business magazine editors and publishers come from the fields their magazines service, some entered it as journalists. One such was William Harrison Ukers, editor and publisher from 1904 to 1954 of *The Tea and Coffee Trade Journal*. Before he engaged in such work he was a reporter for dailies in Philadelphia, New York, and New Haven, including the New York *Times*. He worked on several business magazines, including *The Paper Trade Journal, The House Furnishings Review,* and *The Spice Mill,* before joining that with which he was connected longest. He also became prominent as an author of books of travel and on tea and coffee.

Among executives of recent years are two more brothers, William and Miller Freeman, Jr., of Miller Freeman Publications, San Francisco; Carroll Buzby of the Chilton Company in Philadelphia; Charles S. Mill, formerly of Donnelley and later head of the large trade association, American Business Press, Inc.; and Philip H. Hubbard, of Reinhold Publishing Company, New York. These and other men have developed prominent firms or contributed to the development of the business magazine field through organizations and special services, such as ABP.

Women have had a bigger part in this field than seems apparent. Although relatively few have achieved major executive positions, they have been editors and publishers, particularly of magazines of business in areas important to women, such as beauty shop operation. Women have constituted most of the editorial staff of *Modern Beauty Shop;* they also for long years have been important on the staff of *Publishers' Weekly,* an influential magazine of the book publishing business. Miss Mildred C. Smith for many years served as its editor-in-chief. One of the most widely respected women editors was Miss Alta Ruth Hahn, editorial vice-president of *Sales Management.* She signed herself A. R. Hahn because when she entered the work in the 1920's women were not so readily accepted as today. She was managing editor for a quarter-century before promotion.

The technical publications have not been a barrier to women willing to become familiar with the subject. Mrs. Katherine Clendinning, a Cornell graduate who had edited the university magazine, joined the staff of *Mechanical Engineering* and served as managing editor of that as well as of other publications of the American Society of Mechanical Engineers. Mrs. Lucy Rogers Hawkins became associate editor of *The Journal of the American Oil Chemists Society*. She brought to the position a background of newspaper reporting and feature writing, publicity and advertising writing, and journalism teaching experience.

## Technician or journalist?

These brief biographical sketches bring up the question: Should a publication engage for its editorial department a person knowledgeable in the technical or business area with which the magazine is concerned or should it employ a person who is trained in journalism only?

For many years, publishers of business magazines were obliged to choose, in organizing their staffs, between them and generally hired someone lacking journalistic knowledge. Nor was this difficult to justify at the time. In the early years of business journalism, college preparation for press work did not exist. Few publications of any type actually trained their employes; they put them to work and they learned writing and editing on the job, becoming skilled, therefore, only in the methods practiced by the particular publications on which they served. These practices might or might not be of high quality.

Consequently business journalism was amateurish, for only the outstanding publications were staffed with proficient journalists. Also, the early periodicals boasted no special technical qualities. Editing them was relatively simple. A publication did not suffer so sharply in comparison with general magazines a century ago. But with the increased use in consumer books of color printing, high quality paper stock, striking art work and photography, and artistic design for page layouts, the business periodical could not afford to continue in its drab dress. Even the advertising copy was making editorial copy suffer in appearance.

Because of competition from within the field as well as from the general publication world, the editorial, advertising, and circulation department staffs were obliged to acquire greater technical skill. It was not enough, as frequently was done in the last century, for a business magazine simply to print reports in full; it became necessary, if they were to be widely read, to rewrite and condense them as well as to interpret them so those other than interested executives would comprehend. So arose the need to improve reporting and writing for the business press. And none could make these improvements except journalists.

Business journalists, further, discovered that they no longer could

afford to limit their knowledge to the technical problems of a particular industry or group of businesses. Modern business is so closely related to the whole economic order that wide background, broad education, and correlated technical training are required of the journalist,
not at first but eventually in his development. The best journalism
education programs increasingly include, therefore, special preparation for business writing, editing, and publishing.

### Business magazines at mid-century

It surprises most persons outside the publishing realm to learn
that for decades certain of these periodicals have been carrying more
advertising pages in a year than any consumer magazine. A weekly,
*Oil and Gas Journal,* in a recent year was ahead of all magazines in this
respect, followed by the *Journal of the American Medical Association.*
Third that year was *The New Yorker,* whose advertising also astonishes the person outside the profession, since most persons would name
*Life* or *McCall's* as first in the general group. This lineup is not unusual; it has been thus for years.

The business publication field, largely one of magazines, employs 70,000 people, 14,000 of them in editorial work. Only television
has exceeded the business press in the growth of national advertising
since 1950. Although advertising by page volume has risen about 75
per cent since 1950, it has fluctuated over the years, reaching a peak of
1,218,000 in 1956 to which it never has returned. In 1960 it was 1,194,-
000 and in 1970 hit 1,093,311. But advertising income, because of rising rates, has climbed steadily.

Circulations are up sharply, having more than doubled for the
industry as a whole from 1950 to 1966. By 1966 the aggregate circulation, including those of newspaper format, exceeded sixty-two million.

As American business has changed, so have these magazines. New
industries have led to new magazines to serve them *(Data Processing,* for example). The decrease in activity or progress in an industry or business has altered the number and scope of the periodicals,
accordingly, as in the railroad field.

These business publications have several major types of circulation: paid, controlled, paid and controlled combined, and association (see Chapter 5). A small number, about 5 per cent of the total,
are published by non-profit groups and have certain tax exemptions.
Others are virtually company magazines, but have some characteristics
of business periodicals, for they accept advertising.

Noticeable trends in the industry are the emergence of more and
more group publishers and the amalgamation of publications that
are closely related. As in American business in general, economies
result from group or chain operation. Among the larger multiple
publication firms are McGraw-Hill, Technical, Chilton, Cahners, Mill-

er, Harcourt Brace Jovanovich, Hayden, Geyer-McAllister, Industrial, Billboard, Litton, Bill Buttenheim, Dun-Donnelley, and Vance. Such concentration has been characteristic of business periodicals since their early days but it now is at its peak. Consolidation is not treated as a one-sided advantage. Francis N. McGehee, a media management consultant speaking before an ABP conference in 1966, is reported by *Media/scope* as saying that the growth of the leading multiple magazine publishers has made them more attractive to outside capital; at the same time there have been economies resulting from consolidation. On the other hand, he observed, there is a tendency of the large firms to become larger and to put the smaller, few-unit publishers in a more difficult competitive situation.

The dramatic nature of the growth of large firms Mr. McGehee noted in a tabulation comparing 1956 ownerships with those of 1966 in the cases of ten firms:[6]

| Firm | 1956 | 1966 | Growth |
|------|------|------|--------|
| McGraw-Hill | 42 | 59 | +17 |
| Fairchild | 6 | 22 | +16 |
| Chilton | 13 | 30 | +17 |
| Donnelley | 9 | 22 | +13 |
| Reinhold | 5 | 23 | +18 |
| Conover-Mast | 7 | 16 | + 9 |
| Vance | 3 | 9 | + 6 |
| Ojibway | 8 | 22 | +14 |
| Cahners | 2 | 17 | +15 |

Business periodicals increasingly also constitute an international type of journalism. Like business itself, the magazines are more than ever worldwide in outlook. Several U.S. publishers issue magazines in other languages for sale abroad, particularly in Latin America. One of the largest international operations in magazine journalism, business or otherwise, is the result of the purchase in 1966 by the International Publishing Corporation of 40 per cent of the Cahners Publications, a large U.S. firm. International in 1966 published 134 business publications, 76 consumer magazines, 23 daily newspapers, and is in the book, radio, printing, and papermaking businesses as well. Also, the English language editions are subscribed to from overseas and the similar publications of foreign countries are received here. These are all important means of exchanging technical and business information and knowledge of methods of operation. And it is the business periodical which serves as the transmission belt.

---

[6] A few of these publications are in newspaper format.

*Chapter 19*

---

# Specialized magazines /
# Company and association

T HERE EXISTS quietly within the world of journalism in all countries
with well-developed business and industrial life a large number of
regularly issued magazines and newspapers called industrial publications, company magazines, company newspapers, company publications, association publications, house publications, or house organs.

These thousands of publications, the great majority of magazine
format, are highly specialized in purpose if not so much in content,
never are found on newsstands, are distributed free, and are likely
to be associated in the minds of their readers with advertising and
promotion, although they carry no paid advertising. Consequently
most persons see only those emanating from their own offices, shops,
or factories, are unaware that publishing them is a major business enterprise in itself, and despite the fact that they sometimes are the
equal of the better commercial magazines in format, typography, and
printing, are not likely to consider them magazines in the ordinary
understanding of those publications.

To call them *industrial publications,* however, is misleading, because that name signifies to the hearer a magazine serving an entire
industry, such as railroading or food processing. In fact, it is a classification of a group of business magazines that includes such periodicals as *Pulp and Paper* and *Blast Furnace and Steel Plant.* Adoption
of the label came about because of the dislike for the old designa-

tion, *house organ*. Editors opposing the name said their periodicals were neither musical instruments nor the products of a type of firm that could, in the tradition of British business life, be termed a house; a steel mill, for instance. To avoid *house organ*, preference is for *industrial journalism*, although *company publications* also is accepted.

Regardless of label, these magazines, which number about eight thousand in the United States alone, are classified as internals, externals, combination internal-externals, and association publications. The internals are for employes and others in the company; the externals are aimed at customers, dealers, distributors, and others not within the firm; the combination publication goes to both groups, sometimes with changes in content to create two editions. The association magazines are somewhat apart from the others. They are for groups whose members are persons with similar business interests and are much like the periodicals described in the preceding chapter.

## The internals

Every other month employes of hundreds of manufacturing and other business companies find in their mail a magazine devoted to news and features about themselves and their firm. Such a periodical is classified as an internal house publication. It is sent to the employes' homes so that they receive it regularly, can read it at leisure, and members of the family may better understand the company as a result of exposure to it.

The content of the typical internal includes a regular message from some member of management, often the president or the board chairman, who reports on company progress and affairs. Also there likely is an illustrated article on expansion of operations, such as opening of new plants; numerous vital statistics about employes, like awards they have won for suggestions or long service; and records of births in families, deaths, and retirements. Articles and pictures on unusual persons in the firm's employ are popular, as are news stories, ranging from personals to short interviews and news features sent in by correspondents in branch offices. Increasingly one finds articles on general topics of interest, such as tips on filing income tax forms, gardening, fashions, scouting, health problems, travel, the communities served by the company, and industries that are the sources of supply. Occasionally, however, editors of internals publish special issues devoted to subjects of equal interest to employes and to outsiders. An example is the occasional special issue of the *Parke-Davis Review*.

Internals are the dominant group in the house publication field. The latest survey by the International Association of Business Communicators, reported in 1963, shows that of the about nine thousand in the United States and Canada about 62 per cent are internals, the rest various types of externals and combinations, the latter being 26 per cent and the externals 12 per cent.[1]

Although usually published by the company itself, sometimes the magazines are sponsored by employe clubs. It is not classified as a labor publication, however; organized labor considers the company magazine a representative of management whether owned by management or by employe groups other than labor unions. In viewpoint and content, to be sure, the internal in industry, whatever its source and whoever its sponsor, is totally different from the labor magazine (see Chapter 21). It either avoids labor-management problems or supports management.

Elfenbein believes that the house publication is the forebear of the business paper as well as of the general magazine of today. He traces it to 200 B.C. when court circulars served as internal publications. He also points out that the *Atlantic* and *Harper's* started as houses periodicals for book publishing firms, to which they both still are related. Mott years ago traced the modern magazine to the book catalog, which was in purpose an external house publication and sales tool. Accepted as the forerunner of the modern internal was *Lowell Offering,* published from 1840 to 1847 by a group of women employed by the Lowell Cotton Mills in Massachusetts. It contained the essays and other papers written by members of a society formed by these young women.[2]

### Externals go to the public

Both internals and externals are public relations tools; they are merely directed at different publics. But the externals are more definitely considered a factor in sound public relations because they are among the few channels of communication outside the company.

The externals include numerous handsomely printed and costly magazines considered the aristocrats of the company magazine world: *Service,* of the Cities Service Company; *Think,* International Business Machines; *Ford Times,* Ford Motor Company; *Bandwagon,* H. & A. Selmer Company; and *The Lamp,* of Standard Oil Company (New Jersey). An internal-external of even higher quality than certain of these is *Cascade,* issued by Pacific Northwest Bell.

The gravure-printed *Ford Times* is among the widest known because it has about two million distribution. Pocket-size, printed in four colors, and precisely edited, the Ford publication offers travel articles, hints on driving efficiency, safety counsel, and other informa-

---

[1] *Operation Tapemeasure* (Akron, Ohio: International Council of Industrial Editors, 1963), p. 13.

[2] DeWitt C. Reddick and Alfred A. Crowell, *Industrial Editing* (New York: Matthew Bender & Co., 1962), pp. 17–18.

tion useful to motorists, often written by prominent journalists who are better paid for these articles than most contributors to the specialized magazines on other subjects.

*The Humble Way,* a quarterly issued by Humble Oil and Refining Company, is one of several of a high technical order issued by oil firms. Although it gives major attention to aspects of the oil business, the material includes colored photographs and specially drawn illustrations equal to those in the most attractive consumer books.

A more marked expression of a trend toward general interest material in externals is an entire 48-page issue of *Parke-Davis Review,* a monthly of the Parke-Davis Company, which was given over to short articles and many pictures on the problems of youth. The scope is shown by some article titles: "Profile of a Failure," "Kids in Trouble," "The Law Steps In," "Kids Need Direction," "Terror on Wheels," "What Can the Community Do?" "Teaching Teens About Business," "Citizens to the Rescue," and "When Neighbors Work Together." It included articles on scouting, treatment of exceptional children, and social movements intended to help young people. The standard employe news was printed on an eight-page leaflet insert bound in with this issue, making it an internal-external combination. Single-theme issues of this sort appear occasionally from this firm and others.

Such externals as these are inviting places of employment for persons with journalistic abilities, perhaps more so than the internals since they are able to more easily make use of knowledge of technical and social science subjects. They enable college-trained persons to apply their writing and editing skills to major liberal arts specialties. And the competition for staff positions is much less keen than it is on consumer magazines or the large specialized ones of the arts and sciences and general business. Externals, also, are among the few that buy free-lance copy—written, photographic, or art.

## Functions of the publications

Purposes of internals and externals differ, but all their aims revolve around employe-employer relations, only those externals concerned solely with sales being the exceptions. The function of *Telephone Review,* picture-magazine monthly of the New York Telephone Company, for example, is the same as that of *NI-Gas News,* the Northern Illinois Gas Company four-pager in black and white. That function is to improve the relationships of workers and management. The nature of the improvement sought is not exactly defined, since aims of workers and management are not always identical. Happy labor relations, at least as interpreted by management, are thought to be served by these industrial magazines.

The means used to improve and maintain satisfactory relations
are familiarly journalistic; the magazines carry news to inform; editorials to influence; and features of many types to entertain and to
educate.

The external, although it plays its part in labor-management relations, is far more of an advertising medium. It seeks to better customer or dealer relations with the firm. Its aim is to persuade potential customers to buy a given product and to help them make
better use of it. Also, it seeks to help dealers and distributors sell
more merchandise. In addition, it is a tool for improving the firm's
image before the world.

### Organization of a publication

House magazines are prepared, usually, by one of the following
groups within a concern or engaged by the company: the firm's own
advertising department, an advertising agency accepting the responsibility, a firm of professional house publication editors, the public
relations office of the company, or the offices of industrial relations
or personnel. Generally the internal is edited in the plant and often
by an advertising agency or specialist in production of such journalism, and printed on contract by a firm in the area. Externals, competing as they do more nearly with commercial magazines and advertising leaflets, brochures, and folders, are handled by persons trained
in advertising production techniques. Whichever department is entrusted with the work, executives of the firm ultimately are responsible for both types, a practice necessary to maintain policy but sometimes resulting in production complications, for administrators rarely
are experts in journalistic techniques.

A company-produced magazine centers the work in an editor,
perhaps one or two assistants, one able to take photographs, a secretary, and scores of volunteer plant reporters; exceptionally large and
well-edited periodicals have staffs of four or five trained and experienced editors or writers. Firms with plants that are widely separated
find field writers necessary and have large professional staffs, but these
are the exception. At least the part-time services of a photographer
also are available to most editors of internals, even if the magazine
is small, for the company generally has other photographic work for
him or her.

Externals, being the work more likely of advertising experts, are
produced by people trained and experienced in printing, layout and
design, typography, commercial art, and journalism who spend only
part of their time on a particular publication. As with commercial
periodicals, from one to five full-time editors, associate editors, and
assistant editors are involved. The company publication activities

*Fig. 19.1.* Gathering news for the employe magazine
must be done in all sorts of places.
*(Parke-Davis Review Photo)*

of a large firm, such as the E. I. du Pont de Nemours & Company,
which has forty internals and externals, resemble those of a professional publisher of a group of magazines.

Reporting the news made by the employers and employes who
read the internal cannot be done thoroughly by the average small
staff. Editors enlist the aid of competent employes in each branch
office, shop department, branch factory, and other subdivisions, but
as with the state desks of daily newspapers, it is difficult to obtain
suitable copy from the reporters in outlying areas.

*Cuneo Topics,* company publication of the Cuneo Press, Inc., a
large firm of magazine printers, has an editor and five associate editors
acting as correspondents from six cities where the firm has plants.

Company magazine staffs have found that training classes, held
as often as geographical separation will permit, improve the work
they receive from correspondents or associate editors. Special blanks
intended to encourage systematic gathering and presentation of news
are sent to the reporters, with encouraging letters and suggestions for

stories. Press cards, manuals on news writing and reporting, journalism textbooks, and staff banquets are all intended to help produce more usable copy as well as to keep up interest and morale.

The supervising editors of both internals and externals are active in such groups as the New York Association of Industrial Communicators and others of national or local scope to be noted. Editors, often selected from inexperienced reporting staffs or the industrial relations or advertising office, have shown themselves eager for assistance in technique. Clinical sessions, where experts in journalism and the graphic arts diagnose and recommend improvements in the publications; contests intended to raise quality; and institutes, at which fundamental problems of policy and organization are examined, are arranged.

Few house publications print paid advertising, ordinarily none except for the products or services of their owning companies, and these bring no revenue. Practically all are free, internals being distributed by mail to homes or given to employes on the job; externals always are mailed since no other means of distribution is practical with the exception of branch offices or dealer outlets from which customers can pick them up on visits. Record keeping and other business transactions are left to the business department of the company. In consequence advertising and business divisions are unnecessary; the circulation department, such as it is, is simply organized. The publication is centered on the editorial department. Thus the ideal employe for a company magazine is one who knows the firm and has knowledge of editorial aspects of journalism.

### Organizations

Inevitably, an activity on which $500,000,000 is spent annually for production of magazines with a total yearly circulation in excess of the same figure,[3] gives rise to various organizations. Editors of company magazines are far more thoroughly organized than those of consumer or even all other specialized magazines. One national organization and a half a hundred regional groups are supported.

The International Association of Business Communicators was founded as a "nonprofit organization of local chapters of editors and communicators sponsored by industry, business, and organizations" in numerous countries, to quote its *Members Manual*. In 1970 it was organized as IABC, the result of an amalgamation of the International Council of Industrial Editors, founded in 1941, and the American Association of Industrial Editors, formed in 1938.

The International Association of Business Communicators has

---

[3] *Operation Tapemeasure,* Report by Survey Committee, International Council of Industrial Editors, 1956, p. 3.

chapters in India, Australia, Japan, the Low Countries, Scandinavia, and other parts of the world. It issues a quarterly news magazine, the *Journal of Organizational Communication,* and a monthly newspaper, *IABC News.*

A score of member services include publication critiques, placement, awards competitions, an annual international conference, short courses, and program help to local chapters.

A development of recent years was the establishment at the Department of Journalism at Northern Illinois University, De Kalb, of an Industrial Press Research Center. The Center issues monthly reports containing summaries of studies in the fields of the behavioral and social sciences and in communications that are of value to industrial editors.

The awards program covers the usual areas of design, photography, and writing, but also some less common: one for "excellence in the field of employer-oriented communications, both written and audio-visual" in certain categories. These awards are for an entire communications program, specific, and problem solving.

## Association magazines

Although the regional organizations of company publications editors go by such names as the Upstate New York Council of Industrial Editors, their membership sometimes includes the personnel of college alumni magazines and the periodicals of associations of business and professional people. The line between company and the business magazines considered in the preceding chapter is distinct, for the company magazine is subsidized, carries no advertising, and serves a single firm. But the line between the company and association magazine, on the other hand, is thin. The latter carries advertising, is subsidized, and serves as a publication for a group of companies belonging to an association, rather than an entire industry. The association publication therefore is, in effect, a house magazine within an area served over-all by the business periodical. It is the product of the staff of a trade or professional group, of which there are twelve thousand in this country. These groups were formed by people in such fields as medicine, steel production, hospital operation, banking, and railroading. Virtually all of them issue small newsletters; the more affluent produce magazines often of professional quality, such as *Steelways,* which comes from the American Iron and Steel Institute. Probably the most famous association magazine is *National Geographic,* which has more than 6,800,000 circulation.

The purposes of these periodicals vary with the group producing them. Reddick and Crowell, among the few writers to analyze them, explain that those for business firms are intended to promote trade and sales, which is done by publishing news, "ideas about new developments and techniques in production methods, information on effective promotion and sales methods, special service information, helpful ideas regarding personnel." They also are for promoting public understanding, done by printing "articles showing impact of the industry or business upon the community or the nation, self-improvement stories, reports on research and statistics, human interest."[4] A fourth purpose is to serve as an information center, fulfilled by running question and answer columns, book reviews, and specialized and interpretative news stories. The last three purposes are shared by the magazines of the professional, as distinguished from business peoples' associations.

A common type of magazine in this group is a small one generally issued by each association of newspapers in the states. Publishers of dailies sometimes have their own association with a state, weeklies their separate group, or the two may combine into one organization. A medium of communication is needed. If a newsletter does not suffice, a magazine supported by advertising and a portion of the dues paid by the members is published.

*The New York Press,* one of the oldest in the nation, established in 1852, prints news of that state's weeklies. It also runs accounts of printing and other mechanical developments of importance to readers, stories about the actions of the New York Press Association, plans for conventions, reports on past meetings, and features on individuals.

Association magazine staffs as a rule are small, and their publication is only one of many activities carried on in the offices, which also may have to produce news releases, plan and carry through conventions, develop membership, compile reports, lobby in state capitals, operate a speakers' bureau, a library, and an information bureau, produce special printed matter, such as leaflets and booklets, in some instances scripts for film slides and motion pictures, and cooperate with other associations or those in related fields. Thus the production of an eight- or sixteen-page magazine, even monthly, becomes a small operation in the total of work to be done.

To be engaged in association magazine work, therefore, as with many company magazines, requires far more than knowledge of techniques of magazine writing, editing, and production, except on the largest periodicals of the type. Training as well as business and public relations experience is valuable.

Because until 1969 they were tax free and have low postage rates, association publications are a source of controversy among commercial publishers, who do not have such benefits. Periodicals that are organized to further the work of an association which is intended to be of social value and are non-profit did not pay taxes on the advertising space they sell and cost less to be mailed. These circumstances, said

---

[4] Reddick and Crowell, *op. cit.,* pp. 386–92.

the commercial firms and their organizations, such as ABP, give association magazines an unfair competitive advantage.

Among the better-known magazines of this type is the *Journal of the American Medical Association,* which as already noted has, in some years, ranked second in the nation among all magazines in number of advertising pages sold. Others are *Materials Protection,* published by the National Association of Corrosion Engineers; the *NAHB Journal of Homebuilding,* issued by the National Association of Home Builders; *Modern Maturity,* the magazine of the American Association of Retired Persons; and *National Geographic,* the 6,800,-000-circulation periodical of the National Geographic Society.

An official of a group of association publications has said that there are 4,000 potential members of the organization, most of them magazines. Thus this type of journalism is larger numerically than such commercial ventures as the regular business publications. Doubtless there is considerable overlapping with the educational, religious, and other non-profit organization fields.

When, in the mid-1960's, the commercial business publications described in the preceding chapter more vigorously than ever before objected to the fiscal arrangements of the association magazines, the latter formed an organization as a means of defense and unity. This group is the Society of National Association Publications (SNAP), with its center in Washington, D.C. By 1970 it had 56 members, including *American Paper Industry, Industrial Banker, Public Power,* and *Soybean Digest.*

In that same year the Internal Revenue Service (IRS) adopted a plan to tax such magazines' advertising profits at the corporate rate of 48 per cent. IRS estimated that there are more than 10,000 rather than the 4,000 claimed by the SNAP, also pointing out that most do not carry advertisements, but that 700 had gross advertising revenues of about $110,000,000. Efforts to reverse the IRS ruling failed in 1968.

## *The work is journalistic*

Although not all that a staff member of a company or association publication does is necessarily related to the periodical, much of the work is journalistic. In addition to editing or helping edit the magazine, in the average situation, the staff members may be called upon to use their journalistic skills in other ways.

The preparation of annual reports for the company is becoming an increasingly important function of the public relations or advertising department of a business firm. And logically the journalists on the staff are thought to know the skills needed to produce this document, so difficult to make comprehensible. It is difficult because so much of the content is cumbersome financial information not easy for the average stockholder to grasp and is so detailed that the report is likely to become bulky and perhaps go unread.

# Chapter 20

# Specialized magazines /
## *Educational, juvenile, religious*

Although no other activity has had built around it so large a number of periodicals as business, several others are served well by the magazine press.

These are education, juvenile and youth, religious, farm, regional, the arts, labor, science and medicine, and minority social groups.

Three that are akin—the first three in the above list—are examined in this chapter. Religious bodies are deeply interested in and heavily involved in education; in fact, they contribute many magazines to the list of those concerned with it. And the periodicals for children and youth often are carefully integrated with education. Here, also, religious organizations have contributed magazines. Most magazines for juveniles are issued, it so happens, by church publishing houses.

### *Education magazines*

The range and variety of education magazines seems as great as that of the fishes in the sea. As one looks through the international list of educational periodicals which is part of the yearbook of the Educational Press Association of America one finds everything from four-page newsletters to elaborate, colorful, illustrated magazines as well as serious scholarly journals. This variety results from the definition of an educational periodical used by UNESCO, which has taken the pains to record these publications: " . . . a publication containing material concerning education that appears periodically under the same title."[1]

The subordinate subjects occupy entire magazines and are many. Among the principal ones are: general education, administration, research, pre-school, primary, secondary, higher, special, adult and youth, mass education, community development, teacher training, parent-teacher relationships, teacher status, vocational, and technical. Within most of these are additional, more detailed subjects. The largest sub-group falls under the secondary education classification, which has educational magazines on art, business subjects, geography, health, history, home economics, international understanding, languages, literature, mathematics, music, physical education, philosophy, science, and the social studies.

So segmented a subject naturally would require many periodicals. The *Edpress Yearbook* records 2,500 publications for the United States and Canada. Many are newsletters, not actually magazines; a number qualify by courtesy, such as *Boy's Life, American Junior Red Cross News,* and *Popular Mechanics.* An estimate of those truly qualifying by being genuinely concerned with education as their major subject brings the total to about five hundred.

## Nature of the work

On most consumer and business magazines the publishing operations are professional. But company magazines as well as the smaller business periodicals cannot be thought of as well-rounded operations, in the sense that there are large staffs, well-equipped offices, and thorough procedures of writing, editing, make-up, promotion, research, and distribution. And the majority of all other specialized periodicals to be considered in the remaining chapters, including educational magazines, are small enterprises often unable to operate as professionally as their owners would desire because of lack of budget and editorial talent. They are small, in the sense that a publishing company with three thousand employes producing several periodicals is large, and one with 200 employes and one or two publications on its list is moderate in size. A small one has a staff of four or five at most and a printer's contract, but little more. The magazines of education fall mainly into the latter group. They leave to a few persons the basic procedures. They sell little, often no, advertising space. Preparation of copy is comparatively simple, for many of the publications go to readers unconcerned about anything but the facts and ideas on the pages; there is no money for buying color printing, special art work, or manuscripts from noted writers even on the subject of education.

---

[1] *America's Education Press* (Glassboro, N.J.: Educational Press Association of America, 1963), p. 9.

As with all specialized journalism, the work is put in the hands of persons versed in the subject or associated with the organization responsible for publication. This often necessary practice makes for authoritative but not the brightest, most appealing journalism. Often the editor is an officer of an educational group, such as a state education association, a society devoted to the study of the particular educational specialty, or a member of an education college faculty. He or she has an assistant and may be only a figurehead, the aide being responsible for handling minor advertising duties, since the selling is done by a contracted representative in the field, and for the basic editorial duties—copy editing, title writing, and the like.

The officer in charge, as a reflection of an important trend, may in some instances of large publications coming from organizations be the group's public relations director. This practice is likely to put at the magazine's helm a person with journalistic experience and ability. More and more, also, a professional editor is being placed in charge, but both are small trends.

Over the years, because at first so many magazines were the responsibility of non-professional editors, the staffs of magazines published by the state teacher groups as well as others with similar audiences have been helped in improving their technical work by the Edpress, by the National Association of Secretaries of State Teachers Associations, and by state editors' groups through workshops and round tables.

### *Circulation*

Circulation of many educational magazines is of a type common in most specialized periodical areas: non-voluntary or automatic, i.e., the publication is received as part of a membership payment. This kind is associated not only with these but also with religious, labor, association, company, and other groups.

Such circulation affects the advertisers' confidence in the reading of the publication, usually adversely, and is less likely to mean that readers (better expressed as receivers, under the circumstances) actually read the publication, since they have made no direct, exclusive payment for it.

In the educational journalism world circulations are modest. The non-voluntary is the type for state teachers' association publications and various government-owned magazines. Some samples: *Michigan Education Journal,* one of the largest in its group, 73,500; *Colorado School Journal,* 27,070. Independently owned periodicals often are much smaller or larger. *Today's Education,* for instance, has approximately 1,300,000; *PTA Magazine,* 400,000. Circulation is almost entirely by mail.

## The early magazines

A quarterly, *Juvenile Monitor or Educational Magazine,* was among the first. Published in New York, it was founded in 1811 but lived less than a year. *The American Journal of Education,* which ran from 1826 to 1837, was the first important one. Within twenty-five years, a large number of such journals was founded, as many as 76. Dean Mott learned that between 1850 and 1860, 66 were begun. The increase continued until now educational magazines constitute one of the larger groups among specialized periodicals.

## Portrait of a magazine

Because there is no such publication as a typical magazine of education, the variety being so great, one has been selected to illustrate how virtually all the publishing methods of major firms can be applied to relatively small ones. This brief description should help dispel the all too common notion that because a magazine is not on the newsstands and is not listed in the million or higher circulation class that it counts for little.

*The Instructor* is *Life*-size, published ten times a year, omitting July and August, as do many education magazines, and averages one hundred pages an issue. Its generous size enables it to greet the reader with covers as arresting as those of an art magazine. In fact, many covers are reproductions of paintings by both traditional and modern artists. The size also is attractive to advertisers, as the ad-crowded pages indicate.

Founded in 1891, *The Instructor* is intended for elementary and early childhood school teachers, but contains material as well for their pupils. Its 297,358 circulation makes it one of the larger in its classification. It engages in market research comparable to that of a consumer magazine, but on a smaller scale. "What Are the Facts on School Teacher Travel " is the title of a 16-page brochure reporting on a mail survey which brought a 34 per cent response. This publication differs from many large consumer books in that it is produced entirely at the company's properties in Dansville, N.Y. There copy of all types is received, handled, and edited; art work is prepared, type set, engravings made, plates produced, copies of the issue printed, assembled, and mailed. An editorial staff of eight is employed—editor, production, features, art editors, three associate editors, and one assistant editor. Closely related to them is an art staff of a director and two artists. An editorial advisory board consists of five persons prominent in elementary education. Some of the regular staff members share their time with the book department of the company.

Publication of *The Instructor* is only one of the enterprises of the F. A. Owen Publishing Company, which in 1968 was purchased by Harcourt Brace Jovanovich Inc., a large, New York book publishing firm. It also prints textbooks for other publishing firms and offers an educational service, consisting of teaching materials from business and industrial firms that advertise in the magazine.

### A major group

Group magazine publishing by commercial firms is not common in this specialty; the practice is followed mainly on university campuses, some of which issue as many as a score of scholarly journals each. But one successful business, Scholastic Magazines, Inc., has achieved considerable size. It now issues more than twenty, having developed them, beginning in 1920, from one called *Western Pennsylvania Scholastic.* They have an aggregate circulation in excess of eleven million among junior and senior high school pupils as well as teachers. The more familiar titles are *Senior Scholastic, Junior Scholastic, News Time, Scholastic Teacher, Science World, World Week, Scholastic Coach,* and *Co-ed.* Eight are in Russian, German, Spanish, or French.

### A vocational note

Although all Americans experience the process of education, up to one level or another, and to that extent presumably have some understanding of it, the educational press attracts few recruits.

Explanations are the usual ones of any specialized area. It does not offer the glamour, status, or prestige of the large commercial magazines; it offers comparatively little opportunity for advancement, since staffs usually are small; the same smallness to many people means isolation. The erroneous idea about salary size clings to the educational magazine as to most others of its type; salaries have improved considerably in the past decade.

Perhaps the only explanation peculiar to the education magazine world is that young people, when they leave college, are in the mood to be away from education for a time; those among them who have not been able students naturally desire no more association with the educational world. And those well prepared for that world are more interested, as a rule, in being teachers of their specialty or school administrators. Yet staff is needed and opportunities exist, as in the entire specialized realm.

### Magazines for juveniles and youth

As the publishing program of Scholastic Magazines indicates, publications about education are closely related to those for the persons to be educated. Up the age scale, from small fry who can barely read to college youth who can read even if they cannot spell, the magazines pour from the presses.

Hundreds appear, intended to entertain or to teach. Among them are several money-makers for their publishers, big enterprises, in any case: *Seventeen, Boy's Life, Ingénue,* and *Children's Digest.* More than 150 are published by religious bodies, chiefly Roman Catholic and Protestant. Story papers, they often are called. These include numerous well-edited periodicals, such as *Face-to-Face, Venture, Teens, Upward, World Over, Teen Time, Today, Twelve-Fifteen, Rapport, Youth,* and *Power,* all far from the leaflets once issued by the churches.

Before the days of movies, radio, television, and mass spectator sports, magazines for children and youth not only were popular and influential but also important publishers of notable writing. Our great grandparents enjoyed *Youth's Companion,* which, with a half million circulation, once was the largest magazine in America. And there was *St. Nicholas,* which first printed Kipling's *Jungle Books.* In these two was the work of such story tellers as Joel Chandler Harris, Mary Austin, Mark Twain, Louisa May Alcott, Jack London, William Dean Howells, Frances Hodgson Burnett, Alfred, Lord Tennyson, Jules Verne, Henry Wadsworth Longfellow, Thomas Hardy, Stephen Vincent Benet, William Faulkner, and Edna St. Vincent Millay. Several of these noted authors first appeared in print thanks to these magazines.

An early contributor to *Youth's Companion* was that iconoclast of the 1920's and 1930's, H. L. Mencken.

Today a variety of popular but different magazines is available for children—*Child Life, Jack and Jill, Children's Digest, Humpty Dumpty's.* These are little like others that disappeared when television entered children's lives—*American Boy* and *Open Road for Boys,* for example—and certainly far from the dime novels children enjoyed when there were no comics. There was *Beadle's Half Dime Library,* for example, with its tales like "Davy Crockett—King of the Wild Frontier." Davy was the Superman of his day, although earthbound. Whether today Davy would be preferred to the characters in *American Girl, Boy's Life, Children's Digest, Highlights for Children, Children's Playmate, Teen Time, Teen Age,* and one-shot magazines on popular heroes like singers and sports stars never will be known. As for the comics, they have been some substitute for Davy (see Chapter 14).

The range of the field today is shown further by the specialization within it, for there are publications named *The Junior Musician, The*

Fig. 20.1. *Golden Argosy,* almost the size of a tabloid newspaper in its day, was begun by Frank A. Munsey, at one time owner of many major newspapers and periodicals; its name survives in the men's magazine, *Argosy.*

*National Future Farmer, American Newspaper Boy, Young Crusader,* and *Keyboard, Jr.*

## Special problems

Publishers of these children's and youth magazines have been faced with problems beyond the ones affecting all journalism, such as rising costs of production. They are:

1. Comparative indifference to the field among noted writers, who favor writing books or material for broadcasts. This situation is in strong contrast to the days when these magazines presented the work of leading authors.
2. Difficulty in obtaining, from authors in general, well-written stories, articles, and other kinds of copy for children, such as games and puzzles, because writing for them is more difficult than generally realized. It requires understanding of child psychology and vocabulary.
3. Modern children are better informed than their parents or grandparents were at the same ages as a result of better schools, movies, radio, television, and recordings; they are a new and special kind of audience of our time. They know more about world events, science, and nature, for example. This means that more advanced material is needed for the magazines.
4. Competition for children's and youth's leisure time has been sharpened; much of what they do—watching television, playing games, vacationing, going to sports events, riding in automobiles and boats—reduces time for reading.

## The student press

Pupils and students have their own press, the magazines published for them by primary and secondary schools, preparatory schools, colleges, and universities. Often they are produced almost entirely by the students and occasionally the students are the actual publishers. Although newspapers and yearbooks predominate numerically, literary, humor, or opinion magazines come from all educational levels.

Garwood found that the first United States college magazines appeared about 1810;[2] Mott goes back to 1806, naming Yale's *Literary Cabinet.* These early ones, according to Garwood, were either heavy reviews contributed by faculty and alumni, collections of student chit-chat, or assemblies of student verse, stories, or essays. Yale's *Literary Magazine,* founded in 1836, is the oldest today.

These magazines have been and still are the publications where numerous noted writers first appeared in print. James Russell Lowell neglected his studies at Harvard to edit *Harvardiana* in the 1830's.

[2] Irving Garwood, *The American Periodicals from 1850 to 1860* (Macomb, Ill.: Author, 1931).

*Fig. 20.2.* **A group of small publications for youth issued by various church bodies in recent years.**

Both William Vaughn Moody and Robert Morss Lovett edited the *Harvard Magazine.* F. Scott Fitzgerald wrote for Princeton's *Tiger,* one of his contributions being this ditty:

> *To be on a dais*
> *With Thais,*
> *How nais.*

Robert Benchley started his writing career on the *Harvard Lampoon,* James Thurber his on Ohio State's *Lantern,* Shirley Jackson hers on *The Syracusan.* Alexander Woollcott wrote for and worked on the Hamilton College *Literary Monthly.*

The character of the college magazine is changing. The humor type, consisting mostly of pin-ups and off-color jokes, has been hurt by competition from the men's magazines of like character. An element of seriousness has entered the students as well as the magazines, resulting in periodicals with greater interest in public affairs, literature, or art, such as *Epoch* at Cornell University and *The Husk* at Cornell College, which also are little magazines (see Chapter 17). Those concerned with modern political and social problems include some members of the underground press family; even the authorized college magazine has become something of a rebellious journal.

vol. 7 no. 4 part 1 of 13 parts

# high

► I Was a Teenage TYPEster
IT ALL BEGAN IN HIGH SCHOOL

► The Ugly Neighbor!
SHE WAS A REAL DOG!

A TRUE STORY

# Jungle
## CHAPLAIN

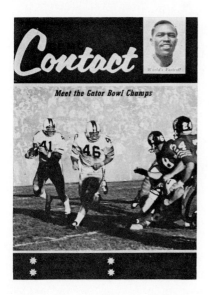

# Contact

Meet the Gator Bowl Champs

World's Fastest

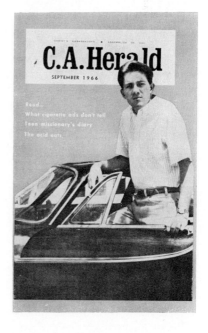

# C.A. Herald

SEPTEMBER 1966

Read...
What cigarette ads don't tell
Teen missionary's diary
The acid cult.

## Magazines of religion

Since the latter part of the eighteenth century, religious magazines have been the core of the churches' efforts to interpret themselves to their constituencies. They have been used by denominations,
interdenominational groups, and non-denominational organizations.

Although at one time they were important general publications,
these magazines have become specialized. They used to deal not only
with current theological and religious problems but also with secular
ones and competed with consumer magazines. But as the commercial
press developed into a costly business, with color printing and high
speed publication, the church press withdrew from the general field.

The publications were reshaped as the churches realized that
the secular press could not give sufficient space to their activities and
was out of harmony with many of their opinions. In the reshaping
process many were lost but new ones acquired. Dean Mott found that
in 1824 there were two dozen magazines of religion, most of them
denominational in source. By the 1850's this number had quadrupled.

"Every denomination had its publications," he writes, "and
usually a full complement of theological quarterly, home monthly,
and regional weekly publications."[3]

Having become magazines of affairs, much like the better known
*The Nation* and *Atlantic,* the denominational publications of the
first half of the nineteenth century were noted for their forthrightness.
Mott compares them with secular publications like *Russell's* and
*Putnam's.* Sometimes they descended to scurrility in their expression
on such controversial issues as slavery and doctrinal differences.
Their growth continued, until by 1870 the weeklies alone had exceeded two hundred. More than six hundred were being published in
1885. Practically all were denomination sponsored.

In the next eighty years, despite many casualties, the number
more than doubled, although it is impossible to determine exactly
how they were divided between formats. A 1972 estimate, based on
Ayer's *Directory,* the membership lists of the Roman Catholic, Jewish,
and Protestant journalism organizations, and other tabulations such
as the Religious Public Relations Council, places the number at about
1,650. Roughly four-fifths are of magazine format, frequency, and
content. Of these about 550 are Roman Catholic, 150 Jewish, and
the remainder Protestant, except for a few that are anti-religious
organs or from other religions.

Circulations, like numbers of titles, rose and fell over the years.
All but a few magazines of any sort had small circulations before the
Civil War, when a ten thousand distribution was large. Following
the conflict, some of the Sunday school publications exceeded fifty

---

[3] Frank Luther Mott, *A History of American Magazines* (Cambridge, Mass.:
Belknap Press of Harvard University Press, 1957), Vol. II, p. 60.

thousand and Henry Ward Beecher's *Christian Union* went past the one hundred thousand level. But the secular press already was climbing into higher figures. Except for leaders, like *Presbyterian Life* (754,000), *Awake* (4,550,000), *The Watchtower* (4,700,000), *The Upper Room* (3,000,000), *Together* (436,000), and *Catholic Digest* (543,000), denominational publications have moderate circulations. A non-denominational magazine, *Christian Herald,* has the leading circulation of that type, about 378,000.

Circulation size is not necessarily a measure of quality, however. Certain smaller church periodicals—*The Episcopalian, The Lutheran, Spirit, Eternity, Home Life,* and *New World Outlook* are only a few of many of professional quality.

Religious magazines sometimes are edited and managed by persons without training or previous experience in journalism, a condition that becomes less true each year as greater hospitality is shown to those with technical preparation for the work. Contributors often are not professional writers, artists, and photographers. Small budgets explain the lack of trained personnel, as does also the difficulty of obtaining persons with a religious commitment, a knowledge of the church and religion, and with journalistic ability.

## Range of format and content

The range of format and content is over all those that are used in the magazine industry. It can be seen in miniature in the products of the printing presses of the Southern Baptist Convention, numerically the largest denomination in the United States. This group, like the Roman Catholic church, the Seventh-Day Adventists, the United Methodist church, and the United Church of Christ, all large bodies, has found it advantageous to issue many different types of magazines for persons of many different ages and interests.

Published under the aegis of the Baptist state conventions are about thirty publications circulating mainly within each state of the South and Southwest. Usually small tabloids or self-cover magazines, they are printed on inexpensive stock, crammed with news of various state official groups, pronouncements by state or church-wide officials, sermonettes, personals, editorials, and cartoons and photographs. The combined circulation of these periodicals is about 1,500,000.

An entirely different type of magazine is that issued by the Foreign Mission Board, *The Commission,* which has attained a circulation of about 90,000. This monthly, size 8 x 11 running to 36 pages, takes the Southern Baptist mission world for its domain and uses photography generously.

Dominating Southern Baptist magazinedom are the more than one hundred publications, all magazines, issued by the Sunday School Board, the chief publishing agency. Included are numerous pupil's and teacher's quarterlies, juveniles for various age groups, a monthly for college students, a general family periodical, another for members of training unions, others for persons interested in missionary education, church music, church libraries, church administration and other specialties, and still others for Sunday school officers. Additional official or unofficial Southern Baptist magazines emanate from other cities, such as three published by the Woman's Missionary Union in Birmingham and one in Memphis for men.

Church magazines achieve complete coverage no more than any others; in fact, on the basis of intensity of interest, they may be said to provide less in proportion to potential readership. Consumer magazines generally claim four or five readers to each subscription or newsstand copy. Denominational and other church magazines can claim some such extra distribution, but it is offset by the inattention from the general membership inevitable from the highly specialized content of many of the magazines and the method of sale and distribution, which is not on newsstands but by mail, often automatically through membership in an organization. Promotion, furthermore, is within the church units only.

### Non-denominational magazines

The loyalty of any particular church group cannot be demanded by a non-denominational magazine. This religious publication must promote itself through organizations that cut across denominational lines or through interests that touch all religious folk. Such support is elicited by the magazines of the David C. Cook Publishing Company and other independent firms and by the business monthly, *Church Management*. But *Christian Century, Christianity Today, Christian Herald, Christian Life,* and *Eternity,* for example, can hope to carry on only through the strength of their editors' ideas or the successful appeal of their special articles, fiction, and features. Circulations usually are comparatively small among the non-denominational periodicals, but technically the magazine includes some of the leaders in the whole area of the specialized magazine.

### Interdenominational magazines

*Spectrum Journal,* a bi-monthly sponsored by the National Council of the Churches of Christ in the U.S.A., is an example of a magazine supported by a combination of denominations and included in a budget provided by various church bodies with a common interest.

Technical standards generally are high in such periodicals, for the union of resources and the cooperative effort is effective. But they are not for the rank and file members of religious bodies, as a rule, and therefore their circulations remain for the most part small.

Interdenominationalism and ecumenicity are expressed also through the numerous organizations of religious journalists, although there is not as yet a national one combining the various faiths. Protestants, Roman Catholics, and Orthodox are joined in the Associated Church Press. This group has a quarterly, *Copy Log*. The Evangelical Press Association, altogether Protestant, represents largely the theologically conservative denominations. A few denominations have their own groups, such as the Southern Baptist Press Association and the Methodist Press Association. The Catholic Press Association, the largest, supports *The Catholic Journalist,* a bi-monthly magazine with an in-between-months newsletter. The American Jewish Press Association serves a small section of the Jewish religious press of the United States, mostly the independent weekly newspapers for communities.

## *The broadening scope*

In the second half of this century the religious press of the United States has shown evidences of returning to its former place of importance in dealing with secular matters. Although the bulk of the periodicals still are house organs for their denominational publishers, needed to promote ideas and events too specialized for the secular press, a substantial and increasing number carry news, editorials, and articles once found in the general publications only.

In thus again reaching out to the secular reader, religious magazines have been slower than the religious newspapers, since the country has for more than a half-century had the Boston *Christian Science Monitor* and for well over a century the Salt Lake City (Utah) *Deseret News*. These papers retained their general appeal whereas the magazines abandoned it.

Only a close reader of *Commentary, Face-to-Face, Fellowship, Liberty,* and *Commonweal* would know the first time through that these are supported either by religious bodies or laymen with religious aims. Others, with more obvious religious names—*United Church Herald, The Churchman, Christianity and Crisis, Sign, Christian Century*—devote much space to what, in the 1930's, were considered strictly secular concerns: unemployment, the narcotics trade, foreign policy, pacifism, government agency practices, racial discrimination, public housing, the homosexual and his problems, marriage and divorce, and many more topics of this sort.

Only a few religious magazines, however, still are available nationally on newsstands, despite this broadening scope and the typographical improvement of many. Only one of consequence is so obtainable: *Catholic Digest,* in format much like *The Reader's Digest* and not, despite its name, open to Catholic writers only. A few others have small distribution, *Unity* and *Ideals,* for instance. These have mainly seasonal or inspirational value.

Growth within the religious magazine world is not evident to the casual reader. Some of it has occurred in the realm of advertising. Realizing that individual circulations generally are too small (some of the most widely distributed do not sell advertising space, such as *Awake* and *The Watchtower* of the Jehovah's Witnesses, the United Methodist *The Upper Room,* and similar devotional periodicals, which are distributed by the millions), the publishers of several of the more influential offer their circulations in combination. Nine such magazines from the major American religious bodies—Roman Catholic, Jewish, and Protestant—call themselves the Interfaith Group. The program received a setback in the late 1960's and early 1970's when the business recession cut into advertising and circulation in these and many other periodicals.

Pressure upon the religious bodies in general to become more relevant to modern life has brought about the broadening. The religious news editors of both *Time* and of *Newsweek* point to the situation. Responding to an interview for the *Long Island Catholic* by Joann Price, Kenneth L. Woodward of *Newsweek* told her, "Theology makes more news than structural things and theological questions are more exciting to readers than any other facet of religion." John T. Elson, a *Time* senior editor and its former religion editor, added that he thought, "We are beyond the day when religious news can be limited solely to the exterior surface of the religious institution."

# Chapter 21

# Specialized magazines/
## *Science, farm, regional, labor*

By now it should be clear that the major groups of specialized magazines follow a pattern. On almost any important subject we find a
few of large circulation and advertising revenue that make a somewhat general appeal. We also find many more that have small distribution and exist to serve the various splinterings of a field or subject.
Either the large or the small specialized periodicals may be owned by
a firm that issues several or, more likely, are individual operations.
Most of them have small staffs and so much advertising or promotion
work it must be left to an outside firm. Technical amateurism per-
sists, but it gradually is fading. Also part of the pattern is the existence of many organizations of both editors and publishers.

A few groups remain to be examined. They conform in general
to the pattern but have some differences, such as extraordinary circulations or remarkable stability. These are the science, farm, regional,
and labor periodicals.

### Magazines of science

Commonly, the moment when the American people took science
more seriously than ever before is thought to be the day Russia
launched Sputnik. Since then, at any rate, the scientific developments
in this country and in others have been so rapid and sensational that
the scientifically unschooled person is overwhelmed. Science maga-

zines naturally have risen on this tide of absorbed interest. They were important before, but now they are both important and more than ever popular. Young people, especially, have been responsible for much of the general interest, but the growth of scientific activity of all sorts in the work scheme of the nation also has helped, for more persons are engaged in technology than ever before.

Science periodicals are published for two groups of people: those who know a great deal about science and those who know little about it. The first is the smaller but has the larger number of publications, most of them with small circulations, which deal with specialties. The second group supports few magazines, but several of them have circulations well into the millions. Informed readers prefer magazines of pure science and laymen patronize the periodicals of applied science. The latter are interested in practical applications rather than in abstractions or theories. Any literate person can understand *Popular Mechanics,* but special training and knowledge are required to comprehend *Nucleonics.*

It would seem that persons who aspire to become science journalists will find places only on staffs of publications that popularize. But this is not true. Laymen of relatively little scientific knowledge help edit highly technical journals. Those magazines that carry news do not require that scientists write it. The scientific experts are in control, to be sure; and the major contributions come from recognized experts.

Many a scientific journal is edited by a renowned scientist. It also has an advisory board which reviews all articles and other major contributions, according to the special knowledge of its members, for the editor cannot be expert in all fields. But assistant and associate editors with only superficial knowledge of the specialty must be journalists if the magazine is to be produced properly.

Clifford Hicks, former editor-in-chief of *Popular Mechanics* and author of children's books of popular science, had studied physics briefly in high school and college as his sole scientific preparation for this work on the magazine, which extended from a beginner's post to the top of the editorial ladder. He advises study of physics and mathematics, however, to avoid "doing it the hard way." These and similar subjects are helpful preparation. Journalists without special science training therefore can serve magazines of either pure or applied science. The objective of the largest publication in this specialty is to make scientific information readable and popular, both of which a competent journalist can do.

## PSM *and* PM

A pioneer in the effort to make science understandable to the general public was Edward Livingston Youmans, first editor of *Popular Science Monthly.* An admirer of Herbert Spencer, he was at

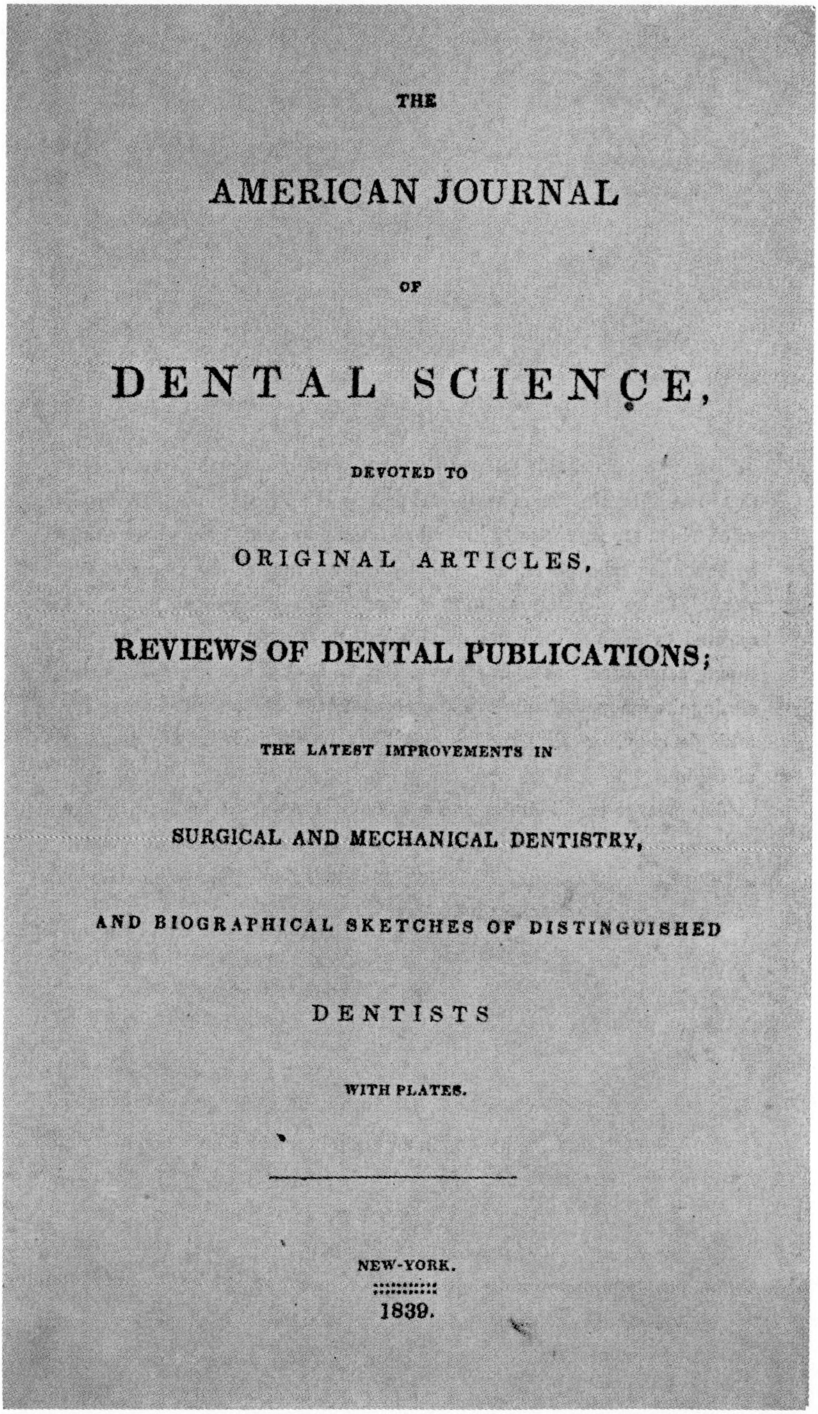

THE

AMERICAN JOURNAL

OF

DENTAL SCIENCE,

DEVOTED TO

ORIGINAL ARTICLES,

REVIEWS OF DENTAL PUBLICATIONS;

THE LATEST IMPROVEMENTS IN

SURGICAL AND MECHANICAL DENTISTRY,

AND BIOGRAPHICAL SKETCHES OF DISTINGUISHED

DENTISTS

WITH PLATES.

NEW-YORK.

1839.

*Fig. 21.1.* A facsimile of the cover of the first dental journal.

first scientific editor of *Appleton's Journal,* a general circulation weekly. When readers objected to scientific articles in a publication bought for literary and art content, Youmans interested the Appletons in publishing *PSM.*

"The work of creating science," he wrote in the first number, issued in 1872, "has been organized for centuries . . . The work of diffusing science . . . is clearly the next great task of civilization."

A believer in the universality of science, Youmans immediately was condemned by some readers as an atheist, this being the time when numbers of Americans still believed that science and religion are incompatible. The Appletons were labelled infidels. The publication continued, nevertheless, growing from 12,000 circulation in the latter part of the nineteenth century to more than 1,600,000 by the middle of the next. Youmans believed—as Godfrey Hammond, a later publisher, wrote on the 75th anniversary of the magazine—that "science is not only the concern of star-watchers and laboratory hermits . . . [it is] more than ever everybody's business . . . science has emerged from the library, through the laboratory, into daily use in our houses and industry."[1]

Transportation experience, rather than a deep philosophical interest in science, was in the background of the founder of *Popular Mechanics,* Henry Haven Windsor, Sr. His magazine, with *PSM,* has come to represent a group of magazines devoted to the popularization of science as well as mechanics, woodworking, and related activities.

This first editor and publisher of *PM* was an official of the South Side City Railway Company, Chicago. To learn firsthand the problems of the drivers, he spent six months, incognito, as an operator of one of the old-fashioned grip cars. He became so much interested in the time-saving devices of maintenance men that he decided there should be a magazine to spread the word about them. After publishing the *Street Railroad Review* and *Brick,* as preliminaries, by 1902 he produced the first issue of *Popular Mechanics* as the embodiment of his idea.

It was an eight-page weekly that within two years grew to a one-hundred-page monthly. Seventy years later the magazine had several foreign language editions and a circulation of more than 1,300,000. Its owners also published numerous handbooks and manuals. By then it also had become one of the group of magazines published by the Hearst company.

*PSM* and *PM* have given rise to several important competitors in presenting news of science and mechanics in popular fashion. *Mechanix Illustrated,* founded in 1928, is a strong third in circulation rank; *Family Handyman* with 1,500,000, *Science Digest, Popular*

---

[1] Godfrey Hammond, "The Editor's Job," *Popular Science Monthly,* May, 1947, p. 81.

*Electronics, Workbench, Electronics Illustrated,* and *Science and Mechanics* all have earned a steady following of subscribers and advertisers.

## Other major magazines of science

Thirty years before *PSM* was founded, Rufus Porter, a versatile inventor, had established a weekly called *Scientific American.* Now a monthly, it is recognized as a leading science periodical. Its history, however, has not been even. Peterson explains that it began in 1845 by covering science news and providing general features about science and technology, especially desiring to encourage inventors. Later, when news of science was given greater place in the general press, *Scientific American* stressed industrial research. Nevertheless, it declined. With a circulation of only 40,000, it was sold in 1947 for an equivalent number of dollars to Gerard Piel, former science editor of *Life,* and two partners, Dennis Flanagan, his successor at *Life,* and Donald Miller, a management expert. Within five years it had pushed its circulation to one hundred thousand and begun to make money. It continued on a program of printing which had been explained in the original prospectus (for a magazine to be called *The Sciences,* for they did not know *Scientific American* was for sale) as coverage of "all science for all who are interested in science." It was to fill the gap between technical publications and the popular type.

Although in its early days the magazine had had several distinguished science journalists on its staff, such as Waldemar Kaempffert, Orson D. and Charles A. Munn, and Austin Lescarboura, it now gained as contributors such scientists as Albert Einstein, Karl Compton, Harold Urey, and Robert Oppenheimer.

In 1888 a magazine of science was founded that long ago equalled the circulations of the newsstand-sold *PSM* and *PM,* although it is entirely a subscription-membership periodical. This unusual publication is *National Geographic,* whose explorations have made history and whose well-illustrated pages are widely known to many an American family.

The *Geographic* is published and owned by a society organized for "the increase and diffusion of geographic knowledge." Because a member's relation to the society is almost wholly through the magazine, the plan is a highly successful mechanism for assuring support. Readers would not continue to subscribe, however, if they were not receiving an attractive publication.

A few months after the founding of the society, its magazine, then but a small scientific brochure, was issued to carry technical papers by members. Irregularly published for several years, it settled down to being a monthly by 1896 and sought newsstand circulation. Dr. Alexander Graham Bell, as society president, decided in 1899 to put the editorship in the hands of Gilbert H. Grosvenor, a teacher of mathematics and science in a boys' school and interested in geography.

Dr. Grosvenor later described his visit to the society's head-quarters. He saw "half of a small rented room on the fifth floor of the Corcoran Building in Washington. . . . The little space . . . [of which] I . . . the only employe, was to assume charge was littered with old magazines, newspapers, and a few books of record."[2] He also found the treasury empty and a debt of nearly $2,000.

Dr. Bell's idea, as Dr. Grosvenor explained it, was to raise this question: "Why not popularize the science of geography and take it into the homes of the people? Why not transform the society's maga-zine from one of cold geographic fact, expressed in hieroglyphic terms which the layman could not understand, into a vehicle for carrying the living, breathing, human-interest truth about this great world of ours to the people?"[3]

Dr. Grosvenor's struggles with the magazine resemble those of editors of more commercial publications. In addition to the usual lack of assistance and inadequate office space was the more unusual problem of obtaining manuscripts from authorities who could write clearly. But he achieved his fiftieth year as editor in 1950, when he also was president. He was retired in 1954, to be succeeded by John Oliver La Gorce, who in turn was replaced by Dr. Grosvenor's son, Melville Bell Grosvenor. The magazine now has handsome new quarters in Washington and a circulation of over six million.

Closely related to the whole range of science magazines are those of medicine. This specialty supports hundreds of technical journals (*American Review of Respiratory Diseases*), association publications (such as the extremely successful *Journal of the American Medical Association*), business periodicals (*Surgical Business*), and general medical publications (*Private Practice*). Dentistry has a similar group.

### Farm magazines

For most of its history, farming has been more a part of agri-culture (the science of farming) than it has been a business. But be-cause of social changes in the United States, cultivating the soil is a rural pursuit which is only part of a much bigger enterprise.

Publishers of farm magazines have had to keep pace with such changes in the world of agriculture as certain trends developed: to larger but fewer farms, to use of bigger and more machinery, to being a business with many special subdivisions, to having a decreasing farm population that is much like that of the urbanites in purchases, tastes,

---

[2] Gilbert Grosvenor, "The National Geographic Society and Its Magazine." Reprint of Foreword to the cumulative index to *National Geographic Magazine*, 1899 to 1946. National Geographic Society, 1948, p. 59.

[3] *Loc. cit.*

and customs. At one time these publishers had the farm market to themselves. It was separate and reachable almost entirely by their publications. But radio, television, consumer magazines, and general newspapers now are part of farm life and advertisers have other ways to gain the farm family's attention than through the printed word. They seek to do so by issuing farm magazines that are national in scope, concentrate on regions (such as groups of states), or are statewide only. Each of these main divisions may have periodicals dealing with one type of farm product, as for example poultry.

Today, therefore, the best edited farm periodicals are concerned with using market research, content analysis, and readability and readership research. Even the most ordinary publication must give its readers agricultural news, reports on new farming methods, and discussions of national policies of immediate import to the farmer's welfare.

The scope of the capably run farm magazine is indicated in the tests of content made by *Wallaces Farmer* and *Wisconsin Agriculturist* magazines, as reported by an executive of both.[4] Among the articles in *Wallaces Farmer* were some with these titles: "Two Price System," "What's Going on in Legislature," "Washington Report," and "Social Security." These were not the most popular, but had substantial reader interest.

Robert H. Williams, in his farewell editorial when *The Indiana Farmer* was merged with the Indiana edition of *Prairie Farmer* in 1963, noted some typical policies of these magazines. He pointed out that his periodical, then the oldest farm publication in the nation, had led a fight for a School of Veterinary Science and Medicine at Purdue. During its final year, the magazine "advocated and helped gain research monies to combat Johnsongrass, sought relief from oppressive property taxes through a state sales tax, and first advocated a new concept in higher education in Hoosierland—the Indiana Vocational Technical College—and saw the idea adopted by the 1963 General Assembly."

Not only are these magazines among the oldest but also several have circulations well over a million and yet remain among the most inexpensive for the reader to buy.

Taking all of the many classifications used by the record keepers,[5] which include everything from the general publications like *Farm Quarterly* and *Successful Farming* to those with such quaint names as *Gobbles* (for turkey farmers) and *The Moos* (for dairymen), the number of magazine format now is about 150 of the commercial type.

---

[4] Donald R. Murphy, *What Farmers Read and Like* (Ames: Iowa State University Press, 1962).

[5] See the farm publications section of Standard Rate and Data Service Reports for the full classification list.

Added to these are the company publications, such as *Business of Farming,* published by the U.S. Gypsum Company, and those serving cooperative associations, such as *Leadership.*

Issuing regional editions has become common, a practice more characteristic of the consumer than the specialized magazines. Group publication also is strong. Home State Farm Publications in Cleveland publishes five; Farmer-Stockman has three; and Mid-West Unit Farm Publications has five such regional magazines. Some of the state and regional magazines are parts of units for advertising purposes. More than thirty are in the State and Local Farm Papers Group.

*Farm Journal,* which is national in appeal, leads all agricultural magazines in individual circulations, with almost 2,800,000 a month; *Progressive Farmer,* despite its name is aimed chiefly at Southern states, and is next, 1,182,000; near it is *Successful Farming,* whose regional editions combine to give it 1,109,000. Several others such as *Farmer-Stockman* and *Prairie Farmer,* run from 340,000 to 400,000.

## The pioneers

*Agricultural Museum,* started in 1810 in Georgetown, D.C., is said by Mott to be the first magazine entirely devoted to agriculture. Wood, however, accepts as first the *Genesee Farmer,* begun in 1831, a predecessor of *Country Gentleman,* perhaps because of the continuity, since the *Museum* lasted less than two years. Many of the pioneers are still published. Among them are *Prairie Farmer,* 1840, now the oldest; *Southern Planter,* 1841; *American Agriculturist,* 1842; *Ohio Farmer,* 1851; and *Farm Journal,* 1877.

Prices of the present publications are a novelty in a day of rising subscription costs and per copy charges for consumer magazines. Some examples of annual rates are: *Farmer-Stockman,* $2; *Progressive Farmer,* $2; *Pennsylvania Farmer,* $2; *Successful Farming,* $1. Per copy prices usually are high, to encourage subscribing. Several of these magazines are large size, with considerable color printing. Such rates are a holdover from the days when farmers had to be induced to subscribe by even lower prices.

Farm journalism, Wood points out, has given the United States government several important officials. James Wilson, editor of *Iowa Farmer,* was the first Secretary of Agriculture; among his successors were Henry C. Wallace and his son, Henry A. Wallace, both editors of *Wallaces Farmer,* the latter also becoming Vice President; and E. T. Meredith, owner of *Iowa Farmer's Tribune* and the more famous magazine of today, *Successful Farming.*

Among the notable journalists in this specialized magazine field have been Luther Tucker, founder of the *Genesee Farmer,* later known as *The Country Gentleman;* Wilmer Atkinson, who started *Farm Journal;* John J. Dillon, editor and publisher of *The Rural New-*

*Yorker;* Orange Judd, editor of *American Agriculturist;* Graham Patterson and Wheeler McMillen, who during the 1940's and 1950's
moved *Farm Journal* into circulation leadership; and Carroll P.
Streeter, formerly editor of it.

Present-day editors and publishers have the standard organizations. The American Agricultural Editors' Association includes farm
newspaper editors and also accepts as associate and affiliate members
others related to farm journalism, such as general newspaper farm
writers. The AAEA in turn is a member of the International Union
of Agricultural Journalists. Publishers have their own Agricultural
Publishers Association.

During the 1950's and early 1960's, U.S. farm publications fell on
bad times because of the effects of the changes noted on pages 364–65.
Circulations and advertising revenue decreased; some consolidations
occurred. An upturn was experienced by the mid-1960's as a result of
heavy promotional efforts by the various units and organizations, the
greater importance of the specialized farm magazines which can provide information no other periodical seeks to offer in depth, and a rise
in rates. Total advertising records in both pages and lines were up
in 1971, over 1970, for many but not all farm magazines, a more meaningful mark of health in this segment of the magazine industry than
revenue gains.

## Regional magazines

Farm and regional publications have in common the fact that
certain farm periodicals have mainly regional circulation, viz., *Pennsylvania Farmer, Ohio Farmer.* Others have regional emphasis not
discernible from their names, such as *Prairie Farmer,* which serves the
Middle West.

The truly regional magazine is not like a replate of a general consumer magazine, which is different only in its advertising content. A
true regional is one indigenous to its geographical area and identified
with no other. The term, *regional magazine,* covers two types: those
*about* a region, as is *Arizona Highways,* and those about some other
subject but published *for* a geographical area, such as *Western Advertising.*

The most famous regional magazine of the first type is *The New
Yorker,* although it long ago moved into the general classification.
Still somewhat regional but rapidly attaining national scope is *Sunset,* a shelter magazine for the Pacific Coast whose circulation now
exceeds nine hundred thousand and is the largest regional issued
outside the farm field. Founded in San Francisco in 1898, it originally
was an external house publication of the Southern Pacific Railroad
and named for a train. Just as it was failing in 1928, having been a
travel type of regional magazine, the Lane Publishing Company
bought it and made it into one of the largest in advertising volume
in the nation.

Still in the regional category are two others that have won national attention, especially for their physical attractiveness: *Arizona
Highways* and *Vermont Life.* Despite their popularity among residents of other states they have kept their attention on their own areas,
a practice *The New Yorker* abandoned, for it may report on New
York City but it does not promote it.

About two dozen state and regional magazines, more or less in
the *Arizona Highway* format, are published, some by private businesses and others by the tourist, highway, or public relations offices
of state governments. Among them are *Nevada Highways and Parks,
New Hampshire Profiles, Yankee,* and *New Mexico Magazine.*

Another fifty-five are individually owned, local enterprises of varying formats, some with a common advertising representative who sells
space in the group. The latter, calling themselves Select Media, are
urban, boosting their communities and local cultural and business activities. Among them are *Palm Springs Life, Twin Citian, Chicagoland,*
and *Nashville.* Most city magazines are recent, but not all. *Paradise
of the Pacific* was founded in Hawaii in 1892. These are growing in
number and advertising. *Philadelphia* and *The Washingtonian* have
been nationally influential.

Chambers of commerce in large cities sometimes publish substantial local magazines, bordering on being business periodicals. Typical
are *Commerce,* from Chicago; *Trenton,* from that New Jersey city;
and *Houston,* from Texas.

Nor are these all. Substantial regional magazines of wide appeal
come from large businesses and associations. *Cascades,* laden with
color photography and original historical articles on the Pacific northwest, actually is the external-internal house publication of the Pacific
Northwest Bell Telephone Company.

*Westways,* almost as colorful, is a monthly published since 1908
by the Automobile Club of Southern California. It has reached three
hundred thousand circulation, and fits into the association magazine
classification.

Of the second type—for a region but about some other subject
than the region—there are hundreds, most of them properly classified
as business magazines. Some typical titles are *Western Fabrics,
Curtains & Draperies, Southern Motor Cargo, Northwestern Banker,
Motor West, Midwest Industry,* and *Texas Fashions.*

Certain city magazines have gone past the booster function accepted traditionally by so many and have become hard-hitting periodicals digging deeply into the life of the communities they serve. Several
are reminiscent of *McClure's* and the *American* in their muckraking
days.

They are concerned with the plight of the people who must live
in the ghettos, with traffic problems, air pollution, and corruption in
local government or business. Among those receiving national atten-

tion for their articles on such subjects are *Seattle, San Diego, Washingtonian, San Francisco,* and *Philadelphia.*

*New York,* an outgrowth of a supplement to the now defunct New York *Herald Tribune,* has managed to set itself up as a rival of *The New Yorker* and like the latter is more of national than a regional periodical, although it gives special attention to New York City events, and has some of the aims of the more vigorous city magazines.

## Labor magazines

Although the labor force of the United States runs between seventy and seventy-five million, labor publications are issued mainly for the approximately fifteen million union members. Employe publications (company or house magazines) are not considered labor journalism, but the products of management.

National labor organization periodicals, like the *Federationist,* are the most elaborate; least pretentious are those issued by local union organizations. Content is heavily on the news side, with considerable attention as well to editorials and articles supporting the labor movement's viewpoints on international and national affairs. Editors and other staff members generally are members of the sponsoring unions.

Labor groups have felt especially the need for establishing their own magazines. The labor movement has been and still is critical of the way the general press handles information about its activities. Examination of what general periodicals have printed about labor shows that, except in times of strikes, lockouts, and layoffs, this area of American life was considered unimportant until about 1935. Since then labor news and views have had considerably better treatment.

The oldest labor periodical is the *Carpenter,* a monthly founded in 1881 by the United Brotherhood of Carpenters. *The Workingmen's Advocate,* issued in Chicago from 1864 to 1879, as the official organ of the National Labor Union, the first large labor federation, was among the earliest magazines.

Biggest labor magazine now in circulation is *Justice,* a semimonthly published in New York by the International Ladies Garment Workers Union. Founded in 1918, it had a circulation of about 400,000 a half-century later. Approximately three-fourths this number has been achieved by the *Butcher Workman,* a monthly founded in 1896 and published in Chicago by the Amalgamated Meat Cutters and Butcher Workmen of North America. The already mentioned *Federationist,* a slick-paper magazine, is sent out from Washington and is one of the few elaborate labor periodicals, with a circulation of about 150,000.

Unlike the rest of the specialized periodical groups, labor magazines are in the minority in labor publications. The newspaper format is preferred, not only because it conveys news more appropriately but

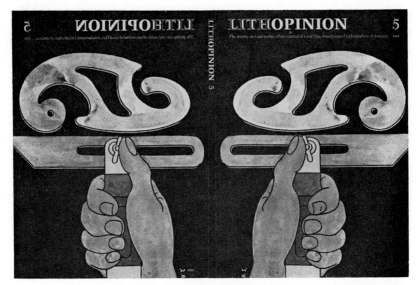

*Fig. 21.2.* A cover of *Lithopinion,* an unusual type of magazine to be issued by a labor union because of its general quality-magazine content. Cover designed by Bernard Simpson for *Lithopinion* No. 5, the quarterly journal of Local One, Amalgamated Lithographers of America. Reprinted by permission. *(Lithopinion Photo by Bill Joli)*

also because it is less expensive to produce, a reflection of the desire of members of the labor movement that their own publications not be extravagantly printed. This characteristic, however, makes it difficult for the magazines to stand up in competition with other periodicals; as with many other types of specialized magazines, these organization periodicals are not given preference in reading time over the consumer magazines.

An extraordinary labor magazine, *Lithopinion,* was founded in 1965 by Local 1 of the Amalgamated Lithographers Union of America. A quarterly without advertising, it is far beyond any other union magazine because of its high-quality art work, breadth of content, typography, and printing.

Sent without charge to selected persons in other occupations, and to the union's members as part of their dues, it takes no subscriptions and cannot be purchased. Each issue has been typographically different in format from the others. (See Fig. 21.2.) Samuel Grafton, for many years a novelist and article writer for consumer magazines, was its first editor. He explained to the author of this book that *Lithopinion* "aims at the quality level of *Harper's* or *Atlantic*—or higher since this is a free country—and is intended to show that the labor movement is entitled to a place at the national council table."

The unusual formula comes from the philosophy of the union, as Grafton explains it: "Local One . . . opposes featherbedding; it favors automation; it believes in technological progress and even does research to foster it. It believes the time has come for full labor participation in the American community, not on a vulgar take-over basis, but as a first-class citizen and participant. The local offers the magazine to the community as, in other circumstances, someone might offer the community a new college or museum."

Originator of the magazine was Edward Swayduck, the local's president who contributes to each issue, which regularly portrays the technological possibilities in lithographic printing by reproduction in color.

Another newcomer is *American Labor,* a monthly founded in 1968 and aimed at business executives in labor and labor executives in business, with a controlled circulation of 100,000.

# Part Five

# *Social and vocational aspects of the magazine world*

# Chapter 22

# Social responsibilities
# and effects

A MAGAZINE PUBLISHING COMPANY decides to reject advertising for a product thought to be harmful to its users. Such a decision is a demonstration of social responsibility.

A magazine editor and his staff adopt a policy of making certain, when writing about any subject, that what they print gives all the legally publishable facts and points of view necessary to meet the reader's needs. This practice, also, is exercising social responsibility.

Magazines of any kind are social institutions and have social responsibility as well as social effect. And the larger the circulation and the more readers the greater the potential influence and hence the degree of responsibility.

So far in this book we have seen how magazine companies are organized and how they operate, what some of their many thousands of publications are like, how they are organized, and what their staff members do. In this chapter we need to consider the obligations to society of such an institution as the magazine business and its effect upon our society.

## Magazines and society

What are the social responsibilities of magazines?

They share with all journalism, whether printed or electronic, the obligation in a democracy to provide the people with a fair presentation of the facts, with honestly held opinions, and with truthful advertising.

Louis M. Lyons, former curator of the Nieman Foundation for Journalism at Harvard, addressing a magazine editorial conference of the Magazine Publishers Association, indicated a difference in the responsibility, however, of the newspaper and the magazine. He said:

> I believe the role of the magazine is quite different from that of the newspaper. I want something quite separate. I think the substance of the magazine should be a quite different fabric. The magazine should give the reader something to chew on, to mull over, something to stir his imagination, to reflect about, not only to broaden his awareness of current issues, but to lead him to consider matters that are not now and may never be current issues, but should engage the attention of the questing mind.[1]

That no medium, and certainly not magazines either as a whole industry or by types, has achieved perfection in fulfilling these and other obligations is evident to anyone who can read. Periodicals, being the result of human work, have numerous shortcomings. Magazines as a whole may come closer to being perfect than the more hurriedly produced media because there is more time in which to eradicate faults or achieve virtue, but this is not yet proved.

No one yet has invented a machine that rings a bell when magazine reading matter or advertising copy is unfair or in some other way unethical. Value judgments must be left to the changing human mind. Intelligent editors make decisions and offer interpretations and opinions based upon facts; and facts themselves, when joined with new facts have new meanings. Readers, being possessed of more or fewer facts than the magazinists themselves, as the case may be with different individuals, arrive at their own interpretations, often entirely different although based on the same facts.

### The meaning of social effect

All publications, as do all institutions and persons, have some social effect. Nothing, in our interdependent world, functions without bearing directly or indirectly upon society or some segment of it. A magazine publishing company may not intend to be a social institution, that is, one with a social purpose, but it cannot escape having a social responsibility. Whether a magazine firm should have a social purpose at all or whether such a purpose should be the main reason for being is a constantly debated matter, settled more by the nature of the economic order than the desires of owners.

A social institution may be defined as one devoted to the whole good of the whole people. Theoretically, that is the purpose of all

---

[1] "Reader's Choice," an address by Louis M. Lyons, March 27, 1963, Washington, D.C., MPA Release, p. 2.

properly run organizations. It is the guiding principle of the school, the church, the professions. This definition is admittedly unsatisfactory because it is vague about what the phrase, "the whole good," means. If, to achieve "the whole good of the whole people," it is thought necessary to destroy some of the people, is such action to be condoned? Obviously not. Yet, for general purposes, magazinists must use some such definition as a working principle and must seek to approximate the ideal.

The magazine world, as we have seen in earlier chapters, is almost wholly within the world of business. At its best, business benefits all of the people. But if a magazine publishing company is part of an economic order which makes it dependent upon public support through purchase of magazines and of advertising space, the magazine can be socially beneficial only to the extent that such dependence permits.

William L. Chenery, for many years editor of *Collier's,* observed while speaking at the University of Virginia that "The national magazine of mass circulation can treat only those national problems about which millions of people . . . are willing to read. . . . [The magazine] is not an endowed educational institution. It is a business operation primarily for profit. If it does not interest its readers, it cannot endure."[2]

Therefore if the public will not read certain types of content, it will not be exposed to ideas and facts in that content. As a result such content is withheld by editors. Here is one of the several points of contact between magazine and public that relate to the publication's social responsibility and effect.

## The attempt at fairness

Frederick Lewis Allen, while editor of *Harper's,* once described a common editorial experience on that and other magazines: "We at *Harper's* are called, from time to time, communists, fascists, New Dealers, reactionaries; brutally savage toward the nation's enemies, pacifistically tender toward the nation's enemies; anti-Russian, anti-British; victims of conspiratorial propaganda of the Russians, of the British; anti-business, anti-farmer, or the tools of each."[3]

The lengths to which readers go in their attacks upon publications that displease them or satisfy them can be illustrated by the experience of *Parade,* magazine supplement to newspapers which distributes eleven million copies a week and therefore has possibilities of

---

[2] William Ludlow Chenery, "The Magazine and Public Opinion," address delivered at the University of Virginia, July 13, 1936. *Vital Speeches of the Day,* Aug. 15, 1936, p. 718. See also "Causes and Effects," *Collier's,* Dec. 15, 1950, p. 70.

[3] Frederick Lewis Allen, "The Function of a Magazine in America," address prepared for delivery at the 36th annual Journalism Week, University of Missouri. *University of Missouri Bulletin,* Aug. 10, 1945.

receiving numerous letters. On an article that appeared in the early
1960's it received twelve thousand letters. About another topic one
reader wrote:

"Your entire reason leads me to believe that you are a lackey of
the Russian embassy. Take your suggestion and go to hell! Now, when
I open my Sunday paper, my first act will be to completely destroy
*Parade* Magazine." And, sure enough, the next Sunday Jess Gorkin,
the editor who relates this incident, received the latest issue, torn up
and the pieces stapled together.[4]

Editors who receive such reactions may think they have been
unfair until they read equally vigorous mail on the other side. Then
they come to conclude that perhaps they have been impartial, after
all, or perhaps not entirely clear. In any case, they are having a social effect; they are reaching people's minds. And since they have
such an effect they have social responsibility.

The owner, publisher, editor, or writer for a magazine does not
work in a vacuum, nor can he for long content himself only with
making or losing money. His presence in journalism, in fact, is likely
to mean that he has other motives: to express himself, to influence
others, to gain power, to assume responsibility. He wants to have
some kind of influence upon the society around him and to be of
value at this time in history, i.e., to have a social effect.

## Attempts at influence

That magazines have not saved the world needs no proving as
we look around at it; that many have made an admirable effort is
easily demonstrated. Over the years since their existence, general as
well as specialized magazines alike have championed numerous socially desirable causes, conducting crusades year after year. Some
have given analysis and advice, others have raised money, supported
political parties, undertaken exploration, or under dangerous conditions sponsored investigations of crime or political corruption. A
segment has explored unpopular social ideas, often surviving to see
them widely accepted.

The effects, good or bad, have been accomplished largely, however, through magazine content rather than organized action. Three
departments have been influential: advertising, editorial, promotion.

The advertising department has offered word, camera, and brush
pictures of new products and services, has conveyed general information and ideas. Through its literature, the promotion department
has supported the advertising. Both have stimulated desires for products and services, influencing the progress of business and industry.
Living standards of readers have been affected in consequence.

---

[4] Jess Gorkin, "Challenges Faced by Mass Media," in John E. Drewry (ed.),
*Better Journalism for a Better Tomorrow* (Athens, Ga.: University of Georgia
Press, 1963), pp. 127–28.

# Credo for a Magazine

**By Norman Cousins**

Fundamentally, to publish a magazine that people will read and respect;

To believe, not as rote or strained slogan, but as rigid fact, that a magazine is by natural right the property of its readers;

That, because of this, editors are but temporary custodians, their tenure related to and dependent upon their confidence in the judgment and intelligence of the reader;

That such confidence is best established by avoiding both the condescension of talking down and the presumption of talking up;

That a magazine, like a person, requires, in order to be effective, certain qualities—readily identifiable and beyond obliteration:

That high among these qualities is a response to values, the capacity to create values, and the passion to defend values;

That other essential qualities include clarity, curiosity, insight, incisiveness, integrity, good taste, good will, conviction, responsibility;

That what is written is believed by the writer and written to be believed by the reader;

That the magazine should reflect a sense of adventure and excitement about life in general and about books and ideas in particular;

That honest sentiments, honest passions, and honest indignations are among the highest expressions of conscience, that there is no need to feel shy or awkward or embarrassed in their presence, and that they are not to be waved aside by mock hysterics;

That cynicism at best is a waste of time; at worst, a dangerous and potentially fatal disease for individuals and civilizations both;

That ideals are the main business of writers, and that people will respond to ideals far beyond the anticipations of their nominal leaders;

That believing all this need neither limit nor inhibit a sense of fun and the enjoyment of laughter;

That editing, finally, is not paring but creating.

Mr. Cousins wrote this editorial while editor of the *Saturday Review*. It is reprinted by permission from that magazine, where it appeared under the head "Credo for SRL," on Aug. 6, 1949.

---

The editorial department has influenced the language of readers, has been a creator or molder of cultural standards and interests, and has purveyed facts and ideas that readers might not otherwise have been exposed to. Editorial content has affected people's dress, eating habits, and use of their spare time.

What might be considered the official concept of the influence of the general magazine has come from the Magazine Advertising Bureau. Placed first among general effects is the shaping of public opinion. "The national magazine does not have the spot news function of either the newspaper or the radio. But being edited with deliberation, it is read with equal deliberation, and therefore has the unique ability to form a *mature* public opinion, nationally." It also is a reflector of American life. Said the MAB: "Life is not the daily headlines of the newspaper, nor is it the artificial dramatics thrown out daily, hourly by radio. The solid values of the lives of millions of American families are reported by the national magazine, unsensationally but vividly and accurately, in articles and fiction, in pictures and illustrations."[5] The contrast with television might be added.

Wood, in his study of American magazines, declares that the magazine is one of "three major forces affecting and controlling national public opinion." With newspaper and radio it "first created the public opinion they affect." He reminds us that the magazine is read more persistently than any other medium, is less perishable, and is read attentively. It provokes results, receives reactions. Much magazine material later goes into books and motion pictures; reprints are made.

"The character of a given magazine limits its audience," he says, "thus, to some extent, the spread of its influence, its educational force, its persuasion to belief, and possibly to individual or social action."[6]

### Effects by types

Wood properly qualifies his generalization by using the word *given*. The effects of the comics are unlike those of literary magazines, and within the specialized magazine world the effects of one technical journal only in a superficial way resemble those of another.

Led by *The Reader's Digest,* condensed material and pocket-size magazines have stimulated popularized reading by the middle-class public, have spread certain social positions and attitudes, and have increased demand for short, quickly read publications. The digests made the portable magazine among the most popular of those published, one of them being of world influence.

With magazines of seven or eight million circulation setting the pace, the women's group, with which may be associated the service and shelter books, has been principally responsible for influence wielded by advertising departments on homes and families of the middle class. They have to some extent standardized housekeeping tools, widened the variety of cookery, introduced or popularized certain habits (such as more frequent bathing and shaving, use of deodorants, and hair coloring), and called attention to books, motion pictures, and art works, considerably broadening their effect. Not a minor result has been the introduction of fictional stereotypes; most heroes and heroines of fiction in women's magazines seldom are like realities. Consumer magazines try to exert influence through their ad-

---

[5] Undated bulletin of the Magazine Advertising Bureau. No. 2, p. 2.

[6] James Playsted Wood, *Magazines in the United States* (New York: Ronald Press Company, 1956), p. 305.

vertising and editorial policies. *Esquire* in 1968, after the assassinations of Dr. Martin Luther King, Jr., and Senator Robert F. Kennedy, adopted a policy of accepting no gun advertising of any kind. This decision came after a campaign against gun advertising launched by *Advertising Age*. *McCall's*, with a circulation of more than eight million, on the day of Senator Kennedy's assassination, stopped its presses and inserted a two-page editorial calling on its women readers to support stronger gun-control legislation, help stop excessive violence on broadcasting programs and in films, boycott certain toys, and follow other policies.

The confession magazine, more and more an imitator of the slick in content, has had a changing influence. In its early days it played a psychological role: it offered spiritual release for uneducated or immature readers (whether adults or adolescents), enabling them to experience adventures of the more daring and unorthodox without personal risk. Now, except for a surviving group offering stories of sex adventures and crime detection, it is achieving on its own economic level a standardization in reader habits and practices similar to the women's slicks.

The circulation and advertising leaders among men's magazines have turned away from tales of wartime bravery to tales of bedroom exploits, holding as admirable man's sexual domination of women and gratification of his dreams of wealth, power, and comfort. They encourage their readers to a hedonistic philosophy of life and to be patrons of entertainment.

The religious magazines, less given than they once were to regularizing moral concepts, now are influencing their readers to apply their religious principles to social concerns as well as to personal conduct. Some have helped bring social movements into existence, such as the civil rights groups, and mustered support for social legislation.

Literary magazines have started movements, erected critical standards and founded schools of criticism, introduced new writers, maintained the following of older ones, and provided an outlet for work not marketable to the public through general or consumer magazines. Henry Mills Alden listed the following famous writers as owing their first publication to magazines: Scott, Johnson, Coleridge, DeQuincey, Lamb, Hazlitt, Shelley, Keats, Wordsworth, Hunt, Eliot, Landor, Trollope, Thackeray, Poe, Twain and Longfellow.[7] In our own day *The New Yorker* alone has nurtured dozens of new writers, as have the little magazines.

Magazines for juveniles have had definite effects, since their readers are in formative years. A youngster's heroes once were provided almost solely by books and magazines; today radio, television, motion picture, and recordings also have strong influence, perhaps

---

[7] Henry Mills Alden, *Magazine Writing and the New Literature* (New York: Harper & Brothers, 1908), pp. 42–52.

stronger. The religious juveniles have built concepts of right and wrong in human conduct and of individual responsibility at home and in the church. They have aroused loyalties. The secular juveniles in more recent times have been simplified versions of magazines for grown-ups—witness the departments in *Ingénue* and *Seventeen,* for example. Their effect has been at once to create little adults and to encourage youthful independence and also standardization of mores among adolescents. The comics have appealed to childish imaginations so effectively, and with so much questionable content, that they have been treated as social phenomena to be studied as seriously as are educational practices and policies.

The effects of specialized magazines are vertical, rather than horizontal. A clothing publication or a food magazine affects the profession, industry, business, or other group it serves by conveying news created by the group, evaluating trends within, providing an outlet for ideas, and stimulating business through advertising. Business periodicals have taken dramatic stands to correct what they consider evils. Among several notable examples in recent years were the successful campaign by *Fleet Owner* against the highway menace of "stay-awake" pills which led to new legislation, and the year-long crusade by *Canadian Fisherman* that brought about regulations concerning greater safety for professional fishermen. The company magazine has established itself as a bulwark or dam against ideas that its publishers deem undesirable or it has helped to stimulate business.

### Evaluating the effects

This discussion of the social responsibilities and effects of magazines has to this point attempted little evaluation. Not much attention has been given by scholars or critics of the magazine to these effects or to their merits. Journalism in general, or specifically the newspaper, radio, or television, has been subject to evaluation, but not much space has been accorded to judging the magazine's performance. For many years there has been an open season for passing upon the effects of journalism as a whole and newspapers in particular. Almost all the judges have been adversely critical of papers, and many have lumped magazines with them, for the term *the press* always has been ambiguous.

Only nine books may be considered evaluations of magazines: John Bainbridge's *Little Wonder,* which is about *The Reader's Digest;* Wood's *Magazines in the United States,* a combination of history and judgment; Helen Woodward's *The Lady Persuaders,* about women's periodicals; Joseph C. Goulden's *The Curtis Caper,* an account of the Curtis Publishing Company's difficulties in recent years; Marty, Deedy, Silverman, and Lekachman's *The Religious Press in America;* Schacht's *The Journals of Opinion and Reportage: An Assessment;*

Peterson's *Magazines in the Twentieth Century;* Otto Freidrich's *Decline and Fall* about the *Post;* and Tassin's *The Magazine in America.* Most are outdated.

During its early days the American magazine was criticized in articles, both at home and in England, for the low quality of its content. But except for complaint about an occasional article, the periodical as an institution has been generally ignored.

Individual magazines or groups sometimes have drawn attack, as shown by the histories of *Woodhull and Claflin's Weekly* or of *The Masses,* to cite two widely different periodicals of distinctly separate periods. The pulps, comics, slicks in general, newsmagazines, digests, and women's magazines have been attacked in this century. Whereas newspapers as a group are evaluated for their ethics or their alleged failure to live up to the guarantees of the freedom of the press, magazines are dealt with more often through appraisals of individual editors and publishers. Harold Ross, Henry R. Luce, William Randolph Hearst, Sr., H. L. Mencken, and George Horace Lorimer have not always been kindly treated in the literature about them.

Insubstantial as criticism of magazines has been, what is its point? A few commonly held views are these.

The adverse critics say: (1) they are too much inclined to give the public what it wants; (2) they deprive the public of the fullest knowledge of facts and ideas; (3) through advertising content they stimulate desires for possessions that cannot be gratified by the average reader's income; (4) they present only conventional or ultra-conservative viewpoints; (5) they evade their duty to provide leadership in solving social problems; (6) they are time-wasting, distracting the reader from more valuable uses of his leisure; (7) they have failed, as employers, to give minority racial groups responsible positions on their staffs; (8) they knuckle in to advertisers; and (9) they deal unfairly with their employes by discontinuing killing on short notice.

The favorable critics counter that: (1) magazines have helped produce the high standard of living in this country through their advertising copy; (2) they have helped stimulate mass consumption of goods and, thereby, mass production; (3) they have therefore contributed toward the lowering of the cost of living; (4) through their popular education materials they have created a better informed public; (5) they have "merchandised," as one proponent put it, new ideas; and (6) they have played an important role in every national crisis, be it war, depression, flood, or recovery from such disasters.

As with so many arguments, this is not a clear case for either pro or con. To begin with, most critics of either side are talking exclusively about the consumer magazine and, as usual, overlooking all the rest, which as we know are fifty times as numerous, and in some instances just as influential. Accepting the consumer scope, some parts of each set of criticisms may be accepted as true. The charge that the magazines are but mirrors of the public mind cannot be disputed; as Godkin of *The Nation* put it long ago in a letter to President Charles Eliot Norton of Harvard: ". . . the press would not be what it is without a public demand for it as it is."

Because magazines depend upon public support, they must gratify public demand to assure support. It follows that unpopular ideas will get short shrift in the mass periodical, such ideas as the consumer cooperative movement, diplomatic recognition of Communist China by the United States, and mental telepathy, for example, either are ignored or presented unsympathetically. The subject of racial and religious intolerance likewise was ignored, except by certain specialized magazines, until progress was begun in the United States toward decreasing such intolerance, and the press ran less risk, as a result, in discussing it. With progress came open discussion in countless magazine articles and even fictional treatment in the women's magazines.

Magazine advertising sometimes does make readers dissatisfied with their present washing machines, cameras, mixers, or vacuum cleaners; the less self-controlled consumers do implicate themselves in endless installment buying. To balance these detriments, however, are the greater sanitation and efficiency made possible in part by the lower prices and greater availability of tools resulting from better merchandising. Magazines are time-wasting to time-wasters; other readers should not be deprived of occasional trivial reading to protect them from themselves.

The charge of knuckling in to advertisers is one of the most often made and of great importance in considering whether magazines are interested in their own welfare rather than that of the commonweal.

Certainly a hat-in-hand attitude toward advertisers was obvious in the policy of the Curtis Publishing Company's management, before the change in control of the firm early in the 1960's. When a new format for the *Saturday Evening Post* was agreed upon by the staff (that is, by those who did not resign in protest), specimens of it were shown to potential advertisers in a much promoted preview. The question arises, since this is common also when new commercial magazines are launched: are magazines intended primarily for readers or for advertisers?

H. W. Kastor & Sons, an advertising agency, has declared that some magazines dropped advertising for Bantron, a smoking deterrent, after tobacco companies had exerted pressure on them. *Advertising Age* looked into the matter and published several statements by unnamed publishers in confirmation. One large periodical said it never carried Bantron advertising "because we decided against it." Taking such copy "would be bad business," for the magazine had much cigaret linage. Size of copy is an important factor here; small purchases of space were accepted.[8]

A vigorous general statement has been made on this general problem by Dean Theodore Peterson of the University of Illinois College of Journalism and Communications:

> One response of magazines to television, I think, has been to treat advertisers with all of the deference accorded a pregnant queen when the crown needs a male heir. Now, magazines must have advertising, I know, and the publishers have been bowing respectfully to advertisers at least since 1896, when Edward Bok of the *Ladies' Home Journal* broke with traditional format by jumping fiction into his advertising pages to increase their readership. But in recent years, their bowing has become lower and lower, and more and more respectful. Let me mention just three manifestations.
>
> First, many publishers have designed their magazines more for advertising exposure than for reader convenience. At their mildest, they simply permit odd-shaped advertisements to chew up their editorial pages. At their most extreme, they dare the reader to find the editorial features. As Louis Lyons has remarked, a reader cannot miss the advertisements in a magazine even though he may have a hard time finding and completing an article he wants to read. Mr. Lyons could have cited the large-circulation magazine that made readers detour around 6¾ pages of advertising to finish the last half of a sentence.
>
> For another thing, many publishers have blurred the distinction between editorial matter and advertising matter by carrying advertisements deliberately designed to trick the reader into thinking they are editorial features.[9]

Examples of editorial independence exist, also, in the consumer magazine world. *The New Yorker*'s thumbing of its nose at advertisers is widely known; in the days of Ross it prohibited its own advertising salesmen from appearing on the floor housing the editors' offices. *Good Housekeeping, Redbook,* and *Saturday Review* in recent years also have demonstrated independence of advertising pressures in specific instances reported in the trade press.

The pressures put upon magazine publishing companies are strong. Typical of what happens occurred when *Life* carried a picture story on the pharmaceutical industry. That business considered it unfair, for it said that consumers are overcharged for drugs. Several important firms then dropped *Life* from their advertising schedules, including Abbott Laboratories and Parke, Davis & Co.[10]

An unnamed magazine publisher, commenting in the Bantron situation described earlier, said: "When the copy runs in small space,

---

[8] "Magazines Confirm 'Cigaret Censorship,'" *Advertising Age,* April 6, 1959, p. 1.

[9] "Where's the Editorial?" from an address before the Periodical Publishers Association of Canada, *Advertising Age,* Oct. 7, 1963.

[10] "Parke, Davis Also Drops 'Life' Ads Because of Article," *Advertising Age,* Dec. 5, 1960.

there isn't any argument. When it appears in full pages, somebody asks one of your salesmen casually why you run 'junky' ads like Bantron, and points out that they don't 'do anything' for the book. And pretty soon you start losing tobacco business. No threats, no intimidation."

During 1963, the Washington State Pharmaceutical Association told its drugstore members: "Check your magazines . . . eliminate those which have articles detrimental to your business." Its special target was *The Woman,* since discontinued, which had published an article encouraging patronage of discount houses.

*The Reader's Digest* has several times been dropped from advertising schedules for its articles that offended certain businesses. The American Tobacco Company, in 1957, removed $1,250,000 in advertising from it because of a cigaret article; in 1961 the American Dairy Association cancelled its schedule because of two articles it considered detrimental to the dairy field. Four pages were dropped and the magazine accused of "lack of courage" because the association was not notified in advance of the articles' publication. But the ADA's general manager of that time said that the Association had "no desire to dictate the editorial policies of any publication."[11]

Such pressures come, also, from other sources than business: local governments, self-appointed guardians of public morals, and patriotic societies. Typical was the banning of *Time, Life,* and *Look* in 1956 from the nine high school libraries of Bossier City and Parish in Louisiana.

Extremely wealthy publishing companies can ignore pressures, but few firms are extraordinarily strong in their resources. Because the majority of publications are issued by small firms there has been sufficient feeling of insecurity in the journalistic world in recent times to produce even more caution than usual. What may be worse is a mind set, resulting from the dependence of magazines upon advertisers, that the advertisers and not the public comes first. Advertisers, after all, bring far more money into the treasury than does the public. On that excuse omission of troublesome facts and ideas is being justified.

Charges about advertiser influence are heard mainly about consumer magazines. But they also are made, if less loudly and possibly with greater validity because so many more could be involved, about the specialized magazines. Because most are small and more vulnerable, the chance of pressures succeeding is greater.

Peter Bart, while an advertising news writer for the New York *Times,* reported that the Society of Business Magazine Editors had surveyed 103 of its members "soliciting their candid opinions about advertiser influence on editorial operations." About 22 per cent of the editors acknowledged that it was accepted policy on their magazines "to

---

[11] "Dairy Men Drop 'Digest' Schedule," *Advertising Age,* April 3, 1961, p. 7.

give preference to advertisers when gathering information for articles."
About 55 per cent said that advertising salesmen exerted "some influence" in selecting and researching articles. One-third said they made
a "special effort" to publish illustrations sent in by advertisers.[12]

Protests came at once, charging slanting by the *Times.* These
were from business magazine associations as well as from a few heads
of companies known, however, for the high ethical quality of their
operations.

The assertion that the public is better informed because of magazines can be accepted if "better informed" is taken relatively. "Better
informed about what?" is a legitimate question. The American people
as a whole may be better informed about current affairs than the inhabitants of many other nations but are they well informed enough
to make democracy work to the limit and to the full advantage of
the people? The revelations of pollsters about what the people do
not know raise doubts.

Yet the magazine does not exist in isolation; it is only one medium
of mass communication. It should not have to carry full blame for
failures shared by all other media. It is blameworthy to the extent
that it makes no attempt to provide facts, to the degree in which
editors and publishers lack interest or courage in dealing with controversial subjects, unorthodox ideas, and topics of limited appeal although important.

A single, all-inclusive statement about the social effect of the
magazine in the United States is difficult to frame. No comprehensive
studies have been undertaken. But it appears that the consumer
magazine has lost the dynamics that made it powerful in the days
when it was a personal organ or a tool for social pioneers. As it has
become the product of a business it has had to follow business methods
and standards lest it not survive. The business periodicals, numerically by far the largest group, naturally are subordinate to the business motive. Any magazine is likely, under such conditions, to invoke
blessings upon the existing social order and warn readers away from
social experiments that threaten to change the fundamental economy
upon which the magazines are dependent.

### The magazine's social role

If the magazine shares its social role with other media, those who
produce and use it must have some idea what that social role might
be.

A business society prevents the magazine from fulfilling the role
of the institution wholly devoted to the welfare of society as are, for
example, church, school, and the professions of medicine and nursing. It is left to play a part short of full devotion to the commonweal.

---

[12] Peter Bart, "Advertising: Loss of Editorial Independence," New York *Times,*
Feb. 12, 1964.

If magazines indiscriminately use the fear motive in advertising, they are not bettering society; if they ignore significant social ideas for fear of adverse reader reaction, they are doing less than their best to help mankind. But where shall they position themselves? How far ahead of the public may they safely be?

Paul F. Lazarsfeld and Robert K. Merton tackle this problem in a general manner and point out a procedure for the magazine, among other media of mass communication. They examine the argument that the level of esthetic taste has deteriorated in "the measure that the size of these audiences has increased." They say there is a fear "that the mass media deliberately cater to these vulgarized tastes, thus contributing to further deterioration." They declare that they have been able to find little knowledge about the social role of mass media and their effect upon the community.

Many critics of mass media make them "targets for hostile criticism because they feel themselves duped by the turn of events." Reformers have helped make available more leisure but people use it in radio listening, movie going, and, the authors might have added later, television gazing. Such media seem somehow to have "cheated reformers of the roots of their victories." Instead of spending time reading Shakespeare or listening to Beethoven's music the public turns to sex novels, television Westerns, or pop singers.

Messrs. Lazarsfeld and Merton ask how best to use mass media "for moving toward designated types of social objectives." They answer by suggesting that propaganda, whether for good or bad social motives, must satisfy one or more of three conditions if it is to be effective: (1) monopolization; (2) canalization rather than change of basic values; and (3) supplementary face-to-face contact. Monopolization they illustrate by wartime censorship in a democracy, the taking over or use of channels of communication for war propaganda. Creation of popular idols by mass media is another example. Canalization perpetuates existing behavior patterns or attitudes. Magazine fiction offers an example. In most short stories the heroine is beautiful and desirable; the hero, handsome and virile. Supplementation is a follow-up on the presentation of a point of view through mass media, achieved through local centers of organized face-to-face contact, such as reading rooms and clubs. It "serves to reinforce the prevailing culture patterns."[13]

Dr. Lazarsfeld went a step further, in an address before the Institute of Communications Research at the University of Illinois, when he said:

> Do we "give the people what they want" or do we believe that there are experts who know the best balance for the total supply which the mass media provide? It is not too difficult to suggest an answer.

---

[13] Lyman Bryson (ed.), *The Communication of Ideas* (New York: Harper & Brothers and the Institute for Religious and Social Studies, 1948), pp. 113–14.

> Obviously we do not want magazines and radio programs in this country to drive audiences away. But almost no one would propose that the media be based on the lowest common denominator; publishers and broadcasters have a cultural responsibility. Their business is affected by public interest. Thus the best solution would be to have mass media aim just slightly above what would be the simplest level at any time. In this way, we shall have a general acceptance of media content, as well as a slow, systematic intellectual progress to which the media, themselves, will contribute.[14]

He admits that the recommendation is more easily made than carried out. Consciously or unconsciously, however, Dr. Lazarsfeld's philosophy seems to be followed by certain editors. The increasing quantity of material dealing with such social problems as divorce, birth control, crime, sickness and disease, and denial of civil rights to minorities has increased the popularity of women's magazines among women who desire more than fiction and advice on everyday household life.

The progress made in introducing new ideas through magazines can be judged by the difference in the climate of public opinion during an earlier period of magazine history.

The social effect of some of the policies of Edward Bok was tempestuous. This editor of the *Ladies' Home Journal* related in his autobiography the medical opposition, in the 1880's, to a department of questions and answers for prospective mothers. He describes, also, the results of a policy of refusing patent medicine advertising advocated by John Adams Thayer, advertising manager, and supported by Cyrus H. K. Curtis, the publisher. Curtis returned a check for the equivalent of five pages of advertising because it came from a patent medicine manufacturer, although the money would have met the magazine's payroll for three weeks. When Bok launched a campaign to improve small-house architecture he found architects unalterably opposed. Finally obtaining the assistance of one, he offered readers full building specifications and plans to scale.

"A storm of criticism now arose from architects and builders all over the country, the architects claiming that Bok was taking 'the bread out of their mouths' by the sale of plans, and local builders vigorously questioned the accuracy of the estimates. But Bok knew he was right and persevered. Slowly but surely he won the approval of the leading architects."[15]

Bok, who wrote an autobiography in the third person, conducted campaigns that would be considered tame today. Far more controversial problems are dealt with now, yet public opinion has so changed that the effect, so far as readers are concerned, is not very damaging.

---

[14] Paul Lazarsfeld, "Role of Criticism in Management of Mass Communications," in Wilbur Schramm, ed., *Communications in Modern Society* (Urbana, Ill.: University of Illinois Press, 1948), p. 195.

[15] Edward W. Bok, *The Americanization of Edward Bok* (New York: Charles Scribner's Sons, 1922), p. 241.

# Chapter 23

# Education and training
# for magazine journalism

Publishers of magazines, like those of newspapers, have in recent years obtained more and more of their personnel from the departments and schools of journalism. The Magazine Publishers Association, American Business Press, Inc., American Association of Industrial Editors, and other such groups have been making special efforts to interest journalism school students, as well as high school pupils, in journalism as a career and in magazine journalism in particular.

New employes of magazine publishing companies, nevertheless, still come largely from the older sources: other publishing companies, firms engaged in specialized manufacturing or services, and from totally unrelated activities. The idea of educating and training people for journalism itself is comparatively new, and preparing them for the magazine field is even newer.

Education for journalism goes back to the beginning of the century, but it was slow to catch on with the businessmen who manage the journalistic enterprises of the nation. This situation was the result of the fact that journalism itself in the United States has struggled to achieve professional status, that salary levels on many publications before the mid-century years were comparatively low, and that publishing was a risky business venture because of the changing nature of the American population and the relative instability of business in times of war and economic depression.

Such specialized education has been dominated by the newspaper industry, for the first deans and directors of the schools and departments of journalism usually were from the newspaper field. Until lately the newspaper business has been far more interested in encouraging journalism education than any other medium and still is in the forefront with its efforts to recruit students for the schools of journalism, provide scholarships, and underwrite research grants. It is still true, also, that most schools and departments prepare students mainly for the newspaper field.

But as the magazine world has shown more interest in obtaining staff members from the student bodies and the alumni of colleges and universities offering special training for its type of journalism, and as the schools themselves have offered more and more courses of direct value to the future magazinist, education for magazine journalism has found a place of its own, small though it be.

Today it is possible for a person to obtain elementary preparation for work in any department of a magazine publishing company and, at the same time, a sound general education. Although magazine journalism is a wide field, highly diversified as we have seen, college preparation is available for advertising, editorial, promotion, research, production, circulation, sales, merchandising, art, photography, public relations, and administration.

## Education and training

*Education* for magazine journalism is relatively new but well organized, for it is offered through accepted and stable educational institutions, i.e., established colleges and universities. At many the school of journalism is on a par with law, medicine, engineering, and other such specialties. *Training* for magazine journalism is not the same activity, is much older, and has little uniformity. At some institutions education and training are combined, but usually training alone is found in short courses and adult education programs.

A person who presents him or herself to be educated in magazine journalism prepares to study general education subjects such as are included in the social and natural sciences and the humanities as well as the general and specialized journalism and communications subjects.[1] Such a student seeks all the values in the experience of attending college. Sufficient specific technical courses that comprise his training for the occupation are included but are subordinated to the general education in such a program, particularly at the undergraduate level.

---

[1] Journalism encompasses the journalistic activities of newspapers, magazines, radio, television, and other media; communications covers in addition the non-journalistic activities; journalism, in regard to television, for example, is concerned with news writing, reporting, interpretation, and programming; communications takes in also all types of programs and what happens between sending and receiving.

A person who seeks only training for magazine journalism does not necessarily go to college at all. He may enroll for a six-week post-graduate program, for instance, consisting entirely of technical preparation, such as the summer Publishing Procedures Course at Radcliffe, which while on a college campus is not a full educational program. Or he may be taken on as an interne for six months or a year to go through one of the few informal training programs at several magazine publishing companies. There the trainee spends varying amounts of time in different departments, sampling them and learning their basic operations. At its end he may or may not be invited to stay on the staff.

In a sound college program the student is taught the basics of the occupation but also to be objective about it, to examine it critically, to think about it creatively. He is taught the best known techniques. In a training program the trainee learns the techniques of the individual firm and to be part of its organization. Usually a questioning and critical attitude is not expected.

## Craft or art?

Because magazine work is a craft rather than an art, it is practical to prepare for most of the duties described in this volume. Virtually all these practices and procedures can be taught. Malcolm Cowley, literary critic and historian, discriminates between teaching an art and teaching a craft, using writing as his example:

> The art, properly speaking, of writing cannot be taught, and neither can the other arts. But the craft of writing can be taught, like the crafts of painting and sculpture, and the craft is a necessary foundation for the art. The craft consists of all past experience and achievement that can be reduced to rules. The art consists of the personal contribution that goes beyond the rules and may some day become a rule in itself. Painters go to schools of painting; even Cézanne spent his years in a Paris atelier. Why shouldn't writers go to schools of writing, where they can produce trial works under skilled supervision, before they are ready to work for and by themselves?[2]

The personal contribution in magazine work is small in circulation, sales, and merchandising operations; it has been reduced steadily by machinery in the production end; it remains important in editorial and art and photography departments. Much advertising copy work cannot be reduced to rules; promotion is still new enough to leave room for the creative imagination. "Past experience and achievement" are sufficient to permit anyone who wishes to enter the magazine field to obtain training for many of the subordinate and even a large number of the supervisory positions.

---

[2] Malcolm Cowley, "The Teaching and Study of Writing (A Symposium)," *The Western Review,* Spring, 1950, p. 174.

*Seventeen*'s editors have sent young girls who aspire to work on the magazine a reprint of an article intended to disabuse them about the interest, romance, and glamour in magazine careers. To the remark that "Magazine work must be interesting" the article's author, Mrs. Alice Thompson, one-time editor-in-chief and publisher of *Seventeen,* said that the editor's unuttered thought is: "I'd better phone Sally to give her those tickets for tonight. It'll be ten o'clock before I finish correcting proofs."

The unspoken comment on the declaration, "I want to do creative work. I hate routine" is "Ten pages to get out today, every one of them to be checked to see if it has the right number of lines, the art work correctly sized, and every statement of fact checked and double checked. I'd like to do some creative work, too." [3]

## *The purposes of preparation*

Although many persons enter a vocation for which they are suited even though they go into it with no clear purpose except to make a living, those who select a more meaningful goal and are guided toward it by some articulate occupational philosophy are more likely to find congenial and widely rewarding employment. Further, persons who add to their clear objectives a knowledge of one or more special areas of knowledge and acquire technical preparation for magazine work go farther occupationally than persons of only broad preparation.

The reasons for choosing a particular career may be idealistic, selfish, or both. The few occupations selected for altruistic reasons are the ministry, priesthood, rabbinate, or some other religious vocation; perhaps government, medicine, social work, nursing, practice of the arts, and teaching. At least social purposes are stronger here if not all-controlling in every instance. These and other occupations like them involve primary concern for the welfare and happiness of others. At the opposite extreme are vocations which permit or require those engaged in them to concentrate on their own welfare, particularly on their own financial gain, with little or no regard for the effect upon others or the institutions in society.

Anyone examining magazine journalism as a possible career has a normal concern for survival and possession of enough material goods to be independent. He also feels normal impulses to live usefully and to engage in work that yields satisfactions beyond those obtainable from money-making alone, even though he may not have attained the moral stature of a St. Francis of Assisi or a Mohandas Gandhi. His motives, in other words, are mixed. If he wishes to clarify them, one way to do so is to ask himself why he is entering a magazine career and

---

[3] Alice Thompson, "I Want To Work on a Magazine," *Seventeen*, September, 1945. A reprint.

to set down his answer in writing, as the highly articulate person occasionally does.

He might note that: (1) Magazine offices have the time to produce better writing than the offices of more rapidly moving media. This means that a person concerned with writing for its own sake will find a hospitable atmosphere. (2) Magazines have more time to interpret and explain events to their readers; thus the work has greater depth. (3) Magazines also have the time to verify and check their material thoroughly and do considerable research on it, resulting in more dependable copy. (4) Magazines are interested in careful workmanship in printing and typography, in the use of color printing, and other technical aspects. (5) Magazines are read in more leisure than other publications except books, being issued less frequently, and therefore more thoroughly, which is gratifying to the serious author and journalist.

### General practitioner or specialist?

The general practitioner in magazine work is the person who understands the periodical world in a broad way but is not an expert on any of its individual operations. He also is a person who does not have command of a particular body of other knowledge on which he can write as an authority or on which he can serve as an expert editor.

The specialist, it follows, is the magazinist who has equipped himself particularly to be a writer of non-fiction, a copy editor, an administrator of magazine properties, a production expert, or a master of some other aspect of magazine work. Or he is a person who has more than usual knowledge of one or another of the hundreds of subject matter fields for which there are entire magazines or which are treated in general periodicals: government, labor, medicine, science, religion, sociology, economics, the arts, and dozens more.

At this time in the world's history the specialist holds the day. Life on this planet has become so complex that knowledge of specialties is imperative, if all people are not in time to be submerged in confusion and incomprehension and finally ruled by a few with superior brains who can understand at least some of the complexities. The ordinary citizen, with room in a lifetime only for basic general education and special training in some area where a living may be earned, depends upon the communicators, who include magazine journalists, to give him understanding of what is taking place in the world outside his own little segment of it.

In deciding whether he wants to become a generalist or a specialist in the magazine world, the prospective magazinist must realize that certain situations exist. One is that it is more difficult to prepare for a specialty than for general work in magazine journalism. The non-specialist, to be sure, must be familiar with common practices, and, in order to meet strong competition for openings have uncommonly good taste, artistic sense, imagination, or energy. But he does not need to know anything about some such technical area as the drug business, steel industry, or soap manufacture to work on, say, *Pageant, American Girl,* or *Ebony.*

As a specialist, he does not need wide knowledge of a given field to handle a routine job on a business magazine, but he must understand that field thoroughly if he is to rise to the top in any except the business department, where also it is an advantage if not a necessity.

In approaching his training for magazine work, the aspirant must realize the difficulty of acquiring a specialty while attending grade school, high school, and college. But it is possible to gain a start on a specialty by working at the same trade or profession in summer or other vacation periods. Not much of a specialty is gained by jerking sodas or working at a resort one summer and hitchhiking across the continent or teaching swimming at a camp another, although there is valuable knowledge of people to be acquired in such work. It is better to accumulate experience in some one field summertimes while studying writing techniques and that field, if possible, during the college year. Then when he is through college the student not only has been helped in knowing how to write but also has something to write about. By all-year-round work on a magazine in his special field or by writing about his specialty for general periodicals, he has given himself background and is ready to begin specialization in earnest.

The place to be sought by anyone in magazine work whether specialized or general depends upon (1) background, (2) ability to acquire a specialty if this is lacking, and (3) natural interests and talents. Opportunities in specialized magazine work have not generally been realized, but journalism school graduates, journalists in non-magazine occupations left stranded by failing or merged publications, and specialists who can write or sell are appreciating them.

## Magazine study

Magazine journalism education is slowly expanding along the lines followed by newspaper training. By 1972 the American Council on Education for Journalism had accredited, at schools of journalism, five specific courses of study or sequences in the magazine. These programs are at Iowa, Missouri, Northwestern, Syracuse, Oklahoma, and Texas. In them, as well as in other programs, are courses in article and short story writing plus others in production, survey of magazines, specialized magazines, company magazines, and management, editing, and publishing of periodicals. Magazine and newspaper studies are often combined in a sequence called news-editorial. Emphasis is on the editorial operations because here is the center of student interest and the strength of teaching staffs.

Typical preparation centers on a group of core courses: news writing and reporting, copy editing and make-up, law of the press, ethics and history of the press and communications, and printing, typography, and photography, to mention only the ones usually required. These are offered in the last three years of a four-year curriculum, with magazine courses available each year but climaxing the final two semesters. Electives cover advertising, marketing, and advanced courses in the core subjects.

All accredited magazine programs lead to a bachelor's degree in journalism or in the liberal arts with a journalism major or joint major. A few schools with graduate programs offer opportunity for advanced magazine study. Whether or not they do depends upon the research courses available for more intensive study of the field. The five-year program of some schools leads to a master's degree.

Those institutions offering the doctor of philosophy degree in journalism or mass communications make it possible to do still further advanced work in the magazine area, sometimes encouraging research in magazine influence, history, and biography.

All institutions that offer journalism courses to some substantial extent provide preparation in part for careers in the magazine field. Most schools and departments of journalism are not so highly specialized as are the larger ones with accredited magazine programs, or those that have selected several specialties on which to concentrate, as have Iowa State University (agricultural, science, engineering, and home economics journalism) and the University of Maryland (industrial journalism), for example.

The author of this book believes that selection of a special area while in college gives the student the advantage of a clear goal and enables him better to fit into an occupation that increasingly is made up of specialists rather than general practitioners. But specialization must be coupled with broad, general studies and enough rudimentary training to prepare him for journalistic work for newspapers, book publishers, and even in small positions in radio and television stations. The best programs of magazine study now available provide this versatility.

Journalism educators realize that magazine careers are possible for people without college preparation. If this were not true hundreds of eminent magazinists of the past (all those before 1900) would not have made their marks. General college education alone and self-study and experience equivalent to college training have been helpful in the past. But today, considering the developments within the industry and the competition between personnel, formal preparation is more than ever valuable.

A gifted and determined journalist will make his career even without preliminary training; it simply is easier and more efficient with the proper preparation. Journalism education quickens a young person's knowledge of background and techniques and helps him discern his aptitudes and talents more rapidly.

With the founding of journalism departments and schools, beginning in the first decade of the present century, more and more would-be journalists combined general college work with special preparation. By the middle of the century it was common to find writers and editors (more often than advertising, circulation, promotion, or other personnel) identified with journalism schools. Among them have been Ben Hibbs (Kansas), former *Saturday Evening Post* editor and later senior editor, *The Reader's Digest;* Wade Nichols (Northwestern), former editor, *Redbook,* and later editor of *Good Housekeeping;* Frederick G. Vosburgh (Syracuse), retired editor, *National Geographic,* and vice-president of the Society; John Mack Carter (Missouri), former editor of *McCall's* and later of *Ladies' Home Journal;* and Dick Hansen (Iowa State), editor of *Successful Farming.*

## Specialized magazine education

Although six universities have fully accredited magazine journalism programs, several others that do not seek accreditation or have not yet been approved have sequences of considerable size and merit. And virtually all of the approximately one hundred institutions that offer majors in journalism teach some courses on the magazine.

Even where there is no specific magazine major, a number of universities offer specialized programs that include some attention to magazines.[4] Taking a few specialties as examples:

Agricultural journalism: Kansas State includes in its program for this specialty a course in magazine article writing; South Dakota State includes magazine editing, and Iowa State University offers feature writing. Usually magazine aspects at these institutions and others offering agricultural journalism preparation, such as Cornell University, Wisconsin (which has a separate Department of Agricultural Journalism), and Texas Agricultural and Mechanical College, are included in general journalism courses as well as certain seminars.

Religious journalism: Since most religious publications are magazines, preparation for this field must include study of the periodical. At Syracuse University, which has a postgraduate program in this specialty as well as a related one called literacy journalism, students usually study the magazine in general, religious writing, magazine article writing and marketing, and editing.

Home economics journalism: At South Dakota State girls studying home economics journalism are expected to enroll in the magazine editing course; at Syracuse they combine their home economics with a

---

[4] Detailed information may be obtained by writing the American Council on Education for Journalism, whose latest address is listed in the *Editor & Publisher International Year Book* or *Journalism Quarterly.*

full magazine sequence, and at Iowa State home economics journalists write and edit a monthly magazine, *Today's Woman.*

Industrial journalism (company publications): Twenty-two schools or departments, by 1965, required an industrial journalism course in certain sequences; 28 more listed such a course as an elective.[5]

## *Education goes higher*

Increasingly it is necessary for persons who expect to arrive at executive positions with certain departments of magazine publishing companies to go beyond the bachelor's and even the master's degree. Especially is such advanced training and education needed in research and marketing divisions. A top official of *This Week,* with one of the larger salaries in the magazine business, went on for his doctorate in marketing while in his 40's. The director of communication for a large automobile manufacturer in Detroit, already author of an authoritative book on company magazines and papers, resumed his college career by working for a doctorate in the field of communications.

In the editorial department, preference is likely to be given to the man or woman possessed of a master's degree in either the magazine's subject specialty or in journalism itself.

An illustration of this trend toward postgraduate study is to be found in the personnel of the Research Department of the Chilton Company, one of the large business magazine as well as general book publishing firms. Here are the educational backgrounds of the department's principal officers:[6]

Director of research (also a company vice-president): B.A.; course work toward Ph.D. in mathematical statistics and quality control engineering; summer study in courses on planning, marketing, strategy, and tactics.

Manager, merchandising research division: B.A., M.A.

Manager, survey research division: B.S., special operations research course.

Manager, industrial research division: B.S., postgraduate courses in marketing; special aeronautical engineering courses.

Manager, communications research: B.S., M.S., Ph.D.

Research associate: B.S., M.A., completing Ph.D.

Research associate: B.S., special courses in physiological psychology and marketing.

Research associate: B.A., advanced study in literature.

---

[5] Richard P. Goodrick, "Industrial Journalism Trends in the Continental U.S." A report compiled in cooperation with the International Council of Industrial Editors, 1965.

[6] "Who's Who in Marketing and Communications Research at Chilton Research Services" (Philadelphia: Chilton Company, 1962).

Research associate: B.S., completing M.B.A.
Study coordinator: B.A., completing M.B.A.
Supervisor of coding and tabulation: B.S.
Supervisor of sampling: B.S., M.B.A., working on Ph.D.

These twelve persons among them all have the B.A. or B.S. degree, four have the M.A. or M.S., one has the Ph.D., three are working toward this degree, two are working for the master's, and five have done other advanced study not leading necessarily to a degree. Of the five in managerial positions, three have or are completing the Ph.D.

## School and college experience

Most high schools and colleges have newspapers; many also have yearbooks. Magazines are no longer common in high schools but humor, literary, and a few public affairs and technical periodicals are to be found on college and university campuses. It should be obvious that young people hoping for places in journalism derive benefit from working on advertising, circulation, editorial, and other staffs of these publications, many of which are better written and produced than some of the commercial periodicals. Obvious as it should be, however, only a small proportion of the journalism students put in time on these papers and magazines unless they are required to by their course of study. Often the qualified personnel are so few that on the typical college campus it is a small group that does most of the hard work of selling advertising space, writing news stories, articles, short stories, poetry, and editorials, editing the copy, and distributing the publication.

Successful magazine writers and artists whose first experience and outlets were on college magazines include James Thurber, Max Shulman, J. P. Marquand, Peter Arno, Robert Benchley, Gluyas Williams, Irwin Edman, Rockwell Kent, Paul Gallico, Abner Dean, Corey Ford, and that noted contributor to the *Harvard Lampoon,* Henry Wadsworth Longfellow. Many another noted name might be listed, for college magazines are nothing new in journalism, as we have seen in Chapter 17. In any case, employers usually are much interested to see, on a job applicant's dossier, if he or she has worked on his college publications.

## Correspondence courses

Journalism education, especially in the magazine field, is relatively so recent that it was not available to many men and women before they began the work in which they are engaged, such as the older, top executives. Moreover, they cannot easily leave their positions for full-time study at colleges and universities offering training or refresher courses. For them, therefore, correspondence work in journalism is of interest. Its value as training is somewhat limited; most journalism techniques are best learned under laboratory and field conditions, by constant practice under skilled supervision, which correspondence courses cannot provide. Article and fiction writing, however, lend themselves readily to mail instruction and have been staples for years. They can help the new writer learn his craft. While not a substitute for more closely supervised work on the campus, they have been useful to commercial writers of both fiction and non-fiction. Several universities offer correspondence courses in professional writing, among the most successful being the Universities of Oklahoma, Minnesota, and Wisconsin. Commercial correspondence schools also offer training by means of their own materials and staff.

## Internships

Since 1967 the Magazine Publishers Association and its associated organization, the American Society of Magazine Editors, have sponsored a summer internship program in New York to introduce college journalism students to magazine journalism.

During the first program, which ran six weeks, this plan placed 35 students on 29 participating magazines. It focused on editorial training. Twenty-three MPA member universities were represented. Later, internees worked for ten weeks. Twenty interns of the first four years were working at magazines by 1971.

Over the past several decades various individual firms have sponsored internships, usually on such specialized periodicals as those issued by the Fairchild Publications, the Reuben H. Donnelley Corporation, *Christian Century,* the Chilton Company, and the publishing arms of the Southern Baptist and the American Baptist Conventions.

Whether the aspiring and inspired magazinist goes to college for a general education or a combination of general and journalism education, or can manage only evening school classes, works with an agent-critic or with occasional courses by correspondence, he benefits from this preparation. And leaders in the field are recognizing the value of special training. Robert E. Kenyon, executive vice-president of the Magazine Publishers Association, told Medill School of Journalism students at Northwestern that "Magazine publishing . . . needs talents of many kinds, but especially editorial talent; that is to say, a talent for writing and a talent for discovering, for encouraging, for inspiring, for guiding—in short, for editing the work of others. It needs mature, experienced talent today. For tomorrow it needs a pool of native, latent talent that can be trained in schools of liberal arts and journalism, serving its apprenticeship in many ways, and come, at the appropriate time, into positions of responsibility and leadership in the craft of creative publishing." [7]

---

[7] "Creative Publishing," an address delivered Nov. 30, 1960, at Northwestern University, Evanston, Illinois. (New York: Magazine Publishers Association.)

# Chapter 24

# Breaking into the magazine world

"J UST WHAT will I be expected to do?"

This question is asked by people thinking of magazine work as a career more often than "What is the salary?" A wise question, the answer may weaken or strengthen the resolve to enter the magazine field as a vocation.

A young woman dreaming of meeting famous writers and seeking her by-line may awaken quickly on being told that for her, long before she gets that by-line, there may be months of proofreading, hunting in the library for material on the origin of tea or peanut oil or the newest types of storm windows. A similar awakening may take place in a man on fire to lead a mad world to the truth as published in magazine editorials he would like to write, when he is told that he must begin by learning to operate a camera and write fillers for the back pages of a business magazine.

In general what the beginner as well as the old hand is asked to do should be evident from the preceding chapters of this book. It may not be what he or she expected but it must be done; few can hope to skip the realities of journalism. It takes time for an employer to discern abilities of employes; if talent and skill are there, they eventually will be recognized and put to use. Few lights remain hidden under magazine office bushels. A department head engages new staff because he needs the manpower; only the inefficient administrator lets discovered talent go to waste. Too many administrators bungle this part of their responsibilities, to be sure, but, by and large, careers are fulfilled despite this.

### Aptitude tests

Before going to work in the magazine world or beginning a course of study in preparation for being an editor, circulation manager, or some other executive, anyone should evaluate his aptitudes for this profession. Although aptitude testing has become more nearly accurate since it was begun earlier in the century, as yet few tests are available for journalists and none specifically for magazinists.

The great magazine writers, editors, or publishers of the nineteenth century never heard of aptitude tests. Given an opportunity in the field, the extraordinarily talented and highly intelligent person can achieve a position of influence or financial success even without prior testing. For years, choice of occupation was dictated or was the result of hit-or-miss choices. Consequently many a square peg went into a round hole. Aptitude testing does eliminate obvious misfits, in journalism as in other occupations, although it does not mean that an individual is necessarily unable to fit himself later if a test shows him unsuited at the time of the testing.

A general aptitude can be established by one or more tests commonly used by educators and applied psychologists. These examinations guide toward a suitable occupation by revealing special abilities.

Interest in or enthusiasm for journalism or some type of magazine work specifically does not necessarily ensure aptitude for it. But anyone who has about the same interests and ability as persons already engaged in journalism is likely to be successful in it. At least a leaning in that direction is indicated.

Persons of many different aptitudes can fit into magazine work. Under the usual misconception of magazine journalism as writing only, anyone determined to find a place in it may submit to tests that measure only literary ability. But general tests of aptitudes as well as of mechanical, artistic, or other abilities may indicate other aptitudes of equal value to magazine journalism. Because magazines are media of communication as well as technical products, more than literary ability is needed by their staffs.

Dr. Walter B. Pitkin, the Columbia University journalism teacher who wrote *Life Begins at Forty* long ago, pointed out that "There is no such job as 'journalism' any more than there is the job of engineering. Within the field of printing and publishing we find almost as many distinct tasks as in the engineering fields." [1]

The few journalism aptitude tests devised so far are either

---

[1] Walter B. Pitkin and Robert F. Harrel, *Vocational Studies in Journalism* (New York: Columbia University Press, 1931), p. 83.

superficial, incomplete, discarded, or experimental. Writers' correspondence schools and writing coaches give tests, but they are of little value. The journalism-literary tests that may be taken at accredited universities and colleges are dependable although not penetrating, for they show only broad abilities.

Employers now place more reliance on testing for specific abilities, such as asking an applicant to compose a critique of the magazine, write a trial article, edit copy, outline an advertising campaign, or rewrite prepared material.

## *The beginner's duties*

The duties and obligations of magazine top brass and immediate subordinates have been examined in earlier chapters. The detailed responsibilities of editors-in-chief, advertising managers, and circulation directors are not a concern of the beginner on a big magazine, at least not at first. The publisher may be seen once a month as he walks through the offices with a distinguished visitor inspecting the surroundings; perhaps the editor is glimpsed only inside a paneled office except when he comes down to earth to socialize at a staff party. True, on some big periodicals exclusiveness is abhorred by the boss, who works in his shirt sleeves surrounded by all the little bosses in their shirt sleeves with the lower ranking staffers near at hand.

The beginner's work is determined by the size of the magazine. If he goes to a small publication, he may be important sooner than anticipated, because there he works more closely with top people to whom he can be more helpful if he understands their jobs. In a month's time, on the medium-size or small magazine, he may edit copy; write headings; prepare captions; write picture story continuity; undertake research; obtain pictures and other illustrations; prepare bibliographies and source lists for authors or staffers; cover assignments, sometimes out of town; review books, plays, or movies; write news stories and news features; read proof; make up dummies; prepare page layouts; copy manuscripts; take dictation; file letters and typescripts; act as first reader on manuscripts; schedule copy; dig for filler; check on picture releases; obtain permissions to use quotations; wrap copies of the magazine; trundle promotion mailings to a post office; and do dozens of other chores that fall under departmental routines. All this may sound overpowering, but the jobs are done one at a time, and the breadth of experience gained is worth the strain. The knowledge acquired is an advantage of working for a small magazine on which the employe gains an overview. This broad approach at first is denied those whose work is on a big periodical, for they are restricted to a few operations done over and over.

Duties on a large magazine must be examined department by department. Secretarial, clerical, and stenographic work is done for all (details of those positions are readily accessible in other sources) and have little to do specifically with journalism and require no journalistic skill. However, the typist, clerk, or secretary with modest journalistic skills needed in the peculiar work of any department possesses a bridge across into journalism, printing, advertising, or some other more specialized occupation than taking dictation or filing letters.

**Advertising department.** Beginners here not classified as clerical or stenographic are few. They serve as assistant to (not assistant) the advertising production manager or the chief copy writer. If the department does research or promotion, the newcomers may aid in this work. They are not expected to do more than prepare copy for simple leaflets, booklets, and display cards; make duplicates of completed advertising copy, even if only via a copying machine; try a hand at direct mail letters; compile reports on assigned subjects; suggest ways to promote products advertising in the magazine; check and verify statistical tables, charts, and graphs; develop simple production ideas; handle routine correspondence; deal with complaints; grant service requests; and, where not done mechanically, address, fold, stamp, and distribute mailings of checking copies or promotional materials.

**Art department.** No beginner could expect to find a place here above the clerical or stenographic level without having artistic talent, skill in photography, or knowledge of the uses made of art and photographic work. If the qualified beginner is not assigned to take pictures or to help an experienced photographer with picture assignments, which on magazines (except those reporting general news) are more static than on newspapers, he may do photo retouching or the smaller drawing and painting assignments.

The assistant in this department helps arrange lights on location; keeps the photographers' schedules; interviews models or temporary subjects; takes notes for captions; makes appointments; goes on expeditions for missing props; keeps track of properties regularly used; sees that they are in proper order; and draws up specifications for materials that must be made or built if they cannot be bought or borrowed.

Assistants working on the art rather than the photo side at first spend their time doing similar work for the artists, all the way from keeping the studio dressing room in order through working with models or serving as a model to helping produce decorations or lettered headings. An art assistant sits in with an experienced staffer when illustrations and typography are being discussed or produced, may be given the task of working out the size of the completed engraving of picture or illustration, and keeps records of art work ordered, checking sizes before and after work is done.

**Business department.** Journalistic personnel as such has no place in this department, at top, center, or bottom. The beginner enters as office boy or girl and messenger; up the scale are clerks, book-keepers, accountants, cashiers, payroll assistants, and other standard business office personnel.

**Circulation department.** Insofar as some types of circulation work are associated with journalism, involving as they do handling of copies of the magazine and important knowledge about the public's reception of it, acquaintance with magazine work in general is desirable and can be used by the beginner through service as subscription salesman or on a solicitation crew or outfit distributing sample copies. Assistants to the circulation manager keep records, do promotion work assigned the department, correspond with field forces or circulation auditing groups to which the magazine belongs, plan copy for mail campaigns, and approach outside sales agencies to smooth the way for cooperation.

The largest magazines have, within their circulation departments, divisions concerned with promotion, work with agencies, art, production, statistics, newsstand distribution, and subscription fulfillment. Says the MPA to college students: "There is room . . . for management men, contact men, writers, artists, statisticians. And most of all there is room for people with ideas."[2]

**Editorial department.** Being the center of magazine journalism, this department offers the new and raw employe several starting places that bring his training and aptitude into early, if not immediate, use.

That lowest common denominator, the editorial assistant, exists like a weed in the magazine garden, but is far more useful. Here is the real general factotum of magazine work, equaled only by the printer's devil of the printing plant and the cub reporter on the newspaper. When Theodore Lustig was an editorial assistant on an engineering magazine he did routine writing and editing, but as he learned more about the business and technical publication worlds' operations and the technical field, he rose to be associate editor of *Construction* and then editor of *Mechanical Contractor.* Among Muriel Friedman's duties the first days she was an assistant on *Seventeen* was toting clothes for the fashion photographer; but after a few months she wrote an article which, while drastically cut, found its way into print with her by-line. The editorial assistant does a little of everything and no great deal of anything until his or her strong points are discovered or an opening in which they are needed occurs.

Here and there the editorial assistant is called a junior editor and may be a beginner in any department. "She handles details . . . gradually builds up know-how," the editors will say to applicants.

---

[2] "Magazine Circulation as a Career" (New York: Magazine Publishers Association, undated).

"She may get her start as secretary, as the winner of a contest, or on the basis of experience," they tell a woman applicant.

Another magazine post connected with the editorial department but of service to others is that of librarian—reference or research, as the case may be. The main duties, which usually but not necessarily always go to persons with some library training, are indexing and cross-indexing books, periodicals, newspapers, and clippings marked by staff members for filing; keeping supplies of magazines, competing as well as home publications; and gathering resource material on subjects within the magazine's specialty. The more a magazine concentrates on one field of knowledge, as does a business or technical journal, the more essential is its library.

On the large consumer magazines catering to women the neophyte may begin as fashion, feature, beauty, or job information assistant. Thumbnail sketches of two of these positions, written by the Condé Nast offices for the information of applicants, are typical:

> The Feature Assistant helps her boss, the feature editor, plan and produce the special articles in the magazine. She reads and edits manuscript . . . does research and writes. She needs wide and informed interests, writing and research experience.
> The Beauty Assistant helps her editor to prepare beauty features, does part of the research herself. She also answers reader mail . . . writes some beauty copy. She can move up to her job from secretary in the department.[3]

If editorial has its own research staff, a college-trained beginner may begin in that branch. Research sometimes is a general service department; wherever placed it is a logical and acceptable starting spot for the newcomer. The prerequisites for research are by now familiar: a broad educational background, a knowledge of reference books and book literature, familiarity with the interview technique, the capacity to be meticulously accurate and extraordinarily thorough. Writing ability is assumed, for without it the research results could not be conveyed understandably.

On small magazines a staff member who is handy with the camera is much appreciated, for the person who can both write and take pictures is possessed of a desirable combination of abilities.

**Production department.** Because most production work is done outside a magazine's own offices, except in the unusual instances where the company owns its own printing and engraving equipment, there are few job openings in this department for the beginner. The apprentice printer and other printing work beginners move along paths separated from journalism.

Editorial, advertising, and promotion may employ proofreaders

---

[3] "Do You Want a Job in Publishing?" (New York: Condé Nast Publications, 1948), pp. 4–5.

who sit in the employing department or work in offices near the mechanical plant in a distant city. Other types of production assistants who rise from clerical ranks may help schedule material and supervise proofreading, do emergency writing, and issue reminders to editorial and advertising department executives on deadlines and overdue material. They check on preparation of editorial and advertising copy for the printer, verifying specifications for type size, and go over make-up and layout plans to be sure everything fits. They are expected to be sharp-eyed copy- and proofreaders and to know the principles of typography and printing. Soon after Robert H. Williams completed his undergraduate work in 1949 at the Syracuse University School of Journalism, where he had taken courses in the basics of the graphic arts and magazine production, he was deeply involved in production of farm magazines whose staffs he joined at Ithaca, N.Y. Before long he was named production editor, and in a year he was able to re-design one of the magazines to give it more modern typography and format. Barbara Love, also a Syracuse journalism graduate, in 1959 went from its magazine sequence to the staff of the *New York Lumber Trade Journal* and then to *Sponsor* as production

*Fig. 24.1.* Five editorial career stories at one table during a Magazine Publishers session: (seated) Mrs. Betsy Talbot Blackwell, then editor, *Mademoiselle;* Robert Stein, then editor, *McCall's;* Edward Weeks, editor until 1966, *Atlantic;* (standing) Richard J. Babcock, onetime editor, *Farm Journal;* and William B. Arthur, while editor of *Look.* *(MPA Photo)*

editor, then to associate editor and production editor. She resigned to become president of a book firm and edit *Foremost Women in Communications.*

**Promotion department.** Serving all other departments as it often does, this one engages personnel with many capabilities. The new and inexperienced but trained employe may begin as an assistant to the promotion director, assistant editor of the company periodical issued for the employes, researcher, copy writer, promotion material writer, or photographer. So diversified is the work that any skill possessed by the magazinist can be put to use in this department.

Promotion assistants help prepare advertising and circulation sales campaign materials—letters, leaflets, booklets, posters. If the firm's publicity work is lodged in its promotion office, they write news stories, magazine articles, radio and television scripts, advertising copy, and slide show scenarios.

The employe publication staff of a magazine publishing company is one of the most desirable spots for the novice, for here small magazine work can be practised in the environment of a big magazine and in sight of opportunities it offers. Transition to the parent magazine's or magazines' staff is comparatively easy for an employe who is on the ground and in position to demonstrate ability under observation by those who make personnel decisions. Lucile Stolteben, for a time editor of the monthly house publication, *Esquire Ink,* brought to the position five years' work on dailies and weeklies in Iowa and Illinois, after attending Clarke College in Dubuque, Iowa, where she majored in dramatics and English. The job with Esquire, Inc., required her, as she sought news, to get in touch every month with people in all departments of the company. The copy, most of which she wrote or rewrote herself, was integrated with material mailed in by reporters in the corporation's offices in other cities. She also obtained and planned a pictorial section for her little magazine.

Then there was Joseph Goodyear, a war veteran who completed a magazine sequence at college. His first duties were like those of many college graduates who go into magazine positions directly from a university. An aviator during the war, Joe was aiming at an aviation journalism career. But when ready for a job, economic conditions in air transport were forcing that specialized magazine field to fire rather than hire. So Joe looked elsewhere and landed on the staff of *Drug Topics Red Book,* a yearbook and directory issued by the Topics Publishing Company, Inc., in New York, publisher of *Drug Topics* and other magazines. The *Red Book's* new staffer knew little more about the drug business than anyone learns from buying toothpaste and aspirin tablets, but he had successfully passed the tests for the job. What was his reaction? Four months later he wrote:

> I have been working here for more than four months now, and I'm quite happy about the whole thing. The beauty of this job is that

I am not a bolt turner. I see my job through from start to finish, picking up much valuable experience en route.

. . . I am responsible for all the text of the *Red Book,* which amounts to about 75 of its 600 pages. About 30 of my pages are concerned with science and research in drugs. The remainder is made up of merchandising features . . . and animal health.

. . . I do all the research, both technical and market. I prepare the rough drafts and follow through to the finished copy. Together with the printer and the big wheel, I choose the type and general layout. I read proof and dummy, etc.[4]

The next year Joe was moved to the editorial part of the main book, *Drug Topics* magazine itself, as associate news editor, continuing some of the duties described, but taking on such new ones as editorial research and the writing of long articles and features. From that post he moved to the editorship of a big industrial company publication, to an advertising agency art directorship, to a prescription drug ad agency, and then to the senior vice presidency of one of the nation's largest advertising agencies.

And it was a company magazine that was the entry into the magazine world for Barbara Michalak, who later was connected with *School Executive, Consumer Reports,* and *Seventeen-at-School* magazines. Here is her story, as she told it:

My first job out of journalism school was typical of one of the largest groups of magazine journalism jobs. I was editor of the 16-page *Echo,* published every month for the employees and customers of Ithaca's Morse Chain Company. If you're thinking that it must be dull writing about drive chains and conveyor belts, you're wrong. It was wonderful fun, because it was about people.

I wrote a whodunit starring the inspector who found out how an order of links skipped an important manufacturing step; I interviewed night-shift men and wrote about their topsy-turvy lives; a combined feature on an employee who drove in stock car races and another who restored antique autos produced one of my favorite headlines: "Some like 'em hot, some like 'em old."

I got intensive, all-round experience. Besides writing and editing, I did my own layout, sized cuts, read proof, dealt with printer, photographer and photo-engraver—and finally ran the mailing envelopes through the addressograph machine. In my spare time, I was secretary to the Safety Director.[5]

### Salaries on magazines

Salary figures are an unsound basis for deciding upon an occupation and even undependable as a clue to actual earnings. Yet many persons incline toward or away from some position on haphazard information.

For many years the whole field of journalism, including the magazine industry, had the reputation of being low salaried, as indeed it

---

[4] Letter to the author.

[5] "Women Have Fun and Future on Magazines," *The ESSPA Magazine,* April 1960, p. 10.

was. The charge was based on a comparison with such other professions as the law, medicine, dentistry, and engineering.

But as non-journalistic fields, and even certain areas related to journalism, such as advertising and public relations, began to win people away from newspaper and magazine work, earnings for staff members were increased. Today journalistic salaries rank among the better ones. A 1960 survey of college graduates with bachelor's degrees received in 1958 reveals that journalism majors ranked tenth in size of salaries received.[6] The only fields standing higher than journalism, in the forty major areas covered, were pharmacy, engineering, military science, physics, health, architecture, business and commerce, earth sciences, and economics. From a Columbia University survey made later we learn that magazine employes led among those who reported they had received better pay than they had hoped. The results were: magazines, 65%; radio-television, 60%; newspapers, 40%; public relations, 35%; teaching, 30%.[7]

Several considerations should be kept in mind when interpreting raw salary figures:

1. Salaries vary widely within the magazine industry. For instance, identical positions may bring far different salaries according to locality. A given position in New York City may have a salary 25 per cent higher than the same position on a magazine in a small city or town because an employer in a metropolitan area must consider the higher cost of living in his area. In the small town there may be little or no transportation expense, lunches may be cheaper, wear and tear on clothing and nerves may be far less.

2. In all journalism, the possibilities of extra earnings through freelance writing, editing, art work, production work, or research are great. Countless numbers of magazines can boast of staffers who also write books, articles, stories, and other journalistic and literary material in their spare time or are paid extra for work done on their own time on sister publications issued by the same firm. Being in a particular position often brings such opportunities.

3. Benefits commonly added to the base salary must be considered, such as commissions and bonuses resulting from achievements in increasing the circulation or greater space sales or advertising revenue. Two magazines offering the same base salary may not, however, offer the same additional benefits when it comes to group health insurance, medical insurance, life insurance, a retirement plan, sick leaves, and vacations.

4. Chances to participate in ownership of the firm are important.

---

[6] National Science Foundation Report, Washington, D.C., 1963.
[7] "Publishers Elect Maier President, Name Milwaukee Executive—Dean Cautions Press," New York *Times*, April 27, 1962.

Some publishing companies award employes shares of stock; later these stockholders may become executives. Another consideration is a more rare benefit, profit-sharing plans.

Some median, raw salary figures follow:[8]

Business magazine beginners in all phases: $4,500 to $6,000 annually; editors-in-chief: $11,000 to $20,000; managing editors: $8,000 to $18,000; other editors: $6,500 to $15,000; promotion, and art directors: $8,000 to $18,000; circulation and production managers: $8,000 to $18,000. The annual survey by the Newspaper Fund in 1967 showed that all journalism areas were paying starting salaries of more than $100 weekly. Magazines stood at $113.27 for those with bachelor's degrees; $141.52 for those with master's.

A report by the Newspaper Guild on some of its magazine members indicates starting and top minimum figures for writers and editors. These range from the $295 a week of an associate editorial director at one magazine to $217 for an assistant editor at another. Second in rank was a newsmagazine writer, with $278.63. Advertising salesmen earned from $238.24 at an opinion magazine to $194.75 at a public affairs and literary periodical.[9]

John Fischer, former editor-in-chief of *Harper's,* while addressing students at the University of Minnesota in 1962, dramatized these differences by saying that one of the two main reasons he moved from newspapers to magazines was money. He had decided that if he continued in newspapers and wire services (he had worked for both the Associated Press and the United Press International and on newspapers in Oklahoma and Texas) he and his wife could not afford to have children or if they did he could not provide for them. The other reason was that he was "increasingly dissatisfied with the kind of reporting I was doing. I found I had to work too fast under certain limitations which made it impossible for me to do the best kind of reporting."[10]

Since the TNG report quoted above was printed, new contracts have raised the figures in some instances. By mid-1970 the new high weekly minimum for writers, and photographers at a magazine for consumers had reached $321.72.

Top minimums for editors at Scholastic Magazines, for example, went to $290 in 1969. Late that year *New Republic* advertising salesmen rose to a top minimum of $260.40 and staff writers to $256.23 a week. Comparable increases were won at *Saturday Review* by the

---

[8] "Careers in the Business Press" (New York: American Business Press, 1967).
[9] "Magazine Top Minimums," *The Guild Reporter,* Oct. 24, 1964.
[10] "Magazine and Newspaper Journalism: A Comparison," in Ralph D. Casey (ed.), *The Press in Perspective* (Baton Rouge, La.: Louisiana State University Press, 1963), pp. 198–99.

Newspaper Guild in 1970. It should be noted how frequently changes occur, shifting with cost-of-living figures and according to contract agreements.

### Some top salaries

As in all areas of communications, the highest salaries go to chairmen of the board, the company presidents, and holders of other high-ranking posts. For an idea of the highest financial returns possible in the magazine industry one need only consult these lists[11] (these persons also often own shares of stocks):

Executives of broadcasting firms receive far higher salaries, however, than those of either newspaper or magazine publishing companies. (See Table 24.1.)

### Job satisfaction

A clue to the reaction of people working on magazine staffs was contained in the study referred to earlier and released in 1962 by the Graduate School of Journalism at Columbia University. Dean Edward Barrett said that the survey, which was of one hundred graduates of the school who had been out from two to eleven years or an average of six, showed that an increasing number of graduates, although trained for newspaper work, are shifting out of it into magazines and other areas.

"How many report the job satisfactions higher than expected?" Dean Barrett continued in his report. "Twenty per cent of those with newspapers and wire services, 25 per cent of those in teaching, 40 per cent of those in public relations, 65 per cent of those in radio-television, and 75 per cent of those on magazines."[12]

In the specialized area of company magazines the Survey Committee of the then International Council of Industrial Editors found evidence of the high degree of satisfaction of magazine work. A report in which 1,600 editors participated brought into view the reasons for liking industrial editing, with these results:[13]

Income, 4.3%; position status, 4.6%; promotional potential, 6.4%; personal satisfaction, 75%; other, 3.4%; no answer, 6.3%. Personal satisfaction is more than ten times higher than any other reason.

### Unions and magazines

Executives of magazines—publishers, circulation managers, advertising directors, editors mainly—have numerous associations for carry-

---

[11] *The Gallagher Report*, Vol. XVI, No. 21, 1968.
[12] *Loc. cit.*, New York *Times*.
[13] *Operation Tapemeasure* (Akron, Ohio: International Council of Industrial Editors, 1963), p. 15.

TABLE 24.1

| Title | Total Annual Remuneration |
|---|---|
| President of firm publishing news, picture, and other magazines and books | $166,800 |
| Editor-in-chief of same firm | 166,500 |
| Editor, weekly public affairs magazine, and vice-president of firm | 139,917 |
| President of firm publishing picture, women's, business, and other magazines and media | 125,596 |
| President of firm issuing business periodicals and in general book publishing | 104,011 |
| President, one of above picture magazines | 90,856 |
| Vice-president, news magazine and picture magazine and other media-issuing firms | 46,267 |

ing out their purposes and helping solve their problems, as we have seen in Chapter 3 and in those devoted to certain types of magazines. They are as general as the Magazine Publishers Association and as specialized as the Association of Screen Magazine Publishers.

Non-executive personnel claim the same right to organize for furtherance of their purposes and unity in solving their problems. They have set up two types of organizations: professional groups and trade unions.

The professional groups include executives as well as rank-and-file employes, are supported largely by writers, editors, and artists, and usually concern themselves with professional standards and social activities rather than economic problems and social welfare. One exception is the Authors League of America, with its subdivisions, Authors Guild, Dramatists Guild, Radio Writers Guild, and Screen Writers Guild. The League is a professional organization rather than a literary club. Among its objectives are obtaining adequate copyright legislation, fair dealings between members and publishing companies, better working conditions and payment, adjustment of disputes, and enforcement of standard contracts between authors and publishers. Writers of all types of magazine material as well as book authors join the League through the Guild.

Trade union groups affecting the magazine industry include chiefly those of the printing industry, which is highly organized. Separate organizations exist for compositors, pressmen, engravers, electrotypers, stereotypers, and binders. Letterpress printers have one union and offset lithographers another, and each is affiliated with a different overhead group. The principal unions are: International Typographical Union, Amalgamated Lithographers of America, International Printing Pressmen's and Assistants' Union of North America, International Photoengravers' Union, Electrotypers' and Stereotypers' Union, International Brotherhood of Bookbinders, and United Papermakers and Paperworkers. All but the lithographers are affiliated with the American Federation of Labor-Congress of Industrial Organizations.

Outside the printing industry are the Office Employees International Union and the Newspaper Guild, both of them AFL-CIO affiliates. The Guild serves employes of newspapers, wire services, syndicates, radio and television stations, and magazines, but only a few employes of the latter. Of the 23,000 members only those on about a score of magazines belong to ANG, including *Life, Time, Fortune, Sports Illustrated, House and Home, Saturday Review, Scientific American, Consumer Reports, Antiques, Parade, Billboard, The Nation, The New Republic, Newsweek,* and the *Scholastic* publications. Formed in 1933 under the leadership of Heywood Broun, New York newspaper columnist who was contributing editor to several magazines and wrote articles and fiction for many more, the Guild at first was affiliated with the AFL but soon shifted to the CIO, before their joining, in its effort to organize vertically within the journalistic world. On magazines with which it has contracts, the advertising, business, circulation, and editorial departments' employes, as the agreement stipulates, are members of the same union. Each plant has its own unit; the units in one city or region in turn form their own local.

Improvement in working conditions, opportunity for professional education, social security, and strengthening of the individual in his relationship with his employer have been aims of the TNG. These objectives have been reached or progress toward them has been made on most of the few periodicals where units exist; as in the newspaper world, standards in general have been raised by the existence of contracts on some publications. Gains have not always been achieved without sacrifice, but magazine strikes and lockouts have been few, partly because of the small number of magazine contracts.

Except on the printing and circulation sides, unions play little part in the magazine industry. Few of the business periodicals are organized; unionization touches company publications only as staff members are organized by craft unions. Undoubtedly there are numerous small magazines whose owners and employes would sign contracts if the owners were economically in a position to do so, as for example certain religious magazines that support the labor movement. In some instances the employes have voted against union affiliation because their wages and working conditions already equal or exceed those called for by contracts.

The nature of a TNG magazine contract is typified by an agreement whose terms fill a 24-page booklet. It covers editorial employes and provides, among other matters, for arbitration, wages, death benefits, expenses, overtime, leaves of absence, hours of work, holidays, dismissal, vacations, sick leave, pay, and part-time employes.

## Women in the magazine field

Magazine work appeals to women more than do some other types of journalism. A woman who shrinks from the fast pace of daily newspapers, broadcast journalism, or wire service offices, thinks of the magazine tempo as more agreeable. In most instances she is right. Men and women alike think of magazine journalism as the entrance to what they call "creative writing," by which they mean a career of writing novels, short stories, poems, and plays. Bewitched mainly by the colorful consumer magazines, they correctly see a long life for their work in periodical form.

Although hospitable to women employes, magazines nevertheless are owned and managed by men and probably will be until more women make magazine work their career and train themselves for administrative responsibility. A few women have made successful careers as top officers of magazine companies but they are the exception. Women have chosen marriage and the rearing of families in preference; they cannot, however, be expected to ignore these choices.

A compromise position is perhaps the one to be followed; it is suggested by some persons concerned with the conflict between career and homemaking. Possibly women can have both if they put them end to end rather than try to put them side by side. A young woman might complete the first stages of her training and education, work for a few years in magazine journalism (preferably while she is single, so she is mobile and can obtain varied experience on magazines in different localities and of different types), and then marry, rear her family, and return to her career when the family is of age. On or before her return she might do part-time study to up-date her skills and knowledge.

More than all other media, magazines have enabled women to rise to leading positions; not many, but more than in the other areas. Since the days of Sarah Hale of *Godey's* fame, a small succession of notable women editors, publishers, and other officials has moved through the pages of magazine history. Women writers for magazines are even more numerous and include virtually all successful novelists, short story, and other writers of inventive material. In our own century among the women who worked within magazinedom itself are the following:

Freda Kirchwey, *The Nation;* Mrs. Beatrice Blackmar Gould, *Ladies' Home Journal;* Mrs. Jean Austin, *American Home;* Mrs. Alice Thompson, *Seventeen* and *Poise;* Christine Holbrook, *Better Living;* Eileen O'Hayer, *Extension;* Fleur Cowles, *Look, Quick,* and *Flair;* Mrs. Clara Savage Littledale, *Parents';* Mildred C. Smith, *Publishers' Weekly;* Amy Loveman, *Saturday Review;* Mabel Hill Souvaine, *Woman's Day;* Mrs. Eileen Garrett, *Tomorrow;* Charlotte Kohler, *Virginia Quarterly Review;* Mrs. Lila Acheson Wallace, *The Reader's Digest;* Era Bell Thompson, *Ebony;* Mrs. Betsy Talbot Blackwell, *Mademoiselle;* Rowena Ferguson, Methodist youth publications; Edna Woolman Chase, Jessica Daves, and Diana Vreeland, *Vogue;* Carmel White Snow and Nancy White, *Harper's Bazaar;* Mrs. Helen Meyer, Dell Publishing Company; Lisa Larsen and Margaret Bourke-White, *Life;* Mrs. Enid A. Haupt, *Seventeen;* Alta Ruth Hahn, *Sales Management;* Kathleen Aston Casey, *Glamour;* Pat Carbine and Shana Alexander, both of *McCall's;* and Genevieve Rhoads, *Woman's Day.*

Also on magazines published or edited by men are hundreds of women in intermediate positions. Although it is true that a few big periodicals and a number of highly specialized magazines do not give women much more than routine places, in general women are no novelty as magazine publishers, editors-in-chief, managing editors, staff executives, advertising officials, critics, reviewers, designers, layout artists, photographers, production editors, and promotion experts as compared with other media.

All this suggests that competition between men and women is greater in the magazine world than in other areas of journalism in the United States, and that opportunities are not sharply limited by one's sex provided one has ability. The literary, journalistic, and artistic creativity needed for magazine pages draws no sex lines but reposes in both men and women. But women, for natural reasons, such as lack of opportunity and education until recent years, have not used that creativity in professional magazine circles as much as have men.

### Qualifications

Editors, publishers, and other employers of staff members for magazines have definite ideas of what qualifications a candidate for a place on a magazine staff should bring. The Education Committee of the Magazine Publishers Association[14] surveyed publisher-members

---

[14] *Report on Magazine Publishers Association Education Committee Survey Evaluating Staff Requirements* (New York: Magazine Publishers Association, 1960).

of the MPA to ascertain their views on these qualifications. Here are some of the conclusions:

1. Young men and women entering the magazine publishing field need a college degree or better. By departmental functions the response of publishers was: Editorial, 77% (that is, that percentage of the publishers said such a degree is needed); administration, 78%; marketing and research, 76%; sales and promotion, 55%; and circulation, 19%.

2. The individual will have investigated the magazine publishing field and will have given more sober thought to his career. By personal qualities: he knows what his immediate and long-range goals are, 93% thought this important (62% scored it *very important*); he knows why he chooses a specific field and has prepared for it, 85% (half said *very important*); he has an acceptable scholastic record, 79% (23% said *very important*); he has had previous work experience, 76% (36% *very important*); he has participated in extracurricular activities and has demonstrated leadership abilities, 73%; he knows what he can contribute to your company, 71%; he has knowledge of your company, 68%; and he is willing to travel or relocate, 58%.

## On the negative side

The magazine field is not Elysium. For some persons who have entered it there has been dissatisfaction; their views should be known to anyone considering the magazine industry as his future place of employment.

Perhaps there are no more complaints from magazinists than from persons working in any other phase of journalism or any other occupation. But they exist and should be confronted.

Beginning salaries, on some publications, are too low. This charge is true about certain large consumer magazines. The supposed prestige value of a connection with a magazine bearing a famous name, the expectations for the future, and the associations with eminent staff members have led some applicants to be content with small wages. This agreeableness has depressed the salary scale for people in the lower echelons of a few large magazines.

Another charge is that employers, especially on consumer magazines, too often fail to take advantage of the applicant's training and education. Young women, in some instances, have been expected to serve as stenographers and clerks for too long before being given the opportunity to write, edit, or do other kinds of specialized work for which they were trained. Once again, this continues because so many girls are willing to take a minor job on a big national magazine for the sake of the connection instead of a more responsible, and sometimes better-paid one, on a specialized periodical with an unglamorous title.

### Editor's complaints

Editors, on the other hand, have their complaints about employes. Ask one what he likes and dislikes about the new staff members and he is likely to have specific reactions. He is seriously annoyed, if not appalled, by a young newcomer's inability to spell correctly, lack of knowledge of grammar, failure to write clear English, tendency to clock-watching, obsession with the coffee break, over-concern for such benefits as retirement plans, group insurance, and sick leaves, insufficient devotion to the work, and inability to be accurate and painstaking.

If he is not an editor but head of a business department, such as advertising or promotion, his complaints usually include the last five, to which he adds a tendency to a know-it-all attitude and lack of initiative.

Almost any department head or publisher complains that hiring young women at the lower ranks is discouraging because girls in a short time marry, or, if married, soon must retire to become mothers. When this happens he must start the search for staff all over again, adjust another new person to his office routines, and renew the battle against some of the faults enumerated above. Here is another reason that men are given preference over women in some instances: they at least stay on the job long enough to repay the employer for his investment in them.

### Seeking the job

Although job-getting in magazine journalism is the same as in other aspects of journalism, this is no guarantee that inexperienced people know the best way to go about it. Six basic steps should be followed:

1. Prepare a data sheet to be sent to periodicals with a brief letter of application.
2. Visit magazine offices.
3. Register with placement services or other agencies.
4. Let friends and relatives know that a position is being sought, even if they are not in publications work, but especially if they are.
5. Answer advertisements found in professional and general publications.
6. Place situation-wanted advertisements.

The usual differences between magazines and other media again should be taken into account. Magazine staffs are smaller, not in the aggregate, but on individual publications. The magazine offers the specialist more opportunity than does the newspaper, which usually is general in its appeal. Magazines are likely to be national in scope and outlook; newspapers and radio-television stations emphasize the local angle. Summer work is not as readily available on national as on local publications. The applicant who recognizes these differences is able to fit himself carefully into the magazine scene. He will know how to make the most of his special training or experience.

Inexperienced job-hunters usually make the mistake of not using simultaneously all methods of handling their problem. If the labor market is slow and job opportunities scarce, it is all the more important to attack the situation from every angle, even though some expense is involved. Visiting offices may be sufficient when personnel is difficult to find, but in a normal situation the beginner cannot count on one approach, for he wants a variety of opportunities, not just one.

Also it should be realized that the job search requires a money investment. Presentable clothes, visits to distant cities for calls on editors, printing of data sheets, mailed applications and reply envelopes, stationery for application letters, and postage for these all mean expense for the applicant. Yet all reliable methods should be used if one can afford them and the job market permits them.

## Data sheets

Use of data sheets (sometimes called resumes and bios) now is an accepted practice, although not all publishers agree that they are essential. The author's students, with few exceptions, have found them to be effective (see Fig. 24.2).[15] The more experience and special ability a data sheet indicates, the more likely it is to be useful. For example, of two young women who had completed their college work in journalism one had combined journalism and liberal arts with home economics, the other journalism and liberal arts alone. Both mailed data sheets to possible employers. The home economics journalist had six job openings within a short time; the second received no encouragement from those same employers. The first had unusual knowledge and skill to offer; the other was too much of a generalist.

The quality of the data sheet also is important. Ideally, it should be individually typed and accompanied with a specially written letter that indicates familiarity with a given magazine and special abilities as a potential staffer. But to send out one hundred individually prepared resumes requires more effort than actually is necessary. Usually they are printed or duplicated in some other fashion and enclosed in an individualized, personal letter that points to the summary of one's life as a source of detailed information. These letters can be written most intelligently when the applicant has become acquainted with the magazine and is able to point out where he might fit into the staff. He must have a sincere interest in it.

The would-be magazinist who prepares a data sheet should keep in mind that a more striking (but not freakish) presentation is expected of him—because he is interested in journalism—than of some-

---

[15] A valuable aid is *Guide to Preparing a Resume* (Albany: New York State Employment Service, 1966), 46 pp.

A Professional Record...

HAROLD DAVID WHIELDON

219 Hobson Avenue
Fayetteville, New York 13066
Telephone: 315-446-6987

Height: 6 feet, 1/2 inch
Weight: 180 pounds
Marital status: single

Date of birth: October 7, 1928
Place of birth: Greenville, Pennsylvania
Church affiliation: United Presbyterian

### Education

**High School**

1940-46  Penn High School, Greenville, Pennsylvania.

**College**

1946-50  Grove City College, Grove City, Pennsylvania. Majored in English. Graduated cum laude, with B. A. degree.

1955-56  Grove City College and Western Reserve University, Cleveland, Ohio. Studied science on undergraduate level.

**Graduate**

1956-57  Hahnemann Medical College, Philadelphia, Pennsylvania. Attended medical school for one year.

1958-61  Syracuse University, Syracuse, New York. Studied journalism on graduate level. Received M. S. degree.

### Journalism Experience

1960-61  Part-time co-editor of The New York Weekly Press, a bimonthly magazine published by the New York Press Association, Syracuse.

1960  Reporter, feature writer, drama critic, and columnist for Summer Orange, weekly newspaper at Syracuse University.

1961  Teacher of graphic arts in School of Journalism, Syracuse University, during illness of regular teacher.

1960-61  Contributor to News for You, easy-reading weekly newspaper published in Syracuse by Dr. Robert S. Laubach for adults with limited ability in English.

1961-64  Communications specialist at Crouse-Hinds Company, electrical manufacturers, Syracuse. Editor of Family Circle, 12-page monthly magazine for employees. Wrote copy, designed layouts, arranged for photographs, read copy and proofs, and processed all copy. Also wrote and edited employee handbooks, designed posters, supervised bulletin boards, and assisted with training programs.

### General Work Experience

1958-60  Teacher at Butler Senior High School, Butler, Pennsylvania. Taught physics, physical science, and space science.

Various  Radio announcer at college radio station.
times  Part-time clerk in retail hardware store. Air Force bombardier-navigator and intelligence officer. Surgical nurse at Cleveland Clinic, Cleveland, Ohio.

### Military Service

1951-55  Served with U. S. Air Force. Completed training as airborne radar operator and commissioned second lieutenant. Flew 19 combat missions to North Korea in B-29 bombers. Served as intelligence officer in U. S. Was honorably separated as first lieutenant.

### Personal Interests

Camping, swimming, handicrafts, travel, geography and maps, history, high fidelity, language, arts, mineralogy, science, and Scouting.

### Awards and Honors

Omicron Delta Kappa national honorary fraternity, Grove City College, 1950.
Scroll and Key academic honorary society, Grove City College, 1949-50.
Air Medal, U. S. Air Force, Okinawa, 1953.
George Washington Honor Medals from Freedoms Foundation, Valley Forge, Pennsylvania, 1963 and 1964.

### Professional and Community Activities

Member, Upstate New York Council of Industrial Editors, Syracuse, 1961-64; secretary, 1962-63; president, 1963-64.
Associate member, Syracuse Press Club, 1963-64.
Member, Syracuse Junior Chamber of Commerce, 1962-64.
Committeeman, Boy Scout Troop 54, Syracuse, 1962-64.

**Fig. 24.2.** Two types of resumes or data sheets. The top one is a folder which will slip into an ordinary business envelope; the other is to be folded similarly or sent flat with examples of one's work.

East Hill Road P.O. No. 288
Canton, Connecticut
OWen 3-4924

**Preparation**

Bachelor of Arts Degree
Magazine Journalism, Sociology
Syracuse University, Syracuse, New York
A General Magazine Course, Magazine Article Writing and Marketing, Magazine Production and Editing, and Critical Writing were courses specific to my major.
Newswriting and Reporting, Graphic Arts, Law of Communications (libel), Principles of Journalism (ethics), and History of American Journalism were additional training.

**Personal Data**

Date of Birth: February 19, 1942
Height: 5'6"  Weight: 125 pounds
Marital Status: Single

**School Address**

(Until June 1, 1965) 825 Euclid Avenue, GR 8-1059, Syracuse, N. Y.
East Hill Rd., Canton, Connecticut. OWen 3-4924

**College Activities**

Judicial Court Justice; Campus Guide; Alpha Xi Delta, social sorority, Association Secretary, Journal Correspondent; Scholastic Advisor to Freshmen; Chapel Representative; Young Republicans Club; Senate Delegate; Floor chairman; Liberal Arts Advisory Council

**Honors**

Theta Sigma Phi, Women's Professional Journalism Honorary; Dean's List (four years); National Honor Society; 2.5 accumulative average (three-point system)

**Experience**

General Reporting for The Athens Daily Messenger, Athens, Ohio, February through May, 1961
Business Staff of The Daily Orange
Literary Editor for high-school yearbook, The Echo
Co-Editor and Feature Editor of high-school newspaper, The Crier
Reporter for The Ohio University Post
Journal Correspondent for national sorority magazine, The Alpha Xi Delta
Summer jobs as: Lifeguard at Avon Country Club, Avon, Conn.; cashier and filing clerk at The Woodland Grocery, 261 Simon Avenue, Hartford, Conn.
Travel abroad in Europe for three months.

**Special Skills**

Typing, photography (developing and enlarging), picture cropping and sizing, copy and proofreading, reporting, typesetting, magazine-dummying and layout, newspaper make-up, knowledge of French language

**Preferences**

Editorial Assistant; writing, editing, layout

**Desired Location**

Hartford, Boston, New York City areas

**References**

Dean W. C. Clark
School of Journalism
Syracuse University
Syracuse 10, New York

Professor Robert D. Murphy
School of Journalism
Syracuse University
Syracuse 10, New York

Professor Roland E. Wolseley
Chairman of Magazine Department
School of Journalism
Syracuse University
Syracuse 10, New York

Gilbert Stuart
81 Briarwood Drive
Windsor, Connecticut

one seeking a position, say, as a metallurgical engineer. He can demonstrate skill with layout as well as ability to write concisely. Data sheets range from single pages to elaborate booklets. All kinds have been proved successful, for employers react differently. For most practical purposes an attractive sheet or two is sufficient. Some applicants have prepared their dossiers or data sheets as small magazines. One young man prepared ten presentation booklets. They cost ten dollars each. He mailed them to ten different offices. Nine were returned but the tenth produced an offer that opened up a career in the field. But equally satisfactory results have been obtained by others who condensed the information into one neat, easily read page.

### Visiting offices

Magazine executives prefer to see job applicants by appointment. The personnel offices of large companies are equipped to handle callers who come without prior arrangement, but the small firms that publish the majority of magazines must ask busy junior editors or others equally occupied to deal with visitors.

Would-be employes should make appointments by letter or telephone and appear faithfully; they may expect courteous treatment, especially if they identify themselves promptly and properly, avoid busy times, as before deadlines, come equipped with data sheets to cut down the need and time for questions, and display samples of work done in other positions or in college.

The applicant stands to profit especially from the visit if he knows something about the magazine whose offices he is entering. He should be able to answer such unexpected questions as, "Well, what do you think of our magazine?" "What is wrong with it?" "What can you suggest as ways to improve it?" An editor, publisher, or advertising manager feels much like a mother in regard to the periodical. He is gratified by every indication of sincere interest in the publication, in his child. Office visits have the merits of permitting personality to speak louder than letters and of making the applicant available exactly when someone is needed. For example: a Syracuse graduate went to the offices of a big firm issuing several dozen magazines. As the assistant publisher was saying good-by to her, having said there was no opening, his telephone rang. The publisher was calling him to tell him that plans to launch several new magazines were completed and that he should hire an editorial assistant to help on basic work. He called the young woman back from the half-open door of his office and asked her to come in again the next morning, as there now seemed a chance for her. The next day she went to work.

If personality is to speak to advantage, the impression it makes must, of course, be favorable. All counselors on job-finding suggest that an applicant be inconspicuously but attractively dressed in business clothes, not party garments, and that he watch details like clean nails and teeth, neat hairdressing, and clear speaking.

Persistence without pestering is another guiding principle. Employers should not be allowed to forget applicants. William Briesky kept the editors of the *Saturday Evening Post* aware of him by occasional letters until the break came and the company hired him, although he was an inexperienced beginner. In a few years he became an associate editor.

Visits with empty hands may be better than none, although if too frequent may do the applicant more harm than good. Better strategy is to present a possibly suitable manuscript, art work, pictures, or suggestions for assignments, advertising plans, or promotion ideas. Copies of journalism projects completed at college are worth exhibiting—term papers, magazine dummies, layouts, and other practical work.

### Registering with bureaus

Placement bureaus are of two general types: services run by commercial firms and by institutions and informal clearing-house work done by professional groups. Companies that make a business of finding jobs exist in all cities. Few handle journalism positions only, and none specializes in magazine work. In the largest cities are some that make an effort to place people particularly in advertising, publicity, and public relations positions, and also will handle magazine, newspaper, and book editorial or art jobs. These charge a percentage or a portion of the first three, six, or more months' salary for their services (in some instances the employer will pay this fee if the applicant is hired).

University and college placement officers assist graduates, although they do not guarantee success, since colleges are not primarily training schools. Seniors and graduate students as well as alumni may register with these officers and will be notified of openings. Few publishing firms send recruiters to campuses; the magazines doing so seek mainly advertising and sales personnel. Some of the trade associations, such as American Business Press, assist by serving as clearing houses and should be notified of one's availability. The college-trained journalist is less on his own in job hunting than others because of such aid. Help also can be obtained from the organizations to which he may belong, such as the professional groups, Sigma Delta Chi and Theta Sigma Phi. These journalism organizations charge small fees, in some instances nothing, for being of help. Many positions are filled by one member notifying another of an opening.

### Help from relatives

A young man, fresh from magazine journalism training, told a cousin working for a national magazine that he needed work. Because the cousin knew of an opening he found the graduate a place. For some months thereafter, each time he told anyone of his position, he was apologetic. He feared, he said, that he had "used"a relative. Other novices who have found their way into the magazine world through friends have been similarly on the defensive.

No one need apologize for accepting the help of relatives and friends, provided he is able to do the work to the satisfaction of his employer and if deserving employes have not been passed over for his benefit. If the boss's young and inexperienced nephew or niece is brought in over the heads of qualified personnel with twenty years' service, the resentment is justified and obvious. Realistically, many positions in journalism are filled by word-of-mouth recommendations, political negotiation, and friendly intervention.

Some offices have rules against hiring employes' friends or relatives in order to avoid cliques. This objection to nepotism sometimes is shortsighted, but the policy may have been established after bitter experience. It must be respected.

### Answering advertisements

> REWRITE man, some scientific or research knowledge preferred. State age, education, experience, salary. KK450 Times.

One morning, a young man experienced in aviation, fresh from journalism school and unsuccessful in finding a place as a writer on flying, spotted this classified advertisement in the New York *Times*. He reorganized his data sheet in relation to the ad and sent it in, freshly retyped. Three days later he was asked by telephone to report to the office of the publishing company. From the men who answered the ad, half a dozen were selected for interviews and given three rewrite assignments on the spot. One was a merchandising story, the second a straight news story, and the third an interpretation of a chemical process patent. Three of the twelve interviewees, including the journalism school man, were asked to return several days later. There were more interviews and finally a decision, for the one-time airman. A career in specialized magazine journalism was launched.

This account illustrates the merits of watching advertisements and of not being too timid about replying even when not completely qualified. This man's qualifications were incomplete, since his scientific or research knowledge was theoretical, but it enabled him to meet practical tests.

Aspiring magazine journalists should watch not only major New York newspapers but also the big dailies, especially Sunday editions, of Chicago, Philadelphia, and Boston, which are centers of the magazine publishing business. It is not necessary to buy them; most usually are received by the larger public libraries.

Newspaper journalists who cannot immediately find suitable openings in their own field often enter the magazine world as a substitute, and remain. Similarly, a magazine journalist offered a place in newspaper, radio, television, or advertising or other phases of journalism or related fields does well to take it if it generally meets his needs. Consulting the want-ad columns of papers in cities where there is not much magazine publishing is worthwhile. Typical ads to watch for, under agency listings or individual placements, are:

MAGAZINE asst cir prom mgr to ..$
_____

CAPTION WRITER, newspaper or smlr
exp resume .......................$
_____

BEGINNER-STENOGRAPHERS (6) for National Magazine, uptown, 5 days.
Fashion Department
Editorial Department
School Advertising Dept.
Circulation Dept. (Dictaphone) ......$
_____

TECHNICAL WRITERS
Expd. engineering reports, manuals on complex electro mechanical devices and equipment. Engineering graduate preferred. Write complete resume including experience and education. Box HT 1268, 113 W. 42 St.

An inexperienced reader may not be able to interpret all these advertisements. The first is for an assistant in the circulation promotion department of a magazine, undoubtedly a large firm. The second, for a caption writer, is for someone with newspaper or similar experience, i.e., magazine, advertising, or wire service office. This opening is in a large plant with highly specialized and segregated duties. The third, longer ad is for stenographers. It is typical of the kind serving to remind young women that stenography is an effective way into the journalistic world, although they run the risk of perhaps not entering more technical work. The advertisement for technical writers is for persons skilled in descriptive and expository writing. Except at colleges that have specialized in technical or scientific journalism, few persons receive training for such work, which is one of numerous specialties profitably combined with journalism.

After the general newspapers in helpfulness come the professional magazines and papers, such as *Advertising Age* and *Editor & Publisher*. In these, advertisements of this type may be found:

ADVERTISING SALESMAN
Aggressive young man with space sales exp. by publisher with leading consumer mags. in specialized fields. Chicago base.

Send letter with resume and salary req. for interview appt.

---

**ASSOCIATE EDITOR**
Growing national magazine needs highly skilled writer to cover socio-economic topics of interest to young doctors. NYC area. To $9,000.

Answers to such advertisements should be complete and neat. Employers have pointed out that even from college trained persons they often receive letters marred by misspellings and inaccuracies. Among the worst offenses is a mistake in the name of the employer or magazine being addressed. Naming references who have not been consulted also breaks down confidence in letters of reply to help-wanted advertisements. Postage for materials to be returned should be included. Newspaper stories, magazine articles, advertisements, leaflets, and other samples of professional work should be sent. Young people who go through their training without working on college or professional publications, who never attempt free lancing, or do not find even a temporary clerical job in a publishing office are handicapped by having little to list or show.

## Placing advertisements

Publishers seeking personnel watch situation-wanted advertisements in the professional publications. Normally these are more numerous than help-wanted notices, especially in editorial work, but in recent years in such key publications as *Editor & Publisher* they have been in balance.

There are good and bad ways to prepare such copy. The dull and routine type reads:

A-1 EDITOR, 36, seeks position in East, preferably New York City. 15 years' experience. $100 a week. Available May 15.

A more original approach was used by a less experienced person:

LET'S FACE IT! Can't get job sans experience, can't get experience sans job, gal recent B.S. Journ—anything creative. New York City only.

When either help-wanted or situation-wanted advertisements result in the would-be employe's being told he has lost out in the race, he should make some reply to this final letter. He should do this for the sake of courtesy and also to keep his name before the employer. Carbon copies should be kept of all correspondence.

## *Using imagination*

Norman Cousins, for many years editor of *Saturday Review,* tells the story of a journalism senior who visited his offices seeking a job. This young man was discouraged. ". . . it's no use," he said. "Either as a writer or editor the chance of breaking in is so slight that there's hardly any point trying."

He told Mr. Cousins that for almost two months he had been visiting magazine and book publishing offices, but no national magazine would have him. He was not sure that even if he could land a job on *Life, Time, Newsweek, Atlantic,* or *Harper's* it would be wise for him to take it. He saw no possibility for advancement because the best spots were filled by persons likely to remain in them. He disliked what he considered the impersonal journalism of the newsmagazines.

He had about decided that he should not have longed for a journalistic or literary career just because, six years earlier, he had enjoyed being editor of his high school paper. What did Mr. Cousins think?

Mr. Cousins thought along less pessimistic lines. He agreed that a writing or editing career is not easy. But, he asked, what profession is not difficult to break into? He also pointed out that the discouraged journalism senior had failed to apply imagination to solving his problem. He had simply written for an appointment and then presented his credentials.

"What else was there to do?" the senior asked.

"One thing he might have done," Mr. Cousins said later, "was to recognize that he had arranged a dead-end tour for himself. There was no reason to believe that his own cold application for employment would stand out in bold relief above the hundreds of other applications—all of them from qualified young people. A job applicant ought to know the history of that publication, a great deal about its format and editorial content, something about the particular audience it is trying to reach and what the problems seem to be in reaching it.

"All this is pay-dirt knowledge. It's not easy to come by," Mr. Cousins went on to say. "But it's worth trying to get, for it can give an applicant a toe-hold on an interview. Most good jobs don't open up; they are created. You create a job by presenting not only yourself but an idea that can fit into an editorial formula, an idea that reveals your knowledge of the publication and your understanding of its audience and its needs."[16]

---

[16] Norman Cousins, "In Defense of a Writing Career," *Saturday Review,* June 17, 1950, pp. 22–23.

# Chapter 25

# The magazine
# of the future

T HE CRYSTAL GAZERS have seen all sorts of futures for the magazines
of the United States. Their forecasts and speculations have ranged
from saying that magazines will continue to be chiefly moderate-cir-
culation, specialized publications to declaring that they will be read
from screens or viewers.

A fair sampling of the prophecies would include these:

The magazine business is halfway through a twenty-year revolution and in ten years, about 1973, will bear "little resemblance" to
what it was a decade ago. This view is that of Robert Stein, then
editor of *McCall's,* uttered in 1963.

"We have already pioneered in adding to our magazines the dimension of sound—in the form of plastic records. We'll go further.
There are two possible values here. We can get an individual step-up
in comprehension and we may well find that group reading—so successful an industrial technique with the Russians—may be encouraged." These are the words of Norman Cahners, president of the
Cahners Publishing Company, also said in 1963.

Magazines and paperback books may be sold in combination at
the newsstands, where several magazines might be sold for a low combination price ("not necessarily by the same publisher"). Magazines
and newspapers also might be sold jointly, and magazines eventually
may be delivered once a month with a subscriber's Sunday newspaper.

Herbert R. Mayes, while president of McCall Corporation, said this the same year.

Lucile D. Kirk, of *Parents'*, in 1959 gathered opinions from several leading magazinists, and found that they think that "magazines of the future will be more artful—have more eye appeal . . . perhaps even combine sight and sound."

Attempts to give magazines more eye appeal are made constantly, ranging from more use of color printing and photographs in the text as well as in the advertising, occasional three-dimensional pictures in color, and larger and more dramatic typography and photo reproduction to a format such as that of *Aspen*. This periodical called itself "the first three-dimensional magazine." Each issue of the bi-monthly, selling for $4 a copy, came as a box. The contents were loose inside—sometimes articles in pamphlet form, each separately bound and shaped appropriately to the subject; a phonograph record; a card kit of modern paintings; a booklet of pictures which appear to move when the pages are flipped; and other attempts to depart from the static nature of the usual periodical.

These are not the only possibilities. Perhaps electronic journalism will crowd out newspapers and magazines altogether. The citizen may be able to press buttons in his home, as he now turns on lights, and bring instant picture reports of events from many parts of the world to a wall screen, thanks to satellites serving as relay points. We all may be wired for sound and be able to communicate at long distance or pick up broadcasts at will without need of even so large an instrument as the hand-model transistor radio. Magazines, under such conditions, would be too cumbersome and slow for popular use.

Or magazines might be produced on film and sold or rented as tiny spools, to be inserted in a projector for viewing on wall screens. [1]

An idea contained in a report of the United Nations Educational, Scientific and Cultural Organization issued in 1964 is adaptable to the magazine. UNESCO forecast as a change in mass communication the possibility of dialing a number which would bring to a television screen a newspaper desired from some other part of the world. Magazines might similarly be read.

In view of the scientific developments of this century, and the plans of scientists for space exploration, nothing any longer can be ruled out as impossible. The future of the magazine could be as fantastic to us as television would have been had it been predicted in 1870.

Whatever extraordinary changes are in store for magazines they are all likely to be in the long range. When radio first became popular it was considered a threat to newspaper reading, but newspapers,

---

[1] For elaboration of this and similar ideas see the author's chapter on "Magazines" in Wesley C. Clark, ed., *Journalism Tomorrow* (Syracuse, N.Y.: Syracuse University Press, 1959), pp. 49–50.

magazines, and books all survived and flourished. Then, when television came onto the scene, gloomy forecasts of what would happen to the print media were numerous, centering chiefly on the fear of the disappearance of reading. The American people continued to be hungry for the printed word; there are more books, magazines, and newspapers being printed and read than ever before. The damage to publications from electronic media has been, not to reading, but to advertising revenue. It is still true that radio and television broadcasts cannot be clipped and filed, reheard or reseen conveniently, mailed to one's friends and relatives, bound for library shelves, or microfilmed.

For the immediate future, the prognostication that makes most sense is this one: a handful of extremely large consumer and specialized-consumer magazines will survive, as the elephant has survived the day of mastodons. A few hundred moderate-size, consumer-type magazines appealing to the wide specialized interests, such as travel, sports, and entertainment, will flourish. All the rest will be thousands of still more specialized periodicals catering to less widely held interests of the people: the trades, the professions, individual arts, and people in specialized groups, as in companies and clubs. There will be shifts and traffic among them, as now, as human activities and interests change. New businesses and hobbies will produce new magazines; as old interests and enterprises die off, their magazines will disappear. And many more U.S. magazines than now will have international and foreign language as well as regional U.S. editions.

We already have seen, in this book, how vast is the field of the specialized periodical; how deeply rooted are many of its units; and how well they have held up through wars, depressions, and competition. These hardy members of the magazine family are more likely to be able to survive whatever rigors the future holds for American journalism than the costly-to-produce, expensive-to-promote, and almost completely advertising-dependent mass magazines.

One of the most astute prophets of the future of magazines has been B. G. Davis, president of a firm with a variety of specialized magazines and at one time an official of the Ziff-Davis Company. As long ago as 1955, two years before the disaster at Crowell-Collier which killed three huge and venerable magazines in a space of months and the later disappearance of more periodicals of mass appeal, Mr. Davis foresaw what would happen.

The magazine publishing industry, he told an interviewer, was then "in a period of dramatic shrinkage, alteration, and weeding out." He said the wheel is turning away from the general magazines and toward the special interest ones. He also anticipated the effect of television. He thought it would hurt the consumer magazines, which it did. But he thought it would stimulate interest in the specialized periodicals, which, in view of their rise, it may have done but which is not yet proved. It is possible to trace the flow of advertising money away from magazines to broadcasting but not to explain the source of new readers of specialized magazines as being because of television any more than adult education, the growth of hobbies because of more leisure time, or the rise in the national income.

Mr. Davis put his finger on a mass magazine weakness which by the end of the decade was to bring anguish for a time to the major women's magazines in particular. For he said that the steady drive for more circulation—"no matter where it came from"—is a symptom of an ailing industry. He was curious as to why advertisers would buy it without reservations. "Circulation by itself doesn't mean anything," he said flatly, "and advertisers should know that. Circulation produced by high-pressure promotion is costly to the publisher and only reduces the productivity of ads." [2]

Supporting Mr. Davis are figures about the growth of the special interest periodicals he had in mind. Between 1942 and 1962 the circulation of such magazines grew from under thirteen million to more than forty-one million. In the early 1950's national distributors of magazines handled thirty for the leading hobby fields of cars, boats, golf, guns, hi-fi, model building, and needlecrafts. A decade later there were 91.[3]

The reasoning behind confidence that the specialized magazine will replace the consumer magazine as the core of the industry also should include a point made by Richard L. Neale, assistant publisher of *Sports Illustrated,* while explaining how his magazine originally was marketed:

> The argument for specialized magazines goes beyond the introduction of new productions. I would like to point out its strengths, limitations, and pertinence to your work. The argument can be simply stated; it is that some people are more important than others, first as customers, secondly, in their influence on other people. For *Sports Illustrated* we carry this proposition two steps further: with the new abundance in America, we say the leaders are more important than ever before both as a market and because they have so many eager and able-to-buy followers; and secondly, sociologically, that what people are most *interested* in learning has to do with the proper use of their recreation and leisure time. We know, or at least there seems to be common agreement among the nation's outstanding economists, that both these propositions are true.[4]

### The sociological background

That the future of magazines rests in the specialized areas is also supported by the concepts of the nature of American life between now

[2] Milton Moskowitz, "Ziff-Davis Head Sees Rosy Future for Specialized Magazine Titles," *Advertising Age,* Aug. 8, 1955.

[3] "Power of Specialized Magazines," *Printer's Ink,* March 11, 1960, pp. 21–30.

[4] "Marketing a New Magazine," an address by Richard L. Neale before the American Marketing Association, Nov. 5, 1956.

and 2000 A.D., as anticipated by scientists, engineers, sociologists, educators, and others who try to foresee conditions that will be brought into existence by present trends and tendencies in society.

**The rising level of education.** Magazines will have to give more substantial fare to their readers, intellectually speaking. The better-educated ones will be more numerous and less content with the lowest-common-denominator type of content now found in many mass appeal magazines. Arnold Gingrich, publisher of *Esquire,* believes that ". . . magazines are inevitably going to be obliged, more and more, to take the calculated risk of meaning more to somebody in particular, as opposed to trying to be everything to everybody. The alternative is to wind up not meaning quite enough to anybody." [5]

Even some of the mass magazine publishers admit this.

And Herbert Mayes, while president of the McCall operations, including the highly successful women's magazine of that name which proved Gingrich's point by experiencing relatively minor financial difficulties by comparison with some of its rivals, in a Chicago address, said, "With the increase in population, with the greater emphasis on education, with the coming improvement in editorial content, magazines cannot and must not stay even approximately at their present levels." To this he added the view, "So it is no longer so much with what attracts the eye as with what attracts the mind that we must make our new advances." [6]

**The rise in population.** Mayes mentioned this, but there are specific facts to be considered. Population trend experts have forecast that the United States will have 282 million people by the year 2000, an increase from 1960 to 2000 of about one hundred million. By the same new turn-of-the-century year, the world's population is expected to more than double, from the nearly three billion of the early 1960's to six billion. India and China together are expected to have as many people by then as the world had in 1960. [7]

The United States Bureau of the Census sees even more rapid population growth than do the United Nations experts. Its figures show that this country is expected to have 259.6 million by 1980 and 285.0 million by 1985. The majority will continue to live in metropolitan areas (196.7 million in metropolitan, 88.3 million in rural and small town areas).

Population growth and location are important to magazine publishers, for where people are to some extent determines their exposure to magazines, their work and play habits, their time for reading, and the kind of distribution needed to reach them.

---

[5] Arnold Gingrich, "The Facts of Life and Death in the Magazine World," *The Quill,* October, 1963, p. 23.

[6] "Herbert Mayes Takes a Look at Where Magazines Are and Where They Are Headed," *Advertising Age,* June 24, 1963, pp. 95–102.

[7] Associated Press dispatch from the United Nations, based on a U.N. survey.

Logically, a greater population should mean more readers for the mass circulation magazines. No doubt it will for those that can survive the problems of the giants. Mayes ventured a prediction. "The larger magazines, I predict, will go on to genuinely great circulations. *The Reader's Digest* may, and can I believe, reach 20,000,000. Perhaps 25,000,000.[8] The women's magazines and the weeklies can go over 15,000,000. And should."

But rising with the few titans will be the bigger special interest magazines which may go to what will be a comparably modest circulation of three or four million. Mayes predicted that an art magazine would reach a million, that a science magazine would have several millions. Possibly *Sports Illustrated, National Geographic, Presbyterian Life, Columbia, Sports Afield, Workbasket,* and some of the other specialized magazines of high circulations now will be joined by several that will rise with popular interest in specialties: *Popular Photography, Motor Trend, Flower Grower, Catholic Digest,* and *Workbench.*

By the early 1970's, however, the publishers of several large magazines were cutting their circulations back deliberately, to avoid the high costs of production and distribution. Thus they might reach Mayes' figures, so far as public demand was concerned, but would not survive economically.

Even if type is set by computers and even if the mechanical editing is done by scanning machines, magazines in some physical form for a long time to come will have, as Dean Theodore Peterson put it at an MPA convention in 1963, "a unique place in a democratic society such as ours. They are a medium well suited to introducing new ideas, to assessing them and, if they have merit, feeding them into the mainstream of thought. We will need a medium like that to help us make sense of the swift and profound changes in the decade ahead."

At the core of the vital magazine world of the future, then, will be the specialized periodicals, with those that once were at the center and dominant—the mass appeal publications—only on the fringe of the industry.

---

[8] He must have meant only the domestic circulation, for in 1965 the world circulation of the *Digest* had reached 25,000,000. Its domestic figure then was 15,000,000.

# *Appendices*

# Appendix A

---

# A magazine glossary

*Compiled by* Ronna Jacobi Telsey*

All entries in this glossary are words used frequently in magazine publishing. They are familiar to persons on magazine staffs who are exposed to the terminology of printers, typographers, engravers, advertising people, newspaper personnel, and persons from other departments of a magazine firm. Certain terms are everyday words included in the vocabularies of those outside the realm of communications.

In addition, pertinent terms were encountered in three journalism textbooks:

Sutton, Albert A., *Design and Makeup of the Newspaper* (Englewood Cliffs, N.J.: Prentice-Hall, Inc., 1957).

Warren, Carl, *Modern News Reporting* (New York: Harper & Brothers, 1959).

Wolseley, Roland E., *The Magazine World* (New York: Prentice-Hall, Inc., 1955), Appendix I, "A Magazine Glossary," compiled by Sally M. Mills.

Furthermore, Webster's *Second* and *Third New International Dictionaries* were consulted for definitions and for identifications of parts of speech. Spellings, except a few words not listed in the unabridged dictionaries, are from Webster's *Third*.

* Mrs. Telsey, at the time she prepared this glossary, was assistant production editor of *Mademoiselle;* she is a graduate of the Syracuse University School of Public Communications, where she majored in magazine journalism.

Staff members of several magazines cooperated by examining the manuscript. The compiler of this glossary as well as the author of the book wish to thank especially Prof. Edmund C. Arnold, chairman, Graphic Arts Department, School of Public Communications, Syracuse, and former editor, *Linotype News;* William A. Phair, editor, *Hardware Age,* and chairman of the editorial board, Chilton Company; and Richard J. Sasso, assistant production manager, *Scientific American.*

*advertisement:* (noun; abbr. "ad") A paid notice or announcement published with the intent of making something known or of selling something. An important source of revenue for many magazines.

*agate line:* (noun) A unit of measurement of page depth; an agate line is 5½ points deep; there are 14 such lines to the inch.

*angle:* (noun) A particular point of view, aspect, emphasis, approach, or attack played up by the writer.

*art:* (noun) Decorative or illustrative elements appearing in a magazine (photographs, illustrations, line drawings, etc.) as distinguished from the text or other parts printed from standard alphabetic types.

*ascender:* (noun) (1) The part of a lowercase letter that exceeds an x-height letter. (2) An ascending letter or character.

*assignment:* (noun) A specific task given to a particular person or group.

**B**

*back issue:* (noun) A copy of a magazine dated earlier than the current issue.

*back of the book:* (noun; "back-of-the-book"—adj.) The section of a magazine following the main editorial portion and consisting of editorial and advertising content.

*backstrap:* (noun) The narrow strip that joins the front and back covers of a magazine and secures the bound inner sections. The *backstrap* is often lettered with the magazine's name, date of issue, and major contents.

*Ben Day:* (noun) A photoengraving process for obtaining different tone values in a line cut.

*bind:* (verb) To assemble signatures in proper order, including folding, trimming, and fastening.

*black and white:* (noun; "black-and-white"—adj.) (1) Printed in black ink on white stock. (2) Photographs characterized by the reproduction or transmission of visual images in tones of gray rather than in colors.

*bleed:* (verb) To be printed so as to run off one or more edges of a page or sheet after trimming.

*block-out:* (noun) A chart filled in before going to press to show the exact positioning of advertising and editorial content on each page in a given issue.

*blowup:* (noun) A photographic enlargement of an advertisement or editorial page which is used for display purposes.

*blurb:* (noun; coined in 1907 by Gelett Burgess, American humorist and illustrator) A brief description, usually set as display matter, designed to whet interest in the piece it precedes.

*boldface:* (noun) A typeface with wide strokes heavier than the normal but usually of same width. **This is boldface.**

*book:* (noun) Synonym for *magazine.*

*broken space:* (noun) Opposite of *display* and *solid.* The front and back sections of a magazine composed of both advertising and editorial content.

*butt:* (verb) To position two printing plates so close together that the printing surfaces meet; or two Linotype slugs.

*by-line:* (noun; "by-line"—verb) A printed line containing the name of the author of a signed story or article.

## C

*caption:* (noun) The body type accompanying a pictorial illustration. Popularly used to refer to either *overline* or underline, although the latter is printed in display size.

*center spread:* (noun) The two facing pages in the center of a magazine.

*character:* (noun) A graphic symbol used as a unit in writing or printing—letters of the alphabet, digits, punctuation marks, etc.

*character count:* (noun) A method of copyfitting. The unit of measurement is a single character. The number of characters, the number of characters that a line of type will accommodate, the number of lines of type required for the copy, the amount of space needed for the total number of lines of type, and the number of words for a given area can be calculated by this method. Spaces count as one character.

*chase:* (noun) A rectangular metal frame into which letterpress matter is locked for printing or plating.

*circulation:* (noun) The average number of copies of a publication sold or distributed over a given period.

*clean copy:* (noun) Opposite of *dirty copy.* Neat manuscript containing few errors or editors' corrections.

*close:* (verb) Same as *put to bed.* To conclude an issue of a magazine; to make the final preparations for printing.

*closing date:* (noun) A date specified when all copy, orders, and plates must be received by the publication so as to appear in a given issue.

*column:* (noun) One of two or more vertical sections of a printed page with a given width and height, usually separated by a rule or by white space.

*commission:* (verb) (1) Same as *solicit.* To authorize a writer, artist, or photographer to execute a piece of writing, illustration(s), or photograph(s) for use in a publication. (2) A form of payment to agencies or salesmen.

*conversion:* (verb) Converting type and engravings to offset printing plates.

*copy:* (noun) Manuscript in typewritten form which is to be used in a magazine.

*copy editor:* (noun; "copy edit"—verb) Same as *copyreader.* An employe who prepares copy for the printer by reading and correcting it, and by processing it (specifying size, style, and positioning of type, etc.).

*copyfit:* (verb; "copyfitter"—noun) To fit copy to a required space. By mathematical formulas the amount of copy needed to fill a given space, and vice versa, can be determined. By cutting or expanding the copy or space and by varying the size of typefaces, measures, leading, etc., the copy can be made to fit.

*copyreader:* (noun; "copyread"—verb) Same as *copy editor.*

*copyright:* (noun; "copyright"—verb; "copyrighted"—adj.) The exclusive, legally secured right to publish and sell the matter and form of a magazine or some part of it for a period, in the United States, of twenty-eight years with a right of renewal for another twenty-eight years. A publication on current U.S. copyright regulations may be obtained from the U.S. Superintendent of Documents.

*copywriter:* (noun; "copywrite"—verb) Employe who writes editorial, advertising, and/or promotional copy. Usually associated with advertising.

*cover:* (noun) The outer part of a magazine. The front cover is known as the "front cover." The inside front cover is the "second cover." The inside of the back cover is the "third cover." The outside of the back cover is the "fourth cover." A "fold-out" cover is oversize, with the excess folded into the magazine.

*cover:* (verb) To get the facts, to be responsible for information, or to report news about.

*cover copy:* (noun) The brief descriptions of content that appear as lines of type on the front cover of a magazine. Used primarily as a selling device to induce the newsstand buyer to purchase and read the issue.

*credit line:* (noun) A line, note, or name that accompanies and acknowledges the source of an item appearing in a magazine.

*crop:* (verb) To cut off or mark out unwanted parts of a photograph or illustration.

*cut:* (noun) An engraving of a photograph, illustration, or type.

*cut:* (verb) To shorten a piece of copy.

## D

*dateline:* (noun) That part of the folio line giving date of issue.

*dead:* (adj.) (1) Art or copy which has been used or is never to be used and is therefore considered *dead*. (2) Metal used in locking up type which is not meant to print and is routed out before publication.

*deadline:* (noun) A fixed time limit when all copy, art, etc., must be in for a given issue, or when the issue must be ready to go to press, etc.

*department:* (noun) (1) A feature devoted to a particular subject and presented regularly in a magazine. (2) A functional division of the staff.

*descender:* (noun) (1) The part of a lowercase letter that is lower than the lowest part of an x-height letter. (2) A descending letter or character.

*dirty copy:* (noun) Opposite of *clean copy*. Sloppy manuscript containing many errors and numerous editors' corrections.

*display:* (noun) (1) Same as *solid*. Opposite of *broken space*. The major editorial section of a magazine void of advertising pages. (2) Composition designed to catch the eye by the use of large and vivid type, unusual layouts, etc. (3) Large prominent advertisements.

*dopesheet:* (noun) A sheet providing factual data for the specialized subject pages of a magazine. Used by the copywriters and researchers.

*double-spread:* (noun) Same as *spread*. Two facing pages in a magazine treated as a single unit and printed with matter that usually runs across the gutter.

*dummy:* (noun) Plan or blueprint for pages of a forthcoming issue showing contents in proper order. When an issue goes to press, a book of duplicate proofs, arranged according to page number, is compiled to insure that proof corrections have been made, that the right photograph appears on each page, etc.

*dummy type:* (noun) Type pasted on a layout for style and positioning only.

*dummy-up:* (verb) Pasting proofs of type matter and/or illustrations on a blank sheet to resemble a page in the magazine. When the issue closes this is sent *OK for press.*

*duotone:* (noun) An illustration or photograph printed in two colors so that a third is produced.

## E

*edit:* (verb) To select, emend, revise, and compile to make suitable for publication.

*edition:* (noun) Same as *issue.* The whole number of magazines with identical makeup and content, and printed from a single setting of type, and made available at the same time.

*editor:* (noun) One who revises, corrects, and arranges the contents and style of the work of others for publication, and who directs or supervises the expressive policies and the preparation of a publication or of a section of a publication.

*editorial:* (noun) An article that is usually given a special or significant place and that intentionally expresses the views of those in control of the publication on a matter of current interest.

*editorial content:* (noun) Of, relating to, or constituting the literary contents of a magazine.

*editorialize:* (verb) To express an opinion in the form of an editorial or to introduce opinion into the reporting of facts.

*editor-in-chief:* (noun) The editor who is the head of the entire staff of a publication.

*editor's note:* (noun) A brief explanation written by an editor that precedes or follows a piece. Tells about the author, gives background information, etc.

## F

*feature:* (noun; "feature"—adj.) An article, often with strong emotional or human-interest appeal, related to but not necessarily news.

*feature:* (verb) To give special prominence to copy, photographs, etc.

*fiction:* (noun) Poetic and prose writing (short stories, fables, novels) which is the product of the imagination with invented characters and situations.

*filler:* (noun) Short pieces of copy (poetry; short, short stories; etc.) set in type and held in *inventory* for use at any time, usually to replace advertisements canceled on short notice just before press time or to complete columns that are running short.

*first bound:* (noun) One of several magazines bound by hand as soon as the press run is completed and sent to editorial personnel before the regular copies are distributed.

*first proof:* (noun) The initial type proof set from copy and returned to the editor for corrections.

*flag:* (noun) Same as *logo* and *nameplate.* The name of a magazine as it is regularly displayed on the front cover.

*flush:* (verb) To align lines of type on the left, right, or both edges, i.e., to justify them.

*folio:* (noun) A page number.

*folio position:* (noun) A set position for the placement of folios.

*font:* (noun) The complete alphabet, including punctuation marks and numbers, etc., of a particular size and style of type face.

*format:* (noun) The shape, size, style, and general makeup of a magazine.

*formula:* (noun) The policies, principles, and purposes which constitute the reasons for publishing a magazine.

*foundry proof:* (noun) A proof of the type and engravings that have been locked in position with dead metal and made ready for plating.

*four-color:* (adj.) Photographs and other art work which run in color and are made from red, yellow, blue, and black plates.

*four-up:* (adv.) Four plates of one page run simultaneously on a press.

*free lance:* (noun) Writer, artist, or photographer who contributes work to a magazine with which he has no affiliation.

*front of the book:* (noun; "front-of-the-book"—adj.) Section of a magazine preceding the main editorial portion and consisting of editorial and advertising content.

*furniture:* (noun) Pieces of wood or metal less than type-high that are placed in printing forms to fill in blank spaces or used with quoins to fasten matter to a chase.

## G

*galley proof:* (noun) A long, narrow proof pulled from type on a galley (an oblong steel tray with upright sides to hold set type).

*gatefold:* (noun) A folded insert in a magazine that is larger in some dimension than the page.

*ghost-writer:* (noun; "ghostwrite"—verb) One that writes for and in the name of another who is the presumed author.

*gutter:* (noun) The white space formed by the adjoining inside margins of two facing pages.

## H

*hairscore:* (noun; "hairscore"—verb) A thin rule used to underscore words for emphasis.

*halftone:* (noun) A photoengraving made from an image photographed through a screen and then etched so that the details of the image are reproduced in dots with the darker areas appearing as heavy and concentrated dots and the lighter areas as fine and diffused dots.

*handout:* (noun) A publicity release.

*hand-set:* (adj.) Individual characters of a particular type face, assembled by hand. Opposite of *machine-set.*

*head:* (noun) Same as *headline* and *title.* The heading of a story, article, or other copy.

*headline:* (noun) Same as *head* and *title.*

*HFR:* (abbreviation for *hold for release*) Information not to be printed until a specified time or under specified conditions.

*house ad:* (noun) An advertisement promoting the magazine in which it appears.

*house organ:* (noun) A publication, typically in magazine format, issued periodically by a company to further its interest among employes (internal) or among customers and stockholders (external); their editors prefer "company publication" or "industrial publication."

*HTK:* (abbr. for *head to come*) Indication to the printer that the heading of a story, article, or other copy will be sent later.

# I

*imposition:* (noun) The order of arrangement of page plates on a press.

*indicia:* (noun) Mailing data required by the post office, usually printed in the magazine or on the wrapper carrying it.

*initial letter:* (noun) A large letter beginning a paragraph, usually capitalized, and extending over two or more text lines, and sometimes ornate and in more than one color. Used for decoration and to break up solid masses of type. (1) An inset, sunken, or stand-down *initial letter* drops down into the body type. (2) A rising, stick-up, or stand-up *initial letter* extends above the body type. This type is used for the chapter openings of this book.

*insert:* (noun) (1) Additional or new copy to be inserted in a manuscript or proof. (2) Preprinted advertisements inserted between signatures during the collating process.

*inventory:* (noun) Reserve material (articles, stories, fillers, etc.) set in type for use at any time.

*issue:* (noun) Same as *edition.*

*Italic:* (adj.; "Italic"—noun; "italicize"—verb) Type that slants to the right, typically used to give emphasis to a word or group of words or to indicate words or phrases foreign to the language of context or to refer to titles of books, plays, etc. Words being defined in this Glossary are set in Italic.

# J

*jump:* (noun) The portion jumped or continued from one page to another.

*jump:* (verb) To continue a story or article from one page to another.

*jump head:* (noun) The title or headline placed over the continued part of a jumped story or article.

*jump line:* (noun) A directional line of print (as "continued on page 102") at the end of the first part of a continued story or article and/or at the start of the continuation (as "continued from page 90").

*jump the gutter:* Said of a title, photograph, or illustration that is continuous from a left-hand to a right-hand page.

# K

*keep standing:* (verb) Reminder to printer to hold type or completed printing forms after the work is finished. Opposite of *kill.*

*kill:* (verb) To delete something designed for publication; to order something (set type, photograph, etc.) to be destroyed. Opposite of *keep standing.*

# L

*layout:* (noun; abbr.—"l.o.") The arrangement of type and art for a page or spread which is to be reproduced graphically.

*lead:* (noun; led) A thin strip of metal ranging from one-half to three points in thickness, less than *type-high,* used as a spacing element between lines of type.

*lead:* (noun; often spelled "lede"; lēd) The first paragraph or introductory section of an article.

*lead:* (verb; led) To add extra interlineal space; to lead out, insert space to fill area.

*lead-in:* (noun; lēdin) Something that leads into something else: as several words of type set boldface to guide the eye into the body matter.

*letterpress:* (noun) The process of printing during which the paper comes in direct contact with the inked printing plate on which the printing areas stand in relief above the non-printing areas.

*letterspacing:* (noun) The spacing between characters in a type word which can be increased or decreased to fit the word into a given space.

*libel:* (noun; "libel"—verb; "libelous"—adj.) A defamatory statement or representation published without just cause, expressed in print or by pictures, that exposes another to public hatred, contempt, or ridicule.

*line cut:* (noun) A photoengraving that contains and prints only solid lines and not shades or tones. A zinc etching is a line cut on zinc.

*Linotype:* (noun) Trade name for a keyboard-operated typesetting machine that uses circulating brass matrices and produces each line of type in the form of a solid metal slug. The Intertype is similar.

*little magazine:* (noun) A literary magazine, often non-commercial, typically small in format, that especially features experimental writing and appeals to a relatively limited number of readers.

*lock up:* (verb) To fasten type securely in a chase or to attach a printing plate to a press.

*logo:* (noun) Same as *flag* and *nameplate.*

*lower case:* (noun) The style favoring lower case or small letters. Sometimes called *down style.*

## M

*machine-set type:* Type set by a machine. Opposite of "hand-set type."

*magazine:* (noun) (1) A periodical that contains a miscellaneous collection of articles, stories, poems, and pictures directed at the general reading public, or special material directed at a group having a particular hobby, interest or profession, or at a particular age group. (In its original sense, the word meant "storehouse"—makhāzin.) (2) The chambers containing circulating matrices in a typesetting machine.

*make-over:* (noun) Same as *recast.* A proof correction, required after foundry, involving the remaking of a press plate.

*makeready:* (noun) A regular series of operations in the press room, including the final preparation and adjustment of plates on the press just before printing.

*makeup:* (noun) The arrangement of type and illustrations on a page, spread, portfolio, and the look of an entire book.

*maquette:* (noun) A preliminary chart showing the tentative positioning of editorial display pages in a future issue.

*mark up:* (verb) To correct and edit copy or proof.

*market:* (noun) The audience for which a magazine is geared.

*masthead:* (noun) A block of matter usually printed beside or near the table of contents of a magazine and consisting of the title of publication, its address, date of issue, names of owners and editors, and subscription and advertising rates.

*matrix:* (noun; "matrices"—plural) A brass mold of individual characters from which type is cast.

*Monotype:* (noun) Trade name for a typesetting apparatus that casts and assembles individual pieces of type.

*must:* (noun) A priority item marked for inclusion without fail in a particular issue of a magazine.

## N

*nameplate:* (noun) Same as *flag* and *logo*.

*non-fiction:* (noun) Factual writing, not fiction.

## O

*offset:* (noun) A planographic printing process in which an inked impression is first made on a rubber blanket and then transferred or "offset" to the paper.

*OK for press:* (noun) Marking on proofs and layouts approving material for press run.

*on-sale date:* (noun) The day on which an issue of a magazine is made available to the public.

*outline:* (noun) Skeleton of an article or piece of fiction.

*overline:* (noun) The title or explanatory matter above an illustration.

*over-the-transom:* (adj.) Fiction and non-fiction submitted to a magazine by free lancers.

## P

*pad:* (verb) To lengthen a piece by the insertion of additional material.

*paste-up:* (verb; "paste-up"—noun) A dummy produced through pasting.

*periodical:* (noun) A publication issued regularly at fixed intervals of more than a day and excluding newspapers.

*photoengraving:* (noun; "photoengrave"—verb; "photoengraver"—noun) A photochemical process for making a relief printing plate. The image is photographed and the resulting negative is placed in contact with a sensitized metal plate. This plate then is photographed and etched, leaving the printing areas in relief; the plates made from *photoengraving*; the prints made from such plates.

*pi:* (noun; "pi"—verb) Type that is spilled, mixed, or incorrectly distributed.

*pic:* (noun; "pics" or "pix"—plural) Usually a photograph, but also can be art work.

*pica:* (noun) A printer's measurement equal to twelve points or one-sixth of an inch, used in measuring the length of lines and the dimensions of cuts and type pages.

*plate:* (noun) A metal sheet from which printing is done.

*play up:* (verb) Same as *feature* (verb).

*point:* (noun) A unit used to measure the size of type and equivalent to one-seventy-second of an inch. Twelve points equal a *pica*.

*policy:* (noun) The official viewpoint of a magazine on various subjects, often made known to the public through editorials.

*portfolio:* (noun) Consecutive pages devoted to presenting a single theme— i.e. an eight-page *portfolio* on vacation fashions.

*position:* (verb) To place type and/or illustrations on a page.

*printer's error:* (noun; "pe"—abbr.) Mistakes made by the printer in setting type.

*progressive proof:* (noun; "prog"—abbr.) A proof made from plates for color printing showing each color separately and then the colors combined, one color added at a time in the order in which it is normally printed.

*promotion:* (noun) Active furtherance of the sale and acceptance of merchandise (including magazines) through advertising and other publicity.

*proof:* (noun) An impression of type or of an engraving made on paper for examination and/or for the purpose of making corrections.

*proofread:* (verb) To read and mark corrections on a proof.

*prop:* (noun) An object used in a photograph.

*pull:* (verb) To make a proof or impression by printing.

*pulp:* (noun) A magazine printed on coarse stock and often dealing with sensational material.

*put to bed:* Same as *close* (an issue).

## Q

*query:* (noun) An inquiry from a free lancer summarizing an article and asking if a magazine would be interested in it.

*query:* (verb) To question the accuracy of something in copy or proof.

*quoin:* (noun) A wedge of wood or metal used by a printer to lock up a form within a chase or to secure type on a galley.

## R

*rag:* (verb) Opposite of *flush.* To stagger the length of lines of copy.

*rate card:* (noun) A card, provided by a magazine for its advertisers, giving data on rates charged for advertisements, closing dates, circulation guarantees, and mechanical requirements for each issue.

*readability:* (noun) The quality or state of being read with ease in large masses; in editorial usage it means ease of grasp of meaning; in graphic arts relates to legibility and physical ease of reading.

*readership:* (noun) The total mass of individuals actually reading or estimated to read a magazine; a particular class of readers. Distinguished from *circulation.*

*recast:* (noun) Same as *make-over.*

*regional advertisements:* (noun) Those included in issues going only to given geographic areas.

*register:* (noun) Exact placement of the successive impressions that make a multicolor illustration.

*rejection slip:* (noun) A small, printed note of regret, enclosed with a rejected manuscript returned by an editor to an author or to his agent.

*reprint:* (noun) An article or extract printed separately and sent to readers, advertisers, organizations, etc., after first being published in a magazine.

*reproduction proof:* (noun; "repro"—abbr.) A clean sharp proof on fine stock made especially from a letterpress printing surface to serve as photographic copy for a printing plate.

*researcher:* (noun) An editorial staffer who furnishes the research for articles and/or who verifies the facts cited in pieces which are to appear in a magazine.

*resumé:* (noun) A brief account of one's education and professional experience given to prospective employers.

*reverse type:* (noun) Printing that gives the appearance of white type on black.

*revise proof:* (noun) Any corrected proof of type or engravings; it is intended to give opportunity to verify corrections made on the preceding proof.

*rewrite:* (noun) One who rewrites copy.

*rewrite:* (verb) To write manuscript over.

*river:* (noun) A white streak running vertically or diagonally through several lines of close-set printed matter and caused by a series of spaces that appear to form a continuous line.

*Roman:* (adj.; "Roman"—noun) Upright type popularly used for body matter and distinguished from Italic; it has serifs, thick and thin lines, and swelling curves.

*rule:* (noun) A metal strip with a type-high face that prints a linear design used as an underscore, or to divide columns of type, or to form boxes, etc.

*running foot:* (noun) The magazine title, date, volume number, slogan, etc., in the bottom margin of the pages of some magazines.

*running head:* (noun) The magazine title, date, volume number, slogan, etc., printed in the top margin of the pages of some magazines.

*runover:* (noun) The portion of a piece continued on another page in the front or back of the book.

## S

*sans serif:* (noun) Style of type face, also known as "Gothic." No serifs, no pronounced variations in thickness of strokes.

*scoop:* (noun) An exclusive story consisting of information of immediate interest or significance.

*scoop:* (verb) To beat: to report an item in advance of or to the exclusion of other media.

*shirttail:* (noun) Several lines of runover type.

*signature:* (noun) A printed sheet, with a specified number of pages, trimmed and folded, to be bound with other signatures to form the complete magazine.

*signature proof:* (noun) The final page proofs pulled while the presses are running. When assembled, they form actual pages in the magazine. *Signature proofs* are always received in multiples of four and are used for checking color register, printing, alignment, positioning, etc.

*sister publications:* (noun) Periodicals published by the same publisher—i.e. *Vogue, Glamour,* and *Mademoiselle* are published by the Condé Nast Publications Inc. and are *sister publications.*

*slant:* (verb; "slant"—noun) To emphasize a particular aspect of an article; to direct written matter to the interest of a particular audience or according to a particular interpretation; to angle; to warp from objective presentation so as to favor a particular bias.

*slick:* (noun) A magazine printed on glossy, shiny, coated stock; commonly the more expensive large-circulation consumer magazine characterized by articles chosen for popular appeal and by fiction limited to formalized stories with happy endings.

*slug:* (noun) (1) A guideline assigned each piece of copy to help the editor and printer identify it. (2) A strip of metal, six points or larger, used for spacing. (3) A line of type that is *machine set.*

*slush pile:* (noun) The stack of manuscripts mailed to a magazine by free lancers.

*solicit:* (verb) Same as commission.

*solid:* (adj.) Set in type without leads or other spacing material between the lines.

*solid:* (noun) Same as *display.* Opposite of *broken space.*

*split run:* (noun) A run of a magazine in which the wording and/or appearance of an advertisement is changed part way through the run while remaining in the same position in the issue—usually for testing the relative effectiveness of the two pieces of copy or for appealing to readers in different geographic areas.

*spread:* (noun) Same as *double-spread.*

*stat:* (noun; abbr. for "Photostat") A photostatic reproduction of a layout which is marked up and sent to the printer with copy.

*stat board:* (noun) Miniature stats arranged in the order in which the pages they represent are to appear in the magazine.

*stock:* (noun) The paper on which a magazine is printed.

*style:* (noun) (1) A magazine's typographical rules to be observed in preparing copy (spelling, grammar, capitalization, punctuation, etc.). (2) The individual manner of expression of an author through writing.

*stylebook:* (noun) Same as *style sheet.* A book explaining the rules of a style governing a magazine.

*style sheet:* (noun) Same as *stylebook.*

*subhead:* (noun) A heading, subordinate to the main title or heading and inserted as a divider between sections of an article or story to break up a long stretch of type.

*surprint:* (verb; "surprint"—noun) To superimpose type over a photograph or illustration by photographic means to make a single plate containing both images; also to print in one color over an area of another color.

## T

*taboo:* (adj.; "taboo"—noun) Banned (words and phrases) from use in a particular magazine on grounds of taste, morality, or as constituting a risk.

*tear sheets:* (noun) Pages from a magazine in sheet form sent to readers, advertisers, and others who request them.

*thirty:* (noun) Used on copy —30— to signify the end of a piece.

*tie-in:* (noun) The coordination of two or more subjects in a single piece of copy—i.e. a fashion and travel *tie-in* describing clothes worn in various locales.

*tint block:* (noun) A printing plate that produces a color area that lacks detail; usually it then is overprinted in darker ink.

*title:* (noun) Same as *head* and *headline.*

*TK:* (verb; abbr. for "to come") A marking on copy to indicate that something more is to come (such as title or caption).

*trim:* (noun) The portion of the outside edges of printed pages of a magazine that is to be trimmed off.

*two-up:* (adv.) Two plates of one page run simultaneously on a press.

*type face:* (noun) The name of a particular style of type, usually bearing that of the person who designed it as, for example, Bodoni or Goudy.

*type-high:* (adj; "type-high"—adv.) Having the same foot-to-face height as printing type and being .918 inch in English-speaking countries.

*type spec:* (noun; abbr. for "type specification") An indication of the size and face of type used.

*typo:* (noun; abbr. for "typographical error") A typographical error.

## U

*upper case:* (noun) The style favoring capitalization. Sometimes called *up style.* Opposite of lower case or down style.

## W

*WC:* (abbr. for "with corrections") An indication on an okayed proof that corrections must be made by the printer before press run.

*white space:* (noun) The blank space on a page, regarded as an essential element in typographic design.

*widow:* (noun) An undesirable short type line ending a paragraph, especially when appearing at the top or at the foot of a printed page or column.

*word spacing:* (noun) The spacing between words in a type line which can be increased or decreased to fit the line into a given area.

*wrong font:* (noun; "wf"—abbr.) A character in a piece of printing that is not of the same font as the other characters or does not match them in style or size or that is contrary to specification.

# *Appendix B*

# Bibliography

CLASSIFIED and annotated lists of most of the books about the magazines and magazinists of the United States may be found in three books, which together cover the bulk of the magazine journalism volumes. These are *The Literature of Journalism,* by Warren Price (Minneapolis: University of Minnesota Press, 1959); *An Annotated Journalism Bibliography,* by Price and Calder M. Pickett (University of Minnesota Press, 1970); and *The Journalist's Bookshelf,* by Roland E. Wolseley (Philadelphia: Chilton Co., 1961). For books published later than 1970 see issues of *Journalism Quarterly* and *Quill and Scroll* magazines.

The books listed below are the principal ones that served as sources for this volume. The numerous periodicals drawn upon are recorded in the footnotes.

Ackerman, Martin S. *The Curtis Affair.* Los Angeles: Nash, 1970.
Alden, Henry Mills. *Magazine Writing and the New Literature.* New York: Harper & Brothers, 1908.
*America's Education Press.* Syracuse, N.Y.: Educational Press Association, 1966.
Angoff, Charles. *H. L. Mencken.* New York: Thomas Yoseloff, Inc., 1956.
Arnold, Edmund C. *Ink on Paper.* New York: Harper & Row, 1963.
Arthur, William R. and Crosman, Ralph L. *The Law of Newspapers.* New York: McGraw-Hill, 1940.

*The Audiences of Five Magazines.* New York: Newsweek, Inc., 1962.

Bainbridge, John. *Little Wonder.* New York: Reynal & Hitchcock, 1946.

Baird, Russell N. and Turnbull, Arthur T. *Industrial and Business Journalism.* Philadelphia: Chilton Co., 1961.

Bakeless, John. *Magazine Making.* New York: Viking, 1935.

Bennion, Sherilyn Cox. *A Study of Diversification of Operations Among United States Magazine Publishing Companies.* Syracuse, N.Y.: School of Journalism, Syracuse University, 1963.

Bird, George L. *Modern Article Writing.* Dubuque: Brown, 1967.

Bok, Edward W. *The Americanization of Edward Bok.* New York: Charles Scribner's Sons, 1922.

Bryson, Lyman (ed.). *The Communication of Ideas.* New York: Harper & Brothers, 1948.

Burack, A. S. (ed.). *The Writer's Handbook.* Boston: The Writer, Inc. 1971.

Burton, Philip Ward. *The Profitable Science of Making Media Work.* New London, Conn.: Printers' Ink Books, 1959.

Busch, Noel F. *Briton Hadden.* New York: Farrar, Strauss & Co., 1949.

Casey, Ralph D. (ed.). *The Press in Perspective.* Baton Rouge, La.: Louisiana State University Press, 1963.

Charnley, Mitchell V. and Converse, Blair. *Magazine Writing and Editing.* New York: Dryden Press, 1938.

Cousins, Norman. *Present Tense.* New York: McGraw-Hill, 1967.

Crain, G. D., Jr. (ed.). *Teacher of Business: The Publishing Philosophy of James H. McGraw.* Chicago: Advertising Publications, 1944.

Crunden, Robert M. *The Mind and Art of Albert Jay Nock.* Chicago: Regnery, 1964.

Culligan, Matthew J. *The Curtis-Culligan Story.* New York: Crown, 1970.

Dembner, S. Arthur, and Massee, William F. (eds.). *Modern Circulation Methods.* New York: McGraw-Hill, 1968.

*Directory of Newspapers and Periodicals.* Philadelphia: N. Y. Ayer & Son, 1963–1971.

Drewry, John E. (ed.). *Better Journalism for a Better Tomorrow.* Athens, Ga.: University of Georgia Press, 1963.

———. *Contemporary American Magazines.* Athens, Ga.: University of Georgia Press, 1938.

Elfenbein, Julien. *Business Journalism.* New York: Harper & Brothers, second edition, 1960.

Elson, Robert T. *Time Inc.* New York: Atheneum, 1968. Vol. 1.

Feitel, Donald. *Secrets of Successful Free Lancing.* Philadelphia: Chilton Co., 1958.

Ferguson, Rowena. *Editing the Small Magazine.* New York: Columbia University Press, 1958.

Finley, Ruth E. *The Lady of Godey's.* Philadelphia: J. B. Lippincott Co., 1931.

Flesch, Rudolf. *The Art of Plain Talk.* New York: Harper & Brothers, 1946.

———. *The Art of Readable Writing.* New York: Harper & Brothers, 1949.

———. *How to Test Readability.* New York: Harper & Brothers, 1951.

Ford, James L. C. *Magazines for Millions.* Carbondale: Southern Illinois University Press, 1969.

Forsyth, David P. *The Business Press in America, 1750–1865.* Philadelphia: Chilton Co., 1964.

Friedrich, Otto. *Decline and Fall.* New York: Harper & Row, 1970.

Garwood, Irving. *The American Periodicals from 1850 to 1860.* Macomb, Ill.: Author, 1931.

Gehman, Richard. *How to Write and Sell Magazine Articles.* New York: Harper & Brothers, 1959.

Goldberg, Joe. *Big Bunny: The Inside Story of Playboy.* New York: Ballantine, 1967.

Gould, Bruce and Gould, Beatrice Blackmar. *American Story.* New York: Harper & Row, 1968.

Goulden, Joseph C. *The Curtis Caper.* New York: Putnam, 1965.

Grant, Jane. *Ross, The New Yorker and Me.* New York: Reynal, 1968.

Gunther, Max. *Writing the Modern Magazine Article.* Boston: The Writer, Inc., 1968.

Hale, William G. *The Law of the Press.* St. Paul, Minn.: West Publishing Co., 1948.

Harper, J. Henry. *The House of Harper.* New York: Harper & Brothers, 1912.

Hendrick, Burton J. *The Life and Letters of Walter H. Page.* New York: Doubleday, Page & Co., 1922, 1925.

Hersey, Harold Brainerd. *Pulpwood Editor.* New York: Frederick A. Stokes Co., 1937.

Hobart, Donald H. *Marketing Research Practice.* New York: Ronald Press Co., 1950.

Hoffman, Frederick J., Allen, Charles and Ulrich, Carolyn F. *The Little Magazine.* Princeton, N.J.: Princeton University Press, 1946.

Kemler, Edgar. *The Irreverent Mr. Mencken.* Boston: Atlantic-Little, Brown & Co., 1950.

Klare, George R. and Buck, Byron. *Know Your Reader.* New York: Hermitage House, 1954.

Kleppner, Otto. *Advertising Procedure.* Englewood Cliffs, N.J.: Prentice-Hall, Inc., 1966.

Kobler, John. *Luce.* Garden City, N.Y.: Doubleday, 1968.

Kramer, Dale. *Ross and* The New Yorker. New York: Doubleday & Co., 1951.

Leckie, Janet. *A Talent for Living: The Story of Henry B. Sell.* New York: Hawthorne, 1970.

*Literary Market Place.* New York: R. R. Bowker Co., 1971–72.

Lyon, Peter. *Success Story.* New York: Charles Scribner's Sons, 1963.

*Magazines Today—Fundamentals of Publishing.* Transcripts of Presentations at Fifth Annual Magazine Publishers Association Conference, New York, 1961. New York: Magazine Publishers Association, 1961.

McClure, S. S. *My Autobiography.* New York: Frederick Unger Publishing Co., Inc., 1963.

Mich, Daniel D. and Eberman, Edwin. *The Technique of the Picture Story.* New York: McGraw-Hill, 1945.

Mott, Frank Luther. *A History of American Magazines.* Cambridge, Mass.: Belknap Press of Harvard University Press, 1957. Vols. I–V.

Murphy, Donald R. *What Farmers Read and Like*. Ames, Iowa: Iowa State University Press, 1962.

Patterson, Helen M. *Writing and Selling Feature Articles*. Englewood Cliffs, N.J.: Prentice-Hall, Inc., 1956.

Peterson, Theodore. *Magazines in the Twentieth Century*. Urbana, Ill.: University of Illinois Press, 1964.

Polking, Kirk, and Emison, Gloria (eds.). *Writer's Market*. Cincinnati: Writer's Digest, 1972.

Price, Matlack. *Advertising and Editorial Layout*. New York: McGraw-Hill, 1949.

Reddick, DeWitt C. and Crowell, Alfred A. *Industrial Editing*. Albany, N.Y.: Matthew Bender & Co., Inc., 1962.

Rhode, Robert B. and McCall, Floyd H. *Press Photography*. New York: Macmillan Co., 1961.

Root, Robert. *Modern Magazine Editing*. Dubuque, Ia.: Brown, 1966.

Schacht, John H. *The Journals of Opinion and Reportage: An Assessment*. New York: Magazine Publishers Association, 1965.

Schoenfeld, Clarence A. *Effective Feature Writing*. New York: Harper & Brothers, 1960.

Schramm, Wilbur (ed.). *Communications in Modern Society*. Urbana, Ill.: University of Illinois Press, 1948.

Tassin, Algernon. *The Magazine in America*. New York: Dodd, Mead & Co., 1916.

Tebbel, John. *George Horace Lorimer and the Saturday Evening Post*. New York: Doubleday & Co., 1948.

———. *The American Magazine: A Compact History*. New York: Hawthorne, 1969.

Thayer, Frank. *Legal Control of the Press*. New York: Foundation Press, 1962.

Thayer, John Adams. *Astir: A Publisher's Life Story*. Boston: Small, Maynard & Co., 1910.

Van, Karyl, and Hahn, John. *Guidelines in Selling Magazine Advertising*. New York: Appleton Century Crofts, 1971.

Villard, Oswald Garrison. *Fighting Years*. New York: Harcourt, Brace & Co., 1939.

White, Theodore H. *The View From the 40th Floor*. New York: William Sloane, 1960.

Wittenberg, Philip. *Dangerous Words*. New York: Columbia University Press, 1947.

Wolseley, Roland E. *The Magazine World*. New York: Prentice-Hall, Inc., 1951.

——— and Campbell, Laurence R. *Exploring Journalism*. New York: Prentice-Hall, Inc., 1949, 1957.

Wood, James Playsted. *Of Lasting Interest*. New York: Doubleday & Co., Inc., 1956, 1967, 1971.

———. *Magazines in the United States*. New York: Ronald Press Co., 1956.

———. *The Curtis Magazines*. New York: Ronald, 1971.

Woodward, Helen. *The Lady Persuaders*. New York: Ivan Obolensky, Inc., 1960.

Wyman, Phillips. *Magazine Circulation: An Outline of Methods and Meanings*. New York: McCall Co., 1936.

# Index